REFILLING HAIG'S ARMIES

Refilling Haig's Armies

The Replacement of British Infantry Casualties on the Western Front, 1916-1918

Alison Hine

Foreword by Professor Peter Simkins, University of Wolverhampton

Helion & Company Limited

Helion & Company Limited
Unit 8 Amherst Business Centre
Budbrooke Road
Warwick
CV34 5WE
England
Tel. 01926 499 619
Fax 0121 711 4075
Email: info@helion.co.uk
Website: www.helion.co.uk
Twitter: @helionbooks
Visit our blog http://blog.helion.co.uk/

Published by Helion & Company 2018
Designed and typeset by Battlefield Design, Gloucester (www.battlefield-design.co.uk)
Cover designed by Paul Hewitt, Battlefield Design (www.battlefield-design.co.uk)
Printed by Lightning Source Limited, Milton Keynes, Buckinghamshire

Front cover: Battle of Poelcappelle. Walking wounded coming down and reinforcements going up a duckboard trench near Langemarck (Langemark-Poelkapelle), 11 October 1917. (IWM Q 3006)

ISBN 978-1-912390-70-0

British Library Cataloguing-in-Publication Data.
A catalogue record for this book is available from the British Library.

Contents

List of Illustrations

List of Maps

NB The maps are not intended as detailed battle maps but simply to aid the reader by showing where specific battalions were on certain dates.

List of Tables

Abbreviations

The following formats have been used in referring to Regiments/Battalions: eg the First Battalion The Cheshire Regiment is shown as 1st Cheshire; the Ninth (Service) Battalion The Cheshire Regiment is shown as 9th Cheshire. Collectively, their soldiers are referred to as Cheshires.

A Branch	Administrative Branch dealing with personnel matters
ACC	Army Cyclist Corps
ACI	Army Council Instruction (January 1916 onwards)
AF	Army Form
AG	Adjutant General
A&Q	Combined Administrative and Logistics branch at a Headquarters
AO	Army Order
AOC	Army Ordnance Corps
APC	Army Pay Corps
ARO	Army Routine Order
ASC	Army Service Corps
AVC	Army Veterinary Corps
BEF	British Expeditionary Force
Bde	Brigade
Bde HQ	Brigade Headquarters
BOH	British Official History
CAB	Cabinet
CIGS	Chief of the Imperial General Staff
CinC	Commander in Chief
CO	Commanding Officer
Col	Colonel
Cpl	Corporal
CRA	Cheshire Regimental Archives
CRAO	Chester Records and Archive Office
DAG	Deputy Adjutant General

DAG & QMG	Deputy Adjutant General and Quarter Master General
DAAG	Deputy Assistant Adjutant General
Div	Division
Div HQ	Divisional Headquarters
DGMS	Director General of Medical Services
DGNS	Director General of National Service
DMO	Director of Military Operations
DOW	Died of Wounds
DPS	Director of Personal Services
DRLS	Despatch Rider Letter Service
FM	Field Marshal
FSR	Field Service Regulations
Gen	General
GHQ	General Headquarters
GS	General Staff
GOC	General Officer Commanding
GOC-in-C	General Officer Commanding-in-Chief
Grad	Graduated (as in Graduated Battalion)
GRO	General Routine Order
HD	Home Defence
HF	Home Forces
HLRO	House of Lords Record Office
HMSO	His Majesty's Stationery Office
HS	Home Service
IBD	Infantry Base Depot
IGC	Inspector General of Communications
IS	Imperial Service
ISO	Imperial Service Obligation
IWM	Imperial War Museum
KIA	Killed in Action
KR	King's Regulations for the Army
KSLI	King's Shropshire Light Infantry
LCpl	Lance Corporal
LofC	Lines of Communication
LHCMA	Liddle Hart Collection of Military Archives
Lt Col	Lieutenant Colonel
Lt Gen	Lieutenant General
Maj Gen	Major General
MG	Machine Gun
MML	Manual of Military Law
MNS	Ministry of National Service
MT	Motor Transport
NCO	Non-Commissioned Officer
nd	not dated
N&MP	Naval & Military Press

OC	Officer Commanding
OH	Official History
OR	Other Rank
PB	Permanent Base
PU	Permanently Unfit
Q Branch	Logistics staff
QMAAC	Queen Mary's Army Auxiliary Corps
QMG	Quartermaster General
RA	Royal Artillery
RAMC	Royal Army Medical Corps
RE	Royal Engineers
RFA	Royal Field Artillery
RFC	Royal Flying Corps
RGA	Royal Garrison Artillery
RHA	Royal Horse Artillery
RMO	Regimental Medical Officer
RO	Routine Order
RSM	Regimental Sergeant Major
RWF	Royal Welsh Fusiliers (reverted to Welch in 1920)
SAA	Small Arms Ammunition
SC	Staff Captain
SME	Statistics of the Military Effort of the British Empire
SMLE	Short Magazine Lee Enfield
SR	Special Reserve
SWB	South Wales Borderers
TB	Temporary Base
TF	Territorial Force
TNA	The National Archives
TR	Training Reserve
TR Bde	Training Reserve Brigade
TRB	Training Reserve Battalion
Vol.	Volunteer and Volume
WAAC	Women's Army Auxiliary Corps (later Queen Mary's Army Auxiliary Corps)
WO	War Office
WOI	War Office Instruction (up to the end of 1915)
YS	Young Soldier

Dedication

To my husband, Nigel, in grateful thanks for his love and support.

It is further dedicated to the memory of my grandfather, Edward Lambert Trehern (1876 – 1955) who served as 97802 Gunner E. L. Treherne RFA between 30 August 1914-4 March 1919.

Foreword

For all those with a serious interest in the British army in the First World War – and, in particular, the story of the British Expeditionary Force in France and Flanders – this excellent book should henceforth be absolutely essential reading. For me personally, it has been an enormous privilege to be part of the impressive progress made in scholarly Great War studies since the late 1980s. Perhaps not surprisingly, however, much of the attention of historians during this process has been devoted to such topics as the personal experiences of front-line soldiers; morale and discipline ; command and control ; officer-man relations ; politics and grand strategy ; medicine and the treatment of casualties ; industry and technology and, of course, battle tactics and the nature of combat. Much valuable work has been done in these areas but, crucially, there has hitherto been a lot less *critical* focus on the organisation, composition and infrastructure of the BEF between 1914 and 1918. It would be broadly agreed, I feel, that we now know a lot more than before as to what it was like to be involved in the fighting at the 'sharp end', and about the exercise of command and planning in various offensives or defensive crises. In contrast, with a few notable exceptions, there has been relatively little detailed analysis of the absolutely vital factors – namely logistics, munitions production and manpower supply – which, when all is said and done, actually sustained the BEF at a level which ultimately enabled it to match and defeat the Imperial German Army in the field. In other words, *without* a reliable logistical chain, the increasing provision of shells and small arms ammunition, and, not least, an adequate, if often variable, supply of manpower and casualty replacements, it would have been impossible for the BEF to be properly supported in action let alone remain capable of playing a central role in the eventual Allied victory. Had it been denied sufficient resources in men and weapons, it would have simply ceased to function as a modern fighting force. Yet logistics and manpower problems do not generally stir the blood of historians and readers to the same extent as battles and command, which probably explains why these topics are rarely covered.

The manpower problems in Britain in the First World War can perhaps be described in terms of a series of vicious circles. During Lord Kitchener's term of office as Secretary of State for War, the nation raised, by voluntary means, Britain's first-ever mass citizen army, which also constituted the largest single organisation in the country up to that time. The vast expansion of the army made it possible for the BEF on the Western Front to bear a much bigger share of Allied offensive operations but, because of the nature of modern industrialised warfare, this inevitably led to a huge increase in casualties which, in turn, had to be replaced to that the BEF could continue to make a significant contribution to the fighting, especially from 1916 onwards.

At the same time, the voracious appetite of the Western Front for weapons and ammunition meant that the means of production also had to be maintained and augmented, making it more difficult for the Government to square these circles and reconcile the often conflicting demands of industry and the respective armed services. Such difficulties were compounded by the fact that, until the National Register was taken in August 1915, the Government had no really accurate picture of what manpower was actually available. Thereafter, its efforts to balance conflicting needs prompted it, first, to abandon its traditional reliance on voluntary recruiting in favour of compulsion and, eventually, to assume much more centralised control over manpower supply by taking responsibility for recruiting away from the War Office and handing it over in 1917 to a new Ministry of National Service. The nature and course of this process, and also its far-reaching effects on the strength of the BEF in France, are brilliantly examined and detailed by Alison Hine in her book.

The various changes to the reserve and drafting system, together with the successive Military Service Acts from 1916 onwards, not only helped to determine the upper and lower ages at which a man (or indeed a youth) was eligible to fight but also the length of time he spent in training and where and when the different phases of that training took place. The flow, or alternatively the relative absence, of reinforcements additionally had a direct link to the strength of units at the front and hence the combat performance of such units. At the same time, manpower problems had major effects on the *organisation* of the BEF, both overall and in the case of individual formations, particularly in 1918. These effects included the reduction in the infantry strength of divisions from twelve battalions to nine; related amalgamations or disbandment of some battalions; and the reduction to cadre or reconstitution of around one-fifth of the *British* divisions on the Western Front, thus robbing the divisions concerned of much of their original composition and character.

It can, I feel, be safely maintained that the *highly localised* character of the BEF of July 1916 – which contained many Territorial Force and New Army units with very close ties to specific communities, was inevitably diluted by the cumulative effects of battle casualties, conscription and changes in recruiting and the reserve and drafting system. On the other hand, a number of historians, including Helen McCartney and Adrian Gregson, have persuasively argued that the measures introduced by the War Cabinet, War Office, Ministry of National Service and other authorities from 1916 on allowed many infantry battalions at the front to retain at least a marked county or regional identity, even if traditional links to a particular recruiting district, town or city were weakened to some extent. In this study, Dr Hine presents a great deal of fresh and compelling evidence which adds powerful support to the views advanced by McCartney and Gregson, though she draws her examples from a somewhat wider geographical area by looking at a range of regiments from the English-Welsh Marches – namely the Cheshire Regiment, King's Shropshire Light Infantry, Royal Welsh Fusiliers and South Wales Borderers. Her findings strongly underline the contention that, in spite of some unavoidable dilution of the closest community links – such as had initially characterised many Territorial or New Army 'Pals' battalions – efforts *were* made, where possible, to uphold the original socio-geographical identity of units by sending out drafts which at least belonged to the same parent regiment or came from the same county or regional home Command. Given the colossal casualty figures on then Western Front and the conflicting demands of war industries, this was no mean achievement.

Alison Hine's topic is decidedly not an easy one which, again, may explain why – with the exception of Keith Grieves – few, if any, previous historians have attempted to tackle it any real detail. Dr Hine should therefore be warmly congratulated for the impressive depth and range of her research and for daring to analyse an aspect of the Great War that nearly all contemporary historians have largely left alone. She has not only raised her head above the parapet but leads us across No Man's Land and guides us skilfully and successfully through the labyrinth of sources on the other side. As a result of her admirable scholarly dedication, she has produced a landmark study which will add substantially to our understanding of the composition, training, strength and combat performance of the BEF on the Western Front.

Professor Peter Simkins
University of Wolverhampton

March 2018

Acknowledgements

There are many people who have played a part in the completion of this book. I would like to thank particularly both Professor John Bourne, who supervised the Thesis upon which this work is based and has continued to give advice and support during the whole process, and Professor Peter Simkins who has so kindly read the work (several times!) and has offered helpful comments and advice along the way.

It has been a long process and many others have been most generous in answering my queries. In particular, I must thank Caroline Chamberlain and Geoff Crump of the Cheshire Regimental Archives; Karen Murdoch and Allan Poole of the RWF Museum; Christine Bernath of the KSLI Museum and Neil Evans and Annette Burgoyne for their knowledge of the KSLI; Peter Lea of the Raven Café, Prees Heath; Alan Culpitt for permission to quote from his grandfather's diary; the staffs of the Cheshire Record Office and the Shropshire Archives; the curator of the AGC Museum; and the staffs of the IWM and the National Archives. I am particularly grateful to the Shropshire Library Service for their assistance in meeting my many requests for books from all over the country.

I would also like to thank Tim Lynch for sharing his work on KOYLI drafts with me at an early stage and also encouraging me to keep going when the task seemed never-ending. Further thanks are due to my friends and colleagues of the International Guild of Battlefield Guides for their support, particularly Clive Harris, Christopher Newbould, Chris Preston and Viv Whelpton. I must also acknowledge the help and advice given by Michael LoCicero of Helion and George Anderson for producing the maps.

Finally, I have also been most grateful for the support and comradeship of fellow members of John Bourne's former PhD cohort: Nick Beeching, Derek Clayton, Trevor Harvey, Peter Hodgkinson and the late Geoff Clarke who sadly died before his own work on the use of railways could be completed.

Introduction

During the First World War almost 5 million individuals enlisted in the British Army. Of these, over 700,000 died in action, of wounds or from disease, more than 170,000 were reported as prisoners of war and the number of wounds received totalled nearly 1,663,000.[1] If units and formations were to continue to function effectively, the gaps caused by the loss of these casualties had to be filled by replacements as quickly as possible.

The British Army had been extensively re-organized during the early part of the century with comprehensive plans being made for its expansion and renewal in time of future conflict.[2] Similarly, detailed procedures for the replacement of the inevitable losses had been developed, although the scale on which they would need to be implemented once the First World War started could not possibly have been envisaged. Far more men than had ever served before would be needed and the plans for their replacement would need adaptation and refinement virtually from the start of the war. Little has been examined in any detail, however, about how the replacements were obtained, who they were, how they were trained and drafted and to what extent their arrival changed the composition of the units they joined.

This book examines how the BEF in France and Flanders was refilled during the second half of the war and to what extent the men of 1918 differed from those of 1916. Broadly, it examines: the impact of successive political initiatives and decisions on the manning of the British Army; how the men were obtained and trained before being drafted; how the replacement of casualties was managed; and the effect of new arrivals on the character and composition of the units they joined.

The subject of Army manpower is vast. It ranges from the political harnessing of the nation's resources, through its management by the War Office and the military chain of command and ultimately to the manning of units on the ground. It is not of immediate interest to those whose key focus lies in the operational and tactical aspects of battles and in the exploits of the units that were involved. Yet to ignore the composition of those units is the same as ignoring the vital importance of logistics: without manpower and matériel the Army could not fight.

1 War Office, *Statistics of the Military Effort of the British Empire During the Great War 1914 – 1920)* London: HMSO, 1922; Naval & Military Press (N&MP) reprint 1999), p. 237 and fn. f p. 240.

2 See Edward Spiers, *Haldane: An Army Reformer* (Edinburgh: Edinburgh University Press, 1980), K.W. Mitchinson, *Defending Albion* (Basingstoke: Palgrave Macmillan, 2005) and Ian F.W. Beckett, *The Amateur Military Tradition* (Manchester: Manchester University Press, 1991).

Very few writers have attempted to do more than address particular aspects of the subject of Army manning. An exception is Keith Grieves who, in *The Politics of Manpower, 1914-1918* (Manchester: Manchester University Press, 1988), notably provided a comprehensive and useful overview of the political level. He drew many of his sources from within the records of the Ministry of Munitions, however, a department whose support for the withdrawal from the civilian workforce of large numbers of men for the Army was, inevitably, limited. The contrasting War Office perspective may be seen in the memoirs of Sir William Robertson *From Private to Field Marshal* (Boston & New York: Houghton Mifflin, 1921) and General Nevil Macready's *Annals of an Active Life, Vol. 1* (London: Hutchinson, n.d.). Both these writers were, of course, equally biased towards the Army's requirements.

Below the political level, some writers have taken as their focus the various constituent parts of the Army: Regulars, Territorial Force (TF) and the New Armies.[3] These works provide useful background but do not always descend to the minutiae of the continuing composition of units. Other writers have concentrated on the histories and exploits of specific units.[4] Many of these are very good but others are often merely recastings of unit war diaries. Some general works have been produced in the last few years, such as Charles Messenger's *Call to Arms* (London: Cassell, 2005) and Richard Holmes's *Tommy* (London: HarperCollins, 2004), but although these touch upon aspects of Army service, they are broad-brush overviews covering a variety of topics, but not necessarily in sufficient depth to give a clear picture. Work has also started on examining the organization, infrastructure and command and control within the BEF.[5] There still exists little, however, on the reserve and drafting system, the training of replacements, the social and geographical composition of units and the extent to which they were filled with conscripts from 1916 onwards.[6]

The lack of information on manning has caused incomplete and even inaccurate conclusions to be drawn concerning the frontline operational experience of formations and units. For example, in *Battle Tactics of the Western Front* (New Haven & London: Yale University Press, 1994), Paddy Griffith commented upon the BEF's practice of withdrawing divisions that had suffered particularly heavy losses from the line, in order that they might recuperate and be refilled. He considered that the ensuing amount of movement this caused within corps was detrimental to the continuity of relationships formed both by and within divisions. The potentially adverse effect of this lack of continuity of command amongst British corps was also noted by Andy Simpson in *Directing Operations: Corps Command on the Western Front 1914-18* (Stroud: Spellmount, 2006). The inference drawn was that the more permanent structure of

3 Ian F. W. Beckett, *Amateur Military Tradition* (Manchester: Manchester University Press, 1991); Peter Simkins, *Kitchener's Army* (Manchester: Manchester University Press, 1985); Ian F.W. Beckett and Keith Simpson, eds., *A Nation in Arms: A Social Study of the British Army in the First World War* (Manchester: Manchester University Press, 2005); K. W. Mitchinson, *The Territorial Force at War 1914 – 1916* (London: Palgrave Macmillan, 2014).

4 Arthur Crookenden *The History of the Cheshire Regiment in the Great War* (Chester: Evans, nd), Jon Cooksey, *Barnsley Pals* (Barnsley: Pen & Sword, 2008); Michael Stedman, *Manchester Pals: 16th, 17th, 18th, 19th, 20th, 21st, 22nd and 23rd Battalions, Manchester Regiment: A History of the Manchester Brigades* (Barnsley: Pen & Sword, 1998).

5 Andy Simpson, *Directing Operations: Corps Command on the Western Front 1914-18* (Stroud: Spellmount, 2006).

6 Peter Simkins, *From the Somme to Victory* (Barnsley: Praetorian Press, 2014), p. 11

the Dominion Corps was preferable and should have been adopted by the BEF. What this view ignores is the reason why British divisions were moved around: namely, the need for time and space to enable them to be returned to full strength. This could only be done out of the line and could also be achieved more quickly for some divisions than others, depending on the availability of replacements. Some divisions could be reinforced close to the front and re-join the line almost immediately, taking part in continuing battles. The 39th Division, for example, was refilled twice and took part in three battles during Third Ypres. Others, however, such as the 38th (Welsh) Division, which suffered 2,922 casualties between 31 July-3 August 1917, had of necessity to be withdrawn after just one action and could not take part in subsequent battles due to lack of suitable replacements. In discussing 38th (Welsh) Division's later success during the Hundred Days, Gary Sheffield notes that the time the Division spent on trench-holding duties, from August 1917 until mid-1918, indicates that it was not regarded by GHQ as an elite formation.[7] This was almost certainly the case, but for GHQ there had also been the difficulty of finding replacements for a Welsh Division, who for political reasons had themselves to be Welsh. Such reinforcements were not always available in sufficient numbers. The availability of casualty replacements was thus another factor affecting the use of divisions.

The limited amount of detailed research into who the replacements were in the second half of the war has also enabled misperceptions to persist. It is often assumed, for example, that the 2,504,183 men who enlisted in the British Army after January 1916 were all conscripts.[8] Since the appointed date for the introduction of conscription was actually 2 March 1916, this view is numerically incorrect (a difference of 164,594). More importantly, it overlooks the fact that throughout the war it remained possible for boys and men to volunteer before they were called up. The *General Annual Report on the British Army 1913-1919* shows that some 208,450 men volunteered between 1 January 1916-30 June 1917. Unfortunately for research purposes, after 30 June 1917 the figures for voluntary enlistments of men coming forward before being called up and boys enlisting under the age of 18, together with all Derby men taken after 1 April 1917, are simply noted as being contained within the figure of 978,354 men obtained between 1 April 1917-11 November 1918.[9]

Yet another perennial and widespread misperception persists: namely that later in the war there was a deliberate intent to 'destroy the Regiment, the immemorial foundation of Armies, and nationalize the Army' by severing the geographical and traditional links that bound soldiers to their home areas.[10] More recently, David French has stated that in the Autumn of 1916, the War Office deliberately set out to break the connection between particular locations and the drafting system in order to 'spread the resulting misery' arising from the heavy casualties of the Somme.[11] He fails to provide evidence for this view and it is at odds with the work of Helen

7 Gary Sheffield, 'Finest hour? British forces on the Western Front in 1918: An overview', in Ashley Ekins, ed., *1918 Year of Victory* (Auckland: Exisle, 2010)

8 For example: Richard Holmes, *Tommy* (London: Harper Collins, 2004), p. 89 and David Stevenson, *With Our Backs to the Wall* (Harvard: Harvard University Press, 2011), p. 256. Enlistment figures are given in War Office, *Statistics of the Military Effort*, p. 364.

9 Army Council, *General Annual Report on the British Army 1 October 1913-30 September 1919* (London: HMSO, 1921), p. 60.

10 J.C. Dunn, *The War the Infantry Knew* (1938; London: Abacus, 1994), p. 245.

11 D. French, *Military Identities* (Oxford: Oxford University Press, 2005), p. 178.

McCartney which puts forward a strongly argued case for continuing homogeneity within units throughout the war, based on her very detailed research into Liverpool Territorial units.[12] There thus remains scope for research into a wider selection of units in order to test the conflicting arguments and the extent to which they are valid for the later years of the war.

Examination of the composition of units requires analysis of the soldiers they contained. This may be obtained from the details contained in *Soldiers Died in the Great War* (SDGW), from personal records, where they still exist, and from personal accounts. It is far easier to find such accounts about volunteers than about conscripts. The first books about the New Armies were published during the war itself: Ian Hay's *The First Hundred Thousand* (Edinburgh: Blackwood, 1916) and Basil Williams's *Raising and Training the New Armies* (London: Constable, 1918). These were followed during the 1920s and 1930s by many personal accounts: Sir William Robertson's memoirs, Charles Edmonds's (Charles Carrington) *A Subaltern's War* (London: Peter Davies, 1929) and Frank Richards's *Old Soldiers Never Die* (London: Faber & Faber, 1933) give some idea of the range but inevitably more were written at that time by officers than by former soldiers. More recently, soldiers' diaries have come to light, such as *Joffrey's War*, edited by John Bourne and Bob Bushaway (Nottingham: Salient Books, 2011) and the transcript of George Culpitt's diaries published on the internet by his son (www.culpitt-war-diary.org.uk/index.htm) Yet more personal recollections have emerged during the current First World War centenary celebrations. The difficulty with the multitude of personal accounts now available, however, in terms of the focus of this work is that they rarely mention the management of manning and few, if any, admit to having been conscripted.

As Gordon Corrigan noted in *Mud, Blood and Poppycock* (London: Cassell, 2003), in later years those who had been conscripted did not advertise the fact. Similarly, Ian Beckett commented that relatively few soldiers who wrote memoirs or left diaries or letters admitted to what was seen as the stigma of conscription.[13] Of those accounts known definitely to have been written by conscripts, Frederick Voigt's *Combed Out* (London: Swarthmore Press, 1920) makes no mention at all of his conscript status while *The Ordeal of Alfred M Hale, The Memoirs of a Soldier Servant* (London: Leo Cooper, 1975), edited by Paul Fussell, reads almost like a spoof document, so different is the treatment he apparently received whilst in training from that normally meted out to recruits. An apparent attempt to research this group of soldiers was made by Ilana Bet-El in *Conscripts, Forgotten Men of the Great War* (Stroud: Sutton, 1999), but she based her work on the false premises that all those who enlisted after January 1916 were conscripted and therefore, by definition, were unwilling soldiers who, on being called up, simply became pawns in an inflexible bureaucratic process. Unfortunately for her arguments, some of the individuals she cites were not in fact conscripts. More recently, the detailed research undertaken by Tim Lynch into a draft of 136 Kings Own Yorkshire Light Infantry (KOYLI) men who arrived in France in June 1918 has shown that the picture is far more complex than the negative stereotype that it has become customary to portray.[14] It is only by analysis of Service Records, where they exist, that it becomes possible to confirm the type of engagement upon which a soldier served.

12 Helen McCartney, *Citizen Soldiers* (Cambridge: Cambridge University Press, 2005)

13 Ian F.W. Beckett, 'The Real Unknown Army: British Conscripts 1915-19', *Great War*, 2 (November 1989).

14 Tim Lynch, *Unknown Soldiers – a 1918 Draft, Stand To! No 98 Western Front Association Journal September 2013.*

In order to examine both the impact of policy changes on formations and the effect on units of large numbers of casualties followed by an influx of replacements a chronological approach has been adopted for this book. It was also decided to concentrate on the British Infantry on the Western Front, as the part of the Army which suffered the greatest losses and hence required the greatest number of replacements; over 80 percent of those Other Ranks who were killed or who died from wounds or other causes on the Western Front belonged to the Infantry.[15] In order to provide exemplars, it was decided to concentrate on selected regiments drawn from a particular area, namely the English/Welsh Marches. The experiences of different Infantry battalions from this area are considered during various actions, with analysis of their casualties. In order to achieve greater granularity, however, twelve specific battalions, one Regular, one Territorial Force and one New Army battalion from each of four Infantry Regiments, were chosen for analysis into their composition as the war progressed. In order to assist comparison, the composition of each of these battalions was considered in detail for the same periods in the second half of each year: August-November 1914 and July-November for subsequent years.

The battalions chosen were:

- Regular battalions: 1st Cheshire, 2nd Royal Welsh Fusiliers (RWF), 1st South Wales Borderers SWB) and 1st King's Shropshire Light Infantry (KSLI).[16] All these battalions were serving at Home in August 1914 and went to France with the first wave of the BEF.
- Territorial Force (TF) battalions: 1/5th Cheshire, 1/6th Cheshire, 1/4th RWF, 1/4th KSLI.
- New Army battalions: 9th Cheshire, 9th RWF, 10th SWB and 6th KSLI. All these arrived in France during 1915.

Although general works have provided pointers, original sources have been consulted to a large extent and cross-referenced wherever possible. Extensive use has been made of the *Official Histories* and original documents have been consulted at The National Archives (TNA), including War Office and Formation correspondence, War Diaries, Army Council Instructions (ACI) and Army Orders (AO). It has been difficult to find some documents and the contents of war diaries are not always completely accurate due to the circumstances under which they were written. Regimental histories have also been used; although many of these are drawn predominantly from the unit war diaries, there are often other inclusions which provide additional information. Personal memoirs, papers and diaries, both published and unpublished, have been consulted including those at the Imperial War Museum (IWM) but it was decided not to use the oral history recordings made later in veterans' lives, partly because memories can unwittingly become falsified after too long a period of time but also because, depending on their rank and role, veterans were really familiar only with their own small area.[17] This work is essentially about management and not 'Everyman' at war.

15 *Statistics of the Military Effort*, p. 249. Total non-commissioned officers and men killed in France 379,450; total number of Infantry non-commissioned officers and men killed in France 307,975.

16 This spelling was the official one during the First World War although the older Welch was the version used unofficially by both the RWF and the Welsh Regiment. It was not until 1 January 1921 that the use of Welch was officially authorised.

17 Dan Todman, *The Great War, Myth and Memory* (London: Hambledon & London, 2005), pp. 187-8

In analysing the composition of units, use has been made of *Soldiers Died in the Great War* (SDGW) and the Commonwealth War Graves Commission (CWGC) website to find the basic data. Using this information in conjunction with the Regimental Numbers of the soldiers concerned, it has been possible to plot roughly the date of enlistment of men joining a particular Regiment. This has been backed up by the examination of Medal Index Cards, Medal Rolls and individual Service Records, where they exist, using www.ancestry.com . Further evidence of the composition of units is also contained in unit War Diaries, which normally refer to the arrival of drafts and occasionally where they have come from.

The chapters of this book follow a mainly chronological sequence. The first two chapters are effectively 'scene setters' containing background information. Chapter 1 covers pre-war manpower planning and the arrival of the BEF on the Western Front whilst Chapter 2 concentrates on 1915 and what were by then 'the realities of war'. Chapter 3 takes the story up to the middle of 1916 whilst Chapter 4 covers the second half of that year. It made more sense to split 1917 geographically so Chapter 5 covers events at Home whilst Chapter 6 considers those on the Western Front. The manpower crisis of late 1917 and early 1918 is covered in Chapter 7 which considers matters up to 21 March 1918. Chapter 8 covers the German Offensives whilst Chapter 9 concentrates on the 100 Days of the Allied advance, from August until November 1918.

1

Planning, Preparation and First Contact

The British Army that mobilized in 1914 was the product of reforms and reorganizations that had been initiated less than a decade earlier. The Army's inadequate performance during the Second South African War had shown that there was an urgent need to review its role and the structures necessary for it to fulfil it. Consequently, between 1905 and 1908, much detailed work on the Army's future shape and requirements was carried out both in the War Office and by the Government. What was then put in place, with some further refinements in the intervening years, would form the basic structure of the Army for 1914.

In the War Office, the General Staff had identified several scenarios which might potentially require the future deployment of the British Army. Each had then been analyzed in order to determine the size of force necessary to meet it. The outcome of these deliberations was circulated in January 1906 in a memorandum.[1]. Five scenarios had been identified as the most likely: namely a Boer uprising in South Africa; wars against the United States, Russia or France respectively; and war against Germany in alliance with France. A further Boer rebellion was deemed at least possible, as were wars against Russia or the United States but it was not thought likely that there would be a war against France. Of all the possibilities, however, war in alliance with France against Germany appeared to be not only 'within the bounds of possibility' but also 'an eventuality to be seriously considered'.

Each of the five scenarios had been analyzed in detail, with potential force levels for each side being identified together with the various external factors that might come into play. The outcome of each analysis was a detailed estimate of the number of troops likely to be required over a possible time frame. Distance meant that war against the United States would require the greatest number of troops but the next greatest force level would be needed for a war against Germany. Since the latter scenario was considered the most likely, it was concluded that for planning purposes the future force level required should be that estimated to be necessary to conduct a war against Germany: 75 Infantry divisions plus Cavalry, Artillery, Engineer and

1 Liddell Hart Centre for Military Archives (LHCMA): Robertson Papers, 1/2/6: Director of Military Operations (DMO) Major General J.M. Grierson, 'Memorandum upon the military forces required for over-sea warfare', dated 4 January 1906.

other supporting units.[2] It was also concluded that the forces to be deployed during the first six months of any Continental War should consist of permanently constituted Regular units, whilst those that might have six months in which to prepare for war could feasibly exist only in cadre form during peacetime. Thus the idea was already developing of Home-based Regular units which could form an Expeditionary Force in the event of war, supported by a second line 'fit for active service abroad after six months embodiment or training', with behind that a 'third line army to be ready, say, 12 months after the commencement of war'.[3]

In December 1905 the new Liberal Government had appointed Richard Burdon Haldane as Secretary of State for War. He had previously been giving thought to the future size and role of the Army and in January 1906 submitted his own Memorandum to the Army Council on the need to create 'a highly organised and well-equipped striking force that could rapidly be transported to any part of the world where it might be required'.[4] Haldane's proposals were inevitably constrained, however, by political demands for financial economies and the need to reduce the annual Army Estimates to below £28 million. Thus in his proposals, whilst any future Army needed to be highly mobile, it would have to be 'on a strictly limited scale, and perfect rather in quality than in expanded quantity'.[5]

Having recommended a future structure for the Army, the General Staff now turned its attention to how it should be maintained in the event of war. Lessons were drawn from studies of recent campaigns, particularly the Russo Japanese War of 1904-5, and a document entitled 'Wastage in War' was published in April 1906.[6] This study concluded that a further 80 per cent of the original Expeditionary Force would be required to replace Infantry losses during the first year of any future conflict. Drafts amounting to 10 to 20 per cent of the Expeditionary Force should be available in theatre within six weeks of the commencement of the war, with subsequent drafts following each month. The drafts required in the first six months should be mobilized with, or immediately after, the Expeditionary Force and consist of men already fully trained and ready for active service. After the first six months, men who had been only partially trained on the outbreak of war ought to be ready to proceed to the front, together with a proportion of men who had been invalided back but who would now be sufficiently recovered to return to active service. The work underlying this study not only contributed to the

2 Ibid., 'The Regular field troops to be maintained as units at home for the purpose of over-sea warfare should, therefore, be:
18 Cavalry regiments
10 batteries Horse Artillery
63 batteries Field Artillery
9 batteries heavy Artillery
3 batteries Mountain Artillery
Cadre of a Siege Train
75 battalions of Infantry
besides Engineers, Ammunition Columns and Departmental Services in due proportion.'

3 Grierson, 'Memorandum upon the military forces required for over-sea warfare'.

4 R.B. Haldane, 'A Preliminary Memorandum on the present Situation. Being a rough note for consideration by Members of the Army Council' National Library of Scotland (NLS) Haldane Papers 5918, cited in P. Simkins, *Kitchener's Army* (Manchester: Manchester University Press, 1988), p.6.

5 Ibid., p.6.

6 TNA WO 32/8813: General Staff Study 'Wastage in War' (April 1906).

thinking behind the imminent Army reforms but would also form the basis for the provision of reinforcements during the first few months of the First World War.

In June 1906, the Army Council decided to abandon the Army's existing Corps structure in favour of creating 'great' Divisions of 18,000-20,000 men. This innovation was not designed specifically to create an Army capable of fighting in Europe; it simply created a Home structure similar to that of the Indian Army. In combination with the other detailed Army staff work of 1905-6, however, this decision enabled Haldane to present proposals to Cabinet for a smaller, more flexible and more cost effective Army.

Haldane's key proposal, presented in June 1906, was for the creation of an expeditionary force immediately available for war service overseas with behind it a territorial organization 'capable of supporting and expanding it'.[7] To create this home-based expeditionary force, the Infantry would be re-structured by withdrawing or disbanding some of its overseas units thus leaving a balance of seventy-four paired battalions, one of each pair being home-based and the other overseas. An Expeditionary Force of 150,000 men would be created from the home-based Regular units, formed into six 'great' infantry divisions, four cavalry brigades, and artillery and supporting arms. In support would be a second line provided by a new Territorial Force (TF). This would consist of fourteen infantry divisions and fourteen mounted (Yeomanry) brigades, formed from the existing Militia, Yeomanry and Volunteers and administered by County Associations under the leadership of the Lords Lieutenant.

Not everyone was immediately in favour of Haldane's proposals and he encountered serious opposition particularly from within the Militia, Yeomanry and Volunteers who saw their traditions and independence being eroded by the proposed subservience to County Associations. The Militia in particular, firmly entrenched within its local areas and wielding significant influence in Parliament, posed the greatest threat to the scheme. The difficulty was ultimately resolved by a suggestion from the new DMO, Major General Spencer Ewart, that the Militia Depots should become seventy-four reserve battalion cadres, which on mobilisation could become draft-producing battalions for the Regular Army. This was agreed and the Militias effectively became the future Special Reserve (SR) battalions.

There still remained questions over the proposed use of the new TF. By the time Haldane's proposals finally went before Parliament, he had been forced into a compromise. Instead of becoming the future source of reinforcements for the Expeditionary Force, a role now filled by the former Militia units, the new TF would be limited to home defence. The County Associations would be responsible for recruiting and organizing their TF formations and units in peace and war with responsibility passing to the War Office only when the TF was called out for training or for actual military service. In March 1907, when presenting the Territorial and Reserve Forces Bill, Haldane was careful to emphasise that Parliament would exercise direct control over the calling out of the new TF and to reaffirm its primary purpose as home defence. It was a compromise but one that enabled the Bill to be passed, receiving Royal Assent in August 1907 and with an effective date of 1 April 1908.

Haldane's reforms created an Expeditionary Force and rationalised the organisation of the auxiliary forces, integrating them more closely with the Regular formations. A draft-finding

7 TNA CAB 3/1/38A: 'Notes on the organization and administration of the military forces of the United Kingdom', 18 June 1906, p.2.

system had been put in place but the restriction of the TF to a Home Defence role deprived the Expeditionary Force of the intended second line support for active service abroad. After the First World War, Haldane would claim that his reforms had been underpinned by a single strategic concept, namely the possibility of sending an army to France in the event of a German invasion. A force of 150,000 was, however, always going to be too small to intervene effectively against the conscript armies of the Continent. As Spiers concludes the size of the new Force bore no relationship to any pre-planned strategy; it simply reflected the peace-time exigencies:

> particularly the restrictions imposed by a financial ceiling of £28 million, the draft-producing requirements of the home army, and the political opposition to conscription.[8]

The new BEF was simply the largest formation that could be made out of the units left at home after the demands of Imperial policy had been met.[9] It was still a very small force, albeit almost twice as large as the entire Army today. The necessary legislation had been passed, however, and re-organization into the new structures proceeded apace from 1908 onwards.

The Regular Army

The Regular Army was little changed other than the Infantry, which now consisted of seventy-four paired battalions, one of each pair serving at home and the other overseas. In 1908 the 1st Battalions of the Cheshire Regiment and the King's Shropshire Light Infantry (KSLI) were both based in Ireland, whilst their 2nd Battalions were serving in India; the 1st South Wales Borderers (SWB) was in Hampshire whilst 2nd SWB was in China; and 1st Royal Welsh Fusiliers (RWF) was in Malta with its second battalion in Dorset.

The traditional recruiting areas for Infantry Regiments remained as laid down in the nineteenth century reforms initiated by Cardwell and Childers, which had created designated areas where Regiments would recruit and have their Depots.[10] These 'Regimental Areas' were numbered with the old Regimental numbers: for example, No 53, which covered Shropshire, Herefordshire and Radnorshire, remained the recruiting area for Regular soldiers of the 53rd Regiment of Foot, now the KSLI.[11] The Regimental Areas were themselves grouped into Military Districts. No 4 Military District, based on Shrewsbury, covered Cheshire, Shropshire, Herefordshire, Monmouthshire, the whole of Wales and that part of South Lancashire

8 Hew Strachan, 'The Continental Commitment, 1904-14', in D. French & B. Holden Reid (eds.), *The British General Staff* (London: Cass, 2002), p. 76; E.M. Spiers, *Haldane – An Army Reformer* (Edinburgh: Edinburgh University Press, 1980), pp. 192-3.

9 J.M. Bourne, *Britain and the Great War* (London: Arnold, 1989, 1994), p. 13.

10 TNA WO 123/23: General Order (GO) 41/1881 of 1 May 1881 amended by GO 70/1881 of 1 July 1881.

11 Regimental Area No 22 (**Cheshire Regt**): Cheshire; Regimental Area No 23 (**Royal Welsh Fusiliers**): Denbighshire, Flintshire, Carnarvonshire, Anglesey, Merioneth and Montgomeryshire; Regimental Area No 24 (**South Wales Borderers**): Brecknockshire, Cardiganshire, Monmouthshire, Montgomeryshire; Regimental Area No 40 (**South Lancashire Regiment**): South Lancashire; Regimental Area No 41 (**Welsh Regiment**): Carmarthenshire, Pembrokeshire, Glamorganshire; Regimental Area No 53 (**King's Shropshire Light Infantry**): covering Shropshire, Herefordshire and Radnorshire.

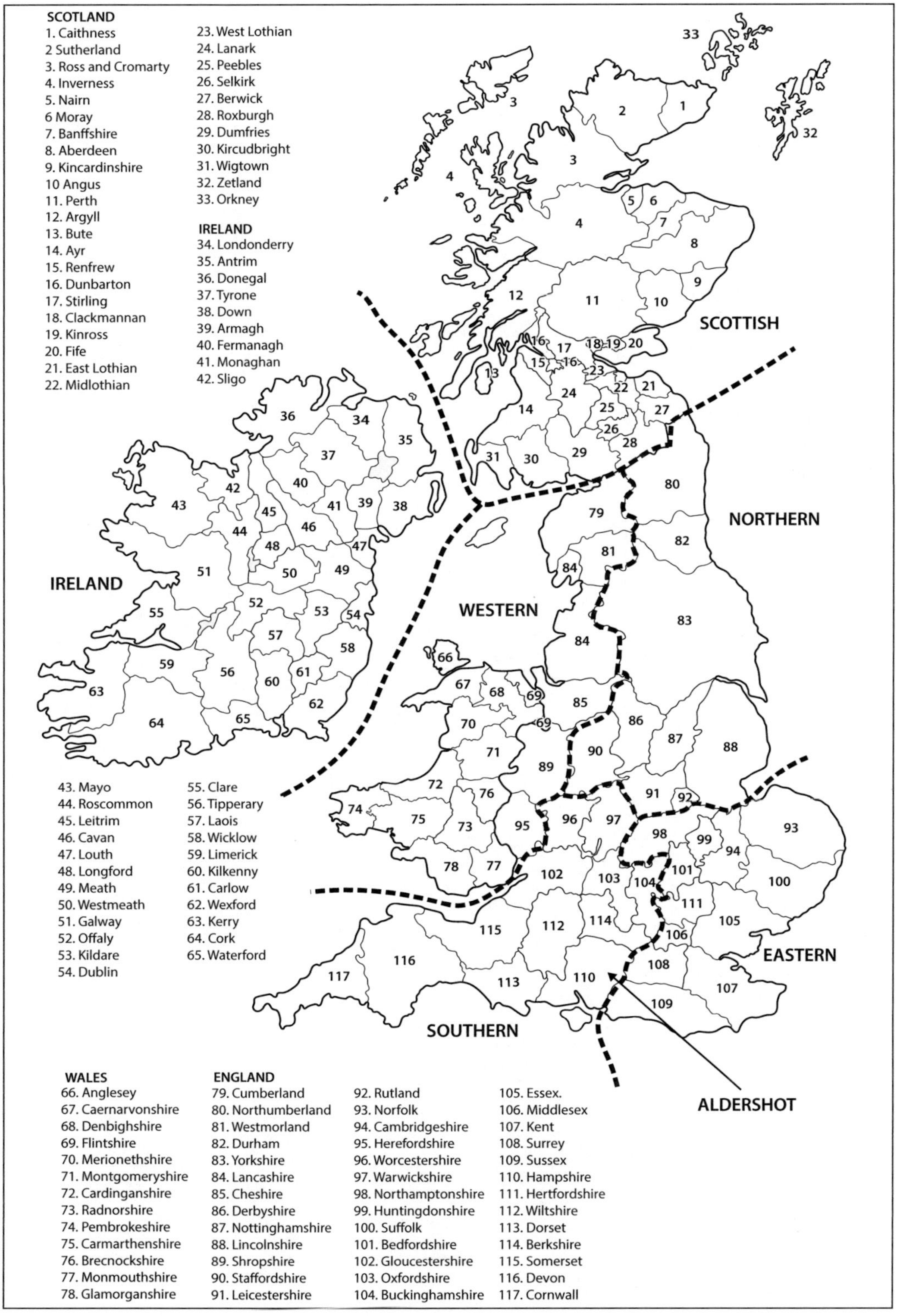

Map 1: Home Commands during the First World War

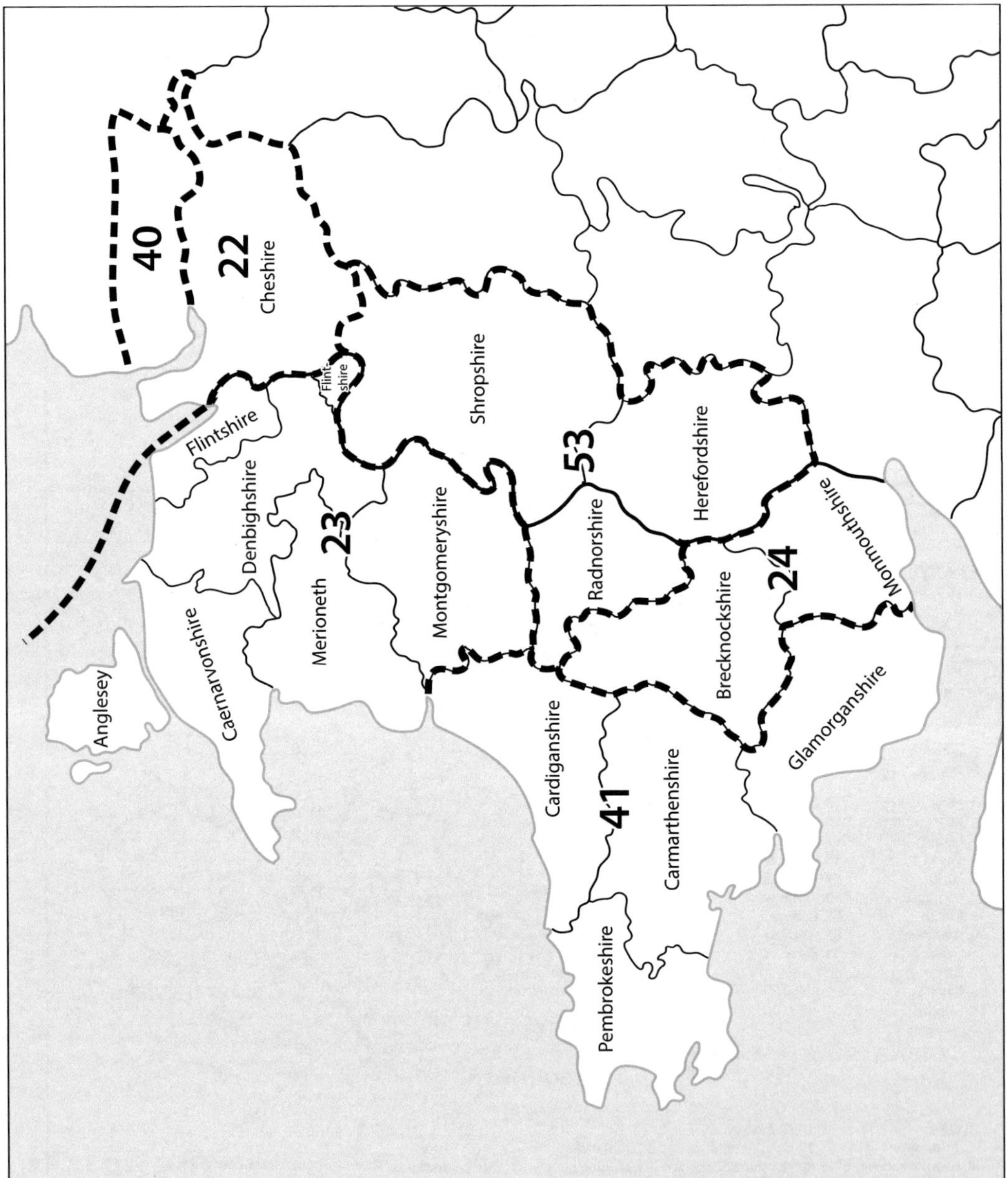

Map 2: Regimental Recruiting Areas in No 4 District

where the South Lancashire Regiment was recruited. Together with No 3 Military District, (Cumberland, Westmorland, Lancashire (except part of South Lancashire) and the Isle of Man) it formed Western Command. This Command thus covered a huge, geographically diverse area of England from the Scottish Borders southwards through the industrialised areas of south Lancashire, to Cheshire and the rural counties of Shropshire and Herefordshire, whilst westwards it included the whole of Wales.

When required, the Home-based battalion of a Regiment would form the new Expeditionary Force of 150,000. The plan looked good on paper but their strengths were seldom up to their effective war establishment. Not only were they perennially under-recruited but they also contained recruits undergoing training before being sent to the overseas based battalion, plus men ineligible for service overseas because they were either under the age of 19 or medically unfit for active service. The units that would form the Expeditionary Force were weakened in order to keep the overseas battalions fully manned.

Recruiting was easier in some locations than others but the individual regimental numbers of soldiers in different battalions indicate that, prior to August 1914, an average of about 200 recruits joined up annually.[12] On mobilization, the under-recruited Home-based Regular battalion would thus be reliant on being augmented by men from the Reserves. In 1870 the then Secretary of State for War, Edward Cardwell, had introduced short service engagements in the Army followed by reserve service. A man could, if he did not want a full career of 21 years, sign on for a shorter period of 12 years in total of which a period would be served with the battalion (known as service with the Colours) and then a further period on the Reserve to make up the total. The Army Reserve consisted of three main sections: A, B and D. Sections A and B consisted of men completing the Reserve term of their original engagement; the difference between A and B was that those serving in Section A had undertaken a higher liability for call-out in any emergency which did not call for general mobilisation. Those in Section A consisted of Reservists within two years of the date of their transfer to the Reserve who had undertaken to rejoin the Colours if required in an emergency not calling for general mobilization. Section B comprised all those who were completing the Reserve term of their original engagement Section D were men who on completion of their twelve years Colour and Reserve service had re-engaged in the Reserve for a further four years. Army Reservists were liable to be called out for twelve days annual training. On mobilization they were liable to serve, as long as their services were required, up to the expiry of their term of service in the reserve and could, under the Army Act, be retained for an additional twelve months or more if a state of war existed or in times of imminent national danger or great emergency. Reservists would expect, on mobilization, to return to the unit to which they had formerly belonged since under Section 83 of the Army Act consent was required before a man could be appointed or transferred to an arm or branch of the service other than that in which he had previously served.[13]

Prior to 1908 the length of time spent on the Reserve was changed frequently and confusingly. In May 1902 the ratio between colour and reserve service of seven and five years respectively

12 It is possible to identify when particular cohorts enlisted by using a combination of *Soldiers Died in the Great War (SDGW)* and Service Records. Examination of the 1911 census also shows, for example, some 200 recruits in training at Chester Castle.

13 On enlistment a soldier was appointed to a Regiment or Corps and was bound to serve in any part of it; he would usually spend the whole of his military life in one part or other of that Regiment.

had been changed to three and nine years, in order to attract more recruits.[14] This did not prove successful and in November 1904, as a result of a growing manpower crisis, the ratio of service was reversed to nine and three years. Then, in September 1906, the ratio reverted to the original seven and five years respectively.[15] There was a potentially serious effect arising out of the rapid changes in length of service commitments: both the 1905-6 and the 1907-8 enlistments would be due to transfer to the Reserve in 1914. In the first decade of the century, this problem would have seemed some way off; certainly no action was taken to address it in advance – thus storing up a problem for 1915.

The 1906 Reserve Forces Act also introduced a significant change. In future, a soldier enlisting after the implementation of that Act could, if called out whilst subsequently serving in the Army Reserve, be appointed to any regiment or corps and could also be transferred within three months to any other regiment or corps. This was a major change and a break with decades of tradition and accepted practice. It is early evidence not only of recognition of the need for greater flexibility in times of crisis but also, and more unexpectedly, of a previously unheard of readiness to sacrifice regimental loyalty. For some reason, the Notice paper signed and given to recruits on enlistment was not amended to show the new liability until 7 July 1908 so the change could not apply to those enlisted before that date.[16] It would thus remain hidden for the next few years since none of the post-1908 enlistments would become eligible for transfer to the Reserve until 1915 at the earliest.

Special Reserve

The second line of the new structure was now the draft-finding Special Reserve (SR), created out of the old Militia and consisting of men with no previous military experience who had signed on for six years' service. On enlistment, the man could join either Section A, thus accepting a higher liability for call out for up to 12 months when war was imminent or in progress, or Section B, which could be called out only by Proclamation in case of imminent national danger or of great emergency. The Special Reservists would undergo six months' full time basic training and thereafter returned to civilian life with an obligation to complete 28 days' training annually. Re-engagement for a further four years was permitted but there was an age limit of 40. In the event of general mobilization, both Sections A and B accepted the same liability for service abroad as did the Army Reservists, namely completion of the unexpired portion of their term of service plus a further period not exceeding 12 months if so directed by the competent Military Authority.[17]

In order to be in a position to provide drafts for the Regular battalions in the event of war, the SR would in the main be organized on a scale of one SR battalion linked to two Regular battalions within each regiment of the line, with the new unit usually being designated simply as the 3rd (Reserve) Battalion. There were exceptions to this, usually for historical and Militia

14 TNA WO 123/44: Army Orders (AO) 73 and 117 of 1902.
15 TNA WO 123/46: AO 209 of 1906.
16 Sir H. Jenkyns, 'Constitution of the Military Forces of the Crown', in *Manual of Military Law 1914* (London: War Office, 1914), pp. 202, 744.
17 Ibid., p. 202.

reasons and the size of the Regiment concerned. Fourteen two-battalion line regiments, such as the North Staffordshire, would have two reserve battalions, designated the 3rd (Reserve) and 4th (Extra Reserve). In Regiments large enough to contain four Regular Battalions, such as the Worcestershire, the Reserve battalions became the 5th and 6th (Reserve) Battalions. The Royal Fusiliers, however, would not only have two Reserve battalions, the 5th and 6th, but also a 7th (Extra Reserve) battalion.

The transformation to the new organizations did not always go smoothly, not just because of vested Militia interests but also due to local rivalries. On learning that it was proposed to disband the Macclesfield-based 4th (Militia) Battalion of the Cheshire Battalion whilst retaining the 3rd Battalion in Chester, the Macclesfield Town Council agreed unanimously to send an appeal to the War Office.[18] The letter, addressed to the Secretary of State for War, was duly published in the *Macclesfield Courier and Herald* on 11 January 1908. It urged the Army Council to reconsider the proposed disbandment, or if there could be only one SR battalion, then to disband the 3rd instead![19] Reasons cited were the lack of employment for men in the town, since its main industry of manufacturing silk goods chiefly employed female labour, and that, being situated in a large agricultural area, the town was a very good area for recruiting. It would also be difficult for the men to travel to Chester as this would involve a two hour train journey each way, via Stockport and Crewe. Furthermore, it was contended that Chester already contained a disproportionate number of units:

> its Line Depot, Yeomanry Headquarters, and Engineer, Artillery and Infantry Volunteers all competing for recruits whereas Macclesfield has only the Yeomanry and 4 Companies of a Volunteer Battalion.

The War Office and Army Council remained unmoved and the paper sadly reports the laying up of the Colours of the 4th (Militia) Battalion on 25 March 1908.

The formation of the SR continued. Although draft-finding for an Expeditionary Force would be its primary role, the SR battalions would also form an integral part of the plans for home defence.[20] For example, the 3rd (SR) Battalion of the Cheshire Regiment would form part of the Mersey Garrison, defending the ports of Liverpool and Birkenhead, whilst 3rd (SR) KSLI, formed out of the 3rd (Shropshire) Militia and the 4th (Royal Herefordshire) Militia, would on mobilization move to its War Station at Pembroke Dock.

Territorial Force

The third component of Haldane's new structure was the TF, created out of the earlier Volunteer and Yeomanry units. Once the re-organization was completed, the TF would consist of fourteen infantry divisions and fourteen mounted (yeomanry) brigades. The new TF Battalions of the Cheshire Regiment were created from Cheshire volunteer battalions: the 1st Volunteer

18 Extract from *Macclesfield Courier and Herald*, Saturday 4 January 1908 (Cheshire Regiment Archives).
19 Ibid., 11 January 1908 (Cheshire Regiment Archives).
20 War Office, *Manual of Military Law,* pp. 202–5, and K.W. Mitchinson, 'The Special Reserve', *Stand To!* 70 (April 2004), pp. 5-9.

Battalion became the 4th Battalion TF; the 2nd and 3rd Volunteer Battalions combined to form the 5th (Earl of Chester's) Battalion TF; the 4th Volunteer Battalion became the 6th Battalion TF; and the 5th Battalion became the 7th Battalion TF. Together these new TF battalions would form the Cheshire Infantry Brigade.

The transformation was not achieved without some bitterness: the *Macclesfield Courier and Herald* reported the farewell order issued by the Commanding Officer of the 5th Volunteer Battalion on Tuesday 31 March 1908:

> After an existence of nearly 50 years, the 5th Volunteer Battalion Cheshire Regiment will tomorrow be merged in a new battalion known as the 7th Battalion Cheshire Regiment. .... I trust that those who served so long in the 5th will not be prevented by [new conditions of service] from continuing their service for another two years at least, to give the new battalion a fair start, and to show the country that England still has some men willing to protect her shores even at the cost of a little personal inconvenience.[21]

Under the TF terms of service, men would enlist for four years during which they would attend regular training and drill sessions plus an annual training camp. Towards the end of the four-year period, they could apply for a further period of four years' service if they so wished. Should they wish to be discharged during their current period of service, application had to be made in writing giving three months' notice and payment of a sum not exceeding five pounds.[22]

The new organisation had come into being but it was recognized that in the event of war it would take six months for the TF to become fully trained. Furthermore, in manpower terms, it also lacked flexibility. Under the 1907 Territorial and Reserve Forces Act a recruit could select the particular TF unit in which he wished to serve and could not subsequently be transferred without his consent. Furthermore, TF soldiers could not be compelled to serve outside the UK.[23] The role of the TF was thus very definitely restricted to home defence and its men protected from being forced to serve in a different unit or abroad against their wishes. This meant that unless the legislation was changed, the TF could not be used to reinforce a BEF serving abroad.

Planning the Use of the New Structures

It was also necessary to define how the newly organized structures should be used in the future. Concern remained focussed, at least initially, on the need to defend Britain against possible invasion. In 1908 the Committee of Imperial Defence (CID) laid down broad policy lines on which plans should be based, concluding that, in the event of the new BEF being sent abroad, it would be necessary to retain at least two Regular divisions for Home defence until the TF was ready.[24] A sub-committee was then tasked to consider the military requirements of the Empire, including the scenario of a war with Germany. The General Staff proposed to the

21 Extract from *Macclesfield Courier and Herald*, Saturday, 4 April 1908 (Cheshire Regiment Archives).
22 War Office, *Manual of Military Law 1914*, p. 761: Territorial & Reserve Forces Act 1907 s. 9.
23 Territorial & Reserve Forces Act 1907 s. 13.
24 Lord Hankey, *The Supreme Command 1914-1918* (London: Allen &Unwin, 1961), pp. 66-68.

sub-committee that in the latter eventuality, an Expeditionary Force of four Infantry Divisions and one Cavalry Division should be sent to operate on the left flank of the French Army.

By 1911, increasing tensions with Germany were giving growing cause for concern. In the aftermath of the Agadir crisis of July, on 23 August the CID discussed the possibility of giving armed support to France in the event of a German assault.[25] Major General Henry Wilson, the Director of Military Operations (DMO), confirmed that the earlier plan to send the BEF to the left flank of the French Army remained extant and had been worked out in minute detail. Although no formal conclusions were reached as a result of this meeting, the Naval Assistant Secretary to the Committee, Maurice Hankey, privately considered that from then on there was no doubt as to 'the Grand Strategy in the event of our being drawn into a continental war in support of France'.[26] It remains debatable, however, whether there was really any 'Grand Strategy' since there was neither the political nor the military will to create the size of army that would be required in the event of a continental war. The CID and the General Staff continued to believe that the appearance of six British Divisions on their left flank would be of immense moral value to the French and thus sufficient.[27] They saw no need to plan for the provision of more troops on European lines as this would have meant conscription.

Conscription had been debated for some years but had few supporters. The National Service League had been created in 1902 to call for conscription in peacetime for the purpose of home defence. Between 1909 and 1912 League membership tripled to almost 100,000 as it continued to lobby for conscription. There was little significant political support, however. Apart from Governmental concern that conscription might precipitate the very conflict with Germany that they were trying to avoid, both the nation as a whole and the Liberal party were opposed on principle to compulsion. The Liberals were also averse to the expense it would incur, which would curtail many schemes for social reform.[28] Nor was there any support from the Conservatives. Electorally it would have been a disaster; conscription was not a vote-winner and thus not an option at that time.

If conscription was not to be considered, increasing anxieties over German intentions meant that existing structures needed to be suitable. Concern remained over the size and viability of the TF, in the event of the Expeditionary Force being mobilised and sent abroad. In 1908 the TF had been set ambitious recruiting targets of just over 312,000 men. Although initially growing rapidly, with numbers in the region of 144,600 in June 1908, 183,000 in July 1908 and 270,000 in October 1909, it would never achieve this target. A pre-war high of about 276,096 was reached in October 1910, but it then steadily declined until it numbered 268,777 officers and men in July 1914.[29] Attention had been diverted from home defence with the result that the TF had suffered delays in the provision of ranges and drill halls, the knock-on effects of which were criticisms over poor training and musketry. In 1910 a third of the force failed the

25 TNA CAB 2/2: Minutes of the Committee of Imperial Defence 114th Meeting, 23 August 1911.
26 Hankey, *The Supreme Command 1914-1918*, p. 82.
27 TNA CAB 2/2: CID 114th Meeting, 23 August 1911, p. 5.
28 Hankey, *Supreme Command 1914-1918*, p. 137.
29 Simkins, *Kitchener's Army*, pp. 17-18.

musketry requirement of firing 23 rounds. Attendance at the annual training camp was poor: in 1912 only 155,000 men had camped for a full 15 days and 6,000 had not turned up at all.[30]

The fundamental problem, however, was the TF's lack of liability for overseas service. Haldane had always rather optimistically hoped that after embodiment on the outbreak of war and six months subsequent training, the TF units would be ready to say 'We wish to go abroad and take our part in the theatre of war'.[31] A more formal footing was obviously required and in 1910 members of the TF were invited to accept liability for overseas service in the event of mobilization by signing the Imperial Service (IS) Obligation. This did not meet with a resounding response and by September 1913 only 7.7 per cent of its 245,779 members had committed themselves. By July 1914, although TF membership had risen to 268,777, the number of those who had committed themselves would fall to 18,683 officers and men, just under 7 per cent of the whole.[32]

Planning for War

Although no further provision had been made for the expansion in size of the Army in the event of war, other contingency planning had continued. On the manning front, this planning had resulted in the preparation and publication of various documents, such as *War Establishments (Expeditionary Force),* detailed *Mobilization Regulations* and new *Field Service Regulations.* All these documents had evolved through several drafts, with some being further amended soon after publication.

The composition of a unit in both peace and war was laid down in Establishment Tables. The *War Establishments (Expeditionary Force),* finally published in early 1914, detailed the numbers of personnel by ranks and trades who were to proceed overseas with each unit.[33] As has already been mentioned, units of the Home Army were perennially under-strength and also contained men who were unready for various reasons to be sent overseas immediately. In order to bring an Infantry battalion up to its War Establishment, which for an Infantry Battalion in 1914 was 30 officers and 977 men, trained soldiers of the Reserve would need to be mobilized.[34]

As with recruiting, the mobilization of units and men was devolved to Home Commands, each of which had been required under the *Mobilization Regulations* to form a Mobilization Committee to oversee local mobilization schemes. These had been drawn up at different levels of the chain of command: by commanders of military districts and stations, such as Chester

30 I.F.W. Beckett, *The Amateur Military Tradition* (Manchester: Manchester University Press, 1991), p. 222.

31 Spiers, *Haldane,* p. 109, quoting Parliamentary Debates, Fourth Ser., Vol. 169 (25 February 1907), cols. 1,286-301.

32 I.F.W. Beckett, 'The Territorial Force', in I.F.W Beckett & K. Simpson (eds.), *A Nation in Arms* (Manchester: Manchester University Press, 1985; 2004), pp. 129-30 and *Statistics of the Military Effort,* p.30.

33 War Office, *War Establishments, Part 1, Expeditionary Force* (London: HMSO, 1 January 1914).

34 The Peace Establishment of a unit was the number of officers, Warrant Officers (WOs), Non-Commissioned Officers (NCOs)., men, animals, guns and vehicles provided for it annually in Army Estimates; the War Establishment was the number in each category required for war. The 1914 edition of War Establishments (Expeditionary Force) laid down the numbers of personnel to proceed overseas.

and Shrewsbury, down to individual units and depots. Such matters as accommodation for mobilizing units, hire of transport, timetable of drawing stores were laid down, right up to the day and hour at which particular units would be required to deploy.

As far as the mobilization of the Reserves was concerned, the Officer In Charge (OiC) of the Records Office in each Military District was responsible for planning the allocation of the personnel under his control 'to the best advantage, with due regard to the efficiency, not only of the regular units and depots affiliated to his record office, but also of the reserve units, including any to be formed on mobilization'.[35] In Western Command, there were two Infantry Record Offices, Preston (No 3 District) and Shrewsbury (No 4 District), for the Regimental Areas within these Districts. Notices for Regular and Special Reservists and the TF to mobilize, together with addressed envelopes, were prepared, kept up to date and held by the Record Offices and the Officers Commanding SR and TF units. On Mobilization, the letters would be sent out ordering Reservists to report to their depots for processing, equipping and training before being sent to their units for deployment. Similarly, TF soldiers would be ordered to report to their units.

In 1911, the production of a 'War Book' had been started. It was to contain a chapter for each Government Department showing the detailed actions to be taken by that department on the outbreak of war, together with a synopsis of the corresponding and simultaneous actions being taken by other departments. The actions were sub-divided into two stages: the Precautionary and the War stages, and the pages organized so that the exact state of preparedness on every subject could be seen at a glance. By July 1914, the final edition had been approved and all routine telegrams, despatches and letters were drafted, awaiting signature or ciphering.

New *Field Service Regulations* for the operation of the British Army in war had been produced in two parts by the War Office in 1909.[36] The second part contained, amongst other matters, the war organization of the Expeditionary Force, outlining the duties and functions of officers, units and commands in the Lines of Communication and at the Base as well as those of formations of the Field Army. It also covered the maintenance of manpower levels in the field and the replacement of casualties, responsibility for which would fall to the Army's administrative, or 'A' staffs, under the Adjutant General (AG). Ranked second in the Army hierarchy, below the Chief of the Imperial General Staff (CIGS), the AG and his department in the War Office was responsible for all personnel matters, including manning, casualties and invaliding. These responsibilities were cascaded from the AG in London to the AG's Branch in the General Headquarters (GHQ) of each operational theatre and from thence down the chain of command to Divisional level. In the field, the work of the AG's, or 'A' branches, covered the whole range of personnel matters including the organization of new units; drafts to replace casualties; discipline; medical and sanitary matters, including the removal and care of the wounded; and later the registration of graves.[37] The maintenance of appropriate levels of manpower and the replacement of casualties would thus fall to the AG staffs of the operational theatres concerned.

35 War Office, *Regulations for Mobilization 1914*, (London: HMSO, 1914), p.18.

36 General Staff, War Office, *Field Service Regulations, Part I Operations and Part II Organization and Administration* (London: War Office, 1909).

37 General Sir Nevil Macready, *Annals of an Active Life, Vol. 1* (London: Hutchinson & Co., 1925?), p. 200.

A sub-branch of AG GHQ's office would be located at the Base, where it would be responsible for the huge amount of personnel administration associated with an army in the field: management of personal records so that casualties could be quickly and accurately traced and reported to the War Office; taking on strength reinforcements, both officers and men, and keeping track of their despatch to the front. They were also responsible for recording and promulgating AG's decisions in order to ensure an identical system for routine personnel matters throughout the BEF. The Branch was known as the 3rd Echelon and would be commanded by a Deputy AG (DAG). It would initially consist of about 200 officers and clerks.[38] Also at the Base, and working closely with the DAG, was the Inspector General of Communications (IGC), the officer in charge of the Lines of Communication (LofC). His organization would be responsible for sending forward all items required from the Base, including reinforcements, and for the evacuation of anything, including casualties, that needed to return in the opposite direction.

Procedures for the maintenance of manpower levels in the field and the replacement of casualties were also laid down in FSR *Part 2: Organization and Administration* (FSR Part 2). The number of reinforcements it was thought would be required once the Expeditionary Force had been mobilized and arrived overseas was based for planning purposes on the 1906 analysis of 'Wastage in War'. An element for each unit, to be known as 'First Reinforcements', was shown in the War Establishment tables, and consisted of 10 percent of the rank and file of the unit plus one officer if the number was over 40. On arrival overseas, these First Reinforcements were to be left at the appropriate Base Depot for the unit concerned. These were holding camps located within easy reach of the ports of entry to the theatre, where reinforcements could be held ready to replace casualties. Within six weeks of the war starting, further drafts amounting to 10-20 percent of the army in the field were to be available in the Base Depots of the overseas theatre. Subsequent drafts were to follow each month, with an additional increase about the sixth month. The intention was that reinforcements were to arrive at the Base before, and not after, losses occurred.[39]

The replacement of manpower depended on accurate and timely notification of the numbers of losses incurred. FSR Part 2 made a very clear distinction between the management information regarding the fighting strength of units or formations, needed by commanders as quickly as possible, and the provision of more detailed and above all accurate information for the notification of casualties to relatives and the public.[40] In order to obtain replacements for casualties, units were required to forward sufficient information as quickly as possible to the AG branch at divisional headquarters. Requirements would then be forwarded to AG GHQ and the DAG at the Base, who would notify the War Office. Small losses of personnel, due to routine wastage, such as sickness, however, were to be notified by unit commanders through divisional headquarters to the IGC, with a copy to AG's office at the Base. These small losses were to be replaced by the IGC at the earliest opportunity. When heavy casualties occurred AG's Branch at GHQ would instruct the IGC as to the priority and extent to which units were

38 Macready, *Annals of an Active Life , Vol. 1*, pp. 199–201.
39 War Office, FSR Part 2, pp. 56-58.
40 Ibid., Part 2 Section 133, pp. 167-8 Casualty reports were to be notified to the AG's office at the Base as soon as they occurred. After verification and confirmation, the names of all officers and men who had been reported as dead, wounded or missing would be telegraphed to the government concerned with the least possible delay.

to be completed. His organization would then issue the orders and timetables for each move to the commanders of the Base Depot concerned, who was then responsible for warning the necessary personnel, ensuring that they were ready to move at the time ordered and sent to the front fully clothed, armed and equipped.[41] In hindsight, the planned information flow, split between AG at GHQ and the IGC at the Base, was bound to cause problems. Until the system was put to the test, however, the full extent of these was unappreciated

In August 1914 the Army was as ready as it could be. Details had been worked out for the mobilization of the Reserves and the TF, the embarkation timings for the BEF's movement to France and the arrangements for it to join the left flank of the French Army. Plans for the provision and drafting of reinforcements and their management on arrival in France had been drawn up, based on the instructions in FSR Part 2. Each Infantry Division would set up a Base Depot at Le Havre to handle reinforcements for its units whilst six General Base Depots at Harfleur would handle reinforcements for the supporting arms.[42]

Even at the outset, however, the manpower numbers did not add up. The Regular Army's Other Rank (OR) strength was some 9,000 short of its establishment of 245,860. The Army Reserve contained 145,347 ex-Regular soldiers but these were men of varying ages, experience and physical fitness and would not all be usable. The Infantry portion of the Reserve numbered 89,575 including the Foot Guards. The SR, specifically created to provide drafts for an Expeditionary Force, numbered 61,376 but was nearly 16,000 below its establishment of 77,238. Its Infantry component numbered 47, 893 against a planned 63,170.[43] Finally, although the Territorial Force (TF) was now effectively the third line there had been little planning for its use in the event of war and the poor training record and attendance at training camps did not bode well for its efficiency. Furthermore, it remained highly questionable whether the restriction of the TF's role to home defence could be overcome. In July 1914 it numbered 268,777 officers and men but less than 10 per cent, and only five complete TF units, had taken the Imperial Service (IS) obligation enabling them to be sent overseas.[44] On the face of it, there might be enough men to bring the BEF up to strength and then to maintain it in the field - but only if the war was over quickly.

Mobilization

War was declared on 4 August 1914 and mobilization began. Regimental depots, in accordance with pre-war plans, split from their respective SR battalions and became separate units ready to receive and process Reservists.[45] In all, some 136,781 non-commissioned officers and men from

41 Ibid., pp. 54, 58-59.
42 No 1: RGA; 2: RHA and RFA; 3: RGA, ASC and RE; 4: RE; 5: RAMC and Cavalry; 6: Corps Details.
43 War Office, *Statistics of the Military Effort of the British Empire during the Great War (SME)* (London, 1922; Uckfield: Naval & Military Press 1999), p. 30 and pp. 158-9.
44 Beckett, 'The Territorial Force', pp. 129-130. *BOH 1914 Vol. II*, pp. 2, 3: Northumberland Yeomanry, Dorset Fortress Company RE, 6th East Surrey and 7th and 8th Middlesex. Full bibliographic citations for the British Official History may be found in the Bibliography, below.
45 Major W. deB. Wood, *The History of the King's Shropshire Light Infantry in the Great War* (London: Medici Society Limited, 1925; Uckfield: Naval & Military Press, n.d), p. 301.

the Army Reserve would rejoin the colours in August, with a further 2,699 in September and 932 in October 1914. Although the Army Reservists were in all states of readiness and fitness, only 1,816 became non-effective almost immediately: 1,528 were unfit, 181 had completed their engagements, 24 were discharged and 83 died from unspecified causes.[46]

The Line battalions implemented their particular mobilization plans immediately. In Londonderry, 1st Cheshire had six days to complete the process. Like other battalions they were under-strength and during the next three days would receive three drafts of Reservists from the Depot, totalling 556 men. Many of these men had seen only two or three years' service, and that as much as nine years before.[47] They would find many differences. In 1913, the organisation of Infantry battalions into eight companies, each of four platoons, had been changed to four companies, each with four platoons and four sections in each platoon: 'We reservists were a little muddled at first by all this'.[48] Most battalions were also now equipped with the new Short Magazine Lee Enfield (SMLE) rifle on which the incoming Reservists needed familiarisation and training. Across Britain, Depots were hastily processing and equipping men before despatching them to the Line battalions. The KSLI Depot despatched drafts daily to 1st KSLI which remained in Tipperary until 14 August, when it left to join the rest of the 6th Division in camp near Cambridge. Once settled in, they were kept continuously at intensive training until 'all ranks had become hardened and were fighting fit'.[49]

After the Regular battalions had been brought up to strength, the remaining Reservists were sent to the SR battalions, now at their pre-planned War Stations. The 3rd (SR) Cheshire had assembled at Chester to draw equipment and stores and was now at its War Station at Birkenhead. On mobilization, it had numbered only 16 officers and 500 men but was soon joined by older trained soldiers, retired NCOs, Army Reservists plus those who had already completed their time on the Reserve, and newly enlisted recruits. The 3rd (SR) KSLI mobilized at the Depot in Shrewsbury and on 11 August, numbering 1,052, left by train for its war station at Pembroke Dock. Within a very short space of time its numbers would be up to 1,600.[50]

The TF was embodied on 4 August 1914 and mobilized as quickly and effectively as its Regular and SR counterparts. The four Territorial Battalions of the Cheshire Regiment, the 4th, 5th (Earl of Chester's), 6th and 7th Battalions, formed the Cheshire Infantry Brigade of the Welsh Division. The Regimental History commented that the:

> response to the order to mobilize was exceedingly creditable, especially as many of the men were clerks and cashiers, holding responsible jobs which they would have to hand over.[51]

Within six days, all four TF Battalions of the Cheshire Infantry Brigade were at full strength.

46 TNA WO 162/23: General Mobilisation: Review of Arrangements 1 November 1914.

47 A. Crookenden, *The History of the Cheshire Regiment in the Great War* (Eastbourne: Rowe, nd), p. 338.

48 F. Richards, *Old Soldiers Never Die* (1933; Uckfield: N&P reprint, nd), p. 11. Frank Richards rejoined the Royal Welsh Fusiliers in August 1914.

49 Wood, *King's Shropshire Light Infantry in the Great War*, pp. 1-2.

50 Ibid., p. 315.

51 A. Crookenden, *Cheshire Regiment in the Great War* (Chester: Evans, no date), pp. 340-1.

Arrival in France and the First Test of the Reinforcement System

The BEF, consisting of I Corps (1st and 2nd Divisions) and II Corps (3rd and 5th Divisions) and numbering about 100,000 men, moved to France between 9th and 17th August. Three Large Rest Camps had been established at the ports of entry, to receive troops on arrival and then despatch them to the appropriate Base Depots. There had been no mention of Rest Camps in FSR Part 2 and plans appear to have been somewhat vague: the designated CO of No 2 Large Rest Camp complained that it was only on arrival at Southampton that he and his men had received some idea of their role – and learned that they would be leaving for France immediately! No 2 Large Rest Camp arrived at Rouen on 10 August and took over two camps previously set up by the French. By 13 August they were ready to arrange the reception and accommodation of troops arriving in France until their departure for the Front by rail.[52]

The first three Regular battalions from the Marches would arrive in France by 16 August. The 1st SWB left Hampshire on 12 August, arriving at Le Havre in the early hours of the following morning. After a couple of days in a Rest Camp, they moved forward and arrived at Leschelle, in the BEF's concentration area, by 16 August. The rest of 3rd Brigade and the 1st Division were close by. The 1st Cheshire left Londonderry for Belfast early on 14 August in order to sail direct for France and arrived at Le Havre mid-afternoon on 16 August. Following a night spent in a Rest Camp, they entrained the next day for an unknown destination and by 18 August were in the Le Cateau-Landrecies area with the rest of 5th Division, as part of II Corps. The 2nd RWF had arrived in France by 13 August and were initially intended as LOC troops. On 21 August, however, they were posted to 19th Brigade at Valenciennes.

The Divisional Infantry Base Depots (IBDs) were slowly getting organized. Having arrived at Boulogne on 20 August, No 2 IBD moved to Le Havre the next day where it took over Camp No 8 containing 100 tents. No 3 IBD also arrived at Le Havre on 21 August. Both received their first reinforcements from England the next day: 15 officers and 1143 ORs for 2nd Division and 13 officers and 1279 ORs for 3rd Division, including 1 officer and 113 ORs for the RWF. The next reinforcements were expected to arrive from England on 27 August

The fighting in the Mons area during 23 and 24 August was the first real test of the FSR Part 2 procedures. Casualties began to flow to the rear areas and by 25 August it was already apparent that the toll exacted by modern warfare was going to be far heavier than expected. On 24 August, 1st Cheshire had gone into action at Audregnies with 27 officers and 934 men; by the time the roll was taken at Les Bavay that evening only 6 officers and 200 men were present.[53] Of those absent, 55 had been killed, 500 taken prisoner and the rest wounded. The Cheshire losses were particularly high owing to their having failed to receive orders to withdraw, but the Infantry as a whole had suffered significant casualties during the first real contact with the enemy.

By late on 25 August, the BEF was retreating with the Germans in close pursuit. The first drafts of reinforcements had been sent closer to the Front and some 6,000 men had been concentrated at Advanced Base at Amiens. At this point the Rest Camps and the IBDs had expected a lull but the BEF's retreat southwards, rather than on its LOC, meant the reinforcements at Amiens

52 TNA WO 95/4116: War Diary of No 2 Large Rest Camp.
53 Cheshire Regiment Archive (CRA), 1st Cheshire War Diary, 24 August 1914.

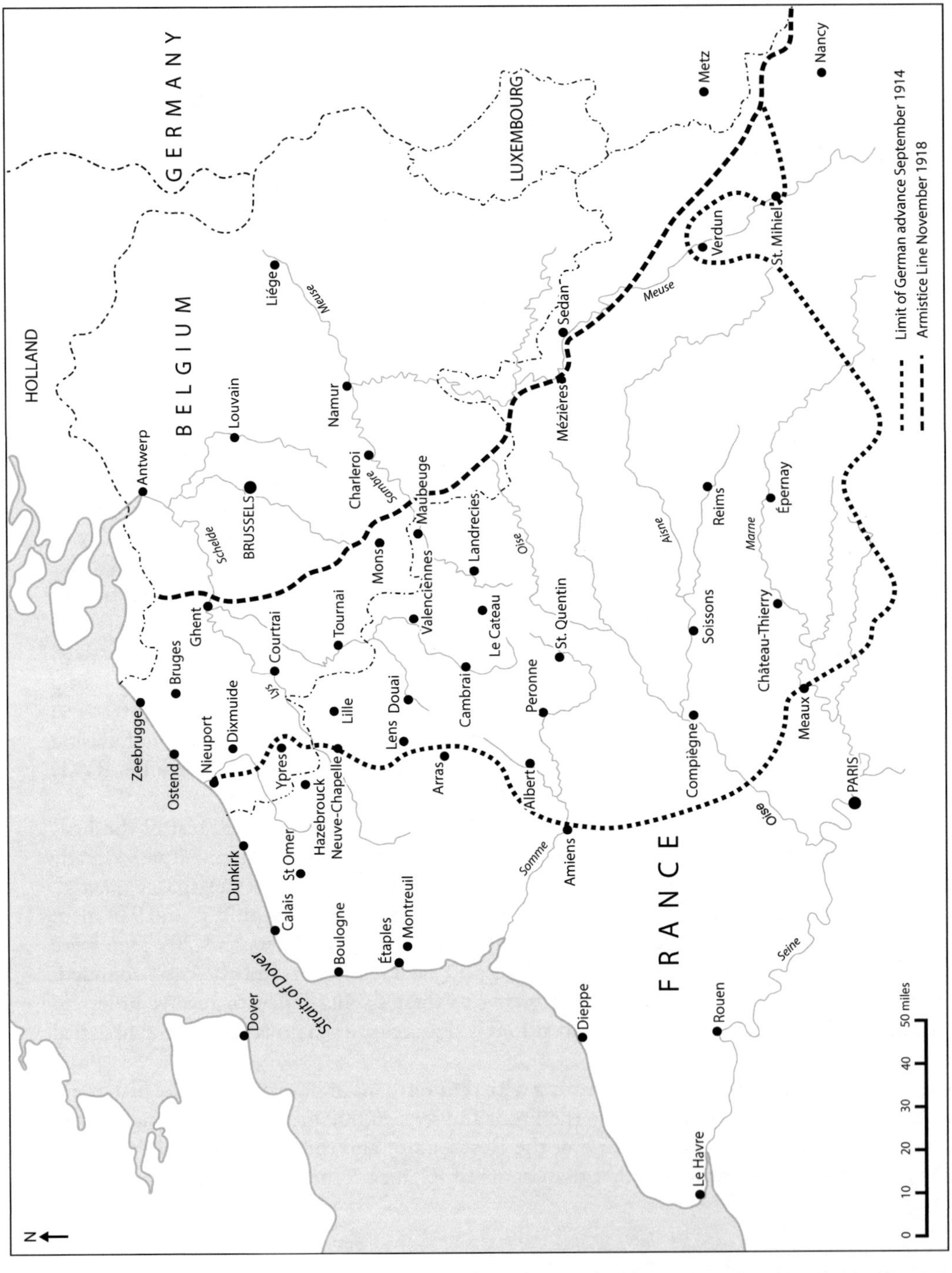

Map 3: Western Front 1914-1918

had nowhere to go. They were hastily returned No 2 Large Rest Camp but matters deteriorated and Rouen was ordered to be evacuated. No 2 Large Rest Camp, with 65 officers and 6000 men, entrained for Le Mans on 30 August, arriving the following day. The IBDs had also been ordered to move and on 31 August were moved by sea to St Nazaire.[54] Huge numbers of men and stores were forced to be moved at speed away from the newly set-up Bases, whilst remaining ready to be sent forward when called for. The 'First Reinforcements' were waiting with the Rest Camps and Base Depots but until a pause could be expected in some definite locality it would be impossible to send them up the line.[55]

The continuing fighting at the front made it difficult to get accurate casualty returns back to the Base and only rough estimates could be made of the reinforcements required. AG GHQ needed a firmer handle on casualty numbers and the first amplification of the FSR 2 procedures was made on 29 August: divisions were to obtain from units the details of officers and the numbers of ORs killed, wounded and missing and to report these by the quickest method direct to GHQ. In slower time, the DAG at GHQ 3rd Echelon would receive direct from units the regimental numbers and names of the dead and missing and from the commanders of medical units the details of those wounded. After the information had been verified, the DAG's office would cable home the names of all individuals reported as killed, wounded and missing.[56]

When a halt was finally called in early September, some 20,000 were missing from the BEF's original numbers. Not all were casualties: on 2 September No 2 Large Rest Camp contained 3,340 stragglers in addition to about 5,970 reinforcements. The reinforcements were sent up on 3 September and on 4 September stragglers numbering 18 officers and 1064 men were re-equipped and despatched back to their units. There was concern about the numbers unaccounted for and GHQ Army Routine Order (ARO) 59 of 4 September notified that in future stragglers were to be given written instructions on where and to whom to report.[57] A proportion of those missing would rejoin later but the official casualty figures for the period up to 5 September still showed just over 15,000 casualties ie killed, wounded and missing. The temporary halt at last enabled the 'first reinforcements' to be brought up from the IBDs, reaching most units by 6 September.[58] By 7 September, all available men from the Base had been used to replenish units but in many cases there had been insufficient replacements available. The Cheshires, for example, had received one officer and 90 men on 5 September but still remained at less than half strength.

The first extended contact with the enemy had revealed significant deficiencies in the pre-war plans and organisations. The AG GHQ, Major General Sir Nevil Macready, realised pre-war casualty estimates needed revision and immediately increased future indents on the War Office. There had also been friction between the respective roles of the AG GHQ and that of the IGC at the Base, Major General F.S. Robb. The latter's designated role had been to anticipate requirements and push as much forward as possible, including reinforcements, in readiness for when required, but in practice this proved unworkable. A tetchy letter of 24 August, from Macready to Robb, illustrates the problems of the passage of information and conflicting roles and responsibilities:

54 Ibid., and TNA WO 95/4185: War Diaries of No 2 and No 3 IBDs.
55 Macready, *Annals of An Active Life, Vol. 1*, pp. 199–201, 203-4.
56 TNA WO 95/25: GHQ – AG Branch War Diary – Army Routine Order of 29 Aug 14.
57 Ibid., Army Routine Order 59 of 4 September 1914.
58 *BOH 1914, Vol. I,* pp. 286-7, 301.

Adjutant General and staff, France 1914. Seated from left to right: Major Childs, Colonel Cavendish, Adjutant General Sir Nevil Macready, Colonel Bunbury, Major Cooke. At Rear: Captain V Davis in centre with clerks on either side of him.

> Theoretically I am aware that your jurisdiction extends to rendezvous points, but I have always held, and present experience confirms me in the idea, that in the area immediately in the rear of the troops it will be better to advise the officer of GHQ concerned before any action is taken, in case we may have information that possibly may not have reached you.[59]

Individuals had done their best and reinforcements had been waiting to be sent forward but all had not gone smoothly. On 4 September Robb wrote to the CIGS in London, General Sir Charles Douglas, concerning mistakes he felt had been made in the replacement of casualties. He had sent reinforcements up to Advanced Base and been most anxious to send them further forward only to be told that until units disentangled from the enemy they could not take them. Eventually they were called forward on 3 September. Somewhat disingenuously, Robb claims to be telling the CIGS this only to show the 'extraordinary difficulties they have in the fighting line'. In a further letter he continues to make the point that he had been ready and willing

59 TNA WO 95/25: GHQ – AG War Diary: Macready letter dated 24 August 1914.

to send men and stores forward but the time taken to fill gaps of all sorts 'is governed by the ability of the unit to receive and not the LofC to send up'. It had also proved impossible to forecast events and to place reinforcements ahead in view of the daily changes and the inability of the Army to retire on its own LofC.[60] That these letters were flying back to London from the Base cannot have endeared Robb to an already hard-pressed GHQ. There was a further difficulty in that Robb reported directly to the C-in-C BEF rather than through the BEF's principal staff officers, AG and QMG. The latter at the time was Major General Sir William Robertson. This dual chain of command caused problems since Robb was independently sending indents for men, stores and matériel to the War Office at the same time as the 'A' and 'Q' staffs were also doing so, thus causing confusion at both ends. This was not something that could be allowed to continue, and the system was changed so that in future Robb would receive his orders from the GHQ Staff, in the same way as any officer commanding one of the larger formations at the front.[61]

The approximate casualty figures for the BEF for August 1914 would later show a total of 14,409, of whom 105 officers and 1,277 soldiers were dead.[62] Fresh drafts of men were sent out to France in early September but the inadequacy of pre-war estimates of the numbers of reinforcements that would be required was already apparent. At home, steps were already in hand to obtain more men but this would take time.

The Expanding Army

The new Secretary of State for War, Field Marshal Lord Kitchener, who had accepted the appointment on 5 August 1914, was well aware of the need for more men. He rejected the prevalent view that economic conditions precluded a long war and instead considered it necessary to plan for at least 3 years, with a consequently significant manpower requirement. On 24 August Kitchener updated the House of Lords on the Government's intention to prepare an Army in the field, stating that he could not at that stage say what its eventual size might be, nor:

> what measures may eventually become necessary to supply and maintain (it). The scale of the Field Army which we are now calling into being is large and may rise in the course of the next six or seven months to a total of thirty divisions continually maintained in the field.[63]

Whilst the ultimate size remained unclear, what was recognised was the need not only to create a large Army but also the requirement for it to be maintained.

60 TNA WO 79/63: Sir A.J. Murray Private Papers. Letters from Robb to CIGS dated 3 September 1914 and 16/17 September 1914. Murray was then COS GHQ so it may be assumed that GHQ had sight of these letters.
61 Macready, *Annals of an Active Life*, p. 210; Field Marshal Sir William Robertson, *From Private to Field Marshal* (Boston: Houghton Mifflin Company, 1921), p. 200; TNA WO 163/45 Minutes of Meeting of Military Members of Army Council of 9 January 1915.
62 War Office, *SME*, p. 253.
63 HLRO: 'Debates on Army Affairs, House of Lords, Session 1914' (London, HMSO, 1915), c. 504.

Much has been written about the raising of the New Armies, in particular by Peter Simkins in *Kitchener's Army*.[64] It is not intended here to re-iterate here the sequence of events except in so far as they had a bearing on the future provision of replacements. The first 'call to arms' for 100,000 men, aged between 19 and 30, for general service for a period of three years or the duration of the war appeared first in the national daily papers on 7 August and subsequently in local weekly papers. During the early weeks of the war large numbers of men enlisted daily.[65] The peacetime recruiting organisation, used to handling fewer than 100 recruits a day in total, found it increasingly difficult to cope and the Regimental Depots and SR Battalions rapidly became over-loaded. Some new form of organization was needed to handle the huge influx of volunteers and it was decided to form new battalions, to be known as 'Service' battalions. On 10 August the KSLI Depot in Shrewsbury received orders to form the 5th (Service) Battalion KSLI whilst on 12 August the Cheshire Regiment raised the 8th (Service) Battalion.[66] Military accommodation was limited in Chester and 8th Cheshire had to set up its Headquarters in the Grand Stand of Chester Race Course, where the men also slept. The 8th (Service) Battalion RWF and the 4th (Service) Battalion SWB were also formed during early August, in Wrexham and Brecon respectively. By 21 August, the 'Service' battalions had been formed into six new divisions.

The flood of recruits was not destined solely for the embryo New Armies. On 22 August the *Cheshire Observer* reported that by the following numbers of men had enlisted:

Enlisted for normal Army Service	950
Joined the 3rd (SR) Battalion of the Cheshire Regiment	600
Enlisted in the Service Battalion, Cheshire Regiment for Lord Kitchener's army	350
Joined the Special Reserve	250
Enlisted in Engineers, Army Service Corps and other regiments	300[67]

The primary role of the SR battalions remained draft-finding, however, and on 28 August Kitchener appealed for a second 100,000 men, which would initially be used to bring each SR battalion up to a strength of 2,000. Any balance above this figure would remain for training at the regimental depots.[68] The following day, the Army Council tasked the AG, General Sir Henry Sclater, to formulate proposals for raising another six divisions. It was at this point that the first six divisions began to be collectively described as K1 or the First New Army[69].

On 1 September Sclater informed his colleagues that new divisions numbered 14 to 19 would be formed as soon as the new influx of recruits had enabled the K1 battalions to reach their war establishments of 1,000 all ranks and the SR battalions a strength of 2,000. The six new divisions would be known as K2, or the Second New Army. By 9 September, the influx of new recruits had been such that the formation of two further New Armies, K3 and K4, had

64 Simkins, *Kitchener's Army*, *passim*.
65 TNA WO 162/3: 'Approximate number of recruits raised day by day from 3rd August 1914'.
66 Wood, *KSLI*, p. 301 and Crookenden, *Cheshire Regiment*, p.343.
67 Cheshire Records Office (CRO) *Cheshire Observer*, Saturday, 22 August 1914 (mf 225/37).
68 TNA WO 163/44: Meeting of Military Members of the Army Council, 27 August 1914.
69 Ibid., Meeting of Military Members of the Army Council, 29 August 1914.

been organised. The speed with which decisions were being taken, however, inevitably led to their being revised, often only days later. The decision to form a new Regular 8th Division from battalions withdrawn from garrison duty in South Africa, India and other overseas stations meant that in early September the divisions of K1 were renumbered 9th to 14th, with the original 8th Division now being designated 14th (Light) Division. It is unlikely that the battalions concerned were too bothered by this change: the 5th KSLI had newly arrived at Blackdown Camp, near Aldershot, and was still trying to sort itself out.

Of more concern, however, was a Kitchener plan concerning the SR battalions, which were already fully occupied in forwarding reinforcement drafts to the BEF whilst manning their war stations. On Wednesday 9 September, the Army Council was informed that the Secretary of State had decided to form the 2nd New Army by organizing the SR battalions into six Divisions. The Armies previously referred to as the 2nd and 3rd New Armies (K2 and K3) would then become K3 and K4.[70] This must have caused consternation amongst the Staff since at a stroke the plan removed the draft-finding units of the Regular Army. Fortunately, by the meeting of Sunday 13 September the plans had been reversed; the Army Council Minutes note simply that Kitchener had 'approved changes in nomenclature'. This almost certainly indicates some fast footwork by the Staff to remind him of the disaster that would be caused by the transformation of the draft-finding SR Battalions into Service battalions destined for the Front. As a compromise, it was decided that the newly enlarged SR battalions would be split, part reverting to Reserve battalions for reinforcement purposes and the other to form the basis of six new infantry battalions. These would be given numbers later and would 'probably' form a Fourth New Army.[71] The revised plan was promulgated by the immediate publication, perhaps in order to forestall further changes, of an Army Order announcing the new titles of 'the several additions to the Army'.[72]

Many more battalions were also being enthusiastically raised by local authorities, industrialists and committees of private citizens eager to play their part in the war effort. The main benefit of the scheme was that it relieved the hard-pressed War Office staff of the burden of housing, clothing and feeding yet more thousands of potential recruits until they were ready to adopt officially these 'locally raised' battalions. These battalions, many of which would become known emotively as 'Pals' battalions, often adopted very specific identities and loyalties to those who had raised them. Although many were raised in specific geographic areas, such as major cities, this in itself did not differentiate them from Infantry battalions raised within their own Regimental recruiting areas. Indeed, the recruiting of 'local squads' was a common approach for the New Armies. For example, in mid-September a recruiting meeting for the KSLI was held in the North Shropshire village of Whixall, where it was stated that it was 'the desire of the Government to form the squads, to get young men from neighbourhoods to go forward for the defence of their country'. Any Whixall lad volunteering at that meeting would have been destined for C Company of 6th KSLI, in the Second New Army.[73] The main difference with

70 Ibid., 30th Meeting of Military Members on 9 September 1914.

71 Ibid., 34th Meeting of Military Members on 13 September 1914. The 'changes in nomenclature' returned K1, K3 and K4 to being respectively the First (9th-14th Divisions), Second (15th-20th Divisions) and Third (21st-26th Divisions) New Armies.

72 TNA WO 123/56: Army Order (AO) 388 of 1914 and AO 389 of 1914.

73 *Whitchurch Herald*, Saturday, 19 September 1914, p. 4.

many of the locally raised battalions, however, was that the men frequently shared common social and occupational backgrounds.[74] Others were recruited from particular pools, such as the Sportsmen's and the Public Schools battalions. Once overseas, however, they would need to be reinforced in the same way as other battalions but their recruiting pool was often more limited.

The TF, which had been embodied on 4 August, was also expanding rapidly. On 10 August TF soldiers were again invited to volunteer for overseas service and on 21 August it was announced that units in which 80 per cent of the men had taken the IS obligation could be sent overseas as formed units. The initial response was not overwhelming with only seventy battalions reaching the 80 per cent mark so on 31 August the percentage was lowered to the more realistic figure of 60 per cent.[75] The County Associations had been authorised, on 15 August, to raise new units to replace those volunteering for overseas service and this now enabled first line TF units to make up their numbers for overseas service whilst those men remaining 'home service only' could move to the second line, forming a nucleus of trained soldiers. Once the First Line battalions went overseas, the Home Service (HS) battalions would replace them at their war stations and also provide drafts for overseas service from new recruits who had signed the IS obligation. By 31 August most of the officers and 80 percent of the men of 6th Cheshire TF battalion had volunteered for overseas service and a home service battalion, 2/6th Cheshire, was created at Stockport in September.[76]

There remained ambivalence over the use of the TF overseas and it is apparent from statements made in August and September that they were not expected to be sent abroad in a hurry, or at least not before they had received considerable training and reached a sufficient level of efficiency.[77] Expediency forced this to change, however, and by October TF units were being rapidly despatched to different parts of the Empire to replace Regular battalions recalled for active service. The 4th KSLI embarked for Garrison duties in India in late October but by then other TF units were already in France. Intended initially as LofC troops, 1/14th London (London Scottish) and 1/1st Queen's Own Oxfordshire Hussars had landed on 16 and 22 September respectively

The arrival of TF units in various parts of the Empire enabled Regular battalions to return home to make up new divisions for France. The newly formed 7th Division landed in Belgium in early October and was followed by a new 8th Division in November. Further Regular Army battalions returning from overseas later in the year were formed into three new Regular divisions, the 27th, 28th and 29th. The creation of these new Regular divisions meant several organizational changes to the New Armies but as yet these would make little impact on the newly formed Service battalions. Of more concern, was that no system for the replacement of their future losses had yet been put in place other than that provided by the already overworked 3rd (SR) battalions. Authority would be given in December 1914 for the locally raised battalions

74 The 15th (Service) Battalion Highland Light Infantry (HLI) (1st Glasgow) contained many recruits from the Glasgow Tramways whilst its sister battalion, the 16th (Service) HLI (2nd Glasgow) was always referred to as the Glasgow Boys Brigade Battalion, having drawn many of its officers and soldiers from graduates of the Glasgow Battalion of the Boys Brigade.

75 Beckett, *Amateur Military Tradition*, p. 228.

76 C. Smith, *War History of the 6th Battalion The Cheshire Regiment* (Chester: 6th Cheshire Old Comrades Association, 1932), p. 2.

77 K.W. Mitchinson, *Defending Albion* (London: Palgrave Macmillan, 2005), p. 62.

to recruit above the War Establishment in order to form additional Depot companies, each 250 strong. There was as yet, however, no provision for reinforcements for the battalions of the first New Armies.

Meanwhile in France and Flanders…

On 6 September the BEF had again turned north in what would become known as the 'Race to the Sea' as the opposing sides tried to outflank each other and gain the crucial Channel Ports. The next few weeks were punctuated by a succession of battles: the Marne 6-10 September, the Aisne 13-28 September, La Bassée 10-31 October, culminating in the First Battle of Ypres from 19 October to 21 November.

The BEF gradually increased in size through what the *Official History* refers to as efforts to 'improvise' armies: on 15 September it numbered 163,897 and by 15 November had grown to 224,647.[78] As the fear of invasion at home receded, the 4th and 6th Divisions had been released. The 4th Division had arrived in France in late August and on 30 August became the III Corps together with the 19th Brigade. The 6th Division arrived in mid-September, making a welcome arrival in the rear of III Corps on 16 September, where the Division was temporarily broken up to provide relief to the weary troops. The 7th and 8th Divisions arrived but other Regular battalions were still in transit from overseas. Only TF battalions were readily available and on 26 October, Kitchener telegraphed the CinC promising six TF battalions to replace six Regular battalions, including 1st Cheshire, that had suffered the heaviest casualties. On 30 October he telegraphed that the battalions were either already on their way or about to leave and the following day notified that a further six TF battalions would be sent.[79] Nineteen TF battalions would arrive in France by early November when 1/6th Cheshire and 1/4th (Denbighshire) RWF landed at Le Havre for use as L of C troops. The 1/6th Cheshire had been augmented by 100 men from its Reserve battalion, which now replaced it in its Home Defence role.[80]

Between 15 August and 30 September some 485 officers and 31,888 men were sent out to the BEF as replacements for casualty losses.[81] The reinforcement system was working but it had already had to provide many more replacements than expected. The heavy and unexpected wastage within the BEF's first month in France had exhausted the supply of Regular reservists for many regiments and men of the SR were already beginning to take their place; the first draft of 100 KSLI Special Reservists had left for 1st KSLI on 15 September.[82] More drafts arrived to fill the weary battalions, but some were only penny-packets. The draft arriving at 1st Cheshire at Sormoise on 24 September numbered four officers but only 21 men and it would be 17 October before a draft of any real size reached them when 3 officers and 248 men arrived.[83] These were a mixture of Reservists such as 6407 George Playfoot, aged 31 and who had originally enlisted in 1900, and new recruits such as 27 year old John William Beard who had enlisted only ten

78 *BOH 1914 Vol. II*, p. 8fn.
79 Ibid., pp. 252 and 276 fn.
80 Smith, *6th Cheshire*, pp. 2-3.
81 *BOH 1914 Vol. II*, p. 467 fn 1.
82 *BOH 1914 Vol. I*, p. 440 and Wood, *King's Shropshire Light Infantry in the Great War*, p. 318.
83 Crookenden, *Cheshire Regiment in the Great War*, p. 25 and TNA WO 95/1571 1st Cheshire War Diary.

weeks earlier, on 5 August 1914.[84] Since Mons, 1st Cheshire had received 359 men to replace the losses of Audregnies but the battalion was still only just over half strength. The delay in providing the reinforcements may be attributed to several reasons. Above all, replacements were required in greater numbers and more urgently than had been anticipated in the pre-war planning. Furthermore, more than half the number of Reservists recalled to the Colours had been needed to bring the battalions of the BEF up to strength before they departed for France and many of those left behind had been unfit or in need of further military training. As for the new recruits of August and September, they would require a minimum of ten weeks of training before being sent overseas.

The lack of reinforcements had made it necessary to start switching particularly depleted units out of the Line for rest and replenishment.[85] Such moves must have been confusing for the divisions and units concerned but an absolute nightmare for the IBDs to know where to send reinforcements. On 9 October, 3 IBD transferred two officers and 199 men destined for the Devonshires, which had been transferred from the 8th to the 14th Brigade, to 5 IBD. In return they received five officers and 351 men of the Suffolks, who were now with GHQ Troops. Similarly, No 2 Rest Camp noted the transfer of 100 men from 3rd to 5th Division between 10-12 October.[86] Men and units were moving in all directions with consequent disruption and disorientation.

The situation was compounded by the IBDs being at this this point still in the temporary locations to which they had been rushed at the end of August during the Retreat. It would be early November before 3 IBD would move from St Nazaire to Rouen and could become properly established. No 2 Rest Camp would remain at Le Mans until 21 December before moving back to Boulogne to fulfil its role of receiving individual reinforcements from UK and despatching them to the base depots that by then were settled at Étaples, Harfleur, near Le Havre, and Rouen.

By late October, II Corps had suffered nearly 14,000 casualties, of whom 10,000 were Infantry. Against its established Infantry strength of 24,000, it could now muster only 14,000, of whom 1,400 had been with their battalions less than a week. The 5th Division numbered just over 7,600 Infantry, but 800 of these had joined as reinforcements only on 25 October. There were grave doubts over whether battalions containing so many new men, Reservists, SR and young soldiers, would be able to withstand a really determined attack.[87] This is the first instance of what would later become regular complaints that the new men were never as good as the old.

The switching around of units and formations continued to cause strain. By early November the Fifth Division history notes:

> a regular jumble everywhere; Brigades, Battalions and Batteries were sent hither and thither to patch up the holes in the strained British front, and many units had no notion to

84 <http://www.ancestry.co.uk/> The Medal Index Cards (MIC) for 6407 Pte George Playfoot and 10103 Pte John William Beard show that both arrived in France on 7 October 1914. Pte Beard's Service Record shows his date of enlistment.
85 TNA WO 95/25: GHQ, AG Branch War Diary 29 Sep 14.
86 TNA WO 95/4185: 3 IBD War Diary and WO 95/4116: No 2 Rest Camp War Diary.
87 *BOH 1914 Vol. II*, pp. 209-10.

> what formation they belonged; Battalions were attached for a day or two to a Division or a Brigade, and then spirited away elsewhere as the circumstances demanded.[88]

It would be the end of November before the component units of the Division would be gathered together again. All units were low in numbers but by then 1st Cheshire, still suffering from the legacy of Audregnies, was again so weak that they were kept back in Corps Reserve. The battalion had lost a further 35 killed, 99 wounded and 65 missing between 5-20 November but no reinforcements are shown as having arrived. Although one officer and 64 men would arrive on 6 December it would not be until 24 December that six officers and 444 men would make a real difference.[89] Meanwhile, divisions were being bolstered by newly arrived TF units: 1/6th Cheshire joined 1st Cheshire in 15th Brigade, 5th Division from the LofC in December whilst 1/4th (Denbighshire) RWF joined 3rd Brigade, 1st Division.

Changes to Procedures

It had become apparent that the FSR Part 2 procedures needed several further amendments as the 'A' staff struggled with the passage of information. Incorrect information had occasionally been passed: in mid-September II Corps units were reminded to ensure that officers 'missing' were not shown as killed or wounded unless this was absolutely certain as there had been several cases of officers reported to GHQ as killed who had subsequently been found alive in England - after the publication of the casualty lists in the Press. Information had also been passed by a variety of routes, causing overlapping demands and delayed replacements. In late October, Army Routine Orders (ARO) 248 noted that **all** demands for replacements, arising from both casualties and normal wastage, were now to be submitted by formations to AG, GHQ, who would pass them to DAG 3rd Echelon GHQ at the Base. Only LofC units were to submit demands for those replacements due to normal wastage direct to DAG, 3rd Echelon GHQ at the base.[90]

Casualty Analysis

Between August and December 1914 the BEF it had suffered a total of 85,046 other rank casualties, of whom 15,735 were dead.[91] The *Official History* notes that the British battalions that fought at the Marne and Ypres scarcely retained an average of one officer and thirty men of those who had landed in August 1914 and claims that 'the old British Army was gone past recall, leaving but a remnant to carry on the training of the New Armies'.[92] It is intended to test that perception and to consider to what extent the composition of battalions changed during the course of the war, by analysis of the deaths in selected battalions of the Marcher Regiments.

88 Brigadier-General A.H. Hussey & Major D.S. Inman, *The Fifth Division in the Great War* (London: Nisbet & Co, 1921), p. 44.
89 1st Cheshire War Diary 24 November 1914 and 24 December 1914.
90 TNA WO 95/25: AG GHQ War Diary September and October 1914.
91 War Office, *SME*, p. 253. NB This does not include 6338 shown as Indian Natives.
92 *BOH 1914 Vol. II*, p. 465.

Analysis of those who died between August and November 1914 in the four Line battalions that had been in France since August will serve as a baseline for future analysis of these battalions through the rest of the war.[93] The results are shown in the Tables below.

Although these were Home-based battalions, recruiting from the Regimental areas seems to have varied, as is shown in Table 1.1 below.

Enlistment Locations	1st Cheshire		1st KSLI		2nd RWF		1st SWB	
Regimental Area	187	82%	63	61%	18	24%	148	42%
Elsewhere in No 4 District - England	1		8		7		8	
Elsewhere in No 4 District – Wales	3		3		5		29	
Total enlisted in No 4 District	191	83%	74	71%	30	41%	185	52%
Enlisted in No 3 District	2		9		3		5	
• Liverpool/Manchester	12		7		2		5	
Total Enlisted in Western Command	**205**	**90%**	**90**	**87%**	**35**	**47%**	**195**	**55%**
Northern Command	5		1		1		16	
Southern Command	5		2		13		33	
• Birmingham	3		3		23		11	
Eastern	7		3		1		17	
London District	4		4		2		81	
Scotland/Ireland			1				1	
Overseas							1	
Total Other Commands	**24**		**14**		**39**		**160**	
Total Deaths	**229**		**104**		**74**		**355**	

Table 1.1. Enlistment locations of soldiers of selected Regular battalions who were killed/died between 4 August – 30 November 1914.

Of the two English Regiments, some 82 percent of 1st Cheshire had enlisted in its own Regimental area but only 61 per cent of 1st KSLI. The latter, however, shows a further 11 percent having enlisted in other parts of No 4 District. When enlistments in their parent Home Command (Western) for these two battalions are considered, the percentages are 90 percent for 1st Cheshire and 85 percent for 1st KSLI. The figures for the two Welsh battalions, however, look very different. Only 24 percent of 2nd RWF and 42 percent of 1st SWB had enlisted within their respective Regimental areas. Even when enlistments within Western Command are considered, the percentages for these two battalions remain low: 47 per cent for the RWF and 55 per cent for the SWB. The RWF had historically recruited in the Midlands and this is

93 Sources of data: *Soldiers Died in the Great War* (Naval & Military Press CD Rom Version 2.5) – Western European Theatre and *Ancestry* <http://www.ancestry.com>

borne out by some 31 percent of those who died in the first months of the war having enlisted in Birmingham. However, of similar note is that some 23 percent of the SWB had enlisted in the London area.

It might be thought for both Welsh battalions that these men were Welshmen who had left to find work elsewhere. The figures for those born in the respective Regimental recruiting areas, however, show that only 11 percent of the RWF and 19 percent of the SWB had hailed from these areas originally (see Table 1.2 below). Even when the figures for those born in the rest of Wales are taken into account, the percentages of native-born Welshmen rise only to 22 percent for the RWF and 35 percent for the SWB. For the two English battalions, around half of those killed had been born in the respective recruiting areas for the Cheshires and the KSLI. So it would appear that none of the Line battalions analysed could be said to have been locally born and bred in their respective areas. When the figures for those born within Western Command are considered, both the Cheshire and KSLI figures show a greater degree of homogeneity, with 82 percent of 1st Cheshire and 76 percent of 1st KSLI deaths having been born within Western Command. The Welsh battalions, however, show just under half having been born in the parent Command.

Birth locations	**1st Cheshire**		**1st KSLI**		**2nd RWF**		**1st SWB**	
Regimental Area	125	55%	51	49%	8	11%	69	19%
Elsewhere in No 4 District - England	3		8		12		14	
Elsewhere in No 4 District – Wales	5		6		8		54	
Total born in No 4 District	133	58%	65	63%	28	39%	137	39%
Born in No 3 District	22		13		4		9	
• Liverpool/Manchester	31		3				4	
Total Born in Western Command	**186**	**81%**	**81**	**78%**	**32**	**42%**	**150**	**42%**
Northern Command	16		7		7		26	
Southern Command	6		4		15		58	
• Birmingham	4		1		16		10	
Eastern	6		4		1		31	
London District	8		2		3		71	
Scotland/Ireland	2		2				8	
Overseas	1		3				1	
Total Other Commands	**43**		**23**		**42**		**205**	
Location of Birth Unknown								
Total Deaths	**229**		**104**		**74**		**355**	

Table 1.2. Birth locations of soldiers of selected Regular battalions who were killed/died between 4 August – 30 November 1914.

Looking at the overall figures for deaths in the light of the claim that the old Army had disappeared, it can be seen that whilst the SWB and the Cheshires had suffered the most fatalities, in both cases these were considerably less than half the battalions. All four battalions had also lost large numbers of wounded and the Cheshires, in particular, had had a large number of men taken prisoner at Audregnies. The prisoners of war would not return to fight but the majority of the injured would recover and rejoin their battalions in due course. Although the perception in late 1914 was that the pre-war soldiers had all gone this was not necessarily the case.

Situation at the end of 1914

The BEF continued to increase in size and on 19 December its estimated British strength was 229,782 officers and men.[94] The losses had been huge, however, and by the end of 1914, it had already received a total of 962 officers and 108,310 men as reinforcements.[95] There were doubts over the quality of some of the men arriving who were alleged by some units to be practically untrained and by others 'to have neither the will nor physique to fight'; one report claimed that many of the men were 'old, worn, drunken wasters' and that no young recruits were being sent. As ever, the truth lay somewhere in between: between October-December the 1st Bedfordshire received as reinforcements 169 serving soldiers, 43 Army Reservists, 745 Special Reservists and 34 re-enlisted old soldiers.[96] Whilst the proportions might have been slightly other than previously anticipated, the sources of these reinforcements were those already planned. The imminent problem, however was that, although the reinforcement procedures had worked, far more men had been needed than had been anticipated. It was now only too apparent that the new industrial form of warfare would require replacement numbers far in excess of the pre-war planning figures.

94 War Office, *SME*, p. 64 (iii) NB This does not include 15,357 British members of the Indian contingent.
95 *BOH 1914, Vol. II*, p. 467 fn 1.
96 Ibid., p. 449 and fn 1.

2

1915: The Realities of War

The War moved inexorably into 1915. With the arrival of the 28th Division in mid-January, the number of British Infantry Divisions on the newly-styled Western Front had risen to eleven, in which the Marches Regiments were already represented by seven Regular and six TF battalions.[1] In manpower terms, the total number of British troops in rations on 15 January 1915 was 326,278. Some 103,957 casualties had been notified up to that date, however, which was some 4,000 more than the total strength of the BEF that had landed five months previously.[2] Pre-war planning estimates of the reinforcement requirement had been proved totally inadequate.

The year 1915 would see various debates and changes in approach to the prosecution of the war. On the political front there would be debates between 'easterners' advocating the opening of other fronts, particularly the Dardanelles, and 'westerners' who were adamant that the war must be won in France and Belgium. At home, recruiting continued but concerns were arising over the effect of indiscriminate recruiting on industry.[3] The Army's manpower requirements continued to escalate but the Government needed urgently to balance them against the demands of the nation as a whole, and the topic of conscription began to be raised at every opportunity in Parliament.

In the War Office, the Army Council was confronted with an Army of a previously unimaginable size and composition, and their staffs were feverishly occupied in trying to work out new organizations to meet the changing demands caused by both the numbers of men coming forward and the different nature of the war that was developing. Many changes, both

1 1st, 2nd, 1/5th and 1/6th Cheshire; 1st, 2nd and 1/4th RWF; 1st SWB; 1st and 2nd KSLI; and 1/1st, 1/2nd and 1/3rd Monmouthshire Battalions.

2 TNA WO 95/25: AG GHQ War Diary for 15 January 1915. Total ration strength, including LoC and Army troops, was 326,278: 9,609 officers (plus 674 Indian) and 270,785 men (plus 12,641 Indian contingent). A further 848 officers and 31,721 were at the Base Depots, sick in hospital and prisoners (presumably German who still had to be taken on the ration strength). Total casualties notified up to and including 14 January 15 were 4222 officers (1021 killed, 2435 wounded and 766 missing) and 99,735 other ranks (11,066 killed, 44,856 wounded and 43, 813 missing).

3 *Parliamentary Debates Fifth Series Vol. XVIII House of Lords 1914-15* cc 231-62 and 352.

political and military, would be made during 1915, some of which would be of an 'ad hoc' nature and need subsequent refinement. On the manning side it would be a year in which foundations were laid for what would come later.

Early Thoughts on the Use of the New Armies

At home, where the threat of an attack on Britain had not as yet been completely discounted, the Home Army needed to be revitalized for its defence role whilst continuing to train the TF and the New Armies. It would be months before the latter would be ready to be sent overseas but in France GHQ was beginning to look covetously at them as a source of extra manpower. Inevitably there were opposing views, fed by both the perennial tensions between an Army in the field and the War Office and personality clashes between senior officers. On 3 January, Sir John French complained to the Army Council that he had not yet been officially informed of:

> the organization, numbers, or composition of what is known as the 'New' Army … It would seem that many brigades formed in this way are now, or shortly will be, sufficiently trained to take their places in the field at once if amalgamated with units composed of troops with tried experience of war.[4]

The next day he further provoked the issue by outlining detailed proposals to completely reorganise the BEF in order to absorb the First New Army. In defence of his cause he cited the growing need, already identified during the early months of fighting, for the temporary withdrawal from the front of units and formations for rest and refit as a result of heavy casualties and battle-weariness. The GHQ proposals were designed to create a margin to provide adequate reliefs by increasing in size all formations from brigades upwards by giving each infantry brigade another battalion, adding a further infantry brigade of four battalions to each division and an additional battalion as corps troops to each corps, including the Cavalry Corps. This would use the 72 battalions of the First New Army, creating an army in the field consisting, apart from the Cavalry Corps and the Indian Cavalry Corps, of two Armies, each containing three Corps of two divisions, each of four infantry brigades. Once the Second New Army became available 'the most convenient plan' would be to form three armies each of three corps of two divisions. Each army would thus have two divisions of the Second New Army to absorb, which it was proposed to achieve by regrouping brigades and divisions in the corps and armies.[5] It was an ingenious plan that looked feasible on paper but was viewed by the Army Council as too drastic a reorganization of a force on active service. It was not that the War Office had been deliberately withholding information from Sir John French and his staffs, but that as yet the Army Council itself was undecided on how to make use of the New Armies. Their response a fortnight later refuted the GHQ proposals in detail but then equivocated:

4 TNA CAB 1/11: Sir J. French, Memorandum dated 3 January 1915.
5 Ibid., Sir J. French, Memorandum dated 4 January 1915.

> the question of how best to utilize and incorporate the New Armies now in course of preparation in this country is in no way necessarily dependent on the points raised in this letter.[6]

In any case, the New Armies were not as yet ready to go anywhere. They were continuing training on the structured programme laid down for them in late August 1914: three months' recruit training, including basic musketry training, followed by five weeks' company training and then battalion and brigade training culminating in a week's divisional training.[7] Although its component elements replicated the annual training programme for pre-war Regular battalions, the compression of this programme into roughly six months inevitably meant that the training was insufficient. Furthermore, lack of equipment and facilities, with many of their training camps still under construction, caused delay and it would be May before any New Army divisions were considered ready to be sent overseas.

Provision of Reserves

The escalating losses on the Western Front made it essential that the SR battalions were kept well up to strength to provide drafts for the Regular battalions. In early February instructions were issued that no more men were to be posted to Fourth New Army or Extra Reserve (ER) battalions until the SR battalions were up to their establishments.[8] This was timely: in February over 24,000 OR reinforcements were sent to France and the number per month was rising.[9]

The experiences of those TF units already on active service showed that an increased provision of TF reinforcements would be needed. In January it was announced that Second Reserve units were to be raised for six TF Divisions by recruiting up to 30 percent in excess of establishment for their First Reserve units 'with a view to forming Second Reserve units later on'.[10] Fortunately this rather woolly provision was soon clarified with the instruction that as soon as a Home Command was notified that one of its TF units had been selected for service on the Continent it was to start raising a Second Reserve unit for that unit.[11] The initial titles, of First and Second Reserve, were somewhat cumbersome and an attempt at clarification was published at the end of January. The original I.S. battalion remained as 1/… as in 1/6th Cheshire, but the First Reserve would become 2/… as in 2/6th Cheshire and the Second Reserve would be known as 3/… as in 3/6th Cheshire.[12] The disparity between the numbering of the battalions and the categories of I.S, First Reserve and Second Reserve rapidly proved confusing, however, so within a month the categories were changed in favour of First, Second and Third Line respectively.[13]

6 TNA CAB 1/11: Army Council letter dated 20 January 1915.
7 TNA WO 123/56: AO 324 dated 21 August 1914.
8 TNA WO 293/2: WOI 16 of 2 February 1915.
9 TNA WO 95/25: AG GHQ War Diary for February 1915. British Cavalry 965, British Infantry 17,946, Indian 3554 and TF 1669.
10 The Divisions indicated were N and S Midland, 2nd London, West Lancashire, Northumbrian and West Riding Divisions. TNA: WO 293/2 WOI 92 of 13 January 1915.
11 TNA WO WOI 151: of 15 February 1915.
12 TNA WO 123/57: AO 54 3 January 1915 and WO 293/2, WOI 258: 30 January 1915.
13 TNA WO 293/2, WOI 228: 24 February 1915.

In March it was confirmed that the TF Third Line's function was to train and provide drafts for both the First and Second line units. All recruits were to be sent in the first instance to the Third Line depots and were not to be transferred to a First or Second line unit until they had completed the recruit musketry course and were otherwise considered as trained soldiers. The Second Line units would replace the First Line units when the latter deployed, or otherwise be employed as directed. They would provide drafts for the First Line units serving abroad only when absolutely necessary and this draft finding duty would cease as soon as the Third Line unit was in a position to carry out these functions.[14]

The New Armies would soon be ready for overseas service but still needed their own source of reserves. This was provided in April by the creation of a Second Reserve through the breaking up of the Fourth New Army and turning its battalions into reserve units. They retained their Regimental designations but their role was now to train recruits to provide reinforcements specifically for the divisions of the first three New Armies. In the Marcher Regiments, 14th Cheshire, 12th RWF, 9th SWB and 9th KSLI now became Second Reserve battalions for their respective Service battalions.[15]

Training and the provision of reinforcements for the Line battalions would continue to be carried out by the existing SR battalions.[16] The distribution of Regular recruits between the Line battalions and those of the New Armies was now confirmed as follows: the SR battalions were to be filled first until they reached their establishment of 2,085 all ranks; then the Second Reserve battalions until they reached 1,500; and then the Extra Reserve battalions, where they existed, until their establishment of 1,020 all ranks was reached. Any recruits over this number were to be retained at the depot until they numbered 300 when the War Office was to be informed so they could be diverted elsewhere.[17]

The Brigades of the former Fourth New Army were re-numbered as Reserve Infantry Brigades, with, for example, 89th Brigade becoming 1st Reserve Infantry Brigade, 90th Brigade becoming 2nd Reserve Infantry Brigade and so on. They were attached to and located within the six Home Commands as units of the Home army and contained the Second Reserve battalions for the respective Regiments of the parent Command.[18] For Western Command, the 11th Reserve Brigade was based at Prees Heath in Shropshire, 13th and 14th Reserve Brigades were at Kinmel Park in North Wales whilst 16th Reserve Brigade was at Altcar in Lancashire. The creation of dedicated reserves for the first three New Armies was timely as by May the 9th (Scottish), 12th (Eastern) and 14th (Light) Divisions were in France and in mid-June 13th (Western) Division, containing 8th Cheshire, 8th RWF and 4th SWB, would embark for Gallipoli.

Although they had been provisionally designated as the Fifth and Sixth New Armies, the War Office had not as yet taken over any of the 'locally raised' units created by private citizens and municipalities. With the breaking up of the original Fourth New Army, the Fifth and Sixth New Armies now became respectively the Fourth and Fifth New Armies. Their constituent divisions were also renumbered, with, for example, the 43rd Division becoming the 38th

14 TNA WO 293/2 WOI 72: 6 March 1915 – L. 121/1720, AG 2a.
15 See Appendix III for more details.
16 TNA WO 293/2 WOI 96: 10 April 1915.
17 Ibid., 18 May 1915.
18 Mitchinson, *Defending Albion*, p. 124.

(Welsh) Division. They would also need reserve units and in mid-1915 the Depot companies of the locally raised battalions were combined to form Local Reserve battalions.[19] These new battalions, 68 in total, took their numbering from their parent Regiment: 17th (Reserve) Cheshire was formed from the depot companies of 15th and 16th Cheshire, 13th (Reserve) SWB grew out of the depot companies of 1st Gwent (10th SWB) and 2nd Gwent (11th SWB) battalions and the depot company of 3rd Gwent (12th SWB) became the 14th (Reserve) SWB. The Local Reserve battalions now joined the same Reserve Brigades as the Second Reserve battalions of their parent Regiments. For the Marcher regiments these were either 13th Reserve Infantry Brigade at Kinmel Park, near Rhyl in North Wales, or 11th, 14th and 17th Reserve Infantry Brigades at Prees Heath in north Shropshire.[20]

Legislative Changes

There was still a need to obtain greater flexibility in the Army's management of its existing manpower but changes to existing terms and conditions of service would require legislation. The first piece of legislation in 1915 was the Army (Suspension of Sentences) Act of 16 March. Its inspiration was claimed by the then Colonel Wyndham Childs, the Assistant Adjutant General (AAG) GHQ, who was responsible for discipline. Walking through St. Omer he spotted a group of soldiers, singing and whistling cheerfully as they were being marched under escort to the Base to serve sentences of imprisonment. Whether Childs was correct in his immediate assessment that 'certain types of men would commit crimes solely to avoid duty at the front' is debatable, but it was certainly true that sentences of penal servitude or imprisonment would remove men from the front line. Under Military Law, the highest penalty was the death sentence, below this came penal servitude for a minimum period of three years, which had to be served in a civilian prison in the UK, and imprisonment, with or without hard labour, for a maximum of two years and which could be served in a military gaol.[21] Childs immediately dusted off a previous proposal for a form of 'probation' for soldiers found guilty of offences. It was submitted to Parliament where it was passed within two weeks.[22]

The Army (Suspension of Sentences) Act enabled a soldier sentenced to imprisonment or penal servitude for offences committed on active service to be placed on a form of probation and returned to his unit to fight. Such suspensions of sentences were to be reviewed every three months and might at that stage be either remitted on the grounds of good conduct or cancelled and the original sentence invoked.[23] In the case of a death sentence, should the CinC, with whom rested the final decision on whether it should be carried out, decide to commute the sentence to a lesser penalty then this could now be suspended.

The Act was promulgated to the BEF on 26 April by means of GRO 300 and an explanatory pamphlet. Rowland Feilding, a battalion commander, thought it good that the bad soldier had

19 TNA WO 293/3 WOI 205: July 1915.
20 E.A. James, *British Regiments 1914-18* (London: Samson Books, 1978), pp. 65-6, 69, Appendix III to Part II.
21 War Office, *Manual of Military Law* (London: War Office, 1914), pp. 110 – 119 Offences and Punishments.
22 Major-General Sir Wyndham Childs, *Episodes and Reflections* (London: Cassell, 1930), pp. 137-8.
23 *Public General Statutes 5 & 6 Geo 5 1914-16* (London: Eyre & Spottiswood, 1916), pp. 47-8.

a threat hanging over his head whilst the otherwise good soldier, who might simply have lapsed momentarily, had the chance of gaining a complete reprieve through good conduct or gallantry on the battlefield.[24] From the point of view of the Manning staffs, it also enabled men to carry on fighting rather than needing to be replaced. It is difficult to arrive at an exact figure for the number of sentences subsequently suspended but it appears likely that around 38 per cent of sentences overseas were suspended.[25] Between 1 October 1915-30 September 1916 some 2417 sentences were suspended but this does not include those that were suspended after the Court Martial proceedings had been finalised. The Act undoubtedly closed a loophole and was a useful tool in retaining men in the frontline, although it is debateable how much of a deterrent it posed to anyone considering transgressing solely to avoid duty; a large number of those subsequently executed for desertion were already on suspended sentences for previous offences.[26]

The second area to be addressed was Section 83 of the Army Act. Under this section a Regular soldier within three months of his attestation could be transferred without his consent to any Regular corps of the same arm or branch; after three months his consent to the move was required. Thus, after completing three months' service a Regular soldier of the Cheshire Regiment could not be transferred to (say) the KSLI without his consent. By early 1915 this was restricting flexibility over the provision of replacements. The first amendment to Section 83 was contained in the Army (Amendment) Act, 1915, of 16 March, which removed the time limitation on transfer between corps of the same arm or branch during wartime but only for Regular soldiers enlisted after 4 August 1914. It thus applied to all men who had joined the New Armies as well as the Line battalions. The amendment was passed with no difficulty.

The War Office now sought to gain greater flexibility in the use of TF soldiers. Under the *Territorial and Reserve Forces Act of 1907*, a TF soldier could not be transferred without his consent from one corps to another nor, when not embodied, could he be posted without his consent to any unit, even one in the same corps, other than the one he had joined on enlistment. He certainly could not be posted without his consent to any regular unit.[27] The War Office had begun trying to chip away at this in mid-January 1915 and had tentatively proposed the transfer of 'IS men in TF reserve formations who may be willing to transfer to the regular army'.[28] This was followed by a similar instruction in February but by March it had obviously proved too difficult and the proposal was retracted.[29]

24 R. Feilding, *War Letters to a Wife* (London: Medici Society, 1929; Staplehurst: Spellmount, 2001), pp. 175-6.
25 War Office, *Statistics of the British Military Effort, Table (x)(g)* p. 666; 1 October 1916-30 September 1917: 2532 sentences suspended; 1 October 1917-30 September 1918: 3078 sentences suspended.
26 Private Evan Fraser's death sentence for desertion in April 1915 was commuted to penal servitude and suspended. He made three more attempts to desert within two months of returning to his unit. There appears to have been insufficient evidence on the new charges of desertion to prove his guilt beyond reasonable doubt but the FGCM invoked the original death sentence, which was subsequently confirmed by the formation commanders and the CinC. Pte Fraser became the first man to be executed for reoffending whilst under a suspended sentence. Cited in C. Corns & J. Hughes-Wilson, *Blindfold and Alone* (London: Cassell, 2002), pp. 338-40.
27 Territorial and Reserve Forces Act 1907, Section 7(4), *Manual of Military Law* (London: HMSO, 1914), p. 760. NB For enlistment and service purposes, the common term 'corps' refers to a regiment or corps. *Manual of Military Law* p. 197.
28 TNA WO 293/2 WOI 118: 16 January 1915.
29 Ibid., March 1915.

It was already proving difficult to reinforce TF units overseas. The ease with which earlier legislation had been passed seems now to have prompted the War Office's first attempt to obtain legislation enabling greater flexibility for the use of TF soldiers. In late April a Bill was proposed, removing the need for TF members to consent to being transferred to other TF units or from one TF corps to another. It was rapidly apparent, however, that it would have a more difficult ride through Parliament since it immediately came up against the strong TF lobby in the Commons. The Bill was seen as yet another attack on TF terms of service. Mr Joynson-Hicks, Conservative MP for Brentford, reminded the House of the 'very great pressure' that had been put upon Territorials to induce them to agree to serve overseas. He continued:

> [I]t seemed to me, even then, a form of conscription on the very type of men who did not need conscription. They had already joined the Army for Home Defence, and pressure was put upon them to induce them to consent to go on foreign service.[30]

There was much more in this vein during a lengthy and heated debate and, considerably bruised, the Government adjourned the matter. It was going to be no easier to change the TF's terms and conditions of service, even during a war, than it had been to create it in the first place.

The following week the Government replaced the TF Bill with a Bill to further amend Section 83 of the Army Act.[31] The differences between this new proposal and the earlier Army (Amendment) Act were significant: it would enable any Regular soldier, irrespective of when he had enlisted, to be transferred to a different arm or branch of the Army from the one in which he had previously been serving. It is apparent from the ensuing Parliamentary debate that some MPs remained, at least initially, a little confused as to which part of the Army they were now debating. Introducing the new Bill, the Under Secretary of State for War, the Rt Hon H. J. Tennant, explained that:

> [I]t is very desirable that we at the War Office should be enabled to ... employ such soldiers as are available in the capacity in which they are most required ...where you have considerable wastage in a particular battalion, and there are not sufficient Reserves in the Reserve battalion for that particular unit, it is desirable that the process of transfer should be made more simple and more easy. The whole object of this Bill is to empower the Army Council to make such transfers.

Various matters were raised during the Parliamentary debate including the position of friends and workmates who had enlisted in the 'Pals' battalions; the reluctance a man might feel to be transferred to 'any Line or Cavalry or Artillery regiment'; Welsh, Scottish and Irish national feelings; the transfer of non-combatants to combat units; and the question of re-transfer at the end of the War. The debate was adjourned but, despite much further discussion in both Houses, the Bill was subsequently passed relatively easily. The only amendment inserted was that a

30 Hansard HC Deb 27 April 1915 Vol. 71 cc. 611-23.
31 Army Act Amendment (No 2) Bill. HC Deb, 6 May 1915, Vol. 71, cc. 1311-20.

soldier who was compulsorily transferred might transfer back to his original cap-badge after the war.[32] The Army (Transfers) Act, 1915 received Royal Assent on 19 May.

Interestingly, the provisions of the new Act were not immediately promulgated to the Army as a whole. It would seem that the War Office, despite having gained the authority, were as yet reluctant to invoke it too widely, perhaps since it was such a fundamental change to a soldier's terms of service. The only relevant AO simply amended the Pay Warrant to ensure that soldiers who were transferred, and remained in the same rank, would retain their existing rates of pay if they were more advantageous than those of the corps which they had joined.[33] The new powers were instead publicised in two War Office Instructions (WOI) which gave details of two War Office letters being sent to the Home Commands concerning transfers to the Infantry from firstly the Royal Army Medical Corps (RAMC) and secondly from the Royal Horse Artillery (RHA and Royal Field Artillery (RFA). Both letters contained space to insert the number of transfers to be made within the Command concerned and an exhortation that whenever possible volunteers for transfer were to take precedence over others. Those selected should also be those least likely to make the grade as medics or artillerymen. Furthermore, 'Scotsmen, Irishmen, Welshmen and Englishmen' should be transferred as far as possible to 'regiments of their own nationality' and men of the same nationality serving together would be transferred to the same regiment of infantry.[34]

By June the effect of the Act was becoming visible. James Jack, serving briefly with 3rd Cameronians, noted on 9 June that 84 volunteers from the RAMC had reached the battalion for training as infantry.[35] Also in June some 200 Gunners were posted to 3rd Cheshire. Harry Parkinson, Wilfred Yates and William Joseph Fleming were part of this group and would find themselves in France in December 1915.[36] Similarly, Pte George William Hall was transferred with a group of about 40 from the RAMC Training Centre to 3rd Cheshire. All these men had enlisted in 1914 or very early in 1915 so were six months through their initial training but would now need training as Infantry soldiers. It would be a further six months before they would find themselves at the Front.

Although men of the same nationality were supposed to be transferred together, there seems to have been less effort in 1915 to post men from the same regional Commands together. A group of about 100 men was transferred from the Sherwood Foresters in Northern Command to 3rd Cheshire in Western Command on 9 July. Many of these men had enlisted in late 1914 or early 1915, although their regimental numbers show that others were pre-war soldiers, presumably Reservists recalled to the Colours. Unlike the medical and artillery transferees, who required further training, some of the Sherwood Foresters would arrive in France within a week of their transfer: a draft of 33 joined 1st Cheshire on 24 July.[37]

32 This sometimes causes confusion when researching a soldier since his unit on demobilization can be different from the one in which he spent the bulk of his Great War service.

33 TNA WO 123/58: Army Order (AO) 211, 25 May 1915.

34 TNA WO 293/2 WOI 199: 23 May 1915 - Transfers from RAMC to Infantry and ACI 200 of 23 May 1915 - Transfer of men from RH and RFA to Infantry.

35 John Terraine (ed.), *General Jack's Diary* (1964; London: Cassell & Co, 2000), p. 106.

36 <www.Ancestry.com> Service records (SR) and Medal Index Cards (MIC) for 28062 Private H. Parkinson, 28113 Private W. Yates, 28275 Private W.J. Fleming and 28024 Private George William Hall.

37 Cheshire Regimental Archives (CRA) – 1st Cheshire War Diary, July 1915.

Minor Changes

In a bid to obtain more recruits, the Army Council decided in May that the upper age limit for enlisting for the duration of the war for men who had no previous service should be raised to 40 and that the minimum height for the Infantry should be lowered to 5 feet 2 inches. Both the age and the height changes were to apply to the TF as well.[38]

There was also a growing need to address the outflow of experienced soldiers at the end of their service. In June it was announced that both Regular and TF soldiers who would complete their periods of service, including the extra 12 months, by 31 December 1915, were to be invited to continue their service.[39] Lists of those to whom it applied would be produced by the manning authorities and forwarded to the units of the men concerned, where they were expected to be interviewed by the CO. Frank Richards of 2nd RWF describes his battalion colonel interviewing some time-expired men only to receive the response from one of them 'that he had every intention of still serving his country but in a safer place'.[40] After nearly a year of enduring the war, it was probably unlikely that a mere invitation would induce a man to serve on. The problem was, however, that changes to terms of service required legislation to amend the Army Act or the Territorial and Reserve Forces Act.

Developments in Medical Administration

There was growing concern over the varying standards of recruits' medical examinations, often conducted by civilian medical practitioners, and the frequent lack of fitness of drafts arriving overseas. In January the CO No 3 IBD commented that, whilst the general behaviour of the troops from home had improved and they were better equipped and of good physique, the pre-drafting medical inspections did not seem to be sufficiently rigorous and many men were being sent to Medical Boards immediately on arrival at the Depot on account of bad teeth. This meant they were practically useless on arrival as they would not be fit for the Front until they had received the necessary treatment.[41] In March instructions were issued for the establishment of Standing Medical Boards (SMB) in all stations providing drafts for service abroad. Composed of two or three medical officers, one of whom was to be a Regular RAMC officer, they were to examine all men reported by their unit as unfit for service abroad. The following classifications were to be applied:

A. Fit for service home and abroad;
B. Temporarily unfit for service abroad;
C. Fit for home only;
D. Unfit for service home or abroad.

38 TNA WO 123/57: AO 217 of M27 May 1915. Under AO 186 of April 1915, the age for joining the TF had previously been changed in April 1915 from 17-35 to 19-38 for the duration of the war, in order to bring it into line with the Regular Army. There were exceptions: the minimum age of 17 still applied to Inns of Court OTC, the Artists Rifles and other stated units.

39 Ibid., AO 252 of 22 June 1915 and AO 253 of 22 June 1915.

40 Richards, *Old Soldiers Never Die*, p. 120.

41 TNA WO 95/4185: No 3 IBD War Diary January 1915.

This was the beginning of classification by medical fitness. Later, in July 1915, the SMBs were augmented by the establishment of Travelling Medical Boards, whose role was to inspect and classify all men reported as being permanently or temporarily unfit for overseas service.[42]

There was a need to find some means of employing those men classified as permanently unfit for overseas service and in late April it was decided that SR battalions should create supernumerary companies or platoons in which they could be placed.[43] Subsequently, in August, these supernumerary companies would be formed into Garrison companies, in order to provide further units for Home Defence. There were some interesting caveats:

> [C]are should be taken ... to compose each company of men drawn from the same class as far as possible ... [and] ... men sent from the locally raised units ... should be formed into separate companies whenever the numbers available render it possible, so as to keep together all men coming from the same class or locality.[44]

In late 1915 these Garrison companies would be expanded to form Home Service (HS) Garrison battalions and allotted to Regiments.[45] Not all Regiments would have such battalions: the only one in the Marches Regiments was the 3rd (HS) Garrison Battalion Cheshire, formed in November 1915.

It was also realized that although men in Medical Category B might not be fit enough for service on the frontline they might still be sent overseas to relieve battalions on garrison duties. This led to the formation of Overseas Garrison Battalions from mid-1915 onwards. The 1st Garrison battalions of the RWF and the Cheshire were formed in July and August respectively and both were sent to Gibraltar in September 1915. Whilst initially the Overseas Garrison Battalions were formed from 'B' men, a revision of medical categories in October also enabled the use of men unable to return to active service at the Front. The basic medical categories were now: general service; field service at home; garrison service (a) abroad or (b) at home; labour; sedentary work; and unfit for any military service. The 2nd Garrison Battalion Cheshire, raised in October 1915, was composed mostly of men who had become casualties earlier in the war but were now fit enough for garrison service overseas. Cheshire soldiers were grouped as far as possible into A and B companies whilst C and D companies were composed largely of men from the South Lancashire and the Loyal North Lancashire Regiments. They were given 'light training, sport – in so far as (their) disabilities would permit – and plenty of good appetising food' and the battalion was soon brought up to standard.[46] In due course it would leave for Egypt in March 1916 along with the 2nd Garrison Battalion RWF thus releasing two TF battalions for the Western Front.

It had also become apparent that there was a need for longer term treatment of sick and wounded men evacuated from the EF, who were unlikely to recover sufficiently to return to overseas service within three months. This led to the establishment towards the end of 1915

42 Major-General Sir W.G MacPherson, *Medical History of the War Vol. 1* (London: HMSO, 1921), p. 120.
43 TNA WO 293/2 WOI 232: 25 April 1915.
44 TNA WO 293/3 WOI 88: 10 August 1915.
45 TNA WO 293/4 ACI 5: of 2 Jan 16; ACI 325, 9 February 1916.
46 Crookenden, *The History of the Cheshire Regiment in the Great War*, p. 348.

of Command Depots, run by the respective Home Commands. The Western Command Depots were in Catterick, Manchester and Prescot, just outside Liverpool. On arrival at the Command Depot, the convalescent soldier would be examined by a medical board and allocated to an appropriate company according to his physical fitness. Every fourteen days he would be re-boarded to assess his progress whilst continuing to receive any necessary medical treatment together with graduated exercises, massage and 'therapeutic gymnastics' designed to 'harden' him ready for drafting overseas. When he had recovered sufficiently he would be posted to the appropriate reserve battalion.[47]

Increasing TF Difficulties

By May there were growing problems with TF manning, both at home and in France. Although the attempt to obtain legislation allowing TF soldiers to be transferred without their consent had failed, the matter continued to rumble on with the War Office seeking ways around the TF's lack of flexibility and the now vigilant TF lobby on its guard against any perceived assault on TF terms of service.

As early as 23 April French had protested to the War Office about the weakness of TF units. In early May he and Macready considered retaining a portion of the Highland Division, which been sent from England in place of TF reinforcements 'which the War Office are not able to find', as a pool of reinforcements.[48] This proposal was not acted upon, but by 18 May drastic action had become necessary. Three of the weakest battalions of the London Regiment, 5th (London Rifle Brigade), 12th (Rangers) and 13th (Kensingtons) were withdrawn to the LofC and temporarily formed into a composite battalion. The 7th and 9th Argyll and Sutherland Highlanders were also temporarily amalgamated as were the three battalions of the Monmouthshire Regiment, which had been particularly badly hit during the recent fighting. On 25 May AG GHQ notified the Army HQs that, since TF reinforcements would be unobtainable for a considerable time, if the strength of a TF battalion fell below 400 ORs then a proposal for its amalgamation with another battalion was to be submitted to GHQ. Should the battalion concerned be part of a TF division, then it would be amalgamated with another in the same division. If possible a TF battalion from amongst those attached to Regular Infantry Brigades would then be transferred to the TF division in order to retain the prescribed number of battalions in the division.[49] There was an immediate outcry at home, particularly from the TF lobby in Parliament, and within a month the Armies of the BEF were notified by AG GHQ of the discontinuation of the policy of amalgamating TF battalions if they fell below 400. In future such TF battalions were to retain their identity unless they expressed a desire to be amalgamated or to be attached to a Regular battalion as a separate company, in which case the matter was to be referred to AG before any action was taken. Meanwhile, the WO had notified that drafts were being prepared for certain TF units.[50]

47 MacPherson, *Medical History of the War Vol. 1*, pp. 91 & 114.
48 TNA WO 95/25: AG War Diary April and May 1915.
49 TNA WO 95/181: First Army DA&QMG War Diary May 1915.
50 Ibid., 28 June 1915. NB The War Diary does not specify which units.

The TF Second Line Divisions were supposed to be dedicated to Home Defence but, although Kitchener appears to have promised not to use them as draft finders, it had proved impossible to hold to this.[51] Although some drafts had been sent overseas by the Third Line, their depots had taken time to create and as yet contained insufficient trained men. Consequently, there had been no option but to send drafts from the Second Line units. In mid-May, Kitchener pessimistically informed the War Cabinet that the Second Line had been 'bled white' by despatching drafts and was now incapable of fulfilling its Home Defence role.[52] In June 'exceptional measures' were imposed: to take from each Second Line TF Infantry Battalion all trained men whose withdrawal would not reduce the battalion's total strength below a total of 700 all ranks. Half of those taken were to be replaced by men from the Third Line Depots. If they were not available, then the Second Line unit was not to be reduced below 800 all ranks.[53] This instruction was followed in July by a further letter reducing the minimum strength of the Second Line battalions to 600 and notifying that any trained men in excess of that number could be taken for reinforcements but that until further orders no recruits were to be sent from the Third to the Second Line to replace the men taken.[54] In a bid to ease the situation, the establishment of all TF battalions in France was also to be reduced to 800 men from 2 July. Even this would cause questions to be asked in the Commons.[55]

Whilst attempts to retain viable TF battalions in France in the face of the lack of replacements, were hampered by the obduracy of the TF lobby in Parliament, it must be admitted that some of the War Office's attempts to gain TF soldiers to serve overseas had been less than subtle. In late May serving Territorials who had previously accepted IS liability were invited to sign an amended version of the original IS declaration (Army Form E 624) indicating their consent to being transferred between corps if necessary. In June, a new version (Army Form E 624A) , to be signed by recruits was also produced, containing the words:

> [A]nd where, with a view to service overseas, my transfer to another corps is required, I hereby consent to such transfer notwithstanding that the corps to which I am to be transferred may be different from that in which I am serving.[56]

The topic of these forms was immediately raised in the House of Commons. Despite Mr Tennant's insistence that signature was voluntary, and that transfers would be made only in exceptional circumstances, MPs remained unconvinced.[57] In early July, the matter reached the Lords with the suggestion that it was desired 'to obtain by a side wind what was directly excluded from the Army (Transfers)) Act itself'. Lord Derby himself noted that something had affected TF recruiting in West Lancashire during the previous fortnight. He could not say if it

51 Mitchinson, *Defending Albion*, p. 100.
52 TNA CAB 22/1/21: War Council Meeting 14 May 1915 cited in Mitchinson *Defending Albion*, p. 99.
53 TNA WO 70/50: Summary of Principal Changes in Organization and Administration of the TF since Mobilization p.35. AG1 letter 121/5441 (AG1) dated 16 June 1915.
54 Ibid., Summary of Principal Changes in Organization and Administration of the TF since Mobilization p.35. AG1 letter 121/5995 (AG1) dated 26 July 1915.
55 HC Deb, 22 July 1915, Vol. 73, cc. 1651-2.
56 TNA WO 123/58: AO 249 and Appendix XXVIII of 15 Jun 15.
57 HC Deb, 9 June 1915, Vol. 72, cc. 249-50 and HC Deb, 22 June 1915, Vol. 72, cc. 1040-1.

was definitely due to the reluctance of recruits to agree to be transferred from one battalion to another but whereas an average of 1,100 recruits per week had previously been joining the figure was now down to 250.[58] Within a week, the forms had been withdrawn and the question of TF transfers had to be dropped for the time being.

There were also concerns over the TF's Home Defence roles. Until March 1915 individuals could continue to enlist in the TF for home service (HS) only. Although many came under pressure to take the IS obligation, some 82,588 HS men would still be shown on TF returns in August.[59] The population of the Second Line battalions was consequently a mixture of genuine HS men, others who had enlisted too late to go overseas with the First Line but still hoped to do so and those who were willing but unfit to serve abroad. The problem was how to use these different categories to best advantage whilst ensuring the Second Line formed an efficient part of the Home Army.

Steps had been taken in late April 1915 to separate HS from IS men by organizing the former in coast protection units and using the latter to complete the Second Line units so that they might be available to serve wherever required.[60] In June the HS men were organized into 56 composite TF battalions, known as Provisional battalions, that were intended to act as front-line anti-invasion units. They were grouped into Provisional Brigades, with other infantry and support units from the same regions, and placed under command of the GOCs of the Home Commands.[61] The intention was that they would be deployed closest to the coast and, should an invasion come, would engage the enemy on the beaches and immediately inland.[62]

These Provisional battalions contained both HS personnel and also soldiers of low medical categories. The prohibition on transferring TF soldiers was circumvented by enlisting the men in Second or Third Line battalions and then simply attaching them to the Provisional battalions, whilst showing them as supernumeraries on the rolls of their parent units. On 5 October, 37 men of the 2nd Monmouthshire joined the 48th Provisional Battalion in Norwich, and on 9 December some 82 men from the 2nd/1st Herefordshire plus a further 113 Monmouthshires arrived.[63] Many of the men originally in low medical categories improved their fitness whilst with the battalions and in October the 44th Provisional Battalion noted:

> During the month a total of 42 recruits have been received from the 7th, 8th and 9th (King's Liverpool Regiment) Depots. These men are shaping very well and will be used for Guard duties as soon as their training is completed. They are all Imperial Service men and will be sent to 2nd or 3rd line units when medically fit and trained.[64]

The problem for the Provisional battalions was their rapid turnover of manpower which made coherent training difficult. Furthermore, their coastal locations were not ideal for exercises

58 HL Deb, 1 July 1915, Vol. 19, cc. 182-99.
59 Beckett, *The Amateur Military Tradition*, p. 230.
60 TNA WO 293/2 WOI 220: of 24 April 1915 – Separation of Home Service men from IS Men in the TF.
61 TNA WO 293/3 WOI 31: of 4 July 1915 Composition of Provisional Brigade; refers to AO 314 of 1915.
62 Mitchinson, *Defending Albion*, p. 101 and Appendix III, p. 208.
63 TNA WO 95/5458: War Diary of 48th Provisional Battalion, September 1915-March 1916.
64 Ibid., War Diary of 44th Provisional Battalion for October 1915.

and they were also very far down the line for the provision of ammunition and equipment. In September 1915 the Norwich-based 48th Provisional Battalion undertook a tactical exercise travelling by train from Thorpe to Melton Constable, a journey of over 2 hours, where they dug trenches before returning again by train. On 8 September it was noted that 193 Japanese rifles were given out to 'A' Company in exchange for 193 Japanese carbines.[65] Men posted from such units and drafted out to the Front were in for a rude shock, as were the units that would receive them.

Events on the Western Front

The organization that had brought it across the channel was inadequate by late 1914 to manage a BEF that had grown to eleven infantry divisions and five cavalry divisions, with more on their way. Instructions were issued on the evening of 25 December 1914 for the immediate re-organization of the BEF's Corps into two Armies: First Army, under General Sir Douglas Haig, would comprise I, IV and the Indian Corps, whilst Second Army, under General Sir Horace Smith-Dorrien, would contain II and III Corps plus the 27th Division. The impact of the new structure on existing systems and procedures appears initially not to have been recognized. On 28 December, Haig produced a note on staff duties in which he advised that the First Army HQ should not become simply a 'post office' and that GHQ would continue to deal direct with Corps on almost all subjects except 'operations'. Corps were to forward to the Army Commander 'Everything that affects operations, and which the Army Commander should know in order to command his forces in action'.[66] On 29 December a GHQ Routine Order stated that the 'A' staffs at Army HQs would deal only with disciplinary matters, courts martial and medical arrangements and that the rest of the 'A' work, including reinforcements, casualties, posting and transfer of officers would 'for the present' be dealt with by Corps direct to GHQ.[67] The introduction of the Army level of command was an innovation so perhaps it is not surprising that there should have been some muddled thinking over what an Army Commander might need to know. The numbers of effective troops under his command and the necessity for reinforcements should, however, have been recognized as key information.

In the meantime, reinforcements continued to arrive and some 23,815 regular Infantry were sent up to the Front during January. They were of variable standards. Some were half-trained SR men, some were time-expired re-enlisted soldiers past military age and some were recruits who had joined since the outbreak of war.[68] Others were simply not fit enough to be sent to the Front. The AG staffs at GHQ attempted to keep units up to strength but it was difficult: on 20 January the Assistant Adjutant General (AAG), Lt Col Cooke, visited HQ 2nd Corps and 27th Division to discuss an unaccountable shortage of men in certain units. There, he learned that

65 Ibid., War Diary of 48th Provisional Battalion September 1915.
66 TNA WO 95/589: 1st Army 'Notes regarding Staff Duties', 28 December 1914, cited in Niall Barr, 'Command in the Transition From Mobile to Static Warfare, August 1914 to March 1915.' in Gary Sheffield & Dan Todman, *Command and Control on the Western Front* (Staplehurst: Spellmount, 2004), p. 31.
67 TNA WO 95/25: GHQ AG War Diary 29 December 1914.
68 *BOH 1915 Vol. I*, p. 54.

a proportion of weak or older men had been removed from units to form corps and divisional reserve 'without the fact having been reported' to GHQ.[69]

New formations were soon to arrive and plans were needed for the creation of their Base Depots. In mid-February, DAG 3rd Echelon attended various meetings concerning the provision of Territorial Base Depots for the TF units due to arrive shortly and for the North Midland Division (TF) 'which are now landing'.[70] In the event, Territorial Camps were established to act as receiving units and IBDS were then created; in mid-March No 6 General Base Depot at Rouen was recycled as No 46 (North Midland) IBD, receiving details from No 2 Territorial Camp.[71]

The split of responsibilities relating to manpower continued to require refinement and the necessity for Army HQs to have visibility of casualty figures was soon realized. New instructions were issued to come into effect on 1 March 1915. In future, Divisions would telegraph daily reports of casualties, as at 12:00 noon, to their respective Army HQ where the reports would be consolidated and forwarded to AG Branch, GHQ and the DAG 3rd Echelon, by 7:15 pm that evening. If heavy fighting was in progress then Divisions or Corps, as previously arranged by the Army HQ concerned, were to telegraph round numbers of heavy casualties in any particular units direct to AG, GHQ. This was to give advanced warning thus enabling immediate action to be taken to obtain reinforcements either from the Base or from England. Under normal circumstances demands for replacements due to casualties and normal wastage such as sickness were now to be submitted directly to DAG, 3rd Echelon by the Army Corps, and no longer through AG, GHQ. The DAG would decide how reinforcements for the same Regiment would be apportioned and would also send weekly tables showing the numbers of reinforcements held at the Bases direct to Army HQs as well as to GHQ. Daily strength returns showing the fighting strengths of brigades were to be compiled and submitted to AG GHQ and a weekly statement showing the strength of each unit together with details of reinforcements at the Base on that date would in future be sent by Corps to Army HQs and copied to DAG, 3rd Echelon and AG, GHQ.[72]

The Battle of Neuve Chapelle 10-13 March 1915

This was the first British planned offensive from a trench system and its outcomes would provide lessons and methods that would form a model for most British attacks for the rest of the war.[73] As well as the operational lessons, much would be learned from this battle on the manning side as the new procedures for the reporting of casualties and the provision of reinforcements were tested in action.

The plan for the offensive, as stated in First Army's Operation Order, was to attack the enemy's lines at Neuve Chapelle and drive back any hostile forces from the line Aubers-Ligny le Grand in order to cut off the enemy's troops holding the line between Neuve Chapelle and

69 TNA WO 95/25: AG War Diary of 20 January 1915.
70 TNA WO 95/43: DAG 3rd Echelon War Diary for February 1915.
71 TNA WO 95/4186: No 46 IBD War Diary 1915.
72 TNA WO 95/25: GHQ AG War Diary GRO 674 Appendix 1 – "A" Staff Duties – Headquarters of Armies wef 1 March 1915 and WO 95/43 DAG 3rd Echelon War Diary for 1 March 1915.
73 Barr, 'Command in the Transition from Mobile to Static Warfare', p.33.

La Bassée.[74] The battle was to start on 10 March, and on that date an Advanced Report Centre for AG GHQ was established at Hazebrouck by the GHQ 'A' staff: the AAG, Colonel Cooke, and the Deputy Assistant Adjutant General (DAAG), Captain Jeffcoat. Arrangements had been made for the rapid reporting in round figures of casualties from Neuve Chapelle and also St Eloi but the contents of the telephoned reports received by GHQ show the steepness of the learning curve and the difficulty of obtaining accurate information. On 11 March, Cooke reported on his visits to the 1st, 2nd, 7th and 8th Divisions' Advanced Reporting Centres. The 1st Division had so far sustained no more than the normal level of losses but three battalions of the 2nd Division had suffered heavy casualties. There were as yet no confirmed figures available for the 7th and 8th Divisions and they had 'promised to wire definite information as they get it direct to GHQ'. Unofficially, the Deputy Adjutant and Quartermaster General (DAQMG) of 8th Division understood that 2nd Berkshires had lost 9 officers and 170 ORs and the Divisional staff considered:

> …that we shall be on the safe side if we indent for 400 men each for the 2nd Scottish Rifles and 2nd Middlesex. In the remaining battalions of the 23rd and 25th Brigades they consider we shall be about right if we ask for 200 men each.[75]

Matters were not much better at HQ First Army. An Advanced Report Centre had been set up on 9 March at Merville, manned by the AQMG, Lt Col Holman, and a clerk. By 11 March another officer had joined him as Holman had 'found he had too much to do' but even then they had difficulty obtaining information. The estimated total casualties for 10-13 March inclusive were given as 463 officers and 13,120 men but accompanied by the comment:

> As, however, practically no casualty figures are available from 4th [sic] Corps, these figures being merely estimates based on remaining strength as far as it is known, the estimate is necessarily very much a matter of guess work.[76]

On 14 March, the report telephoned back from the AG branch's Advanced Reporting centre at Hazebrouck to GHQ shows increasing signs of frustration:

> Col Cooke went out today to the 4th [sic] Corps and the 1st Army Headquarters, and he pointed out clearly that the matter of reporting casualties must be quickened up. He then went on to the 7th Division, and he understands from them that 113 names of officers have been submitted already. As regards other ranks in the 7th Division, estimated casualties are 2448. Col Cooke impressed upon the 7th Division that they must have some better system, on future occasions, of sending out a staff officer to collect information. He then went on to the 8th Division advanced reporting centre. All he could get from the 8th Division was the strengths on this morning. The unofficial figures may be correct, but Col Cooke does not know what they actually include. He thinks they may mean only men in the trenches.

74 *BOH 1915 Vol. 1*, p. 382.
75 TNA WO 95/25: AG War Diary entry for 11 March 1915.
76 TNA WO 95/181: First Army AG&QMG War Diary – March 1915.

> Col Cooke's opinion is that these casualties are not over-estimated. They are gained from quartermasters and transport personnel of the formations mentioned.[77]

The frustrations were not all one-sided, however. Whilst Colonel Cooke and his staff were doing their utmost in the field to collect accurate numbers, the DAQMG of First Army, Brigadier General Hobbs, visited GHQ on 15 March to discuss with Macready the 'present system of collecting casualty returns':

> During the last few days these returns have given rise to very numerous enquiries and telegrams. It is desirable to ascertain if a more speedy and accurate scheme can be devised for rendering these returns without unduly harassing Divisional and other Staffs during periods of active fighting.[78]

Inevitably, this first offensive had thrown up tensions between the staffs operating at different levels of an unfamiliar organization.

On 17 March, the Advanced Reporting Centres closed with AG's returning to GHQ and First Army's moving back to Aire. That several lessons had been learned during the fighting is evident from Cooke's report:

1. That it is very advisable for representatives of AG GHQ to keep in touch with HQ of Divisions during the progress of heavy fighting to ensure early information reaching the AG (and through him the CinC) regarding casualties.
2. That it is essential that Divisional Commanders shall have some organized system of communicating casualties rapidly in round numbers from Brigades to Divisional HQ.
3. That ordinary routine work of the administrative staff of Divisions, Corps and Armies must be suspended to a sufficient degree to enable sufficient numbers of the staffs to deal with the unusual casualty and reinforcement work.
4. That, in order that Division staffs may not be worried with unnecessary questions, the General Staff (GS) Liaison officers should not concern themselves with any figures of casualties, which it is the business of AG's staff to collect.[79]

The official casualty figures for Neuve Chapelle were later shown to have been 583 officers and 12,309 men, which included 544 officers and 11,108 men in the four attacking divisions.[80] Drafts had been sent up from the Base during the battle and, despite the difficulties for the staffs in obtaining accurate figures, the reinforcement system appeared to work effectively with practically all losses having been made good by about 18 March. The total reinforcements sent forward from the Base Depots between 10 – 20 March numbered 387 officers and 19,558 men.[81] At first sight this would appear to have been well in excess of the numbers required. However,

77 TNA WO 95/25: AG War Diary 10-14 March 1915.
78 TNA WO 95/181: First Army A&Q Branch War Diary entry for 15 March 1915.
79 TNA WO 95/25: AG GHQ War Diary entry for 17 March 1915.
80 *BOH 1915 Vol. 1*, p. 151 and fn 1. The total figures include 188 officers and 3859 men of the Meerut and Lahore Divisions.
81 TNA WO 95/25: AG GHQ War Diary – March 1915 Appendix 3.

the total casualties for the Regular Army and the TF shown for March 1915 in *Statistics of the Military Effort* are 992 officers and 20,690 men: 372 officers and 5,875 men were dead; 553 officers and 14,126 men had been wounded and a further 67 officers and 689 men were missing and/or had been taken prisoner.[82] The total British OR reinforcements shown as having been received in March were 743 Cavalry, 28,366 Infantry, 3350 TF Infantry and 49 Yeomanry.[83] For perhaps the only time in the war, the number of reinforcements available in France had exceeded the number of losses. It is likely that this was due to the surge of recruits of late 1914 having finished their training and now being available for drafting.

Although the reinforcement process had worked, there was still room to refine the reporting process. A new instruction on Casualty Reports and Reinforcements, which consolidated and replaced nine previous instructions, was published on 17 March, too soon for it to incorporate all the lessons from the recent fighting.[84] It was still broadly based on FSR Part 2 but the key change was that during actual fighting round numbers of casualties were to be notified to AG GHQ as quickly as possible so that a forecast might be made of the casualty situation and the number of reinforcements required. The importance of speed in notifying casualty numbers was again heavily emphasised, as was also the need for absolute accuracy in the subsequent report to DAG 3rd Echelon of personal details of the dead and missing. Only after further verification would the names of the dead, wounded and missing be forwarded to the War Office.

What can be seen in the new instructions to have evolved from FSR Part 2 was the key role now played by DAG 3rd Echelon. All applications for the provision of reinforcements were to be made through his office and he was the sole authority for submitting demands for manpower to the War Office. Once reinforcements, other than formed units, arrived in theatre their processing remained based on the original procedures: all troops, including casualties now recovered to fitness and returned stragglers, were to be sent to their respective Base Depots where the OC Reinforcements would await the DAG's orders for the numbers to be sent to the Front. Demands to replace casualties and wastage were now submitted directly to the DAG from formation headquarters.[85] On receipt of such demands, if sufficient troops were available in the Base Depots, the DAG would send orders to the appropriate OC Reinforcements to prepare the necessary personnel for entrainment as soon as rail transport could be provided. If insufficient numbers were available to meet demands, the DAG would dispatch what was available and take steps to demand the residue from England. Where the request was for replacements for normal requirements, such as routine casualties and wastage through sickness, the DAG could use his discretion in deciding whether to comply at once or to wait until a sufficiently large number was required in the brigade or division from which the demand emanated. Overall, it was a large and growing area of responsibility. In places it overlapped with the responsibilities of the IGC for the training, administration, interior economy and discipline of all reinforcements,

82 War Office, *SME* p.254. NB The total deaths include those killed, died of wounds or from disease or sickness etc. The figures for the number of wounded are also complicated in that *SME* p. 240 fn. (f) states that 'wounded' means 'number of wound casualties' not 'number of individuals wounded'.

83 TNA WO 95/25: AG GHQ War Diary March 1915.

84 Ibid., AG GHQ War Diary – March 1915 Casualty Reports and Reinforcements Pamphlet, issued with GRO No 720 of 1915.

85 TNA WO 95/181: First Army War Diary 30 March 1915 - correspondence between DAG 3rd Echelon, AG GHQ and First Army on subject of sick wastage reports. In future Divisions were to forward a weekly report direct to DAG 3rd Echelon as before, and a daily report to AAG First Army.

including formed units, and arrangements for their onward movement by rail once orders were received for them to proceed to the Front.

Lessons were still being drawn from Neuve Chapelle and a conference was held at GHQ on 23 March to discuss how the reporting of casualty numbers during heavy fighting might be accelerated in the future. One outcome seems to have been a constant round of visits by 'A' staff officers to explain what was wanted. It was, for example, 'explained to 27th and 28th Divisions that they must have some system of sending staff officers round to collect information as to casualties and let us know at the earliest moment'.[86] A further outcome was the issue in early April of instructions informing Army HQs of future arrangements for dealing with casualty questions during severe fighting, effectively the provision of what today would be called management information.

An advanced report centre would be set up near that of the CGS GHQ and manned by sufficient AG GHQ staff officers to connect with each Army involved in the fighting, together with an officer representing the DGMS. The AG staff officers based at the Advanced Reporting Centre would be out and about during the day visiting the different divisional headquarters and collecting the earliest possible information regarding round numbers of casualties, ascertaining which units had been, or were likely to be, most heavily engaged and generally gaining any other information likely to be of use in forecasting probable casualties and requirements. All useful news concerning casualties, reinforcements or prisoners of war gained from the divisions would be passed back to GHQ by telephone and statements drawn up showing results and figures to date, ready to submit to the CinC when required. A daily report would also be made from the advanced report centre for the CinC giving the latest casualty figures, the strengths of units and the numbers of reinforcements expected. Estimates of casualties to date and reinforcements expected were also to be submitted daily to the General Staff report centre. One officer from those of AG's staff left at GHQ would in future be solely employed in dealing with all casualty and reinforcement work during heavy fighting. He would collect and file under two separate headings all information received from the advance report centre and the divisions: (1) rough estimates of casualties and strengths of units and (2) detailed official figures. Separate tables under headings (1) and (2) were to be kept for each unit engaged. He would also prepare daily: firstly, a summary of casualties by divisions up to 9:00 pm each evening, carrying forward the totals daily whilst fighting continued; secondly, a table of reinforcements received from the Base Depots by Divisions since the commencement of operations, again carrying forward the total daily; and thirdly, a statement in round numbers by divisions of totals of officers and men under orders to move from England or waiting at the Base.[87] He would be a busy man.

For many of the staffs of the newly expanded BEF the battle of Neuve Chapelle had been a first introduction to the requirements for casualty reporting and the provision of reinforcements. Evidence of the refinement needed to earlier plans is shown by the plethora of detailed amendments and new instructions contained in the respective 'A' Staffs' War Diaries for March and April 1915. Such detailed changes do not occur for the periods during which the subsequent battles of 1915 were being fought and it appears that the procedures developed in the light of the experiences at Neuve Chapelle would remain unchanged for the rest of the year.

86 TNA WO 95/25: AG GHQ War Diary late March 1915.
87 TNA WO 95/181: First Army A & QMG War Diary of 5 April 1915 and its Appendix 1.

Training of 'A' Staff Officers

The rapid expansion of the Army had led to shortages of experience at all levels. The *BOH* notes a report from GOC First Army on the shortage of experienced officers and NCOs 'and that in some battalions neither the training of companies nor the general cohesion came up even to a moderate standard of efficiency'.[88] The problem was also acute at the staff level; qualified officers could not be found for the growing number of staff posts created by the increase in the number of formation headquarters at home and overseas. Increased size brought increased complexity. Instead of the previous generalists, specialist staff officers would now be needed who understood the routine of a particular branch or department of the staff.[89] In the 'A' area a programme of 'on the job' training was instigated at GHQ. For example, between 15-26 April Captain C.V.O. Gray, Seaforth Highlanders, was attached to AG's office for instruction in 'A' staff work, before spending a fortnight at the DAG 3rd Echelon's office and then a further period, 9-28 May, at the AG Advanced Report Centre. On 29 May he moved to 2nd Infantry Brigade to assume the duties of a Staff Captain. At a more senior level, Lt Col White, of the Connaught Rangers, spent from 8 June-14 July on attachment to AG's staffs before assuming his appointment as AAG 3rd Army. These were just two of a large number of officers who passed through monthly for training. It might not have been in depth training but at least it gave six weeks' grounding in procedures and, perhaps more importantly, created personal contacts between 'A' staff officers at different levels of the chain of command.

Second Battle of Ypres 22 April-24 May

Almost six weeks after the Battle of Neuve Chapelle, the Germans launched a surprise attack using poison gas in the vicinity of Ypres. Fierce fighting ensued over the next month, in what would become known as the Second Battle of Ypres, and casualties were heavy. The total losses for the period 22 April-31 May were 2,159 officers and 57,125 other ranks. In April, 24,301 plus 3,325 TF were sent from the Base and the May infantry numbers were even higher: 37,774 plus 4,041 TF.[90] Not all divisions were able to be completely refilled, however. The 5th Division figures show a total of 7,994 casualties over the whole period of Second Ypres: 71 officers killed, 209 wounded and 13 missing plus 1,068 men killed, 5,478 wounded and 1,155 missing.[91] Reinforcements were sent up as they became available and between 23 April-4 May 63 officers and 3544 men were received by 5th Division.[92] Unfortunately, what is not shown in the returns is how many replacements had actually been requested.

Fortunately for the BEF, the first divisions of the New Armies were now arriving. The 9th, 12th and 14th Divisions arrived during May followed by five more divisions in July. Kitchener did not want to waste the excellent material of his New Armies and had great faith in their esprit de corps.[93] Consequently he remained reluctant to allow them to be broken up, as GHQ

88 *BOH 1915 Vol. 1*, p. 26 fn 3.
89 Ibid., p. 55.
90 TNA WO 95/25: AG War Diary April and May 1915.
91 *BOH 1915 Vol. 1*, pp. 355-6.
92 TNA WO 95/25: AG War Diary May 1915.
93 Hankey, *The Supreme Command 1914-1918*, p. 260.

had suggested earlier in the year, and the First New Army divisions went to the Front unbroken; in June, for example, the 12th Division replaced the 27th Division in the line north-west of Armentieres whilst on 1 July the 9th Division relieved the 7th Division near Festubert.

The Base

Between 1 January-30 June, 155,000 Infantry reinforcements were dispatched to the Front from the various Base Depots, which were by now well settled into their routine of sending drafts to the Front as and when required.[94] Drafts were allocated to particular units and were not to be diverted to other units without specific authority from GHQ.[95] In early July James Jack commanded 93 men of the 2nd Cameronians at No 8 IBD at Harfleur, where facilities included practice trenches, assault courses and a rifle range. Parades were held morning and afternoon, and training consisted of tactical exercises, route marches, lectures, drill and other training. Reinforcements arrived from various sources: on 8 August Jack noted that 'a smart draft' composed mainly of Cameronians, who had recovered from wounds received at Neuve Chapelle, had arrived on 27 July and a draft of 60 from the 12th (Service) Battalion had arrived three days later. The latter were 'splendid material but insufficiently trained …'.[96]

Training available at the Base depots could not replicate frontline conditions. A partial solution was found by the creation of 'Entrenching Battalions'.[97] These would be located close to the Front and also provide much needed manpower for work such as digging, wiring and trench boarding. By the end of July ten such battalions, each containing 20 officers and 1000 men, had been formed and two were already at work at the Front. For draft-finding purposes they remained under the orders of the DAG and were effectively an 'Advanced Base Depot'. As drafts were posted out to units they would be replaced by further drafts from reinforcements available at Base Depots.[98] Men were normally attached to Entrenching battalions in regimental batches accompanied by their own officers; when they were drafted on as reinforcements it was usually, at least in 1915 and early 1916, to battalions of their own regiment.[99]

Medical facilities were also being refined in order to facilitate the return of men to the Front. The policy was to evacuate as few casualties as possible to England 'in order to avoid general loss of manpower' but the increasing number of casualties caused greater congestion in the Base hospitals than the single convalescent hospital mobilized in 1914 could handle. By July eight convalescent depots had been established on the LofC at Boulogne, Wimereux, Rouen, Le Havre, Étaples, Dannes, Camiers and Le Tréport. Their purpose was to reduce congestion in the hospitals and treat convalescent patients until they were sufficiently recovered to be fit for duty.[100]

94 TNA WO 95/43: DAG 3rd Echelon War Diary June 1915.
95 TNA WO 95/181: First Army RO 57 of 17 May 15.
96 Terraine, ed., *General Jack's Diary*, pp. 106 – 7.
97 C.E.W. Bean, *Official History of Australia in the War of 1914–1918 - Vol. 3 – The Australian Imperial Force in France, 1916* 12th ed. (Sydney: Angus & Robertson, 1941), p. 176.
98 TNA WO 95/43: DAG 3rd Echelon War Diary July 1915 and WO 95/181 First Army DA&QMG War Diary 9 August 1915.
99 K.W. Mitchinson, *Pioneer Battalions in the Great War* (London: Leo Cooper, 1997), pp. 193-4.
100 MacPherson, *Medical History of the War, Vol. II*, pp. 84-5.

The Battle of Loos 25 September-15 October

Planning had begun in June for a British attack in support of the French later in the year. The battle of Loos would take place between 25 September-15 October. On 21 September the indefatigable AAG GHQ, now promoted to Colonel, Cooke, visited the Headquarters of 1st, 2nd, 9th, 15th and 47th Divisions and First Army to discuss arrangements for casualty reporting and on 22 September the War Office was warned to expect about 30,000 casualties. Once the attack started on 25 September, Cooke spent that day and the next two visiting various headquarters; on 28 September he visited 1st Army, 9th and 15th Divisions, arranging for these two divisions to be brought up to strength as early as possible on being drawn back into reserve. By 30 September AG GHQ's Branch was able to note that the system of wiring estimated casualties to GHQ had worked well, enabling the War Office to begin sending out 30,000 reinforcements within three days of the start of the battle. On 4 October, however, following information received from the CinC, Colonel Cooke had to warn AG at the War Office that a further 50,000 casualties were expected before the end of October.[101]

The British casualties at Loos were heavy: 2,013 officer and 48,367 other rank casualties between 26 September-16 October, of whom some 800 officers and 15,000 men were killed or missing.[102] During September and October 75,062 men were sent up from the Base but, unless they were men who had been previously wounded and were now returning, it was impossible to replace the loss of experience.[103] The *Official History* analyzes Loos in some detail and attributes at least part of the problems encountered during it to the composition of the Army. The commanders and their staffs lacked experience and 'their divisions were not yet the instruments demanded by the exigencies of modern war.' The Regular Army had been refilled with half-trained officers and men, the TF were as yet untried in war and also lacked professional officers and NCOs and the Divisions of the New Armies had received 'only hasty and imperfect training', hampered by the late arrival of weapons and equipment.[104] In short, there was a chronic lack of experience at all levels, particularly the NCOs. On 22 October HQ First Army received an enquiry from DAG 3rd Echelon as to whether its battalions would accept Cavalry NCOs from England on condition that these NCOs would be promoted to the next rank on transfer. The answer was that a considerable number of battalions would accept them.[105]

Following the battle, the omission of any mention of further changes to casualty reporting in the relevant 'A' Branch War Diaries may be taken to show that the procedures laid down earlier in the year had worked well. The reinforcement system had also been effective with replacements on hand.

101 TNA WO 95/25: AG GHQ War Diary September and October 1915.
102 *BOH 1915 Vol. II*, p. 391.
103 TNA WO 95/25: AG GHQ War Diary September and October 1915: September: Cavalry 512; Infantry 17,449; Yeomanry 150; TF Infantry 6,183; October: Cavalry 3,784; Infantry 38,017; Yeomanry 348; TF Infantry 8,619.
104 *BOH 1915 Vol. II*, p. 394.
105 TNA WO 95/181: First Army AG&QMG War Diary 22 October 1915.

Analysis of Changes to the Composition of Marcher Battalions

It might be thought that by now the composition of the battalions which had participated in the various battles of 1915 would be gradually changing with the constant cycle of losses and replacements. For instance, five of the Marcher battalions which took part in the Battle of Loos reported the following OR casualties on just one day, 25 September: 1st SWB (121), 2nd RWF (113), 9th Cheshire (54) and 9th RWF (240).[106] The 1/1st Monmouthshire, the Pioneer battalion of the 46th (North Midland) Division, had suffered 147 casualties, including 27 killed, on 13 October.[107] The losses would all need to be replaced.

Some idea of the extent of any changes in composition may be gained by drilling down into the details of individual soldiers using the enlistment and birth locations found in *SDGW*, amplified where possible by individual Service Records.[108] The period chosen for this analysis is 1 July-30 November 1915.

Many of those who died in the second half of 1915 were pre-war soldiers, as evidenced by their Regimental numbers, who had joined a Regiment presumably of their choice: there are numerous examples such as 8269 Pte William Holden who was born and enlisted in Blackburn, Lancashire but joined the Cheshire Regiment. In many cases, however, enlistments also reflected the need for men to move around to find work. Within Western Command that might mean the cotton industries of Lancashire or the mining areas of South Wales. Men frequently joined the local regiment where they worked, as for example 10940 Pte Alfred Hunt from Salisbury who enlisted in Pontypool in the SWB. Sometimes those volunteering reported to their nearest convenient recruiting office with a request for a particular Regiment: 19530 Pte John McKeown was born in Talke and enlisted in Burslem, both in Staffordshire, but chose to enlist in the SWB. At its most extreme, two Cheshire soldiers, 25860 Pte Frank Alden Gallagher and 25854 Pte William Harry McCarty, were born in Canada and enlisted in Barry, presumably straight from the ship. In a few cases in late 1915, the effects of the Army (Transfers) Act may also be seen; some of the men transferred in mid-1915 from the Sherwood Foresters to the Cheshires were killed in October. The information in SDGW simply allows a broad analysis and an identification of trends during the period in question.[109]

The enlistment figures (see Tables 2.1 and 2.2 below) invariably show a higher percentage enlisted within the Regimental areas, as a result of the element of choice involved, than do the birth figures but whilst the KSLI figure of 59 percent remains exactly the same as 1914, the Cheshire's has fallen from 83 percent to 69 percent. This is not such a marked drop as it might

106 *BOH 1915 Vol. II*, pp. 223, 254, 258.

107 The three battalions of the Monmouthshire Regiment which had had to be amalgamated in May due to lack of replacements had been re-constituted in July/August 1915. The 1/1st and 1/3rd Monmouthshire both became Pioneer battalions in September and were posted to 46th Division and 49th Division respectively. The 1/2nd Monmouthshire rejoined 4th Division but would be posted to 29th Division as its Pioneer battalion in May 1916.

108 The data has been drawn from SDGW. Percentages have been used for comparison although this may occasionally obscure the picture due to the differing sizes of the samples analysed.

109 NB Where the figures are low the corresponding percentages may give a skewed picture: e.g. 18 Cheshire soldiers, 69 percent of 26 deaths, enlisted in No 4 District. This rises to 88 percent of enlistments within Western command with the addition of just five more soldiers.

appear, however, since it is caused simply by 3 men (12 percent of the total number of those killed) having enlisted in Northern Command.

Enlistment Locations	1st Cheshire		9th Cheshire		1st KSLI		6th KSLI	
Regimental Area	18	69%	35	92%	67	59%	30	97%
Elsewhere in No 4 District - England					4			
Elsewhere in No 4 District - Wales					4			
Total enlisted in No 4 District	18	69%	35	92%	75	66%	30	97%
Enlisted in No 3 District	2				12			
• Liverpool/Manchester	3		2		6			
Total Enlisted in Western Command	**23**	**88%**	**37**	**97%**	**93**	**82%**	**30**	**97%**
Northern Command	3		1		3		1	
Southern Command					3			
• Birmingham					5	(4%)		
Eastern					3			
London District					6	(5%)		
Scotland/Ireland								
Overseas								
Total Other Commands	**3**	**12%**	**1**		**20**	**18%**		**3%**
Total Deaths	**26**		**38**		**113**			

Table 2.1. Enlistment locations of soldiers of selected English Regular battalions who were killed/ died between 1 July-30 November 1915.

Conversely, local enlistments for the Welsh battalions have increased slightly, although 2nd RWF remains low on 28 percent. Across No 4 District as a whole, 1st SWB seems to be more successful recruiting in the rest of Wales, having enlisted 16 (23 percent) to 2nd RWF's 3 (5 percent); only 2nd RWF has enlisted less than 66 percent from No 4 District as a whole. This trend continues for Western Command where three battalions have enlisted over 80 percent whilst 2nd RWF recruited 19 (29 percent) in Birmingham (Southern Command).

The difficulty with drawing any firm conclusions for the four Line battalions,1st Cheshire, 1st KSLI, 2nd RWF and 1st SWB, is that the differing sizes of the samples, 270 deaths against 765 in 1914, means that some percentages may give a disproportionate picture. However, the overall figures for the Line battalions bear out the finding that they were more homogenous in late 1915 than in 1914, despite the large numbers of replacements that the draft-finding organisations had already had to produce.

It might have been expected that the figures for the New Army battalions, 9th Cheshire, 6th KSLI and 9th RWF, would show universally high recruiting in the Regimental areas. This is the case for enlistments into the two English regiments: 92 percent for 9th Cheshire and 97 percent for 6th KSLI. The 9th RWF, however, shows only 35 (36 percent) recruited within its

Regimental area, although a further 47 (40 percent) were recruited in the rest of Wales making the enlistment figures for No 4 District roughly balance: 9th Cheshire 92 percent; 6th KSLI 97 percent and 9th RWF 81 percent. The Western Command figures are similarly over 80 percent for all three.

Enlistment Locations	2nd RWF		9th RWF		1st SWB	
Regimental Area	18	28%	43	36%	36	*52%*
Elsewhere in No 4 District - England	12	18%	6	5%	1	*1%*
Elsewhere in No 4 District - Wales	3	5%	47	40%	16	*23%*
Total enlisted in No 4 District	33	51%	96	81%	53	*77%*
Enlisted in No 3 District	2		4		3	
• Liverpool/Manchester			1			
Total Enlisted in Western Command	**35**	**54%**	**101**	**86%**	**56**	**81%**
Northern Command	1		7		1	
Southern Command	10		5		2	
• Birmingham	19	(29%)	5	(4%)		
Eastern					10	
London District						
Scotland/Ireland						
Overseas						
Total Other Commands	**30**	**46%**	**17**	**14%**	**13**	**19%**
Total Deaths	**65**		**101**		**69**	

Table 2.2. Enlistment locations of soldiers of selected Welsh Regular battalions who were killed/ died on the Western Front between 1 July-30 November 1915.

The percentages of those born in the respective Regimental areas for 1st Cheshire, 1st KSLI, 2nd RWF and 1st SWB (see Tables 2.3 and 2.4 below) remain similar to those of 1914 although 2nd RWF shows a marked increase from 11 percent to 20 percent. To the latter may be added a further 8 percent for those born elsewhere in Wales; however, at only 28 percent the 2nd RWF could not have been said to be ethnically Welsh in late 1915. Traditionally 2nd RWF had recruited in Birmingham and this is borne out by the 26 percent born in that city. The 1st SWB appears more Welsh with 39 percent having been born in Wales. In contrast, the two English battalions show 61 percent and 50 percent respectively for 1st Cheshire and 1st KSLI having been born within their Regimental Areas, rising to 88 percent for 1st Cheshire and 72 percent for 1st KSLI having been born within Western Command. For the Service battalions, the figures for birth locations are more varied: whilst only 16 percent of 6th KSLI were born in other Commands, this rises to 26 percent for 9th Cheshire and 31 percent for 9th RWF.

Birth locations	1st Cheshire		9th Cheshire		1st KSLI		6th KSLI	
Regimental Area	16	61%	24	63%	56	50%	21	*68%*
Elsewhere in No 4 District – England			1		3		2	
Elsewhere in No 4 District – Wales			1		6		2	
Total born in No 4 District	16	61%	26	68%	65	58%	25	81%
Born in No 3 District	3		1		13		1	
• Liverpool/Manchester	4		1		3			
Total Born in Western Command	**23**	**88%**	**28**	**74%**	**81**	**72%**	**26**	**84%**
Northern Command	3		7		7		3	
Southern Command					7		2	
• Birmingham					5			
Eastern			1		7			
London District					3			
Scotland/Ireland			2		3			
Overseas								
Total Other Commands	**3**		**10**		**32**		**5**	
Location of Birth Unknown								
Total Deaths	**26**		**38**		**113**		**31**	

Table 2.3. Birth locations of soldiers of selected English Regular battalions who were killed/died between 1 July-30 November 1915.

Birth Locations	2nd RWF		9th RWF		1st SWB	
Regimental Area	13	20%	35	30%	14	*20%*
Elsewhere in No 4 District – England	12	18%	7	6%	5	*7%*
Elsewhere in No 4 District – Wales	5	8%	33	28%	13	*19%*
Total born in No 4 District	30	46%	75	64%	32	46%
Born in No 3 District			3		5	
• Liverpool/Manchester			4			
Total Born in Western Command	**30**	**46%**	**82**	**69%**	**37**	**54%**
Northern Command	5		13		4	
Southern Command	10		15		12	
• Birmingham	17		3			
Eastern	2		2		12	
London District			2			
Scotland/Ireland			1		3	
Overseas						
Total Other Commands	**34**		**36**		**31**	
Location of Birth Unknown	1				1	
Total Deaths	**65**		**118**		**69**	

Table 2.4. Birth locations of soldiers of selected Welsh Regular battalions who were killed/died between 1 July-30 November 1915.

Tables 2.5 and 2.6 below show the equivalent data for TF battalions in 1915. The numbers of TF soldiers who died in 1915 were too small for meaningful analysis but have been produced to form a baseline for future consideration. Enlistments show 100 percent from the Regimental area for all the battalions surveyed, which is unsurprising given the local nature of TF recruiting and service and the inability to transfer men between TF units.

TF Battalions – Enlistment Locations	**1/5th Cheshire**		**1/6th Cheshire**		**1/4th RWF**		**1/1st Monmouths**		**1/3rd Monmouths**	
Regimental Area	19	100%	1	100%	14	100%	30	100%	11	100%
Elsewhere in No 4 District - England										
Elsewhere in No 4 District - Wales										
Total enlisted in No 4 District	19	100%		100%	14	100%	30	100%	11	100%
Enlisted in No 3 District										
• Liverpool/Manchester										
Total Enlisted in Western Command	**19**	**100%**		**100%**	**14**	**100%**	**30**	**100%**	**11**	**100%**
Northern Command										
Southern Command										
• Birmingham										
Eastern										
London District										
Scotland/Ireland										
Overseas										
Total Other Commands										
Total Deaths	**19**		**1**		**14**		**30**		**11**	

Table 2.5. Enlistment locations of soldiers of selected TF battalions who were killed/died between 1 July-30 November 1915.

The birth locations for the English TF battalions also show 100 percent as having been born in the regimental areas. The Welsh birth locations are far more scattered, with only around half having been born in Wales.

TF Battalions – Birth Locations	1 /5th Cheshire		1 /6th Cheshire		1 /4th RWF		1 /1st Monmouths		1 /3rd Monmouths	
Regimental Area	19	100%	1	100%	7	50%	12	40%	5	45%
Elsewhere in No 4 District – England					1					
Elsewhere in No 4 District - Wales							5	17%	2	18%
Total born in No 4 District	19	100%	1	100%	8	57%	17	57%	7	63%
Born in No 3 District										
• Liverpool/Manchester										
Total Born in Western Command	**19**	**100%**	**1**	**100%**	**8**	**57%**	**17**	**57%**	**7**	**63%**
Northern Command							1			
Southern Command							2		1	
• Birmingham										
Eastern							2			
London District							1			
Scotland/Ireland										
Overseas										
Total Other Commands							**6**		**1**	
Location of Birth Unknown					6		7		3	
Total Deaths	**19**		**1**		**14**		**30**		**11**	

Table 2.6. Birth locations of soldiers of selected TF battalions who were killed/died between 1 July-30 November 1915.

Growing Manpower Problems at Home

The difficulties of providing TF replacements for the Western Front have already been highlighted but as the year wore on they were beginning to give rise to increasing tensions between the demands of home defence and the BEF. These were highlighted by the situation of the 50th Northumbrian Division which had arrived on the Western Front in mid-April. By 23 April it was in its concentration area around Steenvoorde, to the west of Poperinghe, with 572 officers and 16,858 men.[110] A newly arrived division would usually undergo a period of training but 50th Division's arrival coincided with the German attack at Ypres on 22 April so it was rushed straight into the heavy fighting of the Second Battle of Ypres. It was the only TF division to be involved and suffered heavy losses: 186 officers and 5018 men between 22

110 E. Wyrall, *The Fiftieth Division 1914 – 1919* (1939; Uckfield: Naval & Military Press, n.d.), p. 5.

April-31 May 1915.[111] These were not the heaviest divisional losses for that period, the 28th Division having lost 15,533 and the 4th Division 10,859.[112] The problem for the 50th Division was that replacements would have to come from its Second and Third Line units. However, its Second Line units had originally been full of HS only men and the Third Line units had been very late in forming.[113]

With these constraints the Division was still seriously undermanned nearly six months later when in late September it became the subject of a series of War Office Minutes. The trigger for these was a note from AG's branch, containing drastic proposals to replenish the Division from its Second Line units. Since 1 September 1,474 men had gone or were under orders to join the Division's First Line units in France but this was still inadequate. The only way to increase this figure would be to take every trained man from the Second Line, a total of 1,336. This would leave the Second Line units very weak but would ensure the Division's Infantry units received a total draft of 2,810 during September.[114] The proposal sparked a serious reaction from the then Director of Home Defence (DHD), Major General L. E. Kiggell, who wrote to the CIGS on 27 September warning of the continuing possibility of invasion and the low fighting strength of the HD force which would have to confront such an event with partially trained and inadequately armed troops led by inexperienced officers. The nub of the minute was a request for a decision on whether the already 'dangerously' weak TF divisions at home should be weakened still further for the sake of the BEF.[115] In the meantime, the AG staffs in London were proposing to provide reinforcements for the 1st Northumbrian, 1st Highland, 1st Lowland and the 1st Welsh TF Divisions by amalgamating the Second and Third Lines in some battalions and by abolishing the 1/4th London Brigade, although in the event this did not happen.[116] The Northumbrian matter reached Kitchener, who on 7 October ruled that the Northumbrian Territorials should receive the available reinforcements. The immediate problem for that Division had been eased but the underlying difficulties, caused by the constraints the TF transfer regulations placed on reinforcing units and the conflicting requirements of the Home Army and the BEF, remained.

Recruiting for the Regular Army was also giving rise to concern as numbers dwindled monthly. In the five months from August – December 1914 some 1,186,357 men had been recruited. During the following five months, from January – May 1915, the numbers had fallen by almost 50 per cent to 612,443.[117] During the early months of the year, replacements for losses overseas could be found from amongst the men recruited the previous year who would by then have completed their training. The lead-time for such training, however, was about four months so men to replace the losses of Loos, for example, would have to have been recruited by the end of the previous April.

It was not only the Regular Army and the TF that were encountering manpower problems as the consequences of uncontrolled recruiting were rapidly becoming apparent for the nation

111 *BOH 1915 Vol. I,* p. 356.
112 Ibid.
113 TNA WO 32/5268: The Present Situation as Regards Home Defence.
114 Ibid.
115 Ibid., and Mitchinson, *Defending Albion*, p. 108.
116 TNA WO 32/5268: The Present Situation as Regards Home Defence.
117 *SME* p. 364.

at large. Many industries had been affected by the earlier rush to enlist but the loss of skilled and experienced munitions workers in particular meant that the output of equipment and weapons was failing to meet requirements. The main problem was a lack of any centrally held information on the distribution of manpower nationally. On 1 July 1915, a remedy was sought when a Bill proposing compulsory registration of the capabilities and occupations of everyone in Great Britain, male and female, between the ages of fifteen and sixty-five was put before Parliament.[118] Its purpose was to obtain information on the numbers employed in each industry, from which could then be calculated those needed for essential activities, such as munitions work, shipbuilding and agriculture and the consequent surplus available for the army and navy. Despite some opposition from those who saw it as a precursor to conscription, the National Registration Act was passed in July and registration took place on 15 August 1915. The outcome showed 2,832,210 married and 2,179,231 single men of military age not serving in the forces. Those considered indispensable for work essential for national survival were 'starred' as being in 'reserved occupations'. Some 690,138 single men were thus 'starred', leaving 1,489,093 technically available for military service.[119]

Opposition to conscription continued but there was also a growing realization of the inadequacy of a voluntary system to meet the manpower demands being placed upon it. During the spring of 1915 enlistments had averaged 25,000 men per week but this could no longer be sustained as the year continued. It had become clear that voluntary recruitment was not going to provide the numbers of men required.

This led to a War Policy Committee being set up in early September to examine the existing voluntary recruiting system and 'some general consideration of the alternative of compulsion'.[120] The Committee based its considerations on a projected British Army strength in the field on 1 April 1916 of 1.5 million or about 70 divisions, the figure Kitchener had pledged in discussions with the French High Command at Calais in July 1915, and the need to maintain that force at its full establishment until the end of 1916. In order to meet this figure, the War Office noted that recruiting would have to be raised to 25,000 per week in order to maintain a force of 70 divisions throughout 1916.

Statements were taken from Government departments, which inevitably reflected the responsibility of the Minister concerned. The First Lord of the Admiralty, Balfour, questioned the concentration on the Army when ships were more important; the Chancellor of the Exchequer, McKenna, contended that 50 divisions were the maximum that Britain could afford to recruit and equip; and Kitchener not only needed 70 divisions but regarded 100 as the ideal. He also confirmed that more recruits would be needed to maintain the Army in 1916 than could be obtained under a voluntary system which currently produced about 20,000 men per week, enough to keep only 1,000,000 men in the field.[121]

In early September the War Policy Committee put forward three options: maintain the current system and tell the French that 70 Divisions were unobtainable; increase the number

118 *Parliamentary Debates* (Commons), 5th Ser., Vol.72, cols 1651-55.
119 Report on Recruiting by the Earl of Derby, Director General of Recruiting Parliamentary Papers 1914-16 XXXIX Cd 8149 cited in Peter Simkins, *Kitchener's Army* (Manchester: Manchester University Press, 1988), p 148.
120 TNA CAB 37/134/9: War Policy Committee Report, September 1915.
121 Ibid., p. 8.

of voluntary recruits through a threat of later compulsion; or introduce compulsory service. The report was signed by the six members of the Committee, the Lords Crewe, Curzon and Selborne, and Austen Chamberlain, Winston Churchill and Arthur Henderson. However, in a Supplementary Memorandum dated 7 September, four of the signatories, Churchill, Curzon, Selborne and Chamberlain, broke ranks and offered six more positive conclusions: 70 divisions would be possible and financial arrangements could be made to maintain them up to the end of 1916; sufficient munitions would be available from March 1916; the required numbers of men existed, albeit unobtainable on a voluntary basis, but men could be spared from industry if a proper form of selection was employed; and it would be desirable to increase the number of divisions to 100 for which munitions would be available by August 1916.[122] The signatories considered that the decision required of the Cabinet was clear:

> Whether the 70 division scheme is to be cut down to the limits which can be supplied by voluntary enlistment, or whether it is to be maintained and carried out by compulsion.[123]

Action of some kind was urgently needed as it became increasingly difficult to replace the high level of casualties occurring on the Western Front and elsewhere. A month later, Kitchener informed the Cabinet that the voluntary system was failing to produce the 35,000 men that were now needed each week to maintain the armies in the field.[124]

A final attempt at voluntary enlistment was made in mid-October with the announcement by Lord Derby, who had been appointed Director General of Recruiting on 11 October, of the 'group' or 'Derby Scheme'. Under this scheme, which was not applied to Ireland because of continuing fears of unrest there, men between 18 and 41 not employed in 'reserved occupations' were asked either to enlist immediately or to attest their willingness to serve when required. The attested men would be divided into 46 groups by age and marital status; single men in groups 1-23 and married men in groups 24-46. Groups would be called up as required, beginning with single men aged 19 (Group 2), but no married men would be called up until all the single men had been summoned.[125] Those who attested but chose to defer their service would receive a day's pay at Infantry rates and then be transferred to Section B of the Army Reserve to await call up. This change to the normal form of Reserve service necessitated a hasty amendment to the Army Pay Warrant to ensure that the 'Derbyites' received no further 'emoluments from Army Funds' or any of the normal Reservist entitlements, namely a gratuity under Article 1117 of the Pay Warrant, a suit of civilian clothes or a money allowance in lieu, before being called up.[126] Applications by attested men for further postponements would be considered by specially established Local Tribunals. A network of some 2000 local tribunals was created by the Local

122 TNA CAB/37/134/7: Supplementary Memorandum dated 7 September 1915.

123 Ibid., p. 15.

124 TNA CAB/37/135/15: 8 October 1915.

125 Roy Douglas, 'Voluntary Enlistment in the First World War and the Work of the Parliamentary Recruiting Committee', *Journal of Modern History,* 42 (4) (December, 1970), p. 580; *HC Deb 2 November 1915 vol 75 c520.*

126 TNA WO 123/57: AO 415 of 1915, published 22 October 1915. This amendment ensured that the 'Derby' men would not receive a gratuity under Article 1117 of the Pay Warrant, nor a suit of civilian clothes or a money allowance in lieu. WO 293/3 WOI 221, 23 October noted that they would not be appointed to a Corps or Regiment until actually called up.

Government Board (LGB). They each consisted of five members, drawn mostly from the local registration authorities that had conducted the August registration, and mirrored existing urban and rural council boundaries.[127]

The Derby scheme was initially successful and its original end date of 30 November was extended until mid-December 1915. Enlistment into the TF had been allowed under the scheme and this was also extended until its completion.[128] The processing of recruits seems to have worked well although there were some delays and also resentment of those who turned up only to attest: a 'haughty 'grouper'' who complained of having been kept waiting in the Recruiting Office was greeted by the retort: 'What the devil are you grumbling at, we have been waiting for you for sixteen *** months.'[129]

There was a late rush of attestations before the cut-off date of 11 December but by 24 December 1915 it had become apparent that far fewer men had been obtained than had been hoped for. Almost a third of the 3,145,760 unstarred men were unavailable for various reasons: medically unfit, in Government employment, or their employers had refused their consent. Only 55 percent of available men had enlisted or attested; almost 47 percent of the available married men had refused as had 40 percent of the single men.[130] It was estimated that the scheme had produced only 343,386 single men forcing Derby to conclude that 'it will not be possible to hold the married men to their attestation unless and until the services of single men have been obtained by other means.'[131] The scheme had failed but this was due not so much to insufficient single men volunteering as that the demand for 35,000 volunteers per week was far too high a target for any industrial society to be able to meet after sixteen months of war.[132] The Government was now reluctantly faced with the inescapable conclusion that some form of compulsion was the only way forward.[133]

Overview

The year had started with continuing reliance solely on the recruiting of volunteers but by its end it was clear that the introduction of some form of compulsion was imminent. A National Register had been compiled providing the Government for the first time with information on the employment of manpower throughout the country and the first tentative steps towards greater organisation of the nation's manpower had been taken. The Derby scheme was a last attempt to encourage voluntary enlistments but its introduction of an age-group system to create

127 *Minutes of the Corporation of Glasgow of 5 November 1915* (GCA CI.3.54); TNA: MH 10/195 LGB Circular R1 of 26 October 1915.
128 TNA WO 70/50: Summary of Principal Changes in Organisation and Administration of TF since Mobilization, p. 51; letters 27/Gen No/4507 (AG 2(b)) dated 23 October 1915 and 9/Gen No/5764 dated 9 December 1915.
129 Cheshire Regiment, *The Oak Tree Vol. 1 1915-1916* (Chester: December 1915 edition Vol. 1 No 1).
130 Based on figures cited in Douglas, 'Voluntary Enlistment in the First World War', p. 582.
131 Lord Derby, Report on Recruiting, cited in Simkins *Kitchener's Army*, p. 156.
132 K. Grieves, *The Politics of Manpower, 1914-18* (Manchester, Manchester University Press, 1988), p.22.
133 J. McDermott, *British Military Service Tribunals 1916-1918* (Manchester: Manchester University Press, 2011), p. 13 and Ian F.W. Beckett & K. Simpson, eds., *Nation In Arms: a Social Study of the British Army in the First World War* (Manchester: Manchester University Press, 1985), pp. 12-13.

a pool of manpower that could be subsequently called upon would prove to be the precursor to a system of subsequent compulsion.

Various methods had been tried by the Government, the War Office and the Home Army to obtain and train sufficient men for reinforcements. Legislation had been put in place enabling greater flexibility over the transfer of Regular soldiers between cap-badges, although as yet the TF remained obdurate and consequently its usefulness both overseas and at home was reduced. Reserve units had been created for the New Armies, including the locally raised battalions, and were now organised into Reserve Brigades. More specific medical classifications had been introduced enabling those less than 100 per cent fit to fight to be used in other ways.

On the Western Front, casualty reporting and reinforcement procedures and structures had been refined in the light of experience at Neuve Chapelle and had been tested successfully at Loos. Inevitably the reinforcements arriving as the year progressed were less experienced than their predecessors but the new camps at home contained better training facilities and the Base depots were also better equipped. The creation of the Entrenching battalions was an attempt to give experience near the Front whilst at the same time assisting in basic maintenance work.

Despite the previously unprecedented loss of life and the need for replacements to be found from all available sources, analysis of fatalities during mid to late 1915 shows as yet no marked changes in the composition of battalions in comparison with 1914. Indeed, analysis of the two Welsh Line battalions shows that they were slightly more Welsh at the end of 1915 than they had been a year earlier.

The *Official History*, in referring to operational events, notes that its 'very misfortunes and mistakes make 1915 particularly worthy of study'.[134] It is also worthy of study in the manning and administration spheres, not for mistakes, but for the steady development of structures and procedures which laid foundations for what was to come. These developments had taken place in a BEF commanded by Sir John French but in December 1915 he returned home. His place as CinC BEF was taken by General Sir Douglas Haig. In future the BEF on the Western Front would be Haig's Army.

134 *BOH 1915 Vol. I*, p.vi.

3

1916: The Coming of Compulsion

The prologue for 1916 was the Inter-Allied Military Conference at Chantilly in early December 1915, attended by representatives of the four Allied armies, French, British, Italian and Russian. The main agreement reached was that the Allies would each launch offensive actions on their respective fronts in 1916, if possible concurrently in order to prevent Germany from transferring forces to defend one front after another. For Britain and France the plan was for a major joint offensive in Picardy, on either side of the river Somme.[1]

Governmental agreement to the planned offensive was needed so the Conference outcomes were incorporated in a General Staff paper on the 'Future Conduct of the War' placed before the Cabinet War Committee on 16 December.[2] The ruling principle underlying the paper's recommendations was that 'every possible division, fully manned and equipped in every respect' should be placed in France for 'we require every man we can find to break the enemy's resistance in that theatre'. The crucial question of manpower for 1916 was thus firmly in the spotlight.

On 28 December 1915 the War Committee agreed that France and Flanders was to be the main theatre of operations and that every effort would be made to mount an offensive in the spring in 'close co-operation with the Allies and in the greatest possible strength'.[3] By late December, therefore, and contrary to those who would wish later to portray the Battle of the Somme as a purely military initiative, the British Cabinet had endorsed the Allied military proposals for 1916. There would be some back-pedaling in early January when the War Committee noted that 'it must not be assumed that such offensive operations are finally decided upon', but it was clear that there would be a joint offensive with the French in 1916.[4] All manpower deliberations in early 1916 would be conducted against that backdrop, albeit that the precise intentions were known initially only within the highest echelons of the Government and the War Office.

1 *BOH 1916 Vol. 1*, pp. 4-9.
2 Ibid., *Appendices* pp. 6-27. The War Committee of the Cabinet was formed in October 1915 and consisted of the Prime Minister, the Secretaries of State for War, Foreign Affairs and India, the First Lord of the Admiralty and the Minister of Munitions (Lloyd George).
3 TNA CAB 37/139/59: Meeting of the War Committee held on Tuesday December 28, 1915.
4 TNA CAB 37/140/29: Meeting of the War Committee held on 13 January 1916.

During December 1915 there were changes amongst the senior military men who would handle the events of 1916. General Sir Douglas Haig replaced Sir John French as CinC BEF on 19 December and Lieutenant General Sir William Robertson also moved from his post of CGS BEF, replacing Sir Archibald Murray in London as CIGS. Whilst Robertson's move deprived Haig of the assistance in his new post of an experienced Chief of Staff, it meant that the most senior Military men in London and France not only knew each other very well but also that the new CIGS had had over 12 months' experience of fighting on the Western Front. In February 1916 General Sir Nevil Macready would leave his post as AG BEF to return to London to become AG in the War Office, with the result that the two top military positions in London would be filled by men with recent BEF experience.[5]

Growing Manpower Concerns

The manpower estimate for the financial year 1915-16 was originally 3,000,000 men but on 21 December, even before any decision on 1916 offensives had been made, the Prime Minister sought Parliamentary authority for an additional 1,000,000 to be obtained by 31 March 1916. Wastage at the Front was running at 15 percent per month and extra men were needed for future reinforcements: for every man kept abroad there ought to be 1.8 (sic) at home in reserve. A lengthy debate ensued, covering the perennial topics: the need to recruit all available single men; the merits of the voluntary system over conscription; the demands of trade and industry; and the effect on labour.[6] The urgent need for TF reinforcements was also raised, particularly for the under-manned second line, prompting one MP to ask whether, in the interests of economy in staffing and recruiting, the distinctions between the Regular Army, TF and New Armies should be removed. The Under Secretary of State for War, Tennant, noted that different terms, conditions and lengths of service would make it difficult to implement such a change during wartime but concluded ominously that 'if we have the opportunity before us, (such change) may very properly form the subject of legislation, if legislation is required'. The Vote was eventually passed the day before the Commons adjourned for Christmas, but the debate had highlighted aspects that would re-occur throughout the year.[7]

Parliament might have adjourned for Christmas but the Cabinet continued to meet to discuss various matters, including manpower, recruiting and the disappointing outcome of the Derby scheme. Growing concerns were emerging over the complete lack of co-ordination of military, financial and industrial resources and the issue was raised by the Chancellor, McKenna, during

5 HQ BEF was less fortunate: Robertson's replacement was Lieutenant-General Launcelot Kiggell who until then had spent the war in England, initially as Director of Military Training at the War Office and then as Director of Home Defence. Macready would be replaced by Major-General G.A. Fowke, formerly the BEF's Engineer in Chief. The post of AG BEF would probably not have been his preferred appointment, despite promotion to Lieutenant General, and it seems surprising that despite the efforts being made to train 'A' staff officers for their roles, the most senior personnel officer in the BEF should have no prior familiarity with his new operational responsibilities. Fortunately, the rest of his staff were by now well-experienced in their various roles.

6 *HC Deb 21 December 1915 vol 77 cc213–437.*

7 *HC Deb 22 December 1915 vol 77 cc536–574.*

two Cabinet meetings held on 31 December.[8] The situation was succinctly summed up by Robertson in a letter to Haig:

> There has been no co-ordination of the different departments. I have been working up to 70 Divisions. Lloyd George has ordered material for 100 Divisions. The Chancellor of the Exchequer did not till yesterday know either of these things. Now he says the money will not run to it and I do not think it will.[9]

The outcome of the Cabinet discussions was a decision in January 1916 to create a small committee consisting of the Prime Minister, McKenna and Austen Chamberlain, who was then Secretary of State for India, to investigate the situation immediately. They designated themselves the Cabinet Committee on the Co-ordination of Military and Financial Effort.

The new Committee met several times, taking statements from the War Office, the Treasury and the Board of Trade on their 'respective desiderata' concerning the size of the army, the finance available to fund it and the numbers that could be spared without dire results for the country's trade and industry. The War Office stance was that no limit could be placed at present on the numbers of men which might be necessary for a successful conclusion to the war: 'we should aim at placing in the field every man we can possibly pay for and get'. The Committee accepted this as a general principle, subject to the requirements of the Navy and obligations to the Allies.

The report produced by the Committee on 4 February shows the structure and state of the Army in early 1916 and the extent of the manning problems.[10] Of its 70 British divisions, 50 were abroad (this figure includes one division just about to leave UK), three TF divisions were in India, whilst four New Army divisions were expected to be ready for overseas service within a few months. Thirteen second line TF were allocated to Home defence but contained only weak battalions of about 600 men. A key question was whether any of these Home defence TF divisions should be prepared for active service. As a starting point, the Committee decided to focus on an overall figure of 67 divisions, considering that the three TF divisions in India could be discounted as being unlikely to require many reinforcements. The War Office was requested to produce estimates of the numbers of men required for various alternative allocations of the 67 divisions between active service and home defence, and for their maintenance over different periods of time. Despite Robertson's position that all 67 divisions were required for active service and should be made ready to take the field as soon as possible, the two estimates selected by the Committee for further consideration were the respective requirements for 62 and 54 divisions to serve abroad and be maintained at full strength until the end of September.[11]

8 TNA CAB 37/139/70: PM letter to the King of 1 January 1916 reporting on the two Cabinet sittings of 31 December 1915.

9 Robertson Mss I/22/4, Robertson to Haig, 31 December 1915, cited in Grieves, *The Politics of Manpower, 1914-1918*, p. 23.

10 TNA CAB 37/142/11: dated 4 February 1916.

11 Under the 54 divisions scheme, 13 TF divisions would be retained for Home defence at their weak strength ie 600 and with no reserves. Under the 62 divisions scheme, 8 out of the 13 TF divisions would be brought up to full strength plus reserves ready to be sent abroad by June if needed; the remaining 5 TF divisions would be brought up to full establishment of 1,000 men per battalion and

The War Office's estimates were scrutinized in detail. Since all divisions at home and abroad were below their establishments, the first requirement would be to bring them all up to strength. Some 69,000 (44,000 Regulars and 25,000 TF) would be required for 54 divisions and 148,000 (44,000 and 104,000) for 62 divisions. The reserves needed to cover anticipated wastage during January to March for either force would be 56,000 (39,000 Regulars and 17,000 TF). The numbers needed by the end of March would thus total 125,000 for 54 divisions and 204,000 for 62 divisions.[12]

Wastage after March was estimated at 108,000 all arms per month for 54 divisions and 123,000 a month for 62 divisions.[13] Total manpower requirements for the period January to June were estimated at 648,000 for 54 divisions and 703,000 for 62 divisions, the latter figure having been discounted by 35,000, as some of the TF divisions would remain at home for some months. Finally, a figure of 60,000 was included in order to form new units 'extra to divisions' such as Tank Corps and Machine Gun Corps units. The total estimated requirements for the period January-June came to 833,000 for 54 divisions and 967,000 for 62 divisions.

The monthly requirements were then broken out. January's figures, at 243,000 and 259,000 respectively, reflected the need to bring divisions up to strength so the subsequent monthly figures up to and including June were less: 118,000 for 54 divisions and between 137,000 and 145,000 for 62 divisions. Assuming a decision not to provide reserves for the 5 TF divisions remaining at home, the total numbers for July, August and September would amount to 354,000 for 54 divisions and 399,000 for 62 divisions. The total recruiting requirement up to September would be 1,187,000 for the 54 division scheme and 1,366,000 for the 62 division scheme, which would keep the divisions at full strength until the end of the calendar year.[14]

There were now definite and visible calculations showing the numbers required but it remained to be seen whether sufficient men were available, whether they could be spared from their civil occupations, whether they could be called up as quickly as needed and finally whether they were affordable; in the Report's introduction, the Committee had commented wryly that the 'proposals originally put forward by the Departments were not reconcilable' but compromises were eventually reached.[15] The Board of Trade (BoT) finally agreed that if necessary 250,000 men could be called up so long as certain safeguards were put in place. These were that call up should be by trades rather than by age and marital status; that after 1,275,000 had been taken no more men (beyond the army's proper share of the new crop) should be raised from industry for the last seven months of 1916; and that the BoT should be able to 'watch the pressure

retained for home defence, but would not have the usual three months' reserves ie they would not be available for service abroad unless reserves were subsequently provided for them.

12 TNA CAB 37/142/11: dated 4 February 1916 pp. 4 & 5; a footnote to the pre-March requirements notes that 'These figures are arrived at after credit has been taken for 358,000 Infantry in the depots at home (including 88,000 men returned from the Expeditionary Force who will eventually rejoin their units'.

13 Monthly wastage was calculated at 13.5 per cent for the infantry, 6 per cent for cavalry, 3 per cent for artillery, 4 per cent for engineers and 2 per cent for other arms, making an overall monthly average of 9 per cent. NB: The infantry wastage had been reduced from 15 percent; it was considered that it had previously been inflated by the retreat from Mons and the 'highly wasteful Gallipoli campaign'.

14 Ibid., p. 6. NB: Men recruited at the end of September would not be available for drafting until the end of December.

15 Ibid., p. 1.

gauge' weekly and immediately reduce the rate of enlistment if grave industrial dangers become apparent.[16] The Treasury inevitably continued to state that there was insufficient money to support the increase in manpower.

Despite the conflicting views, the Committee's report concluded that it should be possible to find sufficient men, 'without industrial disaster, though not without grave dislocation of industry, and even some risk', to enable the Army to place 62 divisions in the field by the end of June with three months' reserves, whilst retaining five complete divisions without reserves for Home Defence.[17] To achieve this, however, it would be necessary to adopt financial measures which could only be continued for a short period. They caveated their views, however, with the comment that they considered it unlikely that the Army would meet its proposed timetable to place the divisions in the field and that the War Office should also keep a strategical reserve in case of unforeseen emergencies. As both these aspects would have the effect that men would be required less quickly, the strain on the labour market would be reduced and spread over a longer period, fewer munitions would be required and consequently expenditure would be reduced. This would mean that whatever was saved during the earlier part of the year would enable the Army to be maintained for a longer period. The Committee's final recommendation, noted as

53rd Recruiting Area Staff at The Limes, Shrewsbury 1916 (Shropshire Regimental Museum)

16 Ibid., pp. 7-10.
17 Ibid., p. 21.

'vitally important', that there should be a further review of the whole question in April when the effect of recruiting on trade would be more obvious.

Although the War Office could now plan for an Army of 62 divisions in the field by the end of June, the assumption on the part of the Committee that this would not only be difficult to achieve but that its delay was desirable from a financial point of view was not an entirely satisfactory outcome in view of the large offensive planned for the middle of the year. It was probably the best outcome that could have been hoped for and at least there was the prospect of the further review in April when it was hoped that much would have become clearer.

However, there remained the problem of recruiting the necessary numbers and Kitchener, in agreeing the conclusions of the Committee's report, noted that the intake was much slower than had been hoped for. In January, 259,000 men had been required but only 64,208 had been obtained (34,050 by direct enlistment and 30,158 from the four Groups that had already been called up) leaving a shortfall of about 195,000. It was already estimated that the shortfall against the 473,000 men required by the end of March would be 94,000, which could only be obtained by calling up new sources of men as soon as possible.[18]

The First Military Service Act (MSA)

Running concurrently with the deliberations on the number of divisions to be maintained had been the growing movement towards compulsory service. On 28 December, the same day that the War Committee had agreed to a joint offensive with the French, the Cabinet formally considered conscription and a first draft of a Military Service Bill to introduce compulsion for single men was produced on 30 December.[19] Not all the Cabinet supported it, the Home Secretary, Sir John Simon, resigning over the issue, but work on the Bill continued and it received its first reading in Parliament on 5 January. Key to the debate was the recently received report on the Derby scheme highlighting the disappointingly large numbers of single men who had neither enlisted nor attested.[20] Large numbers of married men had come forward but on 2 November Asquith had pledged that married men enlisting under the Derby scheme would not be sent abroad whilst single men held back. In order to uphold this pledge, it was planned to retain voluntary enlistment for the married man whilst introducing compulsion for the single man.

Unsurprisingly, the Bill did not have an easy ride during four extremely lengthy Commons sittings. Many entrenched positions were aired in great detail: the voluntary system versus any form of conscription, the effects on trade and industry, warnings of industrial unrest, the omission of Ireland in view of the political situation there (and the proposal from one MP that Scotland should also be omitted, which was summarily ignored) and accusations that by introducing conscription the Government would be introducing the very Germanic approach that the nation was fighting against.[21] Despite passionate debate, the outcome was never in

18 TNA CAB 37/142/17: Comment by Kitchener on the Report of the Committee on Co-ordination of Military and Financial Effort dated 7 February 1916.
19 TNA CAB 37/139/58: PM letter to the King of 28 December 1915; TNA CAB 37/139/67 30 December 1915.
20 TNA CAB 37/139/26: December 1915 and TNA CAB 37/14/1 dated 1 January 1916.
21 *HC Deb* 5, 6, 11 and 12 January 1916, vol 77.

any real doubt. The Government gained the support it needed and, despite further lengthy scrutiny in the Lords, the Bill returned to the Commons to be passed on 27 January 1916 as the Military Service Act (MSA). Its effective date would be 10 February and the 'appointed date' 2 March 1916.[22]

The Act applied to single men and childless widowers, who had been aged between 18 and 41 on the date of National Registration, 15 August 1915, resident in Great Britain on or since that date and who had been unmarried on 2 November 1915. From the 'appointed date' all men falling within the terms of the Act would be deemed to have been enlisted in the regular forces for the duration of the war and to have been transferred immediately to the reserve.[23] There were exceptions, listed in Schedule 1, which included those already serving in the Navy or the Marines; men previously discharged from service due to disability or ill-health; ministers of religion; and members of the TF already liable for overseas service. By definition, the terms of the MSA removed the TF HS option for single men but significantly only the Liberal MP, Percy Molteno, had spoken against this whilst the rest of the normally vocal TF lobby had acquiesced.

Under Section 2 of the MSA, applications for exemptions could be submitted to Local Tribunals up to the 'appointed date'. The allowable grounds for such exemptions were clearly defined as: employment on essential war work or in education or training; hardship owing to exceptional financial or business obligations or domestic situations; or ill-health or infirmity. Britain was alone, however, in recognizing a further category, namely conscientious objection to the undertaking of military service.[24] The creation of new Local and Appeal Tribunals to hear the exemption cases was covered in Schedule 2 which laid down that their constitutions, functions and procedure were to be regulated by Orders in Council in order to 'secure uniformity of decision and practice'. The new tribunals might contain as many as 25 members, but the process remained largely the same as that of the previous 'Derby' tribunals which were now abolished. A new layer had now been introduced at the county level, however, which would hear appeals against decisions made at the local tribunals. [25]

A form of compulsion had been introduced but the allowable exemptions and exceptions enabled many to escape the net. The Act applied only to those of age in August 1915 and thus disregarded all who had turned 18 since that date.[26] Moreover, the retention of voluntary enlistment for married men whilst introducing compulsion for singles was always going to be an uneasy compromise. Robertson was certainly disappointed in its provisions and later described it as 'a half-baked measure'.[27]

22 *Public General Acts 5&6 Geo 5* (London: Eyre & Spottiswoode, 1916), Chapter 104.
23 Ibid.
24 Beckett & Simpson, *Nation in Arms: A Social Study of the British Army in the First World War*, p. 13.
25 TNA MH 10/195: LGB Circular R36.
26 Technically the reference in *BOH 1916 Vol. 1* p. 151 that 'By this Act ... all voluntary enlistment even for the Territorial Army ceased ...' is correct only in relation to the single men caught by the first MSA as they had had ample opportunities to volunteer. It would remain possible for all married men and single men not within the provisions of the first MSA to volunteer before being called up until the end of the war.
27 Field Marshal Sir William Robertson, *From Private to Field Marshal* (Boston & New York: Houghton Mifflin Company, 1921), p. 263.

Re-organization of the Reserves

Sir John French had been appointed in January to the new post of CinC Home Forces (CinC HF), responsible not only for Home Defence but also for the home-based training and draft-finding units. It would be useful to have someone in that post who understood the needs of the BEF but balancing GHQ's ever-increasing demands against those of home defence would prove a continuing struggle. The problem for French in trying to produce a coherent plan for Home defence was two-fold: the populations of training and draft-finding units changed constantly as replacements were posted overseas, whilst entire New Army divisions and overseas units of the TF were sent abroad as soon as they became efficient. It made for a very fluid Command.

The creation of the new CinC HF together with the anticipated influx of men, to be obtained through the Derby scheme and the MSA, prompted a detailed review of the Home Forces, including the draft-finding Reserves. For the Infantry, these now consisted of the SR units, the TF Reserves and 18 Reserve Infantry brigades containing the Second Reserve battalions which supported the New Armies in the field. The SR units were settled at their War Stations in their Home defence role but were also busy dispatching drafts as required. Three of the Marcher battalions, 3rd Cheshire, 3rd RWF and 3rd SWB formed part of the Mersey Defences and were based in and around the Liverpool area. At the end of 1915, 3rd Cheshire at Birkenhead numbered over 3,000 men although not all of these were available for drafting as they included convalescents and those awaiting discharge.[28] Similarly, 3rd KSLI was based at Pembroke Dock in South Wales as part of the Milford Haven Garrison, and was sending out each month some 300-400 men, despatched in weekly drafts, plus a further 50 specially selected men destined for the Machine Gun Corps (MGC).[29]

Group photograph (undated) on men of 3rd (Reserve) RWF at Litherland, Lancashire. (RWF Archives)

28 Crookenden, *The Cheshire Regiment in the Great War*, p. 340.
29 Wood, *King's Shropshire Light Infantry in the Great War*, pp. 319-20.

The SR units would continue to fulfill their combined roles of draft finding and home defence but would be augmented in the latter by the creation in early 1916 of Home Service Garrison Battalions containing men unfit for overseas service.[30] Some 20 such battalions would be formed over the following months, including the 5th (Home Service) Garrison Battalion RWF which was formed at Wrexham in August 1916.

The TF second line battalions had taken over the Home Defence roles of their respective first line battalions when the latter left for overseas service: on the departure of the 53rd (Welsh) Division in mid-1915 for Gallipoli, for example, its place had been taken by the 68th (2nd Welsh) Division formed of the second line battalions of the Cheshire, RWF, SWB, KSLI, Herefordshire and Monmouthshire Regiments. The TF Reserves now consisted of the third line battalions, which in February 1916 assumed drafting responsibility for both their first and second line units.[31] They remained largely at the pre-war stations of the First Line battalions.

Group photograph of men of 9th (Reserve) KSLI at Prees Heath Camp, Shropshire 1916 (Shropshire Regimental Museum)

The main area that needed attention, however, concerned the reserve battalions of the locally raised battalions of the New Armies. As locally raised battalions were adopted by the War Office, their depot companies were formed into Local Reserve battalions; for example, in late 1915 when the 1st and 2nd Gwent Battalions were adopted as 10th and 11th (Service) battalions

30 TNA WO 293/4 ACI 5: of 2 January 1916 and ACI 325 of 9 February 1916.
31 In April they would lose the '3/' prefix becoming simply Reserve battalions: 3/4th Cheshire became the 4th (Reserve) Cheshire; 3/4th KSLI became the 4th (Reserve) KSLI; and 3/1st Herefordshire became the 1st (Reserve) Herefordshire.

of the SWB, their depot companies were combined to form 13th (Reserve) SWB. Similarly, when the 3rd Gwent Battalion was adopted as 12th (Service) SWB, its depot company became 14th (Reserve) SWB. Some of the Local Reserve battalions took longer to fill than others, particularly those already refilling battalions abroad. The 13th (Reserve) SWB sent its first draft in January 1916 but as successive ones were required by the 10th and 11th battalions, both of which had arrived in France in December 1915, it was prevented from completing its four companies until June.[32] In early 1916, the Local Reserve battalions were incorporated into the existing Reserve Infantry Brigades, which were now increased in number to twenty-six with an overall establishment of 225,300.[33] The links with the parent Command and Regiment remained. At Kinmel Park in Western Command, 14th (Reserve) SWB and 20th, 21st and 22nd (Reserve) RWF joined 14th Reserve Brigade, where the Second Reserve battalions, 12th (Reserve) RWF and 9th (Reserve) SWB were already located.

The outcome of the changes in the plans for Home Defence in early 1916 meant that there were now the makings of a viable Infantry Reserve organization providing drafts for battalions, both overseas and at home, but linked to the Home Commands and available for Home Defence if necessary. It was also ready to receive the hoped for influx of new recruits. What was now needed, however, was the arrival of these recruits to fill the Reserve units.

Call-Up of the 'Derby' Men and the First Conscripts

The Derby scheme had been re-opened on 10 January until such time as the MSA should take effect. Some 'Derby' men had already been called up: in December single men aged 19-23 in Groups 2-5 were warned for call up on 20 January 1916. This had produced some 30,158 men plus a further 34,050 direct enlistments but the total was already about 195,000 short of the 259,000 required. In early January, the next four groups were warned for call up on 8 February with the rest of the Groups of single men following by 18 March. On being called up men were appointed to a Corps or unit, which could be either Regular of TF and was wherever possible the one for which they had applied on attesting.[34] They still had to be finally approved for service; if not accepted they were retained in the reserve and sent home. Detailed administrative procedures for recording both those accepted for service and those rejected were necessary so that the Registrar-General's records based on the National Register could be updated.[35]

Determined not to repeat the chaos of the early weeks of the war, the recruiting organizations were better prepared this time. In Chester:

32 Atkinson. C. T., *The History of the South Wales Borderers 1914–1918* (London: Medici Society, 1931 N&MP reprint), p. 232.

33 TNA WO 293/4 ACI 205: of January 1916. Colonel T. Cave, 'The Reserve and Training Reserve', *Stand To!* 36 (Winter 1992); K.W. Mitchinson, *Defending Albion* (Basingstoke: Palgrave MacMillan, 2005), p. 125.

34 The attestation form for the Derby Scheme was Army Form B 2512. It contained the following paragraph: '10. Are you willing to serve upon the following conditions provided His Majesty should so long require your services? For the duration of the War, at the end of which you will be discharged with all convenient speed. You will be required to serve for one day with the Colours and the remainder of the period in the Army Reserve, in accordance with the provisions of the Royal Warrant dated 20 October 1915, until such time as you may be called up by order of the Army Council'.

35 TNA WO 293/4 ACI 86: of 12 Jan 1916.

> Frantic plans and preparations were made – rooms set apart for them to don their long deferred khaki – thousands of tickets for their meals printed – complete kits marked in advance for the embryo "Cheshire" lads – recruiting orderlies increased in number – a string of NCOs belted and 'sticked', ready at a moment's notice to scurry to the station to meet arrivals, or to conduct khaki clad recruits safely to their trains – and – all is working smoothly.[36]

Pte Bert Oakes, aged 30, had attested under the Derby Scheme and was warned on 30 January that he would be called up in Group 13 on 29 February 1916. He joined 9th (Reserve) KSLI at Prees Heath and wrote home on 4 March describing his new life at the camp:

> The parade ground is an awful place, up to your ankles in water and as you march it splashes, wetting putties (sic), overcoat and all making them in an a fearful mess. Still it finds us something to do. ... The camp is as large as Ironbridge, Madeley and Broseley all combined...[37]

A normal day's training for the recruits was:

> Six o'clock get out of bed, dress, make bed and tidy room, first parade 6:30 am. Physical training till 7:45 am. Breakfast, buttons cleaned, shaving and boots till 8:45 am. Bayonet fighting till 10 o'clock [sic]. Marching and other drill till 12:00 am. Rest and dinner till 1:45 pm. Musketry till 4:00 pm. The trench digging comes in the drill from 11 till 12:00 am so you see it is a good day. Then some nights we have an hour lecture and others silent marching to the trenches in the dark.[38]

Instruction in the history and traditions of the recruits' regiments would shortly be added to the training syllabus, in order to develop *esprit de corps* in the new men.[39] With a short break in June to get married, Bert Oakes stayed at Prees Heath for six months before leaving for France on 10 July. This was double the 3 months training normally allowed but would hardly equip him for France.

The Derby scheme finally closed at midnight on 1 March but even with the extended period, far fewer single men had been obtained than expected. Consequently, on 7 March the married 'Derbyites' of Groups 25 to 32 were warned by Proclamation for Call Up on 7 April. Although these men had attested voluntarily there was a storm of protest that they should be sent when there were still single men available. Attention now turned to the single men caught by the new MSA who from 2 March were deemed to have been enlisted and passed to the Army

36 'Depot Doings' in *The Oak Tree*, 1 (3) (February 1916), p. 35.
37 Transcripts of Bert Oakes letters provided to the author by Toby Neal of the *Shropshire Star* in December 2013. Letter dated 4 March 1916 to Mrs E Oakes, 5 Barber Street, Broseley from 22219 Private BWO Oakes, D Company, 9th Batt [sic] KSLI, No 28 Hut, 4th Camp, Prees Heath. NB Broseley lies across the R Severn from Ironbridge and Madeley, both of which are now part of Telford.
38 Letter dated 17 April 1916 from 22219 Pte BWO Oakes, No 28 Hut, 4th Camp, Prees Heath.
39 TNA WO 293/4 ACI 850/16: of 19 April 1916 Instruction in History and Achievements of Regiments.

Accommodation Huts along the Prees Road (now the A49) at Prees Heath Camp, Shropshire. (courtesy of Peter Lea)

Training at Prees Heath Camp, Shropshire, in 1916. (courtesy of Peter Lea)

Reserve and procedures were put in place for their calling up. A different Notice Paper to that used for the Derby Groups was to be used and, once called up, men liable for service under the Act were also not attested as such but their names simply noted on the new enrolment form, Army Form B 2513.[40]

On 10 March the first men were called up under the MSA when a Proclamation notified the calling up of men of both Group and Class 1.[41] These were the youngest men; those who were still under 19 would be medically examined and given the option either of returning home or of remaining and undergoing special training until they reached the age of 19; it was to be explained to them that they would not be sent abroad before that.[42] Other Classes followed and the married Derby men also continued to be called up with Groups 33 to 41 being warned for call up on 29 May and the older marrieds of Groups 42 to 46 being warned for call up on 13 June.

The application of the MSA to single Territorials who had not taken the IS obligation before 2 March would appear to have been varied. Instructions were issued by the War Office and notices placed in local papers but there remained an element of confusion. Questions were raised in Parliament to which the response was unequivocal: if TF HS officers and men had not applied for exemption from the MSA by 2 March then they should be discharged, becoming Reservists under the MSA until such time as they should be called up.[43] This administrative process does not appear to have been actioned in many units, however, as no examples of discharges have been found to date. In many cases, single HS TF soldiers also appear to have taken early action to avoid conscription, either by signing the IS obligation or seeking exemption.

Second Report of the Committee on the Co-ordination of Military and Financial Effort

The numbers recruited continued to fall well below those required and manpower continued to form the Army Council's main topic of discussion, following the production on 6 April of the review required by the Cabinet Committee on the Co-ordination of Military and Financial Effort.[44] The situation was gloomy: by 30 June the Infantry would be 179,000 men short. An anticipated 287,000 recruits for April, May and June plus 90,000 earlier recruits delayed for various reasons might cover the shortfall but the 198,000 remaining would scarcely maintain the Infantry to the middle of August and provided 'no margin for any abnormal wastage such as that arising from very heavy fighting'. Furthermore, they anticipated that the flow of recruits would cease altogether before the end of August as a result of the MSA's inadequacies: only

40 Ibid., ACI 336 of February 1916. AF B 2513 - Record of Service Paper – For Men deemed to be enlisted in H.M Regular Forces for General Service with the Colours or in the Reserve for the period of the War, or ex-Soldiers recalled for Service with the Colours, under the provisions of the Military Service Acts, 1916. NB This would later be replaced by Army Form B 2515 – Enrolment Paper and Record of Service.

41 *BOH 1916 Vol. 1* p. 151. Under the MSA men were placed by age in Classes in order to avoid confusion with the Groups of the Derby Scheme; it also avoided the perceived 'slur of compulsion' being cast on the latter.

42 TNA WO 293/4: ACI 839 of 18 April 1916.

43 *HC Deb 07 March 1916 vol 80 cc1340-1.*

44 TNA WO 33/881: Minutes of 176th, 177th and 178th Meetings of the Army Council.

212,000 men had been obtained between January and March, despite the 358,000 considered by the Board of Trade to be available. Other manning issues had been identified but these would require legislative action to resolve them: namely, the compulsory extension of time-expired men, the inclusion within the MSA of all youths reaching the age of 18 after August 1915 and the ability to transfer TF soldiers, from their own arm or branch of the service to any other where their services might more urgently be required. The bottom line for the Army Council remained the need for every fit man not required by the Navy or for essential employment to be made available for the Army.[45] With the impending offensive less than three months away this was now becoming urgent.

The Cabinet Committee produced its own second report on 13 April. Having reviewed the numbers of men available for military service through both the Derby system and the MSA it concluded that there were actually more available than had been demanded but that the War Office's recruiting processes were inadequate. The Committee continued to resist further conscription but did at least endorse the Army Council's proposals for the compulsory extension of time-expired men; compulsion of TF soldiers to serve in any unit where they were needed; and that all youths reaching the age of 18 should be brought within the scope of the MSA.[46] All three of these proposals would, however, require legislative action for their introduction.

The Committee met the Army Council on 15 April to discuss their conclusions and to emphasize how difficult it would be to introduce compulsion for married men of military age. The latest figures provided by the Registrar-General, however, showed that under the present system no appreciable intake of recruits would be available after the end of September. For the Army Council time was of the essence; it was already unlikely that 62 divisions could be in the field by the start of the offensive and the 52 divisions currently abroad were short of 66,000 men. They remained adamant that they required all available manpower, emphasizing the need for haste so that due notice could be given the men concerned and not less than three months allowed for their training.[47] An attempt was made to break the impasse on 19 April, with a compromise proposal from a Cabinet Member, Arthur Henderson, that a further effort be made to obtain men by voluntary enlistment but that if 50,000 unattested married men had not voluntarily enlisted by 27 May then the Government would immediately ask Parliament for compulsory powers. The Army Council could only reiterate the need for haste, placing the onus firmly on the Government to decide the necessary steps to be taken.[48]

The balance was finally tipped by the latest recruiting figures, which would be insufficient to maintain the Army at the agreed size and to replace casualties in the anticipated summer offensive. The subject of general compulsion had already been raised in both Houses of Parliament during April and on 29 April Asquith informed the King that the Government had no alternative but to introduce further legislation as soon as possible. The whole Cabinet was in agreement, although Henderson and Runciman voiced some disquiet over the labour issue.

45 TNA WO 33/881: Minutes of 176th Army Council Meeting of 6 April 1916, Item 2.
46 TNA CAB 37/145/36: Second Report of the Cabinet Committee on the Co-ordination of Military and Financial Effort dated 13 April 1916.
47 TNA WO 33/881: Minutes of 177th Army Council Meeting of 15 April 1915, Item 2.
48 Ibid., Minutes of 178th Army Council Meeting of 19 April 1915, Item 2.

Lloyd George, however, believed their fears and forebodings were exaggerated.[49] On 3 May 1916 the second Military Service Bill was introduced.

The Second Military Service Act

The new Bill extended the first MSA, making all single and married men between the ages of 18 and 41 liable for military service. The exceptions shown in the first MSA remained but the extension of liability to all married men removed home service as an option for married TF soldiers fit enough for overseas service. The 'appointed date' would be thirty days after the Act was passed or 30 days after their 18th birthday for boys turning 18. This latter provision would enable, as the Prime Minister emphasized, boys to enlist before the month was up so that they could come in 'voluntarily without any exercise or threatened exercise of the compulsory powers'.[50] It was clearly stipulated, however, that youths would not be sent abroad under the age of 19.

Further sections of the Bill tidied up various Army regulations. Clause 2 amended the existing Army Act so that for the duration of the war Regular, Reserve and TF soldiers would be required to continue serving beyond their discharge dates unless they had completed 12 or more years' service and had reached the age of 41. Clause 3 enabled the recall of previously time-expired former soldiers who remained within military age and also the re-examination of men previously discharged or rejected as medically unfit for service. Later sections concerned the TF, particularly Section 14 which finally resolved the transfer problem by enabling a TF soldier to be transferred without his consent not only between units but also between TF corps and furthermore to be posted to 'regular units of the corps to which he belongs or to which he is transferred'. Much time was expended in debating the Bill in the Commons, and to a lesser extent the Lords, throughout May.[51] Essentially, however, it received an easier ride than the first MSA since the failings of the latter were only too apparent. It was finally passed as the Military Service Act 1916 (Session 2) (MSA2), receiving Royal Assent on 25 May 1916.[52] The appointed date was to be 30 days later on 24 June.

The new Act was followed by a flurry of AOs and ACIs to enable its implementation. On 8 June AO 202 notified the retention in service of time-expired Regular and TF soldiers unless at their due date they were aged 41 and had served for 12 or more years plus the additional twelve months' war service.[53] The pill was sweetened a few days later, however, by the payment of a bounty for these men and also for those recalled for service by the Act or who had voluntarily

49 TNA CAB 37/146/24: Asquith letter to the King dated 29 April 1916.
50 Hansard *HC Deb* 3 May 1916 Vol. 82 cc 41 – 100.
51 Hansard *HC Deb* 4 May 1916 Vol. 82 cc142-267.
52 *Public General Acts Passed in the Sixth and Seventh Years of King George The Fifth* (London: Eyre & Spottiswoode, 1916), pp. 33-38.
53 TNA WO 123/57: AO 202 of 8 June 1916 - Discontinuance of Discharges on Completion of Engagement. During 1915, soldiers who had come to the end of their engagements or, if they were Reservists mobilised on the outbreak of war to the end of the extra year for which they were liable, had been offered the opportunity to continue serving until the end of hostilities.

re-enlisted.[54] As far as the TF was concerned, it was made clear that all officers and men who had not signed the IS obligation, or applied for exemption, by the appointed date would be treated as civilians.[55] The more contentious issue of compulsory transfer was formally publicized on 9 June.[56] The Army Transfers Act 1915 had already enabled compulsory transfers for Regular soldiers but this had not previously been notified in Army Orders, nor had its impact yet been felt on the Army at large. It was now made absolutely clear that both Regular and TF soldiers of any rank could be transferred without their consent to any Corps. The administrative procedures for such transfers were outlined, and the records of soldiers so transferred were in future to be annotated, 'Transferred under authority of AO 206 and ACI 1166 of June 1916'. For clarity, the changes for a TF NCO or soldier were enumerated: he could now be transferred without his consent from one Corps to another of the TF; if he had taken the IS obligation he could be drafted to serve abroad in any TF unit within the Corps to which he belonged or to which he might be transferred; and he could then be posted to a Regular unit of the Corps to which he belonged or was transferred.

Many TF soldiers undoubtedly had cause to feel aggrieved over the changes to their terms of service. They had originally enlisted for home defence but all who were physically fit were now compulsorily liable for service abroad and, for the duration of the war, they could also be posted without their consent from the unit they had originally joined. Although the TF lobby had fought valiantly to protect their position during the MSA debates, remaining unconvinced by Army Council statements that transfers would be carried out only when absolutely necessary and that they had no intention of allowing 'any injury to the Territorial Force now or in future', but their opposition had been over-ruled.[57] The problem for the AG, Macready, the Manning authorities and the BEF, however, had been that the very inflexibility of the original TF regulations had prevented it fulfilling its originally intended function of providing a force capable of supporting and expanding the regular army. Furthermore, many TF units at the Front could by now no longer be reinforced and had not only been fighting with insufficient manpower but had had to be withdrawn from the front line thus forcing other units to take their places. The two viewpoints were diametrically opposed and would never agree. The second MSA created the necessary tools to address the manning difficulties but the TF grievances arising out of what would become known as the 'Transfer Controversy' would continue for a long time to come.[58]

Review of Medical Categories

At the end of 1915, concerns over the large numbers of recruits rejected on medical grounds had led to the establishment of Recruiting Medical Boards at each Infantry Regimental Depot and at the Central Recruiting Office in each recruiting area. These Boards were to be staffed by

54 TNA WO 123/58: AO 209/16.
55 TNA 293/4: ACI 1140 of 1916 - MSA 1916 Session 2 Procedure for dealing with Home Service Officers and Soldiers of the TF.
56 TNA WO 123/58: AO 204 of 9 June 1916 and WO 293/4 ACI 1166 of 9 June 1916.
57 Hansard 1916 Series 5 Vol. 82, 986-993 – Commons Sitting 11 May 1916.
58 K.W. Mitchinson, 'The Transfer Controversy', *Stand To!* 33 (Winter 1991), pp. 29–32 and K.W. Mitchinson, *Gentlemen and Officers* (London: Naval & Military Press and IWM, 1994), pp. 130–6.

Royal Army Medical Corps Officers and were 'expected to act with much more knowledge and efficiency than the civilian practitioners on whose unsupported testimony many of the earlier rejections were made'.[59] A further innovation was the introduction of medical classifications for recruits as fit for:

i. General Service
ii. Field Service at Home
iii. Garrison Service:
   a. Abroad
   b. At Home
iv. a. Labour (road-making, entrenching, works companies etc) or
   b. Sedentary work, clerks etc.

In early May, to give greater clarity and also in preparation for reviewing men previously rejected for service on medical grounds, these medical categories were further refined: A General Service (ie active everywhere); B Abroad, further sub-divided into B1 Garrison Service, B2 Labour and B3 Sedentary Work; and C Home, further sub-divided into C1 Garrison Service, C2 Labour and C3 Sedentary Work. Even these new categories, however, were soon found to be insufficiently specific for use by Medical Boards in assessing the fitness of soldiers recovering from wounds. In June they were further revised and additional guidelines added:[60]

A. able to march, see to shoot, hear well and stand 'active service conditions'.
   A1: Men fit for overseas service in all respects: training, physically and mentally fit.
   A2: Recruits who will be fit for A1 as soon as trained.
   A3: Returned EF men who will be fit for A1 as soon as hardened.
   A4: Men under 19 years who should be A1 or A2 when 19.
B. free from serious organic diseases, able to stand service on the lines of communication in France or in Garrisons in the Tropics.
   B1: Abroad: Garrison service: able to march 5 miles, see to shoot with glasses and hear well.
   B2: Abroad: Labour: able to walk 5 miles to and from work, see and hear sufficiently for ordinary purposes.
   B3: Abroad: Sedentary work: only suitable for sedentary work.
C. free from serious organic disease, able to stand service conditions in garrisons at home.
   C1: At Home: Garrison service
   C2 At Home: Labour
   C3 At Home: Sedentary Work
D. Men unfit for service in A, B or C but likely to be fit in six months
E. Those not likely to be fit for service in A, B or C

59 TNA CAB 37/139/68: Provisions of an Army Order dated 24 December 1915 cited in Report of the Committee tasked to examine Lord Derby's figures.
60 TNA WO 123/4; *BOH 1916, Vol. 1*, pp. 152-3 and TNA WO 293/4 ACI 1241of 1 June 1916.

The gradual refinement of the Medical Categories during early 1916 would, it was hoped, not only avoid so many potential recruits being rejected on medical grounds but also allow less fit soldiers to be usefully employed, both at home and overseas.

Review of Early 1916 at Home

The story of the first half of 1916 at home is one of unceasing efforts to find more manpower for the Army. Not only was major legislation passed in the form of the two MSAs but there were also administrative and organisational changes brought in, all with the aim of increasing the number of men recruited and streamlining their transformation into the necessary reserves for the Army overseas. It was a slow process but to belittle the efforts of the War Office and the Government would be to underestimate the challenges that had faced them and would continue to do so.

Meanwhile in France …

During early 1916 Haig had had to establish himself in his new role as CinC, whilst at the same time initiating planning for the anticipated offensive. In addition to commanding the BEF and co-operating with the French, one of his main preoccupations was to establish how many reinforcements might be available. Much of his attention and time during the first half of 1916 was consequently taken up by the requirements of munitions and manpower.[61]

By the end of January, the BEF in France consisted of five Cavalry divisions and 38 Infantry divisions in 12 corps and for the first time had a total strength, including Indian troops, of over one million: 874,900 at the Front and 133,500 on the LofC. Of the 38 Infantry divisions, however, nine had been in France for less than four months and 16 had never been involved in anything other than trench warfare.[62] Four more New Army divisions were expected over the next few months but their postings depended 'upon the progress made in arming the new formations with rifles'.[63] Even more tellingly a subsequent letter from Robertson in February noted that the 40th (Bantam) Division's training would be delayed owing to the physical inadequacies of a number of its men and the need to replace them. This would delay completion of the Division's training and it would be unlikely to proceed overseas before the end of May at the earliest. Arrangements were being made to prepare a Second Line TF division, the 61st South Midland, in its place but it was unlikely to be sent before 1 May.[64] By the end of March, Haig was increasingly aware that he had 'not got an Army in France really, but a collection of divisions untrained for the field.'[65]

61 *BOH 1916, Vol. 1*, p.21.
62 Ibid., pp. 19-20.
63 TNA WO 158/21: Letter from Robertson to Haig dated 16 Jan 16 re move of further divisions to France. The four divisions it was holed to send were: 35th Division by end January; 39th Division by end of February; 40th Division by end March and 41st Division by end April.
64 Ibid., Letter from Robertson to Haig dated 10 February 1916.
65 Sheffield & Bourne, eds., *Douglas Haig: War Diaries and Letters*, p.183 Wednesday, 29 March 1916.

In GHQ

The GHQ Staff Branches had been reviewing the conduct of offensives and in early February issued a comprehensive memorandum entitled '*Preparatory Measures to be Taken by Armies and Corps Before Undertaking Offensive Operations on a Large Scale*' was issued. It dealt almost entirely with operational and logistical matters, but at the very end instructed Divisional Commanders that they were to keep AG GHQ constantly informed of estimates of unit casualties, in accordance with instructions issued to Army Commanders.[66]

On the Manning side, business continued as usual for AG Branch GHQ during the early months of the year. No major actions had taken place during January but even so the total monthly casualties numbered 530 officers and 9424 men. Furthermore, many units remained undermanned from the previous fighting and there was a total shortage of nearly 75,000 men. Reinforcements continued to arrive: some 629 officers and 28,198 men in January, 702 officers and 27,030 men in February and a further 43,538 in March, but the BEF would continue to fall below establishment until April.[67] Both at home and in France the 'A' Branches were working tirelessly to gain manpower.

The problem for the Manning staffs was the continuation of trench warfare and raids whilst they were both struggling to replace previous losses and attempting to build up the BEF ready for the anticipated offensive. During the first six months of 1916 there were some nine local actions, including those at Mount Sorrel, The Bluff, St Eloi and Vimy Ridge, plus five more, three of which were German gas attacks. Considerable losses were incurred: for example, in the Ypres area on 14/15 February there were some 67 officers and 1759 OR casualties.[68] Furthermore, G Branch GHQ continued actively to encourage raids as a means of gaining experience and fostering the so-called 'aggressive spirit'. Between 19 December 1915 and 30 May 1916, there were 63 British raids of which 47 were successful. The total battle casualties during this period, however, were 4067 officers and 83,862 men, all of whom had to be replaced. Reinforcements were arriving, albeit slowly. A further 976 officers and 39,496 men were sent up from the Base in April and by 18 May the manpower deficit had been reduced to 46,200. In mid-May AG GHQ and DAG 3rd Echelon visited the War Office to discuss reinforcement questions.

Between January and June some units suffered (comparatively) few losses, depending on their location and the actions they had been in. The 1st KSLI lost 62 dead plus at least 117 wounded whilst 10th RWF suffered 108 fatalities.[69] Conversely 1st Cheshire lost 33 killed but the battalion remained undermanned so had needed 385 replacements for earlier casualties.[70] Amongst a draft that arrived on 21 April was a contingent of about 40 from the Isle of Man

66 *BOH 1916, Vol. 1*, Appendix 16 p. 108.
67 TNA WO 95/26: AG GHQ War Diary January – March 1916.
68 *BOH 1916, Vol. 1*, pp. 155-6 and 242-3; TNA: WO 95/26 AG GHQ War Diary entry dated 17 February 1916.
69 SDGW, 1st KSLI Regimental History and 10th RWF War Diary for January-June 1916.
70 CRA: 1st Cheshire War Diary January-June 1916: drafts received February 80, March 50, April 104, May 104.

(IoM) Volunteers who had volunteered for overseas service and had been posted to 3rd Cheshire in late November 1915.[71]

Replacements for TF battalions continued to be in short supply. On 1 January the Army Council had ordered that priority be given to returning the strengths of TF battalions in France to 1,000 but in many cases the men were simply not available.[72] In mid-February one of Macready's last acts as AG BEF was to interview the COs of the 1/4th and 1/5th Black Watch, the 1/9th Argyll and Sutherland Highlanders (A&SH) and 1/4th Cameron Highlanders. Casualties had reduced each of these battalions to about 500 and insufficient drafts were available to make them up to full strength in the near future. It was proposed to amalgamate the Black Watch battalions and to use the other two battalions as drafts for their respective Regular Battalions. The COs 'thought there would be no great objection on the part of the men to the proposals being carried out'.[73] The Black Watch battalions were duly amalgamated, forming the 4/5th Black Watch which was posted to the 39th Division, whilst the other two battalions were returned to the Base in late February to provide drafts for other battalions.[74] The 1/4th Cameron Highlanders was disbanded with some 300 men being sent to join the 1st Entrenching Battalion whilst a further 100 remained at the Base. Other Scottish TF battalions were proving difficult to reinforce and a further four were amalgamated in May on the orders of the War Office: the 1/5th and 1/6th Royal Scots and the 1/5th and 1/6th Scottish Rifles.[75]

Some Service battalions were also now very weak due to lack of reinforcements. In April War Office approval was given for the amalgamation of 7th and 8th King's Own Scottish Borderers (both K2 battalions), 6th and 7th Royal Scots Fusiliers (K1 and K2 respectively), 10th and 11th Highland Light Infantry (both K1) and 8th and 10th Gordon Highlanders (K1 and K2 respectively). It was not only the Scots who were having difficulties: authority was also received for the disbandment of three Public Schools battalions, 18th, 19th and 21st Royal Fusiliers. These men of these battalions could be drafted to other battalions of the Royal Fusiliers but many were subsequently commissioned.[76] In May the DA&QMG Fourth Army saw the GOC 32nd Division about the state of 19th Lancashire Fusiliers and the next day visited GHQ to discuss with AG the possibility of breaking up the battalion. It was decided that it would be impossible to replace it with another battalion, so the proposal was abandoned.[77]

It is likely that the growing shortage of replacements, particularly for some New Army battalions, was a contributory factor underlying the instruction to the DAG's staffs on 12 May that in future they were to reinforce by Regiment instead of by battalion. This change to previous policy was promulgated by letter to the Army HQs on 22 May.[78] It did not provoke any adverse comment and appears to have been simply regularizing what was already happening. On 1 June 1916, 1st Cheshire received from 8th Entrenching Battalion a draft of 47 former members of

71 <http://www.isle-of-man.com/manxnotebook/fulltext/gw1922/index.htm> B.E. Sargeaunt, The Isle of Man and the Great War (Douglas, Brown & Sons Ltd, nd).
72 TNA WO 163/21: Minutes of 179th Army Council Meeting of Saturday 1 January 1916.
73 TNA WO 95/26: AG GHQ War Diary February 1916.
74 E.A. James, *British Regiments* (Heathfield: Naval and Military Press, 1998).
75 TNA WO 95/26: AG GHQ War Diary May 1916.
76 Ibid., AG GHQ War Diary April 1916 and James, *British Regiments*, p. 50.
77 TNA 95/441: Fourth Army AG & QMG War Diary 21 and 22 May 1916.
78 TNA WO 95/26: AG GHQ War Diary, WO 95/181 First Army AG&QMG War Diary May 1916, WO 95/441 Fourth Army AG & QMG War Diary May 1916

15th Cheshire. Their arrival excited no comment in the War Diary as to their size, presumably because they were already Cheshire soldiers.[79]

Operation and Re-organization of Base Depots

Both the draft-finding units at home and the Bases in France were working flat out to replace losses and build up units before the planned offensive: in May 1,463 officers and 51,685 men were sent forward from the Base areas.[80] The Bases had increased in size exponentially as new divisions and units arrived in France and were now almost the size of small towns. Reinforcement camps for 40,000 each were provided at Rouen, Le Havre and Étaples. At Rouen there were also nine hospitals, plus two convalescent camps each taking 1,000 and depots for supplies, remounts, ordnance and mechanical transport. Similarly, at Le Havre and Boulogne there were supply and remount depots and Boulogne was also the principal base for the evacuation of the wounded.

Drafts going to the Front travelled by a mixture of transport, mostly train and motor vehicles until the point at which they would have to get out and march. Each Army area had 'Tactical trains' kept at six hours' notice to move infantry reinforcements a short distance (15-30 miles). For larger formations there were 'strategical trains': each Army had a timetable for moving a complete division by rail at 9 hours' notice.[81] At each of the Bases, a Railway Transport Officer (RTO) Reinforcement Trains would dispatch troops to the various Armies and places on the LofC. At Rouen, for example, he was responsible for daily dispatching anything from 2,000 to 3,000 men to all four Armies, and then completing and wiring the necessary paperwork to the relevant railway traffic offices, the Corps and Divisions concerned, the HQs of the Armies concerned and the Bases from which the men had left.[82]

An example of the operation of an IBD in early 1916 is No 38 IBD which had landed at Le Havre on 2 December 1915. On arrival at Étaples, the IBD staff spent the next few days putting their camp in order before beginning to receive men discharged from hospitals. The 38th Division battalions were all locally raised in Wales: five RWF, six Welsh and two SWB. On 16 December the first draft of 30 NCOs and men for 10th Welsh arrived, having been sent from 20th (Reserve) Welsh at Kinmel Park. By 29 June 1916, No 38 IBD would have received 2775 men from Kinmel Park and forwarded 2862 men to 38th Division or other Welsh battalions.[83]

One of the men who passed through No 38 IBD was George Culpitt who had joined up in 1915. He had no Welsh connections but had enlisted in the RWF because he had a Welsh

79 TNA 95/1571: 1st Cheshire War Diary entry for 1 June 1916.
80 TNA WO 95/26: AG GHQ War Diary – May 1916.
81 *BOH 1916, Vol. 1*, p. 19 fn. 6
82 *BOH, Transportation on the Western Front 1914-1918*, pp. 514-5 Appendix IV. The particular bugbear of the RTO Reinforcement Trains, Rouen, was not the large numbers of men he had to despatch but officers' luggage: he was frequently besieged just as the train was about to depart by 'a shoal of officers' who had suddenly discovered that they had left their kit at the camp, had not seen it since it was placed in the hold at Southampton, or could not find room for it on the train.
83 TNA WO 95/4186: 38th Infantry Base Depot War Diary for December 1915-June 1916.

A unit arriving at Etaples camp, France. (IWM Q 33323)

Troops going through physical exercise session in the famous "Bull Ring" training camp on the dunes between Etaples and Camiers. (IWM Q 33328)

friend joining at the same time.[84] His diary starts when his draft left Kinmel Park on 27 April 1916 to join 15th RWF. By early afternoon the next day they had arrived at Le Havre where they were accommodated overnight. The following morning, they left for Étaples, where they found a very large tented camp with dining halls in large marquees and one or two wooden buildings dotted about. Having drawn brand new rifles and bayonets from the stores they made their way to No 38 IBD; the No 38 IBD War Diary for 29 April shows a draft of 50 arriving for 15th RWF. The next afternoon the draft started training started on the Bull Ring, on the sand hills some two miles outside the main camp:

> Arriving after about 30 minutes marching, hot and perspiring, because it was mid-day and very hot, we turned off the road and made our way to the position set out for the 38th I.B.D. about half way up the ridge and here awaited the coming of the sergeant instructors. … During the afternoon under the supervision of the sergeants and closely watched by the officer we went through rapid loading, extended order drill, and bayonet fighting and we were much relieved when we finally made our way back to the road, the instructors took their leave and we made tracks for the Depot.

For the next two weeks the draft practised bayonet fighting, bombing and extended order drills, apart from two days when they went on route marches to the coast and a single day live-firing at targets some 75 yards away on the Sandhills Range just outside the camp. It did not take long and they had returned to camp before lunch. The following day, 11 May, Culpitt and his draft learned they would shortly be leaving for the Front to join 10th RWF. He was one of a draft of 80 men who left the IBD on 13 May having been diverted from 15th to 10th RWF to replace casualties suffered by the latter battalion in a German gas attack on 30 April.[85] This transfer of drafts between RWF battalions confirms that reinforcement by regiment was already happening in early May. As far as Culpitt was concerned, he does not appear to have been disturbed by the switch of unit; he was simply relieved to find himself in the same company as seven others of his original draft from Kinmel Park.

The change to reinforcement by regiment would be inoperable under the previous system of divisional IBDs since, for the new system to work, drafts needed to be centralized by regiment. In mid-June the IGC, Lt Gen F. T. Clayton, informed the War Office that GHQ had authorized the re-organization of the IBDs in France and attached details of their intended amalgamation by regiments and military districts.[86] In noting that '1 July would be a suitable date on which to commence sending out reinforcements to their new Base Depots', the letter's purpose was simply to request that from that date the WO should direct all Infantry reinforcements to the new IBDs. Agreement was given, and the changeover was rapidly implemented: 38th IBD began to receive men of the Royal West Surrey, East Surrey and East Kent Regiments in early July. The last Welsh draft, nine men for the SWB, was sent forward on 10 July.[87]

84 <www.culpitt-war-diary.org.uk/index.htm>
85 TNA WO 95/4186: 38th IBD War Diary – 13 May 1916.
86 TNA WO 95/3969: IGC letter AD 2074 dated 13 June 1916.
87 Ibid., Letter 121/8528 (AG2a) dated 20 June 1916 and WO 95/4186 38 IBD War Diary for July 1916.

Under the new organization the IBDs continued to be split between Rouen, Le Havre and Étaples. At Rouen, No 4 IBD would serve the Cheshire, KSLI and Monmouth Regiments, No 5 IBD the RWF and SWB and No 6 IBD the Welsh and South Lancashire Regiments. The IBDs serving the No 3 District Regiments were all at Étaples with Nos 23, 24, 25 and 30 IBDs serving the regiments recruited in Lancashire, Westmorland and Cumberland. The TF Base Depots at Rouen and Le Havre continued to be linked to the TF Divisions, but TF reinforcements for units not within the TF Divisions would be allocated by the regimentally affiliated Base Depots. The final list of Base Depots in France with their affiliated units was sent to the War Office at the end of July.[88] Although the dates of the re-organization coincided with the start of the Battle of the Somme, the cause of the change was clearly the inability to continue to reinforce by battalions and divisions.

Preparations for the Battle of the Somme

In early January Haig had instituted weekly meetings with the three Army Commanders and had set them to working out operational schemes both to wear out the enemy and a decisive attack.[89] At this time, General Sir Herbert Plumer's Second Army occupied a 20 mile front from Boesinghe to Armentières, First Army, temporarily commanded by General Sir Henry Rawlinson, held the next 25 miles south to Loos after which the French Tenth Army occupied a gap of 20 miles before the Third Army, under General Sir Edmund Allenby, covered the 22 miles from Ransart down to the Somme near Curlu. The task of working up an attack in the Third Army area initially fell to Allenby, who was instructed that it might be either an isolated attack with 15 divisions on a 13-14 mile front for about the 20 April or a later attack astride the Somme in co-operation with the French using 25 divisions.

The continuing expansion of the BEF now necessitated the creation of a Fourth Army, to be commanded by Rawlinson. Its HQ was formed on 5 February and its troops arrived from March onwards. These were obtained in the first instance by taking over three Third Army Corps, XIII, X and VIII, and the 20 mile stretch from the Somme to Fonquevillers that they had been holding.[90] Rawlinson and the new Fourth Army staffs took over planning for the offensive. On 6 March he outlined to his Corps Commanders the general nature of the undertaking, although as yet there was neither a clear objective nor a definite date. He expected to receive more troops and planning was to proceed on the assumption that there would be 15 infantry divisions if the offensive opened on 1 May or 17 divisions a month later, plus in either case a cavalry division. A further three divisions and one or more cavalry division would be held in GHQ reserve.

It was still not definite that there would indeed be an offensive and Haig was coming under pressure from the French. On 4 April he wrote to Robertson asking for confirmation that he

88 TNA WO 95/3970: IGC War Diary and IGC letter A.D./2074 dated 31 July. See Appendix VII for details of the re-organization.
89 Sheffield, & Bourne, *Douglas Haig, War Diaries and Letters*, p. 178, diary entry for Saturday, 8 January 1916.
90 This initially gave Rawlinson just eight divisions: XIII Corps: 7th, 18th and 30th; X Corps: 32nd, 36th, 48th and 49th; and VIII Corps: 31st. It also enabled the rest of Third Army to take over the line from the French on their left and join up with First Army near Vimy.

had the Government's authority to agree 'to co-operate with the French armies as requested.'[91] Robertson replied by wire on 7 April that the War Committee had given authority, sending a letter on 9 April confirming the War Committee's conclusions:

> The War Committee approve of the Chief of the Imperial General Staff informing the British Commander-in-Chief in France that he is given the authority for which he asks in the last paragraph of his letter No O.A.D 679 of the 4th April 1916.

All now seemed clear but Robertson sent a further personal letter on 10 April:

> I desire, in order to avoid any possible misunderstanding, to make it clear that the approval of the War Committee extends only to your co-operation with the French in offensive operations and not to the force to be employed by you, which is a matter entirely within your discretion. I am not at present able to guarantee that you will receive any troops beyond those already notified to you.[92]

Haig now had authority for an offensive in conjunction with the French but it came with a warning over the number of troops available. This reflected that the Army Council was at that precise time embroiled in discussions with the Cabinet Committee over the need for greater compulsion in order to obtain the necessary recruits. The outcome remained as yet uncertain.

Meanwhile, Fourth Army was gradually building up.[93] Rawlinson would eventually have five Corps but none of them would have had stable organizations for more than a couple of months; only one contained four divisions; and two would not receive third divisions until mid-June. There was very little time for the staffs at all levels to establish procedures and relationships in the new organizations. Not all the divisions were at full strength: in April VIII Corps was joined by the 29th Division, which had fought at Gallipoli and had arrived in France only at the end of March. Concerns about its strength meant that on 11 April the DA & QMG Fourth Army visited GHQ to discuss urgent reinforcements for it.[94] Furthermore, although the divisions of Fourth Army contained some Regular and first-line TF battalions, most battalions were New Army, many of which had been in France for only a matter of months. Despite the 'stiffening' process that had been carried out after Loos, with the insertion of Regular battalions into some New Army divisions, of Fourth Army's sixteen divisions, three (17th, 18th and 19th) remained totally New Army and a further three (31st, 34th and 36th) were completely locally raised. Replacements for their future losses would have to be found from the Second Reserve and the newly created Local Reserve battalions, respectively.

91 TNA WO 158/21: Haig letter OAD 679 dated 4 April 1916.
92 Ibid., Robertson correspondence with Haig dated 7, 9 and 10 April 1916.
93 *BOH 1916, Vol. 1,* p. 254 fn 1. In early March Fourth Army contained VIII Corps (4th, 31st and 48th Divisions), X Corps (32nd, 36th, and 49th Divisions) and XIII Corps (7th, 18th, 21st and 30th Divisions). HQ III Corps arrived on 24 March with 8th Division but the 19th and 34th Divisions would not join until early May. A new XV Corps was also formed, taking over the 7th and 21st Divisions from XIII Corps on 29 April, but it would not be joined by 17th Division until 11 June. The XIII Corps now retained only the 18th and 30th Divisions; the 9th Division would not arrive until mid-June.
94 TNA WO 95/441: War Diary Fourth Army A&Q Branch.

Seven of the divisions had yet to see action on the Western Front, other than trench warfare, and many of their officers were inevitably inexperienced in battle. Equally, in those units that had seen previous action, many officers and NCOs had been wounded and replaced. It was thus a simple statement of fact when Rawlinson noted on 19 April that many of the battalions contained:

> [N]ew troops with little experience, and amongst whom the standard of discipline, leadership and tactical training of company commanders is not what obtained in our troops of a year ago.[95]

Haig was also concerned and on 4 May noted in his diary that, whilst he stood ready to support the French in case anything catastrophic happened at Verdun, 'My divisions ... want much careful training before we could attack with hope of success.'[96] He reiterated this to Rawlinson a couple of days later, making it clear that he had no intention of attacking in force until the Armies were as strong as possible, the divisions adequately trained and the ammunition supply ample.[97]

It had been decided that Fourth Army's Corps would attack the five objectives of Montauban, Contalmaison, Pozières, the Miraumont spur and Serre respectively. A simultaneous attack to the north by part of Allenby's Third Army at Gommecourt would form a diversion whilst First and Second Armies and the rest of Third Army would carry out wire-cutting operations. On 17 May Rawlinson informed his corps commanders of their precise objectives and issued 'Fourth Army Tactical Notes', based on a GHQ Memorandum dated 8 May entitled 'Training of Divisions for Offensive Action', which were to form the basis of training whilst troops were in reserve. It was again emphasised that the inexperience and lack of previous training of officers and troops meant that it could not be assumed that military skills had become sufficiently second nature to take over automatically in unforeseen circumstances. Divisional and Brigade Commanders were therefore to hold special training exercises to equip subordinate commanders at all levels to react to unexpected situations. Brigades were to be trained over the same kind of ground as they would advance across with the distance of the various objectives being marked out and also to practise passing through other Brigades during attacks.[98]

The training objectives were highly laudable but the problem for those trying to implement them was that, whilst in reserve, troops were constantly required to provide labour for numerous preparatory tasks necessary for the offensive.[99] A Fourth Army A and Q staff conference in

95 *BOH 1916 Vol. 1,* Appendix 10, p.77.
96 Sheffield, & Bourne, *Douglas Haig: War Diaries and Letters*, p. 186.
97 *BOH 1916, Vol. 1*, p. 258.
98 *BOH 1916 Vol. 1*, pp. 131, 262, Appendix 18.
99 In 1915 eleven RE labour battalions containing elderly labourers and tradesmen had been formed for defence works such as roads and water supply. In early 1916 Infantry Labour battalions began to be raised from men of Reserve Infantry units unfit for service at the Front who were without specialist trades or professional qualifications. The Cheshires formed two such battalions: 18th (Labour) Cheshire in March and 19th (Labour) Cheshire in April, both of which were sent to France; on 26 May 19th Cheshire was temporarily allotted to XV Corps for work on the Dernancourt railway. None of the other Marcher Regiments formed such battalions although some of their recruits were cross-posted to the Cheshire Labour units. By June there were in France 11 RE Labour battalions, 12 Infantry Labour battalions, 30 Labour Companies ASC (for the disembarkation of stores and

early March was informed that GHQ could allot only two RE Labour battalions and three Infantry labour battalions to them. Consequently, in the months preceding the attack the 'troops wore themselves out in digging assembly and communication trenches, cable trenches and dug-outs', vast dumps of ammunition, material and warlike stores of all kinds had also to be collected and miles of railways and trench tramways to be built. At the same time the line had to be held and 'most important of all, tactical training of the new levies had to be carried on.'[100] The adverse effect on training was noted on 28 May by Captain Jack of the 8th Cameronians:

> Training Programmes, submitted to a zealous High Command even before we left the line, are scheduled to cover 6½ hours daily, commencing on our first day in reserve...But the fine-looking programmes, all neatly typed, have been pretty well ruined. Since the 26th half our dutymen have been required to spend the whole of most nights on fatigues near the line, and although they proceed there and back in motor transport the men are too tired on their return for more exercise that morning.[101]

The 8th Cameronians moved back to the Front on 4 June, following their fortnight's training. Jack noted that they had done their 'level best to instruct all ranks and tune them up for the battle ahead' but in his opinion they were still not 'PROPERLY TRAINED'(sic).[102]

Medical Arrangements

The Medical Services would also play their part towards making manpower available; their role, in bluntest terms, being to return those who had been wounded or sick to active duty as soon as possible. Plans were reviewed, based on anticipated numbers of casualties, and improved arrangements set in place for the rapid evacuation and treatment of casualties at the earliest appropriate stage in the system so that lives might be saved and earlier convalescence encouraged. Although some 61,000 hospital bed spaces existed in a total of 58 hospitals on the LofC and in convalescent and stationary hospitals in the front area, on 1 July only 36,237 vacancies would be actually available. As a matter of urgency a large number of wounded were sent back to UK in order to free up space before the battle started. To avoid sending slightly wounded men back, however, the convalescent depots, of which there were seven, were now enlarged to cater for as many as 5,000 at a time. Their role was the same as that of the Command Depots in England, namely to free up hospital beds and to prepare convalescents for return as soon as possible to their units at the Front.[103] Work on a further large convalescent depot had started at Cayeux which would open on 24 July.

formation of depots), 3 Naval Labour companies and 8 Non-Combatant (conscientious objectors) Labour Companies. The units were thinly spread, however, and labour would continue to be a problem throughout the offensive, necessitating the use of Infantry soldiers.

100 Crookenden, *Cheshire Regiment in the Great War*, p. 64.
101 Terraine, ed., *General Jack's Diary*, pp. 136-7.
102 Ibid., p. 138.
103 MacPherson, *Medical History of the War Vol. III*, pp. 24, 48.

Final Arrangements for Reinforcements

On 14 June AG GHQ requested that the War Office send out 20,000 men per week, preferably ordinary trained reinforcements but partially trained men could be sent provided they had fired their musketry course. On 20 June the War Office wired that 20,000 Regular and New Army and 17,500 TF reinforcements would be sent out, leaving the next week. Of these the TF were only partially trained but had at least completed their musketry training. During June some 1823 officers and 72,131 men were sent from home – huge numbers but still short of the 20,000 a week requested. The War Office telegraphed on 28 June that 2,500 partially trained men were being sent at the end of the week, 15,000 partially trained men would be sent on 2 July and a further 15,000 partially trained men would be sent during the first fortnight of July.[104]

On 14 June Rawlinson issued his formal Operations Order and on 22 June held his final conference with his Corps commanders. The planning was over and on 26 June Advanced GHQ opened at Beauquesne in readiness for the attack. It now remained to be seen whether the arrangements for reinforcements were both sufficient and timely.

Mid-1916 Diversity

By mid-1916 the various changes since the beginning of the war meant that British soldiers serving with the BEF could fall into some nine distinct types: surviving pre-war Regulars; reservists, both SR and Army, mobilized on the outbreak of war; 'Kitchener' volunteers; TF soldiers, both IS men and those HS men caught up for overseas service by the MSA; Derbyites whose enlistment had been delayed; conscripts; and those continuing to volunteer rather than be called up. The Battle of the Somme would be fought for the most part by volunteers, including the Derby men. The lead time from reporting for duty to completion of training for the Infantry soldier continued to be twelve to fourteen weeks and it would thus be June before the earliest men called up under the MSA might be ready for drafting.

Differing perceptions of the relative capabilities of the conscripts were inevitable and widespread. An early and somewhat naïve comment was that of Lieutenant Eric King, who had written home in January 1916:

> [N]o man who is dragged into the Army through Conscription will ever be able to look the world in the face with a clear conscience. … one feels such contempt for the miserable slackers who wait until they are fetched.[105]

Others felt that conscripts had at least shown the courage of their convictions by waiting until they were forced to enlist, in contrast to the 'Derby' men who had attested but then gone safely home again to await call up: to be called or even thought a 'Derby' man in some units was an insult.[106] Walter Williamson, who was attested in late 1915, would not be called up until June

104 TNA WO 95/26: AG GHQ War Diary for June 1916.
105 Lieutenant E. King, 'A Ripping Lot of Fellows – Letters from a Grenadier Battalion Officer', *Stand To!*, 70 (April 2004), p. 17.
106 Feilding, *War Letters to a Wife*, p. 47.

1916. On joining 6th Cheshire at the end of the year he was relieved to find that 'We were made very welcome and knowing that the battalion had been in France since 1914, it was a pleasant surprise to hear no remarks about 'Derbies'.[107]

The reality of the conscripts would be as diverse as the men themselves: 3rd (Reserve) KSLI would find that the introduction of conscription brought 'men of superior education, drawn from all kinds of trades and professions' into the battalion. They were not physically of so high a standard as the farm hands and ploughmen who had enlisted after the 1915 harvest 'but training quickly improved them in all ways'.[108]

Whatever the terms under which they had been recruited, the men of the BEF were now about to take part in the first large-scale British offensive of the war.

107 W. Williamson, edited by D. Priddey, *A Tommy at Ypres: Walter's War* (Stroud: Amberley Publishing), p.46.

108 Wood, *The King's Shropshire Light Infantry in the Great War*, p. 317.

4

1916: Into the Melting Pot

The Battle of the Somme began at 7:30 am on 1 July. Recent research by Robin Prior and Trevor Wilson has discredited the traditional view that all battalions left their trenches at that moment and advanced in successive lines and at walking pace towards the German parapets.[1] Instead, the majority of battalions, some 53 out of the 80 that took part in the first attack, crept as close as possible to the German wire before the attack began and then rushed the enemy line. A further ten battalions rushed from their own parapet whilst only twelve appear to have advanced at a steady pace, in some cases following a creeping barrage. The method of advance is unclear for only five battalions. Whatever tactics were adopted, however, in most places the troops were attacking undestroyed machine guns and were at the mercy of unsubdued German artillery. The outcome was that casualties on 1 July were far higher than had ever been anticipated. Eighteen divisions were shown in the order of battle for that day of which thirteen participated in the actual assault; of their eighty battalions thirty-two battalions suffered more than 500 casualties each.[2] A total of 19,240 men were killed and 37,646 wounded or missing. Horrific in themselves, the casualty figures posed a massive challenge for those responsible for replacing the men that had been lost.

The procedures followed were those that had evolved earlier in the war. Estimated casualty figures were wired daily to AG's office in GHQ by all divisions actively involved in operations. At 9:00 am each morning AG's staff closed the previous day's list, totaled it up and forwarded the figures to DAG at the Base and to the AG in the War Office. Every night a list of casualties by division was telegraphed to Advanced GHQ.[3] Throughout the battle, there was frequent contact between the 'A' staff and the Armies, with the new AG GHQ, Lt Gen Fowke, visiting Advanced GHQ almost daily and his staff making frequent visits to the Fourth and Reserve Armies.

1 R. Prior & T. Wilson, *The Somme* (New Haven & London: Yale University Press, 2005), pp. 114-115. NB the reference is the same in the updated version published in 1916.
2 M. Middlebrook, *The First Day on the Somme* (London: Allen Lane, 1971; Penguin edn., 1984), p. 330.
3 TNA WO 95/26: AG GHQ War Diary for 1 July 1916.

As the battle continued, the system continued to function as previously planned although it occasionally required a slight tweak to ensure its smooth running. On 25 July the AAG Reserve Army, Lt Col C. F. Hunter, notified all Reserve Army Corps and Divisions that, whilst divisions were to continue to send estimated casualty numbers by wire to AG GHQ, Reserve Army 'A' Branch and their parent Corps, they were in future, in order to reduce telegraph traffic, to send the long 'actual' casualty returns by Despatch Rider Letter Service (DRLS) to the parent Corps and Reserve Army 'A', marking the envelopes 'Casualty Return Urgent'.[4]

Sometimes there were difficulties in obtaining the casualty figures. Reserve Army 'A' staff tried to pre-empt problems by meeting incoming Corps staff and briefing them on casualty reporting requirements.[5] This did not always work: diary entries from 26 July-1 August continually note the non-receipt of casualty figures from the Australian Divisions. On 31 July the A&QMG staff called a conference with the Australian Staff Captains and the figures soon began to appear.[6]

The estimated casualty figures were essential for the reinforcement system to operate as quickly as required. On receiving the consolidated lists, the GHQ GS Operations Branch would each evening notify AG and DAG Base of the priority for reinforcements. On 9 July, for example, it was notified that 70th Brigade should be brought up to strength as soon as possible and on 16 July divisions were grouped into priority categories. Sometimes a general policy was laid down, for example on 24 July it was noted that 'as a general rule, divisions holding defensive fronts should not be allowed to fall below 9,000 and should receive priority to that extent'. The system would continue unchanged throughout the battle: on 19 November the message to AG and DAG Base was that reinforcements were to be prioritized for 3rd, 31st and 32nd Divisions for Fifth Army and for 17th, 50th, 33rd and 8th Divisions for Fourth Army.[7]

Despite the disastrous first day, sufficient reinforcements seem to have been available, at least to begin with. On 7 July Rawlinson impressed upon Fowke the need to refill 7th Division as soon as possible; on 10 July the Fourth Army 'A' staff reported the satisfactory arrival of drafts for 7th and 21st Divisions, and that 7th Division was now practically back up to establishment. As casualties mounted, however, their replacements inevitably began to take longer to arrive. On 16 July Colonel Nation, AAG GHQ, informed DA&QMG Fourth Army that some 2,000 reinforcements might be expected daily. In the event, however, these figures fluctuated: on 21 July they received 2,742 men but for the last seven days of July the daily average had fallen to 1,338. From 12 July, when Fourth Army started recording incoming figures, to 31 July they received just 30,605 men against estimated casualties for the whole month of 4,428 officers and 116,270 men.[8]

The provision of replacements was made more difficult for AG GHQ by the fact that losses were not limited solely to those on the Somme, which for July were estimated to be 5,054 officers and 146,130 men. The rest of the BEF was not unscathed and the total losses for July

4 TNA WO 95/523: Reserve Army A&QMG War Diary entry 25 July 1916.
5 Ibid., Reserve Army A&QMG War Diary entry 27 July: 'VIII Corps being relieved by XIV Corps. Met XIV Corps advanced staff and discussed reports of casualties etc'.
6 Ibid Entries for 26 July-2 August 1916.
7 TNA WO 95/5, 95/6, 95/7, 95/8, 95/9: GHQ GS War Diaries for July, August, September, October and November 1916.
8 TNA WO 95/441: Fourth Army A&QMG War Diary July 1916.

on the Western Front were 9,228 officers and 180,115 men: battle casualties accounted for 7,835 officers and 155,767 men and a further 1,375 officers and 24,348 men were classed as 'sick wastage'. Reinforcements from home numbered just 1,669 officers and 106,552 men.[9] Battle casualties were to be expected, and many of those shown in the overall casualty figures would recover sufficiently to return to the line, but nonetheless the figures for July were high. Summarizing his views on the present situation in a letter to Robertson on 1 August, Haig rationalized the figures somewhat cavalierly:

> Our losses in the last month's very heavy fighting – totaling to about 120,000 more than they would have been if we had not attacked – cannot be regarded as unduly heavy, or as sufficient to justify any anxiety as to our ability to continue the offensive … our ranks have been filled up again and our troops are still in excellent heart.[10]

Had all the divisions involved in the previous month's fighting been expected to remain in the front line then there might well have been anxiety over their ability to continue the offensive. From the earliest days of the war, however, the BEF had as a matter of course withdrawn weakened divisions from the line so that they might be rested and refilled with reinforcements. During the Somme battle, divisions were not only withdrawn from the frontline for short periods but could also be sent right away from the battle area by swapping them with divisions from First, Second and Third Armies. Orders for such moves of divisions were given by GHQ. For example, GHQ GS Ops letter (O.A.D.41) of 4 July initiated the following merry-go-round:

- II Corps was to transfer from GHQ Reserve to Fourth Army
- 3rd Division was to transfer from II Corps to XIII Corps, Fourth Army
- 12th Division transferred from III Corps, Fourth Army to X Corps, Reserve Army
- 8th Division (II Corps) to be held in readiness to entrain for I Corps, First Army,
- 1st Division (I Corps) to be held in readiness to entrain to II Corps, Fourth Army
- 35th Division, Third Army to move to VIII Corps, Reserve Army[11]

As a result of this instruction, on 7/8 July 3rd Division, newly arrived from the Ypres area and containing 7th KSLI and 10th RWF, relieved 18th Division, which had been in the line since the start of the offensive and had already lost over 3,400 all ranks. The 12th Division, originally in GHQ Reserve, had been called forward overnight 1/2 July to III Corps and on 3 July had attacked Ovillers, losing nearly 2,400 officers and men. It would now move to X Corps, in the Reserve Army. The 8th Division, having lost 4,921 officers and men on 1 July, was warned for a straight swap with 1st Division and would entrain on 6 July for First Army area where it would remain until mid-October. Of necessity, however, plans had to remain flexible. The 1st Division, although wanted for II Corps, would be diverted on its arrival on 8 July to III Corps. The 35th Division moved to VIII Corps but was to be held in Reserve and not employed

9 TNA WO 95/26: GHQ AG War Diary entry for 31 July 1916.
10 TNA WO 158/21: GHQ OAD 90 dated 1 August 1916.
11 TNA WO 95/5: GHQ GS War Diary dated 4 July1916.

without agreement from GHQ.[12] Such movements of divisions would continue throughout the battle as divisions needed to be withdrawn from the line to rest and recuperate: on 13 November GHQ instructed Second and Fifth Armies that 7th Division was to be transferred from Second to Fifth Army by 'march route' during 15-19 November and that 39th Division would subsequently transfer by rail from Fifth Army (II Corps) to Second Army (VIII Corps).[13]

Occasionally brigades were switched. On 5 July GHQ ordered the 110th, 111th and 112th Brigades of 37th Division to be transferred to the Somme as quickly as possible. On arrival, 110th Brigade exchanged places with 63rd Brigade from 21st Division whilst 111th and 112th Brigades replaced the 102nd and 103rd brigades of 34th Division, III Corps, which had lost 6,811 all ranks in the first three days of the battle. The 111th and 112th Brigades immediately went into the line with 34th Division on 10 July. The Brigades leaving the Somme (63rd, 102nd and 103rd) joined 37th Division in Third Army on Vimy Ridge.[14]

Such switches of Brigades were few, however, quite possibly because, apart from dislocating divisions, it became too difficult to manage. It was hard enough keeping track of whole divisions and the Fourth Army staff created a brightly coloured chart, referred to as the 'Tartan', to plot which division was doing what, when and where. A check was also kept on the number of days up to 31 October that each division spent in the front line, including whether those days were in the more difficult area north of the Ancre.[15] The extracted example below refers to 3rd and 18th Divisions:

Division	Days in the Line-First period			Days in the Line-Second Period			Total Days in the Line to 31 October
18th Division	1-7 Jul	13-17 Jul	12	26 Sep-5 Oct	16 Oct-31 Oct	26	38
3rd Division	8-25 Jul	15-19 Aug	23	8-19 Oct (north of Ancre)	22-31 Oct (north of Ancre)	22	45

Table 3. Number of Days in the Line for 3rd and 18th Divisions 1 July-31 October 1916.

On 20 July 18th Division, which had lost 5,437 all ranks in just 12 days in the line, was warned for transfer from Fourth Army to Second Army.[16] It would not return until mid-September when it would join the Reserve Army. In late August the 3rd Division was also sent north to recuperate, having spent a total of 25 days in the front line and lost about 8000. It had spent 18

12 TNA WO 153/1265: Fourth Army 'Tartan' and Days Spent in the Line 1 July-31 October 1916; WO 95/5 GHQ GS War Diary for 4-8 July 1916; and *BOH 1916 Vol. 2*, pp. 4, 8, 12, 40.
13 TNA WO 95/9: GHQ GS War Diary dated 13 November 1916.
14 TNA WO 95/5: GHQ GS War Diary for 5 July 1916, E.A. James, *A Record of the Battles and Engagements of the British Armies in France and Flanders 1914 – 1918* (1924: London: The London Stamp Exchange, 1990), p. 11, fn. 1 and *BOH 1916 Vol. 2*, p. 13 fn 2. The 34th Division would be reformed as originally constituted on 21 August.
15 TNA WO 153/1265: Fourth Army 'Tartan' and Days in the Line for Each Division 1 July-31 October 1916.
16 TNA WO 95/5: GHQ GS War Diary entry for 20 July and WO 95/26 GHQ AG Table of Estimated Casualties for July 1916.

days in the front line until 25 July, taking part in the battles of Albert, Bazentin and Delville Wood, and had lost 248 officers and 5854 ORs. Reinforcements had been received, for example on 21 July 7th KSLI received a draft of 130, including Bert Oakes who had finally left Prees Heath on 10 July, but the Division as a whole was still much below strength.[17] Despite this it went into action again on 15 August, losing nearly 1900 before being withdrawn on 19 August and sent north. It would not return to the Somme until early October, when it would go into the line again as part of V Corps in the Reserve Army.

In early August GHQ notified Second and Third Armies of further divisions that were required to reinforce the Somme battle front and those with which it was intended to replace them. Details were also sent to the Reserve and Fourth Armies with forecasts of the replacement divisions they might expect.[18] An established system was obviously in place for the rotation of divisions but it cannot have been easy to operate and also inevitably caused dislocation of relationships and established patterns of working. It was deemed necessary, however, to give divisions a rest and to enable them to be refilled and re-equipped out of the line.

Problems over individual reinforcements were becoming increasingly apparent. In response to a complaint by the Minister for Munitions, Montagu, Macready explained the reinforcement process:

> France indents on us for the number of men required per battalion, and we send them out by regiments. That is to say, we may send out to France 1,000 men belonging to one regiment and when they arrive in France they are drafted to such battalions of that regiment as are likely to require to be made up to full strength at once in conformity with the plans of the General Staff. Also it may be necessary where the supply of men for any particular regiment is short to supplement it from other regiments in the same recruiting district ...[19]

Despite the caveat in the final sentence above, units continued to expect drafts belonging to their parent Regiment. This did not always work as planned and Fourth Army complained in early August that

> [R]einforcements do not appear to be coming up very satisfactorily, and in two or three cases drafts appear to have been sent to units to which they do not belong – apparently without reason. DAG Base has in some cases asked that these drafts should be sent back to the Base, but it has been decided to ask that these drafts may be readjusted within the Army.

Fowke, together with the Director of Organization at the War Office, Woodward, visited Rawlinson on 14 August to discuss the matter. Rawlinson stated that 'there was a great deal of apparently unnecessary mixing up of reinforcements for various units' and urged that slightly wounded men returning from the Base should be posted to their original units, as was supposed to happen. He also proposed a pool of reinforcements for Fourth Army but this was not agreed by Fowke, presumably because it would cut across existing systems and also reduce GHQ's

17 *BOH 1916, Vol. 2*, pp. 88 and 193.
18 TNA 95/6: GHQ GS War Diary for 4 and 6 August referring to letters OAD 94, 95, 96 and 97.
19 Macready, *Annals of an Active Life, Vol. I*, p. 256.

flexibility.[20] In practice HQ Fourth Army appears to have turned a blind eye to the transfer to their own regiments of men who had arrived at other regiments. Captain Dunn, the RMO of 2nd RWF, describes the arrival in late July of 'men recruited and trained for the Cheshires, Shropshires and SWB … resentful of their transfer and unwanted by us.' When the opportunity occurred, the Shropshires 'were bartered for half their number of RWF from a neighbouring division'.[21]

Part of the problem was that by now some regiments were so short of reserves that it was necessary to use the authority and procedures granted by both the Army Transfers Act of 1915 and MSA (2) of 1916 and publicized in AO 204 and ACI 1166 to transfer men to them from other regiments.[22] The recent streamlining of the Base Depots now necessitated further administrative procedures when these men were transferred and posted on arrival in France. On 31 July ACI 1499 announced that IBDs were to be issued with blocks of 5,000 Regular regimental numbers for each of the regiments they managed together with 1,000 numbers per TF battalion. Further blocks of numbers would be issued as required. On being posted from the IBD, new regimental numbers would be issued to those regular soldiers transferred to other corps and to TF soldiers posted to both regular or TF units of their existing corps or transferred to regular or TF units of other corps.[23]

Casualties for August were fewer than the previous month enabling Haig to write to Robertson that they had 'not been more than some 28,000 greater than would ordinarily have occurred during three weeks of normal trench warfare …'.[24] Nonetheless, the numbers were still high and the Manning authorities were struggling to bring many Infantry battalions and divisions back up to strength. The official (established) Infantry strength of a division was 12,000, made up of three brigades each containing four battalions of 1000 men, but during the Somme the average divisional strength dropped to 10,000. On 30 August AG GHQ was instructed to bring all battalions of certain (unspecified) divisions up to full establishment at once. All other divisions in Fourth and Reserve Armies, except for those going to defensive fronts, were to be kept over 10,000 strong and no battalion was to be under 850 strong. The strength of battalions in divisions on defensive fronts was to be not less than 700.[25] The figures for August show that great efforts were being made to supply reinforcements with some 1431 officers and 74,414 ORs having arrived from home, of which 34,727 had gone to the Fourth Army. However, although the total estimated casualties for units engaged in active operations for August were 1155 officers and 36,330 ORs, the total BEF casualties, including sick wastage,

20 TNA WO 95/441: Fourth Army A&Q War Diary of 8, 14 and 17 August 1916.

21 Ibid., Fourth Army A&Q War Diary of 12 August 1916 and Dunn, *The War the Infantry Knew*, pp. 245-6. NB Dunn's claim is not totally corroborated by 2nd RWF's War Diary (TNA 95/2561) which shows that between 20-31 July the battalion received 388 reinforcements, but does not indicate that these men were anything other than RWF soldiers.

22 TNA WO 123: AO 204 of 9 June 1916 and WO 293/4 ACI 1166 of 9 June 1916.

23 TNA WO 293/5: ACI 1499 of 31 Jul 1916. ACI 1840 of 23 September subsequently stipulated that documents of individuals posted or transferred to different corps were to be annotated 'under authority of AO 204 and ACI 1499 of 1916'.

24 TNA WO 158/21: GHQ OAD 119 dated 23 Aug 16: Letter from Haig to Robertson.

25 TNA WO 95/6: GHQ GS War Diary entry dated 30 August 1916.

were 5197 officers and 101,965 ORs.[26] Whilst most of the minor wounded and the sick could be returned to duty as soon as they were fit enough, there still remained immediate gaps to fill.

September was a month of successes but also heavy losses: estimated casualties noted by AG Branch GHQ were 18,900 for Martinpuich, Flers and Courcelette; 5,000 at Mouquet Farm; 1270 at Morval and Lesboeufs; and 7,200 at Gueudecourt, Thiepval, and Combles. Divisions continued to be moved around and reinforced according to the GHQ priorities. For the first time, however, AG Branch's September end of month figures showed that more reinforcements had been received (4167 officers and 107,625 ORs) than the total battle casualties (5254 officers and 105,588 ORs).[27]

Battle of Flers-Courcelette. Reinforcements crossing the old German front line during the advance towards Flers, 15 September 1916. (IWM Q 188)

The War Office was obviously finding men from various sources and the timing is such that many would by now have been Derbyites and single conscripts called up earlier in the year. The influx had had an effect on training, however. On 16 October it would be learned that 15,000 recruits due to arrive gradually from England would need to be trained to shoot the short rifle before being sent forward.[28]

26 TNA WO 95/26: AG GHQ War Diary entry dated 31 August 1916. The Medical History notes the appearance of a considerable number of cases of diarrhoea and dysentery during August. It blames this on the constant movement of divisions which meant that divisional sanitary sections were unable to maintain permanent sanitary arrangements in the areas through which they passed. MacPherson, *Medical Services General History Vol. III* p. 49-50.

27 Ibid., AG GHQ War Diary for September 1916.

28 Ibid., AG GHQ War Diary for 16 October 1916.

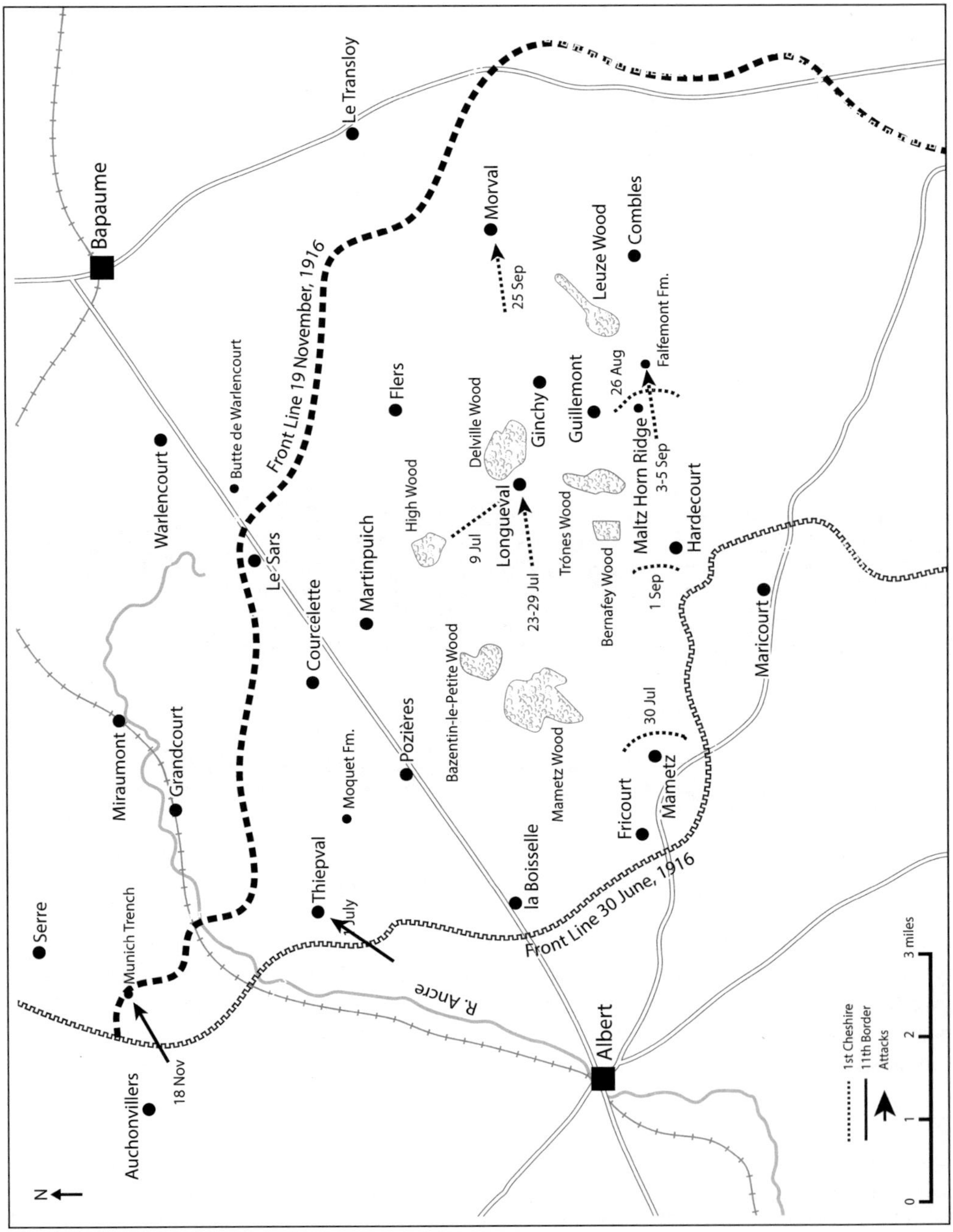

Map 4: Battle of the Somme 1916: 1st Cheshire and 11th Border

The experiences of 1st Cheshire from July through to September provide an illustration of the casualties suffered by a battalion and their subsequent replacement. As part of 15th Brigade of 5th Division, 1st Cheshire arrived on the Somme from Third Army in mid-July and moved into position between High Wood and Longueval on 19 July. At 3:30 am on 23 July 15th Brigade, including 1st Cheshire, advanced on Longueval from the west, penetrating some distance into its orchards and enclosures before the attack was broken up by machine gun nests and they had to withdraw. The 5th Division History shows 'the Cheshires losing heavily' on 23 July, although this is not borne out by 1st Cheshire's War Diary which notes that it was on subsequent days that the battalion suffered 45 casualties plus seven deaths whilst in the support trenches.[29] The 15th Brigade's main attack on Longueval went in on 27th July, led by the 1st Norfolk and 1st Bedfordshire whilst 1st Cheshire carried out a separate attack on an alleged German strongpoint: the Regimental History notes some doubt about its existence! At 8:38 am, three parties, each led by a Second Lieutenant, went forward. The leading two parties made strenuous attempts to reach their objectives but were met by cross fire from machine guns at High Wood and Longueval. Both officers were killed and nearly all the men killed or wounded; a party sent in support was forced to retire. The objective was not reached, although an advanced post was established, and heavy fighting continued all day. The CO, Col M. F. Clarke, had been wounded, some 24 ORs had been killed and a further 12 would be lost over the following two days as the Cheshires moved up and occupied the northern and western edges of Longueval. By the time 15th Brigade was relieved on 30 July and back in Divisional reserve near Mametz, the Cheshire's remaining strength was under 300 all ranks; during July a total of 44 soldiers had been killed in action with a further four dying of their wounds.[30]

Analysis of the 1st Cheshire deaths shows that one third (16) of the men had been with the battalion since 1914 and that almost all the rest (27) had arrived in 1915, with only five, two of whom had been posted from 8th Cheshire, having arrived in early 1916. All except two men had enlisted originally in the Cheshire Regiment; fifteen had been pre-war Cheshire soldiers with varying lengths of service and engagements.[31] The majority (26) were in their 20s whilst thirteen were over 30. Six NCOs were amongst the dead, two Sergeants, two Corporals and two Lance Corporals. Of the 48 who died, 41 had enlisted in Cheshire, two in Lancashire, two in the IoM and one each from Nottinghamshire, Essex and Derbyshire; all except three had thus been recruited originally in Western Command.[32] Despite the battalion's previous undermanned state, its composition in July 1916 would appear to have been very similar that of previous years.

Replacements were quick to arrive. A draft of 70 reinforcements joined on 31 July bringing the total received that month to 100. During August a further 5 officers and 189 men arrived,

29 Hussey, A. H. & Inman, D. S. *The Fifth Division in the Great* War (London: Nisbet & Co Ltd, 1921 N&MP reprint), p. 112, TNA: WO 95/1571 1st Cheshire War Diary for July 1916.
30 *SDGW* and <www.ancestry.com>
31 8641 Pte Frank Ernest Fox had joined the SR in 1910 and was mobilized on 8 August 1914 with 3rd Cheshire. On 19 September he deserted rather than be sent to France and was not arrested until March 1915. A District Court Martial (DCM) in April sentenced him to 1 years' detention which was mitigated to 56 days detention. On 29 May 1915 he rejoined 3rd Cheshire and was posted to 1st Cheshire in France in early July after which he seems to have stayed out of trouble until being killed a year later on 28 July 1916.
32 *SDGW* and <www.ancestry.com>

including a draft of 50 from the Shropshire Yeomanry. These men had initially been attached to 1st Cheshire on 19 August and were then compulsorily transferred on 1 September. The Regimental History notes that the dismounted ex-Yeomanry needed intensive training to become fit for trench warfare but 'once they realised there was no alternative, they soon learnt the work and made excellent reinforcements'. Once the battalion could be got together in a rest area, 'these [new] men soon became one with the unit'.[33] It presumably helped that they came from the neighbouring county.

The 5th Division spent the next few weeks training near Abbeville before returning to the Somme on 26 August and relieving 35th Division on the eastern slopes of Maltz Horn Ridge. It was now part of XIV Corps in Fourth Army and would participate in the attack on Falfemont Farm, on the high ground between Combles and Guillemont. The attack was postponed until 1 September and on that morning 1st Cheshire moved into Chimpanzee Trench, immediately northwest of Hardecourt. The War Diary notes that 'casualties during the day were not very heavy but amounted to about 23 OR'. At 3:10 pm the attack was again postponed but two hours later the Brigade ordered the sending out of strong patrols at 8:30 pm, to establish strongpoints if no opposition was encountered. It obviously was encountered as the Cheshire's final casualty toll for the day was 67, including one officer and seven ORs killed. The soldiers who died had all, with just one exception, been with the battalion since 1915.[34]

Late the following day 15th Brigade was withdrawn into support with the exception of 1st Cheshire which, having been relieved by 14th Warwickshire, was detailed as immediate reserve for a 13th Brigade attack on Falfemont Farm on 3 September. The attack went in at 9:00 am but soon failed due to lack of artillery support which was to have been provided by the French. At 10:45 am 1st Cheshire was ordered forward to reinforce 13th Brigade but on reaching the front line found a very confused situation: 'the KOSBs and the Warwickshires had suffered heavily and did not seem to be in a position to fully explain the situation'. In mid-afternoon the Cheshires were told to push forward patrols to try to 'clear up the situation'. Messages were received that the enemy was retiring; then that the enemy was not retiring but being reinforced with 5000 troops, which figure was later corrected to just 50. At about 5:00 pm the battalion was ordered to send a company to support the West Kents, whilst keeping two companies in the front line and one in support. At 6:00 pm the Commander 13th Brigade ordered 1st Cheshire to attack the still strongly defended Falfemont Farm at 6:30 pm. This attack failed within five minutes, with heavy machine gun fire having caused many casualties, and the Cheshires regrouped in the front-line trench. By now the Cheshire casualties were estimated at over 300, including one officer and 20 ORs killed, and they reported to 13th Brigade that the front line was now full of various regiments and asked 'for some other battalion to take over to enable us to re-organize'.[35]

Overnight 13th Brigade was withdrawn but despite their request 1st Cheshire remained in the front line to be joined by the rest of 15th Brigade: Norfolks on the right, Cheshires in the middle and Bedfords on the left. During the morning, orders were received for the

33 TNA WO 95/1571: 1st Cheshire War Diary for August 1916 and Crookenden, *Cheshire Regiment in the Great War*, p. 77.
34 Ibid., 1st Cheshire War Diary for 1 September 1916 and *SDGW* 1st Cheshire deaths for 1 September 1916.
35 Ibid., 1st Cheshire War Diary for 3 September 1916.

three battalions to attack Falfemont Farm mid-afternoon. Despite their depleted numbers, the Cheshires were to attack the Farm and the trenches immediately to the north of it, whilst the Norfolks would attack the south side of the Farm and the Bedfords the German trenches to the west of the Farm and south of Wedge Wood. The attack went in at the planned time but on the right the Norfolks and 'A' Company of the Cheshires ran into difficulties under heavy machine gun fire and the attack soon failed. On the left, the Bedfords and the Cheshires' 'C' Company succeeded in entering the German trenches to the north of the Farm and then Lt Gwynne-Jones of 'C' Company led a bombing party which, with the help of the Bedfords, eventually gained a footing in the Farm itself. By dark the position had been won but the Cheshire casualties had again been heavy: 3 officers killed and 7 wounded plus 43 ORs killed and 407 wounded. The Regimental History estimated that only 280 men remained untouched.[36]

The Divisional History would refer to the action at Falfemont Farm as 'one of the finest exploits of 5th Division during the war' and the Cheshire Regimental History also calls it a 'brilliant success' and 'the second of two prolonged and successful offensive movements by the 15th Brigade since they came into the Somme battle'. For 1st Cheshire, however, the losses had been heavy and the battalion that was withdrawn during late afternoon on 5 September was only some 280 strong. Reorganization began immediately with the return of those officers and men who had been left behind with the transport, bringing the strength up to 442. Fortunately, two large drafts of reinforcements also arrived: 8 September a draft of 136 from 2/6th Cheshire and three days later 102 men arrived, mostly from 2/7th Cheshire. The transfer of these TF soldiers had been enabled under the second MSA. They had arrived at No 4 IBD during August and were transferred, under AO 204 and ACI 1499 of 1916, to 1st Cheshire in early September when the scale of the battalion's losses became evident.[37] Even so, the battalion's total strength still numbered only 680.

Later in September 1st Cheshire found themselves 'very worn out and wet and of no fighting value' holding the line on the right of the attack on Flers-Courcelette.[38] Their next objective would be Morval, on the right of a much bigger British attack heading north-east towards Bapaume on 25 September. The 15th Brigade's task would be in three stages: the first objective was the German front line in the valley between Ginchy and Morval; the second objective was the German support line halfway up the slope towards Morval; and the Cheshires were to capture the third objective, the eastern edge of Morval itself. The attacks went well and 'objectives were taken in every case at the first assault'.[39] Morval itself was captured by 1st Cheshire at about 3:00 pm with relatively light casualties, although 23 had been killed. The battalion consolidated its new position but the following day the trenches were steadily shelled and a further eight killed. Altogether 1st Cheshire had sustained 140 casualties during the events around Morval, of whom 31 had been killed. Fortunately, the Battalion was relieved by 10:30 pm on 5 September. It now left the Somme area, moving by train to south-east of Abbeville, and would play no further part in the Battle of the Somme.

Between 19 July and the end of September the 5th Division had suffered 559 officer and 11,186 OR casualties. The Cheshire Regimental History noted that 1st Cheshire had taken part

36 Crookenden, *Cheshire Regiment in the Great War*, p. 83.
37 <www.ancestry.com> Service Records for 1st Cheshire soldiers.
38 TNA WO 95/1571: 1st Cheshire War Diary 21 September 1916.
39 Ibid., 1st Cheshire War Diary 25 September 1916.

in three separate operations and had suffered about 20 officer and over 1,000 soldier casualties but they had received large numbers of reinforcements after each action, although many of the men received 'having no connection with the county'.[40] The 1st Cheshire War Diary, however, shows that large drafts had been received from Cheshire TF battalions. Detailed analysis of the 140 soldiers killed 1–26 September also shows that geographically 92 had enlisted in the county of Cheshire and 122 had originally enlisted in the Cheshire Regiment itself, either as Regular or TF. A further six had enlisted elsewhere in No 4 District which, with 29 in No 3 District, made an overall total of 127 enlistments in Western Command. Of the 13 who had enlisted outside Western Command, six had served with the Cheshires for over a year having been transferred in 1915 from other Regimental Depots as a result of the Transfers Act. Whilst these figures might be taken to indicate that those killed had been pre-Somme reinforcements, in reality 29 of the 32 men killed during September were originally Cheshire TF soldiers who had arrived in France only a few weeks before. The other three were from the Shropshire Yeomanry who had arrived in August. Overall, analysis thus shows that during September 1916 drafts for the Cheshire Regiment had continued to come from their own Regimental reserves, although many were TF soldiers, who had joined under the Derby scheme and had been transferred to the Regular battalion on arrival in France.

The Somme offensive continued into October with the battles of Le Transloy, 1-18 October, and Ancre Heights which lasted the whole of the month and into November. The 5th Division took no further part in the Somme battle having been moved from Abbeville northwards to the area around Givenchy for rest and refit. Other divisions which had previously been sent north to recuperate were now being returned to the Somme, with some 12 divisions that had last fought there in July and August returning to the line.[41]

By November the weather had turned, with continuous rain between 24 October-3 November and further bad weather after that. The Reserve Army, now retitled Fifth Army, continued the battle of Ancre Heights whilst Fourth Army attacked Le Transloy. The offensive was drawing to a close although it was still intended to exert pressure on the Germans to avoid their reinforcing other theatres with troops from the Western Front.

Divisions that had last been on the Somme in the summer continued to be brought back once they had been refilled. One such was the 32nd Division, which had been badly mauled on 1 July in the attack on the Leipzig Salient. The 11th Border (Lonsdales) of 97th Brigade, raised in Cumberland and Westmorland and therefore within Western Command, had lost 100 killed, 371 wounded and 19 missing on that day and even after re-organization their OR strength on 7 July was only 480.[42] The other battalions of 32nd Division were in much the same state and consequently the Division had been sent north to the area of Bethune and Cambrin where it recuperated and reorganized amid 'conditions of comparative serenity' whilst waiting

40 Crookenden, *Cheshire Regiment in the Great War*, pp. 87-8.

41 TNA WO 153/1265: Days in the Line per Division 1 July-31 October 1916. NB. Some divisions, such as the 36th (Ulster) and 38th (Welsh) Divisions, which had left the Somme area in July would not return as there were insufficient reinforcements available to refill them.

42 Colonel H.C. Wylly, *The Border Regiment in the Great War* (Aldershot: Gale & Polden, 1924), p 85 and TNA WO 95/2403: 11th Border War Diary for July 1916.

for reinforcements.[43] There were frequent minor moves and some spells in the trenches but very little action.

Between 1 August and 22 October, the Lonsdales received 378 men, including a draft of 212 TF soldiers from the 1st Reserve battalion of the Herefordshire Regiment.[44] This draft was a mixture of former TF HS men, who had joined 3/1st Herefordshire between August 1914 and May 1915, and Derby men who had enlisted in the 3/1st Herefordshire Reserve Battalion and had since been called up. Most of the HS men, roughly one third of the draft, were in their late twenties and early thirties and almost all came from Herefordshire. From mid-June 1915 they had been defending the Norfolk coast with the 48th Provisional Battalion where many of them had pre-empted compulsion by signing the IS Obligation before the appointed date of MSA 2: 3064 Pte Joseph Loader and 2786 Pte Henry Pryce signed the IS Obligation at Cromer on 21 June.[45] On 19 July 1916 they had been returned to their parent battalion. The other two thirds of the draft were 'Derby men', mainly from Herefordshire but with a few from Radnorshire, Monmouthshire and South Wales, who had now been called up. Both the HS and the Derby men were compulsorily transferred to 3rd (SR) KSLI on 22 September and, after being medically examined and pronounced 'Fit for Draft', they had become part of a draft of 250 which arrived on 1 October at No 4 IBD in Rouen. They had been earmarked for 5th KSLI, which was then near Arras having left the Somme area in September, but on 11 October some 212 were posted to 11th Border Regiment. Although the KSLI and the Borders belonged to different Military Districts both were recruited in Western Command.

In late October the Lonsdales and the rest of 97th Brigade moved south again, carrying out some training at La Vicogne during the first two weeks of November. The 16th HLI spent the fortnight under canvas in bitterly cold weather, and there is no indication in their war diaries that the other battalions in the Brigade fared any differently.[46] By 15 November 32nd Division was part of Fifth Army, and preparing to take part in the final operations of the Battle of the Ancre. On 17 November, they received orders for an attack on Frankfurt Trench to take place early the following day.[47] The 97th Brigade's objective was to take the Munich Trench, using all four battalions 'by the express desire of the corps'.[48] The Brigade accordingly planned its attack on a frontage of 1125 yards, with its battalions from left to right: 2nd KOYLI, 11th Border, 16th HLI and 17th HLI.

On 17 November, the 32nd Division took over the front-line trenches and later began to move up to the start-line. They had difficulty getting there due to very swampy ground caused by the recent heavy rains and the situation was compounded by the men having no previous knowledge of the area and the layout of trenches.[49] The 11th Border were ready in their trenches by 4:00 am, moved into position on the tape by 5:00 am and at 6:10 am on 18 November the attack was launched. It was not a success. On the right, 17th HLI was checked by rifle and machine

43 T. Chalmers, *History of the 16th H.L.I* (Glasgow: M'Callum & Co, n.d.), p. 47.
44 TNA WO 95/2402: – 2nd KOYLI War Diary; TNA 95/2403: 11th Border War Diary August – October 1916.
45 Service Papers searched using <www.ancestry.co.uk>
46 Ibid p 48.
47 TNA WO 95/2368: Appendix 16A - Narrative of Operations 18 November 1916.
48 *BOH 1916 Vol. 2*, p. 521.
49 TNA WO 95/ 2402: 2nd KOYLI entry for 17/18 Nov 16.

gun fire and to the left 2nd KOYLI and 11th Border were held up by an enemy redoubt. Some Borderers managed to get into Munich Trench and some even reached Frankfurt Trench but were driven back to hold a line about 200 yards in front of it.[50] By noon the attacking force was back in the front line, except for a party of 7 officers and some 120 Other Ranks of 11th Borders and 16th HLI who had reached Frankfurt Trench and would hold two dugouts there for a further few days before being taken prisoner.

The attack had cost 97th Brigade 491 men killed and many others were wounded and missing.[51] The 11th Border had lost 141 men killed, of whom over a third (53) were Herefordshire TF soldiers who had been part of the draft of 212 rushed out just five weeks earlier.[52] It would be tempting to say that the failure of the attack was due to the large proportion of newly arrived former TF HS men in the battalion. Many other reasons might be cited, however, but a key one must be that this was a division that had spent just 10 days on the Somme front line in July before being sent north.[53] Since then it had been effectively rebuilt and having played no part in actions on the Somme during the intervening months had been thrown in November into an attack for which it was patently ill-prepared.

The Battle of the Somme 1916 officially ended on 18 November. It is difficult to say with any certainty how many casualties had been taken by the BEF during its course. The *Official History* shows that the BEF suffered 419,654 casualties up to 30 November 1916, although this includes some absentees who had returned.[54] The *Statistics of the British Military Effort* gives a figure of 498,054 (excluding sick) during the period of the Somme Offensive, of whom 108,724 were dead, 343,431 were wounded and 45,899 missing or prisoners.[55] Prior and Wilson give a total casualty figure of 432,000 for divisions based on an untitled document in the Australian War Memorial.[56] All these figures are at odds with the estimated casualties given at the time in AG GHQ's War Diary:[57]

The disparity between the total figures both during and after the event shows the huge difficulty of obtaining accurate data, which inevitably compounded the problem for those responsible for providing reinforcements. Initially the high battle casualty figures of July, even without including those for the sick, exceeded the number of replacements sent out. It was only in September that the balance started to swing the other way although it was not until December that the number of reinforcements arriving exceeded the total losses for that month. On paper, the overall GHQ figures show that by the end of December some 576,235 reinforcements, not including those for the RA, RE and RFC, had been received from home, enough to cover the

50 TNA WO 95/2368: Appendix 16A.
51 *SGDW*: 2nd KOYLI 107; 16th HLI 162; 17th HLI 81 and 11th Border 141.
52 Ibid 11th Border deaths for 18 November 1916 and *SDGW*.
53 TNA WO 153/1265: Days in the Frontline 1 July-31 October 1916.
54 *BOH 1916 Vol. 1*, p. 497.
55 War Office, *Statistics of the Military Effort of the British Empire*, p. 324.
56 AWM 252/206 'Casualties by divisions', untitled document in the Australian War Memorial, cited by R. Prior & T. Wilson, *The Somme* (New Haven & London: Yale University Press, 2005), p. 204 fn 2 and p. 300.
57 TNA WO 95/26: GHQ AG Branch War Diary for July-December 1916. NB Estimated casualty figures shown are overall whilst the replacement figures do not include those for the RA, RE and RFC.

battle casualties but short of the overall number required when the sick/wastage figures are taken into account.

	July	August	September	October	November	December	Total
Total strength of BEF	1,465,200	1,520,000	1,539,584	1,520,900	1,524,110	1,590,700	
Total battle casualties (k, w, m)	163,602	77,191	110,842	70,812	47,887	11,290	481,624
Total sick wastage	25,723	29,970	37,660	32,209	47,093	55,660	228,315
Total losses	**189,343**	**107,161**	**148,502**	**105,021**	**94,980**	**66,970**	**711,977**
Reinforcements from home (excluding RA, RE and RFC)	108,221	75,845	111,792	88,732	71,786	119,859	576,235
Estimated casualties by Divisions engaged in Active operations (Somme)	151,184	37,485	90,249	31,015	26,604	(no separate figures shown)	336,537

Table 4. Estimated numbers of losses and reinforcements July-December 1916.

The replacement figures were augmented, however, by the sterling work of the medical services in retaining in France many less seriously wounded or sick men who would recover after a short period in hospital or convalescent depot and then be fit to return to duty. A third of all those wounded and over half of the sick were treated and returned to duty within theatre.[58] Whenever possible, men were supposed to be returned to their own units. The policy was reiterated by the IGC on 31 July, namely that as far as possible less seriously wounded cases were to be retained in France for treatment and then to rejoin their own units as soon as they were fit enough.[59] The policy was certainly applied as far as Bert Oakes and George Culpitt were concerned. Bert Oakes had finally arrived with 7th KSLI on 21 July but on 22/23 was buried by a shell bursting over the trench. He survived but was badly shaken and was back at the Base recuperating by 28 July where he remained during early August. He was fit enough to return to his Battalion by mid-August and wrote home on 21 August that he had been in action the previous week 'but

58 *BOH 1916 Vol. 1* pp. 91-94.
59 TNA WO 95/441: Fourth Army A&Q War Diary 16 July 1916 and TNA WO 95/3969: IGC War Diary 31 July 1916.

am glad to say I came through safely although had many narrow escapes'.[60] George Culpitt of 10th RWF had been in action with 3rd Division but in late July was evacuated with influenza. After nearly three weeks in hospital he was declared fit enough to go to the recently established No 5 Convalescent Camp at Cayeux where he spent a further three weeks before being returned to the IBD at Rouen. Those who had been wounded or sick did only light training 'and did not train with the new recruits from England'. After about a week he and eleven others were warned for the line, six each for 10th and 9th RWF. By now it was about 24 September and 10th RWF was near Bethune, where Culpitt was happy to rejoin 'A' Company.[61] Admittedly these are just two men during the early months of the battle, but there is no reason to suppose that they were especially unusual at that time.

Not all the men arriving in France or those who had recovered from slight wounds or sickness could be sent to the front line. Men were medically examined again on arrival at the IBDs and classified as: 'A' fit for General Service; 'TB' Temporary Base until fit for general service; 'PB' Permanent Base but fit enough for service on the LofC and in Army Corps; or 'PU' Permanently Unfit: never likely to become fit for active service but could be employed in the same way as PB men. With the Manning problems back home, there was constant pressure from both the War Office and GHQ for fit men in the Base Areas to be 'combed out' and sent forward to fight, their places being taken by PB men; in July the IGC was employing 16,000 PB replacements at the Bases, Casualty Clearing Stations and the various hospitals. These men could also be employed by Armies at Ammunition Railheads and also to relieve men of fighting units on such duties as 'sanitary fatigues, Officers and Mess Servants, cooks, charge of Divisional recreation rooms etc'.[62]

It was all a bit piecemeal, however, and a definite organization was required to administer the PB men, both on the LofC and with Armies. On 7 September the CinC requested authority from the War Office for the creation of units to administer the PB men at each of the Bases, Le Havre, Rouen, Étaples and Calais. At this point the proposed units were simply intended to organize and administer the constant flow of large numbers of PB men rather than to form them into battalions of a particular size. It was recognized that such units would be less viable with the Armies as the PB men were scattered over very wide areas so there it was proposed to have seven NCOs per 100 PB men and one officer at Army Headquarters, responsible for their administration, periodical re-classification and the replacement of casualties.[63] By early November, however, it had been realized that a more formal organization was needed and battalions of 4,000 and upwards were now created to administer PB men at Le Havre, Rouen and Étaples with a further battalion of up to 2,000 at Calais. On 11 November No 3 Employment Base Depot confirmed the formation of the PB battalion with 4,300 men. Two

60 Letters dated 10, 17, 28 July and 3, 11 and 21 August 1916 from 22219 Pte Bert Oakes; *KSLI History*, p 229.
61 <www.culpitt-war-diary.org.uk/index.htm> Chapter 5.
62 TNA WO 95/3969: IGC War Diary of 22 and 25 July 1916.
63 Ibid., IGC War Diary of 7 and 21 September 1916.

weeks later the camp strength was 1,472 and the 4,906 men of the PB battalion were providing labour for POW camps, Schools of Instruction, Bases and Army Headquarters.[64]

New units were also brought out for work behind the Front line; in August the 2nd Garrison battalions of the Oxfordshire and Buckinghamshire Light Infantry and the Kings Own Yorkshire Light Infantry arrived for employment on traffic control work.[65] Further dedicated labour units, both skilled and unskilled, arrived in the form of Army Service Corps (ASC) Labour Companies and Infantry Labour battalions. By the end of August six more Labour battalions would arrive and the War Office considered that the deficiency of 9,000 unskilled labourers in France would then be practically made good.[66] However, yet more were required and on 5 October the 14th (Labour) Devonshire and the 21st (Labour) Cheshire arrived at Le Havre. Altogether, thirty-three Infantry Labour battalions were formed in 1916 of which thirty went to France for employment mainly on road maintenance.

Other sources of labour included large numbers of German prisoners of war who were formed into companies and set to work, primarily repairing roads, guarded by PB men.[67] A further group were the non-combatants. Although liable for service, these were men who had been accepted by the Tribunals as conscientious objectors. Authority had been given for them to be formed into a Non-Combatant corps for employment on roads, hutting, timber cutting, quarrying, sanitary work, in the loading and unloading of ships and vehicles and in digging, provided it was not in the firing line. Their officers and NCOs were PB Regular Infantry.[68] There were also labour units drawn from various parts of the Empire: India, South Africa, the West Indies and elsewhere. Both the British and the French also recruited large numbers of Chinese labourers. The purpose behind the provision of skilled and unskilled labour was the reduction of demands on the fighting troops whilst out of the line but there was never enough labour to achieve this aim.

Analysis of Battalions' Composition

The total number of deaths during 1916 for Marches battalions on the Western Front, both Regular and TF, was 5,763, an increase of 2,439 over the previous year, reflecting the greater intensity and length of the Somme battle.[69] It is not possible to calculate the total number of casualties but taking the deaths at roughly 20 percent, the total casualties could have been in the region of 28,000. Some of these would have been minor, and their recipients soon treated and returned to duty, but other casualties would have taken longer to recover and some might never again have been fit enough. Whatever the outcome it seems fair to say that the Marches Regiments on the Western Front had probably required well over 20,000 replacements during 1916, the equivalent of over 20 new Infantry battalions. A view of quite where these

64 TNA WO 95/4186: No 3 Employment Base Depot War Diary for November 1916.
65 TNA WO 95/26: GHQ AG War Diary for 18 and 23 August 1916.
66 TNA WO 95/3970: IGC War Diary for 1 August 1916.
67 TNA WO 95/26: GHQ AG War Diary for June-September 1916.
68 *BOH 1916 Vol. 2* p. 67.
69 SDGW figures for Marches Regiments serving in Western European Theatre during 1916.

replacements had been obtained may be gained from detailed analysis of deaths in selected battalions for the period 1 July-30 November 1916.[70]

Details of the enlistment locations for the English battalions are shown in Table 3.1 below.

Enlistment Location	**1st Cheshire**		**9th Cheshire**		**1st KSLI**		**6th KSLI**	
Regimental Area	146	71%	100	66%	66	57%	89	*82%*
Elsewhere in No 4 District (England)	3		7		9		2	
Elsewhere in No 4 District (Wales)	3		3		20		7	
Total enlisted in No 4 District	152	73%	110	72%	95	83%	98	90%
Enlisted in No 3 District	19		8		5		8	
• Liverpool/Manchester	16		19		4		0	
Total Enlisted in Western Command	**187**	**90%**	**137**	**90%**	**104**	**90%**	**106**	**97%**
Northern Command	13		8		2		2	
Southern Command	1		2		2		1	
• Birmingham	1		1		2			
Eastern	2		1		2			
London District	1		3		2			
Scotland/Ireland	2				1			
Overseas								
Total Other Commands	**20**	**10%**	**15**	**10%**	**11**	**10%**	**3**	**3%**
Total Deaths	**207**		**152**		**115**		**109**	

Table 5.1. Enlistment locations of soldiers of selected English Regular battalions who were killed/died between 1 July – 30 November 1916.

For 1st Cheshire enlistments in the regimental recruiting area remained roughly the same at 71 per cent but those for 9th (Service) Cheshire had dropped from 100 percent in 1915 to 66 percent. The figures for those recruited in No 4 District, however, remain around 72 percent and in both cases the numbers enlisted in Western Command were 90 percent, largely due to the proximity in No 3 District of the conurbations of Liverpool and Manchester and the rest of Lancashire. Similarly, the composition of the KSLI remained recognisably similar to earlier

70 Tables drawn from SDGW figures for the Western European Theatre between 1 July-30 November 1916.

years. Enlistments in the Regimental area had dropped for both 1st and 6th KSLI but those in Western Command as a whole stood at 90 and 97 percent respectively. Some 17 percent of 1st KSLI had been recruited in Wales reflecting its proximity to mid-Wales and fewer men were recruited from No 3 District.

Poor recruiting in Wales made reinforcements for the two Welsh regiments more problematical although greater efforts were being made to post Welsh recruits to Welsh regiments.

Enlistment Location	**2nd RWF**		**9th RWF**		**1st SWB**		**10th SWB**	
Regimental Area	44	23%	28	22%	54	45%	46	94%
Elsewhere in No 4 District (England)	18		12		6		1	
Elsewhere in No 4 District (Wales)	43		41		21		2	
Total enlisted in No 4 District	105	54%	81	64%	81	67%	49	100%
Enlisted in No 3 District	16		3		4			
• Liverpool/Manchester	9		6		2			
Total Enlisted in Western Command	**130**	**67%**	**90**	**71%**	**87**	**72%**	**49**	**100%**
Northern Command	9		17		10			
Southern Command	12		3		2			
• Birmingham	26		11					
Eastern	2		1		4			
London District	15		4		17			
Scotland/Ireland	1				1			
Overseas								
Total Other Commands	**65**	**33%**	**36**	**29%**	**34**	**38%**		
Total Deaths	**195**		**126**		**121**		**49**	

Table 5.2. Enlistment locations of soldiers of selected Welsh Regular battalions who were killed/ died between 1 July-30 November 1916.

By late July 1916 2nd RWF had become recognisably more Welsh with 46 percent having enlisted in Wales as opposed to 32 percent in 1915. In 1915, 45 percent of those who died had enlisted in Southern Command, mainly from the Birmingham area, but this had decreased to 19 percent in 1916. Western Command enlistments had risen to 67 and 71 percent for 2nd RWF and 9th RWF respectively. Conversely, some 62 percent of 1st SWB had enlisted in Wales, a slight drop on the 1915 figures, and 72 percent in Western Command. The 10th SWB had arrived in France in December 1915 and its 1916 deaths were those of original Kitchener recruits, all except one of whom had enlisted in Wales.

The figures for those born in Cheshire (see Table 3.3) were more varied but again comparison of those born in Western Command show that the percentages remain high at 78 percent for 1st Cheshire and 81 percent for 9th Cheshire. The Cheshire Regular battalions thus remained recognisably the same as they had always been. Births in the regimental area and Western Command for 1st and 6th KSLI also remained similar across 1915 and 1916.

Birth location	**1st Cheshire**		**9th Cheshire**		**1st KSLI**		**6th KSLI**	
Regimental Area	92	44%	79	52%	57	50%	74	*68%*
Elsewhere in No 4 District (England)	5		5		8		2	
Elsewhere in No 4 District (Wales)	9		5		11		4	
Total born in No 4 District	106	51%	89	59%	76	66%	80	73%
Born in No 3 District	25		16		7		7	
• Liverpool/Manchester	30		18		3		1	
Total Born in Western Command	**161**	**78%**	**123**	**81%**	**86**	**75%**	**88**	**81%**
Northern Command	19		11		6		6	
Southern Command	2		4		5		3	
• Birmingham	2		1		1		2	
Eastern	3		5		2		5	
London District	6		2		2			
Scotland/Ireland	6		2		1		3	
Overseas								
Total Other Commands	**40**		**25**		**17**		**19**	
Location of Birth Unknown	6		4		12		2	
Total Deaths	**207**		**152**		**115**		**109**	

Table 5.3. Birth locations of soldiers of selected English Regular battalions who were killed/died between 1 July-30 November 1916.

It is thus fair to say that both the English county regiments in the Marches remained remarkably homogeneous in late 1916.

The picture changes again for those born in Wales, however, since in 1916 fewer than half the soldiers from either 2nd or 9th RWF battalion had actually been born there, although the surnames of most were Welsh (see Table 3.4). Roughly half of 1st and 10th SWB had been born in Wales, many of the rest having been born just across the border in Gloucestershire or else in London. The composition of the Welsh battalions thus reflects both regional recruiting problems and the growing emphasis on posting Welsh recruits to Welsh regiments. Roughly one third had enlisted in England for service in Welsh battalions but scrutiny of the Medal Index Cards (MIC) does not as yet indicate previous operational service in English battalions for these men.

Birth location	2nd RWF		9th RWF		1st SWB		10th SWB	
Regimental Area	53	27%	26	21%	31	26%	24	49%
Elsewhere in No 4 District (England)	17		9		7		3	
Elsewhere in No 4 District (Wales)	26		33		22		4	
Total born in No 4 District	96	49%	68	54%	60	50%	31	63%
Born in No 3 District	15		7		9		0	
• Liverpool/Manchester	7		4		1		0	
Total Born in Western Command	**118**	**61%**	**79**	**63%**	**70**	**58%**	**31**	**63%**
Northern Command	18		22		10		2	
Southern Command	19		10		12		12	
• Birmingham	14		6		1			
Eastern	3		6		4		1	
London District	11		1		18		1	
Scotland/Ireland	6				3		1	
Overseas					1			
Total Other Commands	**71**		**45**		**49**		**17**	
Location of Birth Unknown	6		2		2		1	
Total Deaths	**195**		**126**		**121**		**49**	

Table 5.4. Birth locations of soldiers of selected Welsh Regular battalions who were killed/died between 1 July – 30 November 1916.

The Marches were a fertile recruiting ground for the TF and consequently, with the exception of 1/4th RWF, Table 3.5. shows a continuing high percentage of enlistments from within the regimental areas. Although less than half of 1/4th RWF had enlisted in the Regimental area, roughly two-thirds had at least enlisted in Wales. This probably reflects traditional custom in crossing county and regimental boundaries. For example, the Stockport-based 1/6th Cheshire had always contained men from Glossop in Derbyshire, nineteen of whom show up as the 17 per cent enlisted in Northern Command. Overall, in 1916 TF enlistments from within No 4 District remained almost universally high.

TF Enlistment Locations	1/5th Cheshire		1/6th Cheshire		1/4th RWF		1/1st Monmouths		1/2nd Monmouths	
Regimental Area	104	*93%*	90	*78%*	20	*49%*	34	*92%*	64	*91%*
Elsewhere in No 4 District (England)	5		4		2		1			
Elsewhere in No 4 District (Wales)			1		7		1		5	
Total enlisted in No 4 District	109		95	83%	29	71%	36	97%	69	99%
Enlisted in No 3 District	1								1	
• Liverpool/ Manchester			1							
Total Enlisted in Western Command	**110**	**98%**	**96**	**83%**	**29**	**71%**	**36**	**97%**	**70**	**100%**
Northern Command	2		19	(17%)	5					
Southern Command										
• Birmingham										
Eastern					7		1			
London District										
Scotland/Ireland										
Overseas										
Total Other Commands	**2**	**2%**	**19**	**17%**	**12**	**29%**	**1**	**3%**		
Total Deaths			**115**		**41**		**37**		**70**	

Table 5.5. Enlistment locations of soldiers of selected TF battalions who were killed/died between 1 July – 30 November 1916.

The birth locations for TF soldiers are more scattered, as shown in Table 3.6. although the large number of unknown places of birth for some of the battalions make it difficult to draw any firm conclusions. It had not been a requirement to note places of birth on enlistments before the war.

Birth locations	1/5th Cheshire		1/6th Cheshire		1/4th RWF		1/1st Monmouths		1/2nd Monmouths	
Regimental Area	75	*67%*	48	*42%*	12	*29%*	23	*62%*	28	*40%*
Elsewhere in No 4 District (England)	5		4		2		2		2	
Elsewhere in No 4 District (Wales)	2				6		2		11	
Total born in No 4 District	**82**	**73%**	**52**	**45%**	**20**	**49%**	**27**	**73%**	**41**	**59%**
Born in No 3 District	7		9							
• Liverpool/ Manchester	6		8				1			
Total Born in Western Command	95	85%	69	60%	20	49%	28	76%	41	59%
Northern Command	5		16	(14%)	7				4	
Southern Command	5		1				2		6	
• Birmingham					1					
Eastern	1				3		1			
London District	1				1		1		2	
Scotland/Ireland			1				1		1	
Overseas	2						1		1	
Total Other Commands	**14**		**18**		**12**		**6**		**14**	
Location of Birth Unknown	3		28		9		3		15	
Total Deaths	**112**		**115**		**41**		**37**		**70**	

Table 5.6. Birth locations of soldiers of selected TF battalions who were killed/died between 1 July – 30 November 1916.

Of those whose birth locations are known, however, fewer had actually been born within the Regimental areas and Western Command.

Developments at Home July-December 1916

During the second half of 1916, the continuing demand for casualty replacements together with the longer term requirement for future recruits meant that manpower remained at the forefront of both the Army Council's and the Government's attention at home. There were two aspects to be addressed: reorganization of the training and drafting organization and the longer term management of the nation's manpower for the future.

Creation of the Training Reserve

The reinforcement process was working but there was room for further refinement within the Home training and drafting organization. The move towards reinforcement by regiment rather than battalion earlier in the year, with the consequent streamlining of Base Depots in France during June/July, prompted re-organization of the home draft-finding units. In early August it was announced that a new Infantry corps, to be known as the Training Reserve (TR), would be created on 1 September.[71]

The main Regimental reserves, the SR, the ER where they existed, and the TF Reserve battalions, were to remain in their current forms and continue to provide drafts for the battalions of the regiments they supported. They were to be brought up to strength immediately with men from their respective Second and Local Reserve battalions and thereafter were always to be kept at full strength by being allocated recruits as required from the Infantry general service recruits raised in their regimental areas. When a regiment's reserve battalions were full, surplus recruits would firstly be allocated to other regiments of the same Command which had been unable to obtain sufficient recruits from their respective recruiting areas. Once all the Command's regimental reserves were full, surplus recruits who had enlisted within its recruiting areas, would be posted to TR battalions affiliated to it. The ACI initiating the new organization was very clear that only when insufficient trained men were available from the Regimental Reserves would they be drawn from a TR battalion.

The battalions of the new corps were to be formed from the former Second Reserve and Local Reserve battalions which would now lose their regimental designations and be numbered consecutively as TR battalions. They would, however, be affiliated to the Districts within a Command. From 1 September men remaining in them after the regimental reserves had been filled received new regimental numbers, prefixed by 'TR/', the number of the District in which the Record Office of the unit was situated and then the actual number eg TR/4/12345.

The existing Reserve Infantry Brigades were now reduced to twenty-four, each containing between four and six TR battalions, and with an overall establishment of 208,500. This reduction in number necessitated the disbandment of nearly a quarter (33) of the 145 Second and Local Reserve battalions, and was inevitably unpopular as was the loss of regimental designations. In the Marches area, four RWF battalions were combined into two TR battalions but otherwise the changes for No 4 District units were simply of nomenclature with the brigading and locations remaining the same. The 9th (Reserve) KSLI, for example, now became the 48th TR battalion but remained within 11th Reserve Brigade at Prees Heath.[72] In total, 29 TR battalions were affiliated to Western Command, 14 for No 4 District and 15 for No 3 District. Those for No 4 District continued to be located at Prees Heath and Kinmel Park but the TR battalions serving No 3 District remained more scattered with five at Altcar in Lancashire, five at Prees Heath and two apiece at Cannock Chase and Wareham in Dorset and one at Seaford in East Sussex.

The TF Reserve was also to be reorganized and rationalized. The 194 TF Reserve battalions in their 14 Groups became, through amalgamations, 87 battalions in 14 TF Reserve Brigades.[73] For the Marches this meant the absorption of the 5th, 6th and 7th TF (Reserve) battalions

71 TNA WO 123/58: AO 259 of 1 August 1916 and WO 293/5: ACI 1528 of 6 August 1916.
72 See Appendix III.
73 Mitchinson, *Defending Albion*, p. 142.

NCOs of 64th Training Reserve Battalion at Kinmel Park, Flintshire. (RWF Archives)

Gym staff of 57th Training Reserve Battalion at Kinmel Park, Flintshire. (RWF Archives)

of both the Cheshire and the RWF by their respective 4th (Reserve) battalions; 1st (Reserve) Monmouthshire absorbed its 2nd and 3rd Reserve Battalions. All the No 4 District TF (Reserve) battalions remained part of the Welsh Reserve Brigade TF based at Park Hall near Oswestry.

It is clear from careful reading of the whole of ACI 1528 that the intention was to preserve regimental and territorial connections as far as possible, with TR men being drafted only to those battalions which could not be reinforced by men from their own regimental reserves. The wording of the first paragraph of ACI 1528, however, that 'the recruits ... appointed to the training reserve ... will be available for drafting when trained to any regiment overseas requiring drafts' inadvertently encouraged misperceptions as to the purpose of the new corps which would be repeated in works written after the war. In writing of 1st Cheshire's reinforcements in late July/August 1916, the Regimental historian ignored the ACI's subsequent statement that 'there will be retained as regimental reserves in each regiment the [SR, ER and TF] battalions' and noted inaccurately that in future 'Battalions were to receive men from a pool formed by recruits and reinforcements from units whose recruiting areas were contiguous' which it was felt would destroy 'esprit de corps'.[74] He was not alone: Captain Dunn's comment that the rumour that some 'hairy-eared theorist' had told the new War Lord 'that the way to win was to destroy the Regiment ... and nationalize the Army' subsequently proved to be true, has often been quoted by more recent writers.[75] At the dates referred to by both these writers, however, the TR had yet to come into being and its true impact remained to be seen. In the event, some Regiments would find little difficulty with the new TR battalions: the KSLI noting that 'when the personnel [of 49th TR Battalion] became mixed with officers and men of other regiments, the spirit and traditions of the KSLI were always preserved'.[76]

Monthly posting ACIs had been started in January 1916 to give details of the distribution of recruits. Further weight to the continuing emphasis on regimental connections is given in the amendments now made to show that men fit for general service and appointed to the Infantry were to be posted firstly to the 'Regimental Infantry Reserves (Reserve, Extra Reserve and TF Reserve battalions including dismounted yeomanry reserves') and secondly the Training Reserve.[77] Maintenance of the emphasis, however, relied on there being sufficient recruits for all regiments.

Creation of the Manpower Distribution Board

The main conflicting demands for manpower in the longer term were those of the War Office and the Ministry of Munitions and there was some concern when on 8 July, following the death of Lord Kitchener in June, Lloyd George moved from Munitions to become Secretary of State for War. Within a couple of weeks, however, and much to Macready's relief, he had been persuaded that many men employed on munitions could be spared for the Army without

74 Crookenden, *History of the Cheshire Regiment in the Great War*, p. 77.
75 Dunn, *The War the Infantry Knew*, p. 245 diary entry for 28 July 1916.
76 Wood, *King's Shropshire Light Infantry in the Great War 1914 – 1918,* p. 323.
77 TNA WO 293/4: ACI 212 of 1916 Posting recruits of Groups 6, 6, 8 and 9 of Class B Army Reserve and WO 293/5: ACI 1839 of 23 September 1916 Posting recruits who are called up from Class B Army Reserve, or who come forward for service before being called up, on or after 1 October 1916.

jeopardizing the output of material.[78] On 28 July the Army Council, including Lloyd George, decided that the War Office should press for the creation of a strong central committee to organize the distribution of manpower, and that a sound working agreement should be reached with the Ministry of Munitions over the release of skilled men from the military for civil work.[79] Macready had first proposed a strong central committee for the distribution of manpower in May 1916 but nothing had come of it.[80] He now re-submitted the proposal for a small Board, with a Chairman and two civilian Members, 'able to determine the relative importance of competing demands and [possessing] powers of final and absolute decision as to the allocation of men available', in a Memorandum to the Cabinet on 2 August.[81] The War Committee discussed the matter favourably on 5 August, creating a small committee to draft Terms of Reference for what would become the Manpower Distribution Board (MPDB).[82] Specifically, the Board was to:

> [D]etermine all questions arising between Government Departments relating to the allocation or economic utilization of manpower for the purpose of the successful prosecution of the war and … to direct the Government Departments concerned to create the machinery necessary to co-ordinate their activities in regard to the distribution or utilization of men and women.

It was also to decide on the feasibility of any future large-scale demand for manpower by any Department. Although agreement to its creation had been given, it would be 12 September before its composition was finally agreed and work could begin; by now it had grown to five members. The Army Council considered it was all taking too long and Robertson continued to stress the need for urgency. Recruiting was the 'reverse of satisfactory' with a large number of men rejected as unfit and many employers releasing older men rather than the younger ones needed. Some 400,000 men would be required by 15 March 1917 to keep the present number of divisions up to strength and provide for RA and RFC expansion.[83]

On 26 September, Macready and Brigadier-General Auckland Geddes, Director of Recruiting, informed the MPDB that British forces in France were short of 80,000 men and it was estimated that no more than 105,000 would be sent to France over the next three months. Macready blamed the shortage on the lack of co-ordination between departments, the demands of the Ministry of Munitions and the actions of the Tribunals.[84] Over the next few days evidence was taken from Government Departments and the MPDB's first report was submitted

78 Macready, *Annals of an Active Life, Vol. 1*, p. 252.
79 TNA WO 33/881: Minutes of the 184th Meeting of the Army Council held on 28th July 1916.
80 Macready, *Annals of An Active Life, Vol. 1*, p. 253.
81 TNA CAB 37/153/12: Memorandum on Proposed Establishment of a Manpower Distribution Board.
82 TNA CAB 37/153/19: War Committee Meeting of 5 August 1916 and CAB/37/154/11 War Committee Meeting of 22 August 1916.
83 TNA CAB 37/155/17: War Committee Meeting 12 September 1916 and Appendix III dated 11 September 1916.
84 IWM: MPDB 77/66/1, Manpower Distribution Board, First Day, evidence of C.F N. Macready, 26 September 1916, cited in Grieves, *Politics of Manpower*, pp. 45-7.

to the War Committee on 3 October.[85] There would be two subsequent reports, on 12 October and 9 November respectively, but ultimately Macready felt that 'nothing effective developed from its activities'.[86] The situation between the War Office and the Ministry of Munitions was eventually resolved through a series of bi-lateral meetings between Montagu, the Minister for Munitions, and Lord Derby and agreement that, through a process of de-badging, some 50,000 semi-skilled and unskilled munition workers, aged under 30, could be made available for general military service by the end of January 1917.[87] Their places in munitions factories would be filled by substituting women and men unfit for general service. Most importantly, there was to be 'close co-operation' between the two Ministries.[88] However, this addressed only part of the problem.

In France, planning for the following year had already begun. The Allied military heads agreed at Chantilly in mid-November that minor operations would continue over the winter whilst coordinated offensives on the Western Front were planned to start again in the spring with attacks by the French between the Oise and the Somme, and by the British between Bapaume and Arras. Joffre, the French Commander-in-Chief, intended that they should be ready to launch the joint offensives by 1 February. Haig felt he could, if necessary, launch attacks in February but would much prefer to wait until May when the BEF would be in a better position. It had to be a joint decision so it was agreed that both the British and French should be ready by the first fortnight of February but that so long as the enemy remained contained they might delay the offensives until a more favourable date.[89]

That gave a scant three months to rebuild the BEF ready for an early Spring offensive. Haig raised the question of future reinforcements in a report to Robertson dated 21 November, which the latter attached as an Appendix to a note to Lloyd George.[90] The Infantry strength of the 55 divisions on the Western Front was 576,079 against an establishment of 689,680, although 22,881 reinforcements at the Base reduced the deficit to 90,500. Looking ahead to 1 March 1917 it was estimated that some 302,500 infantrymen would be needed to provide a surplus of 10 per cent with units, cover estimated winter wastage of 113,000 and enable adequate drafts to be available at the Base on 1 March 1917. Haig continued to regard 'the prospects of success on this front next year as most favourable' but emphasized that the first essential was 'an adequate supply of men, sufficiently trained, and on the spot, to fill vacancies in the ranks immediately they occur'.

The Army Council recognized the need to set its own house in order and on 24 November discussed the need to scrutinize men employed at home: as at 1 November there were nearly 400,000 men employed within Home Forces. Macready was tasked to reduce this number by 100,000 by the end of current year. It was also proposed to send a senior officer 'familiar with the man-power situation and the difficulties which have to be overcome in providing reinforcements for the fighting troops' to France to examine the number of fit men employed on

85 TNA CAB 37/157/4: War Committee Meeting 3 October 1916 and Appendix dated 29 September 1916.
86 Macready, *Annals of an Active Life, Vol. 1*, p. 253.
87 TNA CAB 37/159/48: War Committee Meeting 17 November 1916.
88 TNA CAB 37/160/33: War Committee Meeting 30 November 1916.
89 *BOH 1917 Vol. 1*, pp. 9-10, 24.
90 TNA CAB 37/160/15: Memo by CIGS to Secretary of State dated 24 November 1916.

the LofC and at the Bases with a view to their replacement by others. Finally, it was agreed that Macready was to prepare 'a complete survey of the recruiting prospects for the next 12 months' for submission by the Army Council to the War Committee.[91]

Macready's survey took the form of a strongly worded Memorandum on the Supply of Men for the Army which warned that:

> [U]nless steps are taken at once by His Majesty's Government to introduce some better system of utilizing the manhood of the nation untrammelled by conditions that in practice now nullify to a great extent the objects of the Military Service Acts, it will be impossible after April next to keep the armies up to strength.[92]

It was estimated that, with the monthly intake running some 20,000 below requirements, the total number of recruits obtained in 1916 would be 95,000 below the number agreed the previous February. The Army's anticipated requirement for 1917 was 940,000 men and a further 250,000 to 350,000 would be required by Munitions. To raise these numbers, it was suggested that all men up to 55 'should be utilized for such national service as HM Government deem to be essential to the effective prosecution of the war'. The Army Council submitted the memorandum to Lloyd George for presentation to the War Committee but he, presumably for reasons of his own, now decided that it should be sent by the Military Members only so that the 'Parliamentary members of the Army Council (held) themselves free to press its adoption on the Cabinet'.[93]

Matters were reaching a head. The MPDB may not have made universally accepted or indeed effective proposals but a passage in its Third Report initiated a step towards national service. On 30 November the War Cabinet agreed unanimously that the military situation overall was such that the time had come 'for the adoption of compulsory national service' for all men up to the age of 60.[94] It was hoped that once the necessary details had been worked out the necessary legislation could be enacted before Christmas but this did not happen, not least because on 5 December Asquith resigned as Prime Minister. His place would be taken by Lloyd George, who in turn would be replaced at the War Office by Lord Derby. The fall of Asquith's government would delay consideration of compulsory national service until 1917.

Overview of 1916

Much had changed during the year as the demand for men became ever greater. The first tentative moves in January towards compulsory service for single men under the age of 41 had by December approached the realization that national service was required to ensure that best

91 TNA WO 33/881: Minutes of 194th Meeting of Army Council on 20 November 1916.
92 TNA CAB 37/160/25: Memorandum by the Military Members of the Army Council to the Secretary of State for War dated 28 November 1916.
93 Macready, *Annals of an Active Life, Vol. 1*, pp. 253-4.
94 TNA CAB 37/160/7: War Committee Meeting 21 November 1916 and CAB 37/160/33 War Committee Meeting 30 November 1916 (the President of the Board of Trade was the only absentee at the meeting of 30 November 1916).

use could be made of the nation's population. How quickly and in what form this might be implemented remained to be seen, however.

The legislation that brought about compulsory service for both single and married men had also had a major effect on the TF, allowing TF soldiers for the first time to be transferred without their consent between units and corps, and into Regular units. This legislation had enabled TF replacements, many of them former HS and Derby men, to be used to fill gaps caused by Somme casualties. The side-effect, however, was deep-seated resentment against the way in which their terms of service had been changed which would continue to fester for years.

The need for men had also prompted re-consideration of how existing Army manpower should be used. The Medical Services had played a significant part in this by introducing more accurate classifications enabling better use of less-fit men in order to release fit men to fight. Improvements had also been made in the treatment of casualties, enabling more men to be returned to duty in theatre.

The Army's procedures for casualty reporting and demanding replacements had continued to prove effective under the severe testing of the Somme but a need to streamline the reinforcement organization had been identified before the battle started. Replacements were now drawn from regiments rather than battalions and the Base Depots had been re-organized to implement this. At Home further streamlining of the Reserve organization had occurred in September. Regimental reserves continued to be maintained as the first port of call for replacements but once the regimental reserves were full surplus recruits could fill up other neighbouring regiments; only when all the Command's regimental reserves were full would surplus recruits be sent to the new TR battalions for use where needed. Despite perceptions in the Army at large, however, emphasis remained on preserving regimental affiliations.

Analysis of selected battalions from the Marches regiments during the period 1 July to 30 November shows their composition remaining remarkably similar to that of earlier years. The English county regiments continued virtually the same whilst the Welsh battalions had become more Welsh. The numbers enlisted in the parent Command remained high overall: over 67 percent of those who died had enlisted in Western Command and nine of the fourteen battalions analysed showed 90 percent or higher.

By the end of 1916, manpower remained problematical but steps had been started towards its better use across the nation. The Army was attempting to make better use of the men that it had but as yet there is no evidence that the localized regimental system was being eroded, either by design or circumstances.

5

The 'Man Question'

The provision of manpower for the Army would become increasingly difficult during 1917 as the Government struggled to find means by which the labour requirements of the nation's industries could be balanced with the demands from the War Office. This chapter outlines the War Cabinet's continuing attempts to address the manpower problem without actually resorting to universal compulsion and the Army Council's various efforts to make better use of the manpower that it did have. Inevitably, some of the decisions and actions taken would cause tension between the Government and the Military hierarchy and also between the War Office and GHQ in France. For the sake of coherence, some initiatives, such as the implementation of the Lawson Report and the employment of women, have been approached as discrete topics rather than attempting to split them between home and France. It remains more appropriate, however, to consider chronologically the events on the Western Front and their impact on manpower so these are covered in the next chapter.

Tentative Steps towards National Service

In late November 1916 the War Committee had agreed, albeit reluctantly, to the introduction of compulsory national service for all men up to the age of 60 and to the drafting of the necessary legislation.[1] Any further action was delayed, however, by the fall of the Government on 5 December. Lloyd George was to become the new Prime Minister, but it appeared that his previous interest in the Army's manpower whilst Secretary of State for War had now waned. Robertson, in writing to General Sir Charles Monro, complained:

> The one thing I cannot get [the War Cabinet] to touch is the question of men and that happens to be the most important of all. Before Lloyd George became Prime Minister he was very keen on the Man Question. He now declines to touch it.[2]

1 TNA CAB 37/160/7: War Committee Meeting 21 November 1916 and CAB 37/160/33 War Committee Meeting 30 November 1916.
2 K. Grieves, *The Politics of Manpower* (Manchester: Manchester University Press, 1988), p. 90, citing

The new War Cabinet formed by Lloyd George comprised just five members: himself; Lord Curzon, the Leader of the House of Lords; Andrew Bonar Law, the Chancellor of the Exchequer; Arthur Henderson, representing the Labour Party; and Lord Milner. Only Bonar Law had Departmental responsibilities; the other three had no specific portfolios. Neither Lord Derby, who had succeeded Lloyd George as Secretary of State for War, nor Dr. Addison, the Minister for Munitions, were now Cabinet members and consequently attended Cabinet meetings only in an advisory capacity when the topics under discussion fell within their respective remits.

On 14 December 1916, the draft bill introducing compulsory National Service, that had been initiated by the previous administration, was discussed by the newly constituted War Cabinet but no firm conclusions could be reached since Lloyd George was not present. All that emerged was a 'useful preliminary survey of the question' and provisional agreement was given to the appointment of a Director-General of National Service (DGNS) who would take charge of both military and civilian compulsory National Service.[3] By the War Cabinet meeting of 19 December, however, it had already become apparent that resistance from the Labour movement towards anything implying industrial compulsion could jeopardize the existence of the newly created Coalition Government if it were to press ahead with proposals for compulsory National Service. Consequently, it was agreed that voluntary enrolment and transference of labour would continue for the time being; only if the voluntary effort failed would the Government ask Parliament to release them from previous pledges and enable the introduction of measures to make better use of the nation's manpower. No time limit could thus be set for the introduction of compulsion. The creation of a DGNS would go ahead, Neville Chamberlain having been appointed to the post. His first task would be the creation of machinery and processes for voluntary enrolment and transference, albeit in such a way that they could also be used for compulsion should it subsequently prove necessary. During the Cabinet's discussion, Lord Derby wished it placed on record that not less than 100,000 men fit for general service must be obtained during January and that in his opinion it would soon become necessary for the Government to amend the 1916 MSAs.[4] Later that day, Lloyd George made a lengthy speech to the Commons on the new government's war policy. On manpower, he announced Chamberlain's appointment to head up a new Department of National Service but emphasized the voluntary nature of enrolment for the proposed 'industrial army'.[5] It was clear that, for political reasons, compulsion was a long way off.

Although the creation of his new Department of National Service (DNS) had been announced, Chamberlain lacked any clear definition of his powers and responsibilities and could make little headway. Without a parliamentary office, he lacked the authority to confront Government Departments whose autonomy would be affected by greater centralization of manpower control through his Department. Concerned by the lack of progress, Lloyd George called a conference on 12 January at which Chamberlain was tasked to prepare a memorandum setting out proposals for an organization, to operate at both central and local levels, for obtaining and

Robertson's letter to Monro dated 12 January 1917. Robertson mss I32/52, Robertson to Monro, 12 January 1917.

3 TNA CAB 37/161/26: War Cabinet Meeting No 7 of 14 December 1916.

4 TNA CAB 37/161/42: War Cabinet Meeting No 11 of 19 December 1916.

5 <http://hansard.millbanksystems.com/commons/1916/dec/19/prime-ministers-statement>

enrolling National Service Volunteers; the method by which such volunteers could be allocated to different branches of National Service, 'with special regard to the possibility of the same organization being hereafter required for compulsory purposes'; and the measures to be taken to meet the Army's requirements for recruits.[6]

Chamberlain's first report identified, as 'the greatest and most urgent requirement', the need to provide 450,000 men (350,000 Category A and 100,000 Category B and C) for the Army by the end of March if the forces in France were to be maintained during April, May and June.[7] Consequently, he proposed the release for military service of all men aged 18-22 and the cancellation of all Exemption Certificate already issued to men born in the years 1895 – 1898. No further exemptions would be issued to men in these age groups, other than in cases of exceptional hardship or their real importance to the nation in civilian life. Such sweeping measures would inevitably have an impact upon industries vital for both the nation's well-being and the war effort, but Chamberlain could offer no alternative solution in the short time available if the 100,000 men required for January were to be obtained. The withdrawal of such a large number of men from civilian life would create an urgent demand for substitutes which it was proposed to meet by making a 'great patriotic appeal for recruits' which the DNS would allocate to Government Departments and firms as required. The second part of Chamberlain's report outlined proposals for a National Service organization, containing both a Military and a Civil Section. The Military section would be formed by the existing Army Recruiting organization whilst the administration of the Civil scheme would be based on existing Employment Exchange Divisional Areas. The Local Government Board would also be involved so that local authorities' staffs might be used in the enrolment of recruits at town halls. Finally, Chamberlain sought further powers:

> [T]o determine all questions … relating to the organization, utilization and transfer of male and civilian labour for the purpose of providing the necessary man and woman power for naval and military operations … and the continuation and development of industries.

The War Cabinet discussed Chamberlain's report at some length on 19 January.[8] It decided that 100,000 men should be released for General Service by the end of January: 30,000 from agriculture, 20,000 from mining and 50,000 semi-skilled and unskilled men from munitions. The Board of Trade was also tasked to consider measures for releasing a further number of men from the railways. The release for the Army of all men aged 18-22 was also agreed, but with the exception of those employed on work of vital national importance, namely those employed in steel production, in occupations covered by the Trade Card Scheme or in agriculture, mining and quarrying, railway shops, transport work or shipyards. The proposed new National Service Organization was not fully agreed, however, since the Employment Exchanges were to remain under the control of the Ministry of Labour and the War Office's Directorate of Recruiting was not to be transferred to the DNS. Indeed, Macready had lobbied strongly against the

6 TNA CAB 23/1/33: War Cabinet Meeting No 33 of 12 January 1917, Appendix IV: Proceedings of a Conference held on 12 January 1917.

7 TNA CAB 23/1/39: Minutes of War Cabinet Meeting of 19 January 1917, Appendix I: Report by Director General of National Service to the War Cabinet.

8 Ibid., Minutes of 39th War Cabinet Meeting of 19 January 1917.

latter proposal, considering it unsafe to hand over the whole Army Recruiting machine until the DNS was able to assert its authority over all Government departments.[9] Finally, although Chamberlain was given authority to require Government Departments to transfer or release labour, this was subject to appeal to the War Cabinet and thus fell far short of the powers he had requested.

At the same meeting, the War Cabinet also discussed a proposal submitted by Macready to lower the age for call-up from 18 years 7 months to 18 years 1 month, 'for immediate training and to hold them available to be sent abroad before 19, if diminution of other sources of supply of men for the Army renders this course necessary'.[10] An early decision was requested since it would take at least a month's warning when the notices were issued. The change was agreed but in return the War Office was tasked to produce a report on the number, classification and use of the men retained for Home Defence.

The War Cabinet's decisions failed to produce the promised manpower. An Army Council memorandum submitted for the War Cabinet meeting of 5 February noted that only 50,000 recruits fit for General Service had been produced, just half the number required for January. Consequently, the requirement for February had now increased to 170,000 with a further 130,000 and 120,000 needed for March and April respectively; a total of 420,000 Category A men was required by the end of April. Although the Army Council recognized the difficulty of the man-power question and the many conflicting factors affecting Departments other than the War Office, it proposed that legal powers be obtained to cancel all existing exemptions and also 'to compel all men up to the age of 55 or 60 to engage in work of national importance where and when required'.[11] Chamberlain's second report was also before the Cabinet and similarly questioned the War Cabinet's previous decisions: the stipulation regarding excluded occupations had meant that the number of 18 to 22 year olds released had been negligible. The need for 'prompt and drastic measures' was reiterated with the proposal for a short Act of Parliament to cancel all exemptions up to the age of 31. Confronted by these two documents, the Cabinet confirmed their original decision on releasing men aged 18-22 but stopped short of cancelling exemptions, deciding instead to instruct the Home Secretary to draft a Bill providing simply for the review of all Tribunal exemptions held by men aged 31 and under. The War Office was required to provide an estimate of the number of men who might become available for the Army if such a bill were to become law. It was also at this meeting that the War Office was also instructed to consider the effect of reducing the number of battalions in divisions.[12]

9 Macready, Sir N. *Annals of an Active Life, Vol. 1* p. 265.
10 TNA CAB 23/1/39: Appendix II to Minutes of 39th War Cabinet Meeting of 19 January 1917 and WO 293/6 ACI 189 of 31 January 1917 Calling up of men in Groups and Classes A and B.
11 TNA CAB 23/1/55: Minutes of 55th War Cabinet Meeting of 5 February 1917 and Appendices I -Note by the Army Council on the Supply of Men.
12 Ibid., Minutes of 55th War Cabinet Meeting of 5 February 1917 and Appendix II. Having consulted GHQ on the feasibility of reducing the number of battalions per division, the Army Council responded in March that no such reorganization should be made until it had become clearly impossible 'to obtain the number of men required to maintain divisions at their present establishment'.

Failure of War Cabinet's Earlier Decisions

By mid-February, it was patently apparent that some of the Cabinet's earlier decisions had either been ineffective or were causing problems. The Army Council reported back that the number that might be generated by the proposed review of Tribunal exemptions was only 25,000. Furthermore, the Minister for Munitions, Dr. Addison, called attention to the effect on output of the calling up of skilled munition workers. Notices for men aged between 18 and 22 to present themselves for medical examination had been sent in error not only to semi-skilled and unskilled men but also to highly skilled men. The loss of such skilled men would cause problems throughout his area: for example, the likely reduction in the output of brass would mean the loss of 300,000 fuses and 200,000 cartridge cases per week. There were also serious delays in implementing the previously agreed release of 50,000 semi-skilled and unskilled men under the Substitution Scheme due to the slowness of medical examinations. In Barrow, for example, there were 12,000 men ready to be medically examined but a Medical Board had manged to examine only 1,700 during the preceding three weeks. The Munitions Ministry was quite prepared to release the 50,000 men, provided there was a sufficient supply of suitable substitutes, but could make no progress until they knew which men were fit enough for General Service.[13]

Faced with these unwelcome outcomes, the Cabinet created a series of committees, thus further delaying any immediate action.[14] One committee was to examine how many men had actually been made available for the Army by the Cabinet's previous decisions.[15] The proposed bill for the review of Tribunal exemptions was dropped but a small committee under Lord Rhondda was to consider what amendments to the MSAs were necessary and also to frame fresh instructions to Tribunals 'for the purpose of accelerating the release of men for military service'.[16]

Rhondda Committee

Lord Rhondda's committee acted rapidly, producing revised instructions for Tribunals which were approved by the War Cabinet at the beginning of March.[17] The new instructions included the revision of exemptions held by those men up to the age of 31 who were not employed in certain specified occupations. They also reduced, from two months to two weeks, the period within which an application for the renewal of an exemption previously given on the ground of certified

13 TNA CAB 23/1/64: Appendix IV to Minutes of 64th Meeting of War Cabinet on 13 February 1917.
14 Ibid., Minutes of 64th Meeting of War Cabinet on 13 February 1917.
15 Its members were to be Lord Derby (Secretary of State for War), Lord Rhondda (President of the Local Government Board), Dr Addison (Minister for Munitions), Mr Hodge (Ministry of Labour) and Neville Chamberlain (DGNS). They reported on 24 February that the maximum number of general service men made available by previous Cabinet decisions was 50,000.
16 The other members were Lord Derby and Neville Chamberlain.
17 TNA CAB 23/2/2: Minutes of 84th Meeting of War Cabinet on 1 March 1917. The additional members of the Rhondda Committee were the Minister of Munitions, the Secretary for Scotland, the Secretary of State for India, and Mr. David Shackleton, Permanent Secretary to the Ministry of Labour.

occupation might be lodged. The Committee had also produced a draft report on amendments to the MSAs and it was agreed that this should be circulated to the Departments concerned for their consideration. In the meantime, the same Committee, augmented by additional members, was now further tasked to consider and report back on the general position on the supply of men for the Army, the policy to be adopted over future legislation and the modification of existing methods of exemption (including the Trade Card scheme). A small Sub-Committee was to prepare and submit to the main Committee a schedule of the occupations from which men over certain ages should not be withdrawn for military service, with an estimate of the numbers that might be made available if all other forms of protection (apart from Tribunal exemptions) were abolished.

A Bill to create a Ministry of National Service 'for the purpose of making the best use of all persons, whether men or women, able to work in any industry, occupation or service' had finally been submitted in early March. It did not have a particularly easy ride and the ensuing Commons debates continued to foster unease in the War Cabinet over anything that might lead to compulsion. It was eventually passed on 28 March. It conferred no greater powers on Chamberlain, however, and those he had were circumscribed by the inclusion of specific pledges; there would be 'no compulsory employment or transfer of any person in or to any industry, occupation, or service'.[18]

In the meantime, Lord Rhondda's Committee had submitted its second report on 21 March.[19] It was brief but comprehensive. In order to meet the Army Council's requirement for 555,000 men in Categories A and B(i) during April-July, the Committee had found that some 330,000 would have to be taken from protected industries. The removal of this number of men would endanger the supply of essential requirements and they therefore recommended that, during the four months concerned, the number to be released from these industries should be limited to 250,000. This figure was to be made up by stipulated quotas, for example 55,000 from coal mining and 21,000 from the railways. In order to release these men, it would be necessary to ensure 'an adequate supply of reasonable competent substitutes' but the Committee admitted to some doubts as to whether sufficient replacements would be forthcoming without the introduction of compulsion. The majority of its members had felt, however, particularly in the light of the recent discussions in the House of Commons of the National Service Bill, that 'any measure of compulsion … was at present impracticable', preferring instead to support a proposal by the DGNS for special appeals for 'Substitution Volunteers'. Only if, after a further limited period, these appeals could be shown to have failed would the case for compulsion be deemed to be overwhelming.[20] The report also proposed that the Trade Card Scheme should be replaced by a Schedule of Occupations, with age limits and that liability to serve should be extended to friendly aliens of Allied countries resident in in this country with reciprocal arrangements for Allied countries. Finally, a draft Bill containing some minor amendments to the Military Service Acts was attached. In conclusion the Report noted the growing severity of the strain on the manpower of the country, stressing that the number of men taken for military

18 *Public General Acts Passed in the Seventh and Eighth Years of the Reign of King George V* (London: Eyre & Spottiswoode, 1918), pp. 6 & 7: Ministry of National Service Act, 1917.
19 TNA CAB 23/2/21: Appendix II to Minutes of 103rd Meeting of War Cabinet on 23 March 1917.
20 Although Lord Rhondda had signed the report as Chairman, he noted that both he and Shackleton disagreed with the Committee's view on further delaying the introduction of compulsion.

service should be limited to those really needed and that there should be 'the fullest economy in the use of manpower, not only in industry but also in the Army'.

The War Cabinet began its consideration of the Rhondda Report on 23 March.[21] Its first reaction was yet again:

> that it was impossible to proceed with any scheme for the compulsory transfer and allocation of civilian labour until it had been demonstrated by experience that voluntary enrolment … was incapable of yielding the necessary supplies.

It did decide, however, that the Trade Card Scheme should be superseded by a new Schedule of Occupations and age limits but noted that its introduction should be delayed until consultations had been held on how it should be communicated to the Trades Unions and the machinery agreed by which 'workmen engaged in the scheduled industries [should be protected] from wrongful enlistment, with special reference to the case of men employed in shipbuilding and repairing, and marine engineering shops'.

Other matters contained in the report were reserved for later consideration, namely the quotas to be released from the protected industries, the draft Bill to amend the MSAs, the extension of liability for military service to resident aliens of Allied countries and the question of economy in the use of manpower by the Army. To take some of the pressure off the War Cabinet it was subsequently agreed that Lord Milner and Arthur Henderson should be delegated full authority to determine the outstanding questions from the Rhondda Report.[22]

One of the first follow-up actions taken was to introduce in late March a Bill amending the 1916 MSAs but by then it had been reduced to a single clause enabling the medical re-examination of men who had been discharged from the Navy or Army due to disablement or ill-health, previously been rejected for service, or exempted from overseas service.[23] On 5 April, the Military Service (Review of Exceptions) Act 1917 was passed.[24] Although it produced some 70,000 'A' men and 60,000 'B' men for military service during its first six weeks of operation, it was to prove a highly unpopular Act in operation and would subsequently cause questions to be raised almost daily in the Commons.[25] One example given was that of Mr. Sam Leigh of Hyde who had lost his left arm some years previously. He had notified the Military Authorities of this but was still summoned to Chester Castle on 17 May for re-examination 'where he was ordered to strip in the usual way, although it was obvious that the arm was missing, and he could only do it with great difficulty'. Another case cited was that of a former soldier, William Jones of Salford, who had been discharged from the Army in February 1914 as medically unfit for further service but who had subsequently tried on two occasions to re-enlist, each time being rejected on medical grounds due to a heart murmur and varicose veins which left him unable to perform

21 TNA CAB 23/2/21: Minutes of 103rd Meeting of War Cabinet on 23 March 1917.

22 TNA CAB 23/2/26: Minutes of 108th Meeting of War Cabinet on 29 March 1917. It would not be until July that the Military Service (Conventions with Allied States) Act 1917, enabling the conscription of British subjects living abroad and of Allied citizens living in Britain, would be passed.

23 Ibid., Appendix 1.

24 *Public General Acts Passed in the Seventh and Eighth Years of the Reign of King George V* pp. 13–15: Military Service (Review of Exceptions) Act 1917.

25 Figures cited by Grieves, *The Politics of Manpower*, p. 131.

hard physical work of any kind. Despite his documented medical history, he had been passed on 11 May and classified 'A' for service abroad.[26] Many of the examples cited were not necessarily completely accurate but there was sufficient commonality for a growing groundswell of concern over the stringent application of the Act by the Army recruiting authorities. The complaints multiplied to such an extent that at the end of June a Commons Select Committee would be set up to report on the method, conduct, and general administration of medical examinations under the Military Service Acts.[27]

Despite having taken decisions on the advice of the Rhondda Committee, the Cabinet appeared powerless to impose them in full. The release of 55,000 miners had been agreed but this was now reduced to 20,000 on the understanding that the Coal Controller would release as many miners as possible for iron-stone mining and timber cutting. The Schedule of Protected Occupations was also amended to protect men employed in shipbuilding, repairing and marine engineering although Dr Addison placed it on record that this might make it impossible to produce the quota of 124,000 required from Munitions.[28] The expected implementation date of the new Schedule was to be 1 May.

Hankey Memorandum

In mid-April, Maurice Hankey, the Cabinet Secretary, produced a document reviewing the state of the war in all its aspects. He had produced a similar review for Lloyd George when the latter became Prime Minister but since then many things had changed, notably the enemy's adoption of unlimited submarine warfare, the German withdrawal on the Western Front, the entry of America into the war and the Russian revolution. The specific purpose of the new document is unclear, Hankey simply noting that a fresh review might be useful, his 'sole object ... being to indicate the direction in which it is desirable that the War Cabinet should focus its energies'.[29]

It is a lengthy and extensive review, covering recent events, the outlook for the Allies, which is seen as dependent on a solution of the shipping problem, and the military situation within the various theatres. Then comes a shorter section entitled Economic Policy in which Manpower, although identified 'as the most difficult of the problems which the War Cabinet has to face under the economic head', is covered in just three paragraphs (41, 42 and 43). Hankey notes that, as policy in this respect had never been explicitly defined, this might 'in time lead to a difficult parliamentary situation'. Noting specifically the conflicting demands of the War Office and the ever more insistent ones emanating from the shipbuilding industry and agriculture, he comments that, with the increasing probability of a prolonged war, 'the Government feel it to be more and more dangerous to mortgage the future by reducing our manpower by any drastic

26 HC Deb 07 June 1917 vol 94 cc300-4300.
27 HC Deb 26 June 1917 vol 95 cc217-26217.
28 TNA CAB 24/9/37: GT 336 Minutes of a Meeting held on 29 March 1917 in Pursuance of War Cabinet Minute 108 (1) to Determine Outstanding Questions Arising Out of the Report Of Lord Rhondda's Committee.
29 TNA CAB 63/20: Minute by Hankey dated 18 April 1918. It is obvious from other documents in this file that Hankey, as Cabinet Secretary, attempted to influence and organise the work of the War Cabinet

steps'. Some relief might perhaps be obtained from the National Service scheme now being overhauled Lord Milner and Mr Henderson but the number of drafts for the Army would remain low over the summer. In Hankey's opinion: 'relief can eventually only be obtained by the adoption of compulsion … but this is recognised to be difficult in the existing political situation until the voluntary scheme is proved a failure'.

The next two paragraphs, although often cited as evidence of a deliberate policy to keep the Army short of manpower, are nothing like as definite as has been claimed, being heavily caveated with 'it is understood' and 'if this is the policy'. Paragraph 42 states that:

> 42. Although it has never been formulated in the War Cabinet Minutes it is understood that the policy of the Government is first, by keeping the War Office short to compel the soldiers to adopt tactics that will reduce the waste of manpower. … Some British Generals are known to be far more careful of human life than others, and these are not the least successful leaders. The War Cabinet, it is understood, intend to force this fact upon the Higher Command, in order that they in turn may compel subordinate leaders to exercise great care in this matter. …

The same paragraph also goes on to mention the War Cabinet's wishes to see partially fit and 'coloured' [sic] men being substituted for fit men currently being employed behind the lines and the reduction of the number of battalions per division to nine. Paragraph 43 continues:

> 43. If this is the policy of the Government it might be as well to place it on record in the War Cabinet Minutes at an early date. The army is making efforts to adopt part of the policy, and is doing a great deal in the importation of foreign labour, and something, it is understood, in the direction of substitution, but has hitherto resisted the reduction of battalions in a division.

And there the Manpower section ends. Even if it was felt by some War Cabinet members that it should be a matter of policy to keep the Army short of manpower, nothing to that effect was ever placed on record in the War Cabinet's Minutes. Furthermore, there is no evidence that the actions of the War Cabinet were anything other than those of a Government vulnerable to prevailing political pressures and unable at this point to impose its decisions on the great Departments of State. In fact, contrary to the construction that might be placed upon Paragraphs 42 and 43 by taking them out of context, Hankey is actually advocating the early introduction of national compulsion.

Growing Distrust Between the Army Council and the Government

An example of the War Cabinet's dilemmas may be seen in the protracted negotiations necessary to achieve the supersedure of the Trade Card Scheme by the new Schedule of Occupations. The change required lengthy consultations with the Trades Unions and had encountered some opposition, particularly from the Amalgamated Society of Engineers. In late April, the matter was brought back to the War Cabinet and subjected to a lengthy discussion.[30] There was already an atmosphere of general unrest in the country, which had been deepened by the Russian Revolution, and there were fears of strikes if the change was made as planned. A delay of a week would allow the Engineers' Executive further time to consult with its constituencies and also move the date away from the original one which had unfortunately been set as 1 May (Labour Day). This delay, whilst intended to smooth the way with the unions, would, however, cause problems for the Army's recruiting processes as these had already been changed from a geographical to an occupational basis in anticipation of the new approach. The only way the delay could be applied would be to grant a week's leave for all and obtain no recruits for that week, thus effectively delaying the training of about 120,000 men by a week. It was recognised by the War Cabinet that any action that stopped the flow of recruits, when the Army was not only short of drafts but also involved in an offensive, 'was to be deprecated' and that hardship would be caused to those men who had already given up their jobs. The alternative of sticking to the original timing could potentially not only increase resentment amongst the workforce but also cause a strike that would delay shipbuilding and the output of munitions, which would be 'a still greater evil'. The outcome was that, whilst the War Cabinet stood by its earlier decision concerning the new Schedule, its introduction was to be delayed for a week until 7 May and its implementation until 31 May.

By late May Macready, who had no need to keep the Trades Unions on side, considered that the situation had become impossible. He submitted a Memorandum for consideration by the Army Council which clearly showed his frustration with the lack of definitive action over the preceding months. On 12 May the divisions in France had been 82,783 men below strength 'while the outlook with regard to recruiting [was] even worse than that of the supply of drafts'.[31] The bottom line was that by the end of May the number of men required to maintain the Army should have been 570,000 Category A men and 130,000 of other categories. By 28 May, however, only 309,506 Category A men had been recruited; an extra 50,000 had been obtained in other categories, but these had been swallowed up by an expansion in transportation services overseas. Macready proposed: that the War Cabinet should instruct Government Departments to release the quotas agreed in January and March as quickly as possible; that a Bill be passed raising the military age to 45 and subsequently 50 so that older men might then be used to release younger men to fight; the introduction of another Bill to make various changes to the operation of Tribunals; and finally the creation of a statutory limit on the powers of all Government Departments and Tribunals to protect men under 25. He continued to believe that the necessary numbers of men did exist in the country at large but that, unless drastic changes were made to the present methods of obtaining manpower, 'labour troubles would be fostered, the manufacture of war necessities delayed and the recruiting of men who can and should be made available for the Army effectually paralysed'. The Army Council fully endorsed the Memorandum and it was submitted to the War Cabinet by Lord Derby. In his covering note, he complained that it appeared that the Army was now being provided with men only after all the other needs of the nation had been met and that the consequent diminution in its strength would correspondingly reduce the chances of winning the war. Derby endorsed the

30 TNA: CAB 23/2: Minutes of War Cabinet Meeting 127 of 27 April 1917.
31 TNA CAB 24/15/66: Army Council Memorandum by the Adjutant General Regarding the Position and Prospects of Recruiting dated 31 May 1917.

measures outlined by Macready and reiterated the call, that the Army Council had been making since November 1916, for the adoption of a system of general liability for National Service.[32]

The War Cabinet discussed Macready's Memorandum briefly in mid-June but with no outcome, other than a slightly waspish suggestion that 'the Navy and the Army should set an example by releasing for active service all their officers and men of military age who are engaged upon work of an easy nature which could be just as efficiently done by men who are over military age'.[33] Neither side felt that the other was really trying to help find a solution. From the Army Council's perspective, during the first half of 1917 the War Cabinet's consideration of the manpower problem had appeared to consist solely of examination of the DGNS's various recommendations and their referral to 'committees without end [which] sat and investigated the needs of various trades and requirements of Government departments (and) recommendations were made only to be put aside or watered down owing to pressure from various interests'. In short, 'much apparent activity [was] displayed, but the net result of it all was that the men were not forthcoming …'.[34]

The Army Council members were not the only people frustrated by the 'Man Question'. In his Tenth Report, a disgruntled Chamberlain complained that men were still not being released for the Army.[35] In accordance with the Rhondda Report, his Department had been preparing the necessary processes for obtaining and allocating substitutes to take the place of the men who would be released but there had been no demand for them and nor did there appear to be 'any likelihood of such a demand in the near future'. This had led him to consider the whole position of his Department. The proposals made in his First and Second Reports had either not been acted upon or circumscribed in such a way that the results were negligible. He reiterated his conviction that the only policies which would quickly provide the men required for the Army were the cancellation of Government exemptions for men in the younger age classes and the introduction of calling up of men for military service by age groups without regard to occupation, and subject only to Tribunal appeals. If such decisions were not taken, he could see no prospect of demands being made on his National Service organization, nor could he see any justification for the continued existence of his Department.

By now, it was proving difficult for anyone who had not been involved from the start to keep track of the various manpower deliberations. The War Cabinet had recently been augmented by the addition of George Barnes, a Labour Minister, and in early July his Private Secretary, G. M. Hodgson, attempted to compile a general review of Manpower.[36] Tellingly, he noted that the subject was 'one of the utmost difficulty, as events (had) not followed one another in any ordered sequence', and hoped that his memorandum might be useful 'as a guide to our contemporaries and a warning to those who come after us'. It was a comprehensive document which Maurice Hankey, the Cabinet Secretary, asked to be circulated to the War Cabinet and

32 Ibid., Army Council Memorandum Regarding the Position and Prospects of Recruiting submitted to the War Cabinet by the Secretary of State for War on 7 June 1917.

33 CAB 23/3/10 Minutes of 163rd Meeting of War Cabinet of 14 June 1917.

34 Macready, Sir N. *Annals of an Active Life, Vol. 1,* pp. 263-4.

35 CAB 24/17/76 Tenth Report of the Director General of National Service to the War Cabinet dated 22 June 1917.

36 TNA CAB 24/19/97: Memorandum on Man Power dated 12 July 1917.

all officers concerned in Manpower.[37] It is of note that it makes no reference to any intentional policy, written or unwritten, of keeping the War Office short of manpower.

Only two Cabinet Members, Lord Milner and George Barnes, were present on 13 July when the War Cabinet discussed Chamberlain's Tenth Report.[38] It was suggested that it was still too early to tell the effect of the Rhondda Committee's proposals which had been in effect only since May and it seemed likely that matters might be delayed yet again. In discussing the position regarding recruiting, however, the Army's Director of Recruiting, Brigadier-General Auckland Geddes, tried a different approach. He stated that there was a disproportionately large number of younger men amongst the 3,900,000 men of military age remaining in civilian employment in Great Britain. In his opinion, the existing policy was hitting older men, many of whom were professionals or had their own businesses and were married, whilst the younger men, the majority of whom were unmarried, 'had been caught in the factory system, [and] were being protected'. He considered that the policy being forced upon the War Office was 'anti-national' in that it was actually fostering antagonism. Not only was there no possibility of maintaining the Army under the existing system but it was also 'destroying the independent class of the nation and protecting those not so worthy of being preserved'. His views were endorsed by Macready; the Army wanted the younger men but the recruiting situation was so serious, in terms of the numbers obtained, that the 'Army authorities could not afford to reject any man they could legally obtain, however, old he might be'. After further discussions with the representatives of the key industries concerned, it was agreed that the recent undertakings given to the Trades Unions had further complicated the whole problem of recruitment and substitution. The question of what action should be taken on Chamberlain's Tenth Report would be left for discussion by a fuller meeting of the War Cabinet.

In an effort to end the deadlock, Geddes undertook a comprehensive analysis of the factors affecting recruiting in a modern industrial state. Although he had had military experience during the Boer War, Geddes was by profession a surgeon and brought a civilian outlook to his role as Director of Recruiting. He had been involved in the earlier creation of the Trade Card scheme and was present at many of the trades union meetings with the War Office and at the frequent bi-lateral talks with the Ministry of Munitions. As such he had a broader outlook than a purely military one and was able to understand the political context surrounding the allocation of labour and its effect on the country as a whole. The paper he now produced was broken down into four parts: Theory, Administrative Principles, the Existing Position and Practical Steps.[39] The key proposal contained in the final section was the transformation of the administration of recruiting from one based on age to one based on occupation. If this was agreed, he believed it could be carried out in about two months. He also proposed the continued release of the quotas already ordered, an end to all Government protection of youths between 18 and 19 and that legislation should be introduced to abolish age limitations and to recast the powers of Tribunals. Finally, by noting that that the effect of the MSAs was to 'present the War Office to the Nation as an industrial compulsitor [sic]' and that it would be preferable if men could be obtained by a different system, Geddes was by implication supporting the transfer of the Army's

37 Ibid., covering note dated 14 July 1917.
38 TNA CAB 23/3/33: Minutes of 185th Meeting of War Cabinet on 13 July 1917.
39 TNA CAB 24/20/83: Memorandum by Brigadier General Auckland Geddes on the Theory and Practice of Recruiting dated 23 July 1917.

recruiting organization to civilian control. This was not such a maverick suggestion from within the War Office as might be supposed – in March 1916 Macready had unsuccessfully proposed to Kitchener the formation of one central authority to be responsible for the distribution of the nation's manpower.[40]

It did not take long for the War Cabinet to agree to the transfer of Army recruiting to a civilian organization although there was to be some debate as to quite which department should assume responsibility.[41] Yet another committee, to be composed of Lord Milner, General Smuts and George Barnes, was now formed and given authority to decide on this and other questions concerning recruiting and manpower. Their decisions were to be reported back to the War Cabinet but in the event the only one taken was that the recruiting organization should become part of the MNS. All other outstanding questions of detail concerning manpower and recruiting were to be left until the DGNS had had time to address them.[42] That this individual would no longer be Chamberlain was by now patently apparent and he finally left office on 10 August. On 11 August Auckland Geddes was offered the post but before accepting he made sure of a clearly defined role from the outset with a seat in Parliament and the status of a Cabinet Minister. These increased powers would allay the War Office's previous concerns and give the new DGNS a better chance of balancing the demands of the fighting services with those of the civilian world. By now, however, the position of the Army was serious as by August the total deficit was 347,560 physically fit men and 39,143 men of lower physical categories.[43]

Although agreement had been reached that responsibility for recruiting was to pass to the MNS this would take some time to put into effect. The Solicitor General had initially advised that the transfer of any of the Army Council's statutory powers for recruiting would require legislative action but the Council decided that, in the short term, an ACI of limited duration should authorize the DGNS to act on its behalf.[44] Although it seems to have remained unclear whether legislation would be needed, the War Cabinet agreed on 8 October that one of the functions of the DGNS should be 'to obtain for the Army, Navy and Air Service such men as could be withdrawn from civilian life without detriment to the maintenance of essential public services'.[45] The Army Council now agreed to the transfer of its statutory powers for recruiting and concluded a formal agreement with the MNS as to the future division of responsibilities.[46] The need for legislative action had been circumvented. On 1 November the MNS assumed responsibility for 'recruiting, enlistment, the call up of men of the Reserve Forces individually and otherwise in relation to the provision of men for the Army'.[47]

There would be differences between the War Office and Geddes in the future but there was now confidence that the latter understood the needs of the military and that whatever he might

40 Macready, *Annals of an Active Life, Vol. 1*, p. 238.
41 TNA CAB 23/3/49: 201st Meeting of 1 August 1917.
42 TNA CAB 23/3/58: 210th Meeting of 10 August 1917.
43 War Office, *Statistics of the British Military Effort*, p. 369.
44 TNA WO 163/22: Minutes of Army Council Meeting of 27 September 1917 and WO 293/7 ACI 1483 of 28 September 1917: Ministry of National Service and Recruiting. ACI to remain in effect until 31 October 1917.
45 TNA CAB 24/4/10: Minutes of War Cabinet Meeting No 246 of 8 October 1917 and Appendix I.
46 TNA WO 163/22: Minutes of Army Council Meetings No 232 of 11 October and No 233 of 22 October.
47 TNA NATS 1/859: Press release of 1 November 1917.

decide in the future 'would be in the best interests of the nation, whether those interests were civil or military'.[48] Geddes' knowledge of manpower issues and his increased powers would enable him to assess the relevant merits of the conflicting demands for manpower and address problems that up to now had been systemic rather than deliberate.

Army Council Actions

Although the increasing dearth of recruits could be addressed only by political measures, the Army Council had already been taking action to ensure better use of the men already obtained. The measures introduced ranged from the release of fit men for duty on the front line to improvements in the allocation and training of recruits. A women's corps had also been created with the aim of releasing fit men from roles that could be fulfilled equally well, if not better, by them.

The Lawson Reports

For months, the War Office had been under pressure from the Cabinet to ensure that men obtained for the Army, and particularly those sent overseas, were being used to best advantage. In late 1916 the Army Council had sent a senior officer 'familiar with the man-power situation and the difficulties which have to be overcome in providing reinforcements for the fighting troops' to France to take a radical look at the situation.[49] The officer selected, Lt Gen H.M. Lawson, spent most of December visiting various locations in the Base areas and scrutinizing the manpower figures. On 3 December there had been 10,084 officers and 241,589 men on the L of C, of whom over half (7596 officers and 126,069 men) could be classed as effective.[50]

Reporting on his return, Lawson concluded that it would certainly be possible to reduce or reorganize the many units which had gradually collected at the Base and on the L of C in order to comb out manpower for the Front. He had found the physical conditions in the rear areas to be much less severe than at the Front and concluded that only 'B' men (those fit for garrison service, labour and sedentary work abroad) need be employed there. Any TF battalions that it was necessary to retain in the rear area should be converted to contain only 'B' men. The men of the four Garrison battalions should also be medically re-examined at regular intervals with any 'A' men being combed out for duty at the Front:

> Experience has shown that men enlisted with Cat B physical qualifications improve owing to physical training and good food and develop in no small proportion into the higher category.

Overall, he considered that better organization and supervision could reduce the numbers in the rear areas, estimating that some 26,000 'A' men could be combed out and sent to the Front

48 Macready, *Annals of an Active Life, Vol. 1*, p. 267.
49 TNA WO 33/881: Minutes of 194th Meeting of Army Council on 20 November 1916.
50 TNA WO 95/43: DAG War Diary 14 December 1916 and WO 95/26 GHQ AG War Diary 30 December 1916.

plus a further 12,100 if their places were taken by women, but that a constant watch would be necessary to ensure 'co-ordination and co-operation with the consequent prevention of overlapping and waste of manpower'.[51]

It took two weeks for Lawson's report to be received in France, the delay probably being the first of a series of irritants for GHQ.[52] A holding response was received from them a month later, noting that some parts of the report could be actioned at once whilst others would require more detailed investigation 'as to the most economical method of replacement of fit men by men of a lower category and women'.[53] As a first step the GHQ staff had considered how best to allocate non-'A' men. With the Armies, it would be possible to release 'A' men to fight by employing Permanent Base (PB) men in newly created Labour Companies and with POW companies in the rear parts of the Army areas. PB men not required by the Armies could be employed on the L of C as could Permanently Unfit (PU) men not required at the Base. Those PU men unable to be employed at their trades in France should be sent home. Garrison battalions, currently split up between the Army Railheads and the L of C, should be withdrawn and any 'A' men made available as reinforcements, their places being taken by PB men. Other possibilities for employment on the L of C and at the Base were also 'coloured labour' (sic) and women.

By 11 March, tension between the War Office and GHQ is visible in Haig's personal covering letter to a thirty-one page report from GHQ:

> There is every wish and intention on my part to comb out fit men, and the Army Council may rest assured that the importance of this matter is fully appreciated, and that elimination will be carried out to the limit compatible with safety.[54]

A thorough investigation had now been carried out and such of Lawson's recommendations as were considered 'advantageous and feasible' were already being implemented. It was necessary to make the changes gradually, however, and there was also a limit:

> [T]o the extent to which replacement by unfit men, women and coloured labour can be carried out with safety, and this limit can only be decided in this Country. Conditions in England and France differ, and the failure of any service in this Country through inefficient personnel may directly affect the troops, and even endanger operations.

Pressure to release men in lower medical categories for service in France was also being applied at home, both in the HD organization and through greater substitution of women for men.[55] The greatest losses were being suffered amongst the Infantry and a conference to discuss how to obtain as many 'A' men as possible for the Infantry took place at the end of March.[56] The

51 TNA WO 106/362: Report by Lt Gen H M Lawson on the Number and Physical Categories of Men Employed out of the Fighting Area, dated 16 January 1917.
52 TNA WO 32/5093: WO letter No 121/France/287 (AG1) dated 27 Jan 17 and TNA WO 95/26 AG GHQ War Diary entry for 1 February 1917.
53 TNA WO 32/5093: AG –C94 dated 25 February 1917.
54 Ibid., GHQ letter dated 11 March 1917.
55 Ibid., Lawson letter dated 14 March 1917 covering Memo on 'Urgent Need of Setting Free for Service in France of trained men of B & C Categories in the Home Establishments'.
56 TNA WO 162/34: Calling notice for conference on Manpower to be held on 29 March 1917.

Agenda was lengthy, covering topics including: economizing in personnel at home and abroad; the employment of women 'in every possible sphere'; the release of lower category men at home for work on L of C abroad; and reduction in the categories of men accepted for the Technical Corps. Every possible avenue was being explored but there were constraints: skilled men in technical units in Engineering Trades could not be combed out for the Infantry.

In April a further pool of men for overseas service became available at the stroke of a pen: conditions on the Western Front were really very similar to those at home and the definition of Category C was now amended to read 'Fit for service at home or in North Western Europe'.[57] This enabled 'C' men to be posted to the Base for employment in garrison or labour units or on sedentary work, thus releasing fitter men for the Front.

Work on Lawson's proposals continued in France, where it had been decided to revise the classifications: 'A': men fit in all respects for fighting and who would be kept exclusively for fighting units; 'TU': temporarily unfit men likely to be reclassified A at the periodical inspections; and 'PU': permanently unfit men who for some reason would never be upgraded to 'A'.[58] The 'TU' men were waiting to go to fighting units as soon as they were passed fit and could in the meantime be used on work being carried out by 'A' men, thus releasing the latter for service at the Front. The 'PU' men would replace 'A' or 'B' men on the L of C but any not fit for work in France would be returned to England in order to release others for France. It was noted, however, in an irresistible dig at the War Office, that large numbers of 'A' men continued to arrive in units intended solely for duty on the L of C and the process of combing them out was often delayed since it was entirely dependent on supply from home of 'an adequate' number of 'B' men, 'coloured personnel' and women.

Progress reports and instructions on the implementation of Lawson's proposals continued to pass between GHQ and London. In early July, the War Office stated that AG GHQ should be authorized to investigate the numbers, category and nature of employment of all BEF personnel and should issue all instructions concerning the allotment and distribution of such personnel.[59] In return, GHQ noted that the replacement of fit men by those of lower categories was continuing, with the men so released being sent for training before being posted to the Infantry.[60] In August the Army Council demanded monthly statistics from GHQ on the progress made on the various measures adopted.[61] The staff in GHQ obviously felt that London was labouring the point unnecessarily; the clerical effort entailed was considerable and by December GHQ declined to send any more such reports.[62]

Creation of the Women's Army Auxiliary Corps (WAAC)

Even before Lawson reported that the employment of women in France could release over 12,000 men for the Front, consideration was being given to their greater use by the Army. By

57 TNA WO 293/6: ACI 679 of 26 April 1917.
58 TNA WO 32/5093: GHQ letter dated 8 April 1917.
59 TNA WO 95/26: AG GHQ War Diary for 7 July 17: receipt of War Office letter 121/France/872 AG1.
60 TNA WO 32/5093: GHQ letter O.B/1070 dated 16 July 1917.
61 Ibid., AG1 letter 121/France/287 (AG1) dated 12 August 1917.
62 Ibid., GHQ Letter dated 6 December 1917.

1917 women were already serving overseas in various capacities, mainly medical, and many more had taken on new roles at home. Voluntary organizations had grown up, including the Women's Legion. This was a private organization which hired out cooks from its cookery section to the War Department; by the end of 1916 detachments totaling 2,000 cooks and kitchen staffs were working in 200 camps in England, where the standard of catering had been improved, with less wastage.[63] The only people not delighted were the men who would now be posted overseas. The Women's Legion had also formed a mechanical transport section and the QMG's Department was only too happy to hire 'ready made chauffeurs … uniformed and clothed and paid at a certain rate'. They were a great success although inevitably there were pockets of resistance: it was noted that some Home Commands were not happy with ladies driving staff cars at night.[64]

The suggestion of employing women clerks in France had been mooted in August 1916 but discounted, ostensibly due to lack of suitable accommodation.[65] By December the increasing seriousness of the manpower situation caused the question to be raised again, and on 4 December Macready gained Haig's acceptance to the introduction of women for duty in the rear areas.[66] The way was further paved by Lawson, who explained wherever he went how successful the substitution of women for men in many roles had been in England. That is not to say that he was totally enlightened as his views were inevitably coloured by the prejudices of the time: 'It does not look well, nor is it fair on the men themselves, to have quantities of men in khaki doing work which all over England is being done by the other sex'. To the obvious objection being raised, he simply noted that results at home had shown 'that the sex difficulty has not been anything like what some have predicted'.[67]

On 5 January Macready called the first of a series of conferences to discuss the future employment of women by the Army.[68] It was already clear that it was a question of when, and not if, women should be employed with the Army but what Macready wanted to establish was how that 'woman power' could be organized simply, and controlled centrally, in order to avoid the proliferation of small groups. Initially the proposed employments were clerical, housekeeping and driving, and several requests for these services had already been received, including female clerks for Rouen and elsewhere. Although catering staff and drivers for employment at home had previously been obtained from the Women's Legion, it was anticipated that in future women should be recruited through DGNS and 'belong more or less to the Army'. That raised the question of potentially differing terms of service and the thorny question of rates of pay.

Further conferences were held, chaired by Macready, and attended by members of his staff plus the heads of the Women's Legion Sections: Cookery and Housekeeping; Motor Drivers; and Clerks.[69] Discussions covered terms of service, discipline and the proposed enrolment form, concerning which the Head of the Cookery and Housekeeping Section stated that 'as far as

63 S. Bidwell, *The Women's Royal Army Corps* (London: Leo Cooper, 1977), p. 6.
64 TNA WO 162/31: Conference on the Organization of Women Employed by the Army – 5 January 1917.
65 TNA WO 95/3970: IGC War Diary - 15 August 1916.
66 Dame Helen Gwynne-Vaughan, *Service with the Army* (London: Hutchinson, 1941), p. 12 and Bidwell, *Women's Royal Army Corps*, p. 10.
67 TNA WO 106/362: Lawson Report, 16 January 1917.
68 TNA WO 162/31: Conference on the Organization of Women Employed by the Army.
69 TNA WO 162/33: Conferences on Organization of Women Employed by the Army held on 10, 15 and 17 January 1917.

she could speak for her women, they were willing to sign anything, and that what they wanted was to be soldiers, that they wanted to take the place of a man in every sense'. The need for central organization effectively meant a new corps for which an interim title was decided upon: Women's Army Service Department.

Lawson's first report in mid-January identified 12,100 posts in France that could potentially be filled by women. This gave further impetus to what was already moving forward very positively and on 6 February Macready outlined full details of the proposed scheme.[70] By now a new AG branch, AG11, had been formed and the corps' first head appointed: Mrs Mona Chalmers-Watson, the sister of Sir Auckland Geddes, Director of Recruiting, and Sir Eric Geddes, then DG Transportation in France.

The GHQ response to Lawson's report opened the way for women to be employed in France.[71] With the proviso that more detailed investigation would be required, it confirmed that 2,430 women clerks could be accepted for work in different locations, including Étaples, Rouen and GHQ Montreuil. It was understood that they would come out with their own officers and be employed in parties of not less than one officer to twenty women. 'As an experiment' a domestic section consisting of eleven cooks, six waitresses, two scullery maids and a clerk was requested for each of Calais, Étaples, Rouen, Le Havre and Boulogne, and it was also noted that women drivers could be used.

Armed with GHQ's agreement, Mrs Watson visited France at the end of February, together with the newly-designated Chief Controller overseas, Mrs Gwynne-Vaughan, in order to see where women could be employed and accommodated.[72] On returning to London, feverish planning ensued to establish what it was now confirmed would be known as the Women's Army Auxiliary Corps (WAAC) and to start recruiting women. Aspects requiring attention were the corps organization, areas of employment, rates of pay and the design of a khaki uniform and badges of rank. One area examined in detail was the legal status of women posted to a theatre of war to replace combatant soldiers since, unlike medical personnel, they would not be protected by the 1906 Geneva Convention. Rather unflatteringly, it was agreed that women serving overseas could be defined as 'camp followers' and as such be covered by the Army Act whilst those serving at home would be covered by civil law. It was thought necessary, however, for there to be a written contract, so female recruits were required to sign enrolment forms confirming their agreement to serve for twelve months or the duration of the war, whichever was the greater, to fulfil the rules, regulations and instructions laid down from time to time for the Corps, to work wherever the Army Council required, to obey all orders, to perform any work, and finally to be discharged at a week's notice (later extended to a month) if their services were no longer required, or without notice for breach of conditions.[73]

In mid-March Mrs Gwynne-Vaughan took up her post in France with the immediate task of organizing accommodation suitable for use by women. She toured locations in the rear areas, including Abbeville, Rouen, Le Havre, Dieppe and Étaples, meeting Commandants, inspecting accommodation and discussing possible employment with the employing officers. She was disconcerted to find that however helpful the officers she met were during the official

70 TNA WO 162/34: Conference on Organization of Women Employed by the Army 6 February 1917.
71 TNA WO 32/5093: GHQ AG – C94 dated 25 February 1917.
72 Gwynne-Vaughan, *Service With the Army*, p. 14.
73 Ibid., p. 21.

side of the visits, she would later be told that wherever it was 'was the one place where women ought not to come'. Indeed, she discovered almost universal objection to the employment of women, largely because the military distrusted the complications that working with women might bring and disliked 'the intrusion into their offices and workshops of an alien element'.[74] It would take time for the new Corps to be accepted but the manpower situation meant that there could be no turning back.

On 28 March details were announced of how the women were to be employed at the Base and on the L of C.[75] There would be six categories of trades: clerical, typist and shorthand typist; cooks, waitresses and domestic staff; motor transport services; storehouse women, checkers and unskilled labour; telephone and postal services; and a further miscellaneous category covering any employments not falling into any of the above. The publication of the ACI was not a moment too soon because the women were about to start arriving in France.

The first detachment of fourteen cooks and waitresses for the Officers' Mess in Abbeville arrived on 31 March. They were followed almost immediately by a draft for the Officers' Club in Boulogne and a further twenty-two clerks arrived on 7 April for the Forestry Directorate at Le Touquet. By mid-April the first of the big camps for females was nearly finished: a collection of hutments just outside Abbeville to accommodate clerks and others at the Advanced Mechanical Transport Depot (AMTD) where spares for all kinds of vehicles were stored and distributed.[76] In mid-May a detachment of women clerks would arrive for the DAG's office in Rouen.[77] Pay clerks were also arriving for the Command Pay Office at Wimereux, where there would soon be several hundred women, and a request was received in mid-May for twenty-four domestic staff for the Fourth Army School.[78] Also in May, the first draft of postal workers arrived for employment in the Army Post Offices in the rear area and at Le Havre, Boulogne and Calais. These women had answered a notice in the *Post Office Circular* for female Sorters, Sorting Clerks and Sub-Office Assistants with at least four months service with the GPO to enrol in the WAAC for service in France with the Army Postal Service. They were under the impression that their duties would be similar to those back home, so were somewhat shocked to find they were working on the counters in the Army equivalent of an ordinary post office.[79]

Accommodation, thought originally to be a major obstacle, in fact proved perfectly manageable. It varied according to locality: where available, hotels and villas could be used, as at Wimereux, but elsewhere large wooden huts accommodating twenty or thirty women or Nissen huts holding eight women were used. It would soon become necessary to create female Base Depots in France. Eventually there would be two depots, one at Étaples and a second one outside Le Havre. The big camp at Étaples, housing over 500 women, would eventually have between 70 – 80 Nissen huts as well as dining huts, recreation huts and washing facilities.

74 Ibid., p. 26.
75 TNA WO 293/6: ACI 537 of 28 March 1917: Employment of Women with the Armies Abroad.
76 Gwynne-Vaughan, *Service With the Army*, p. 31. In later years the Mautort MT Camp would be remembered nostalgically as the 'old camp built on the high hill on the Ancienne route de Blangy'. AGC Archives: *QMAAC Old Comrades Gazette*, 8 (February 1921).
77 TNA WO 95/43: DAG War Diary 14 May 1917.
78 Gwynne-Vaughan, *Service With the Army*, p 34.
79 AGC Archives: Extract from the Forces Postal Historical Society Newsletter, No 247 p. 199.

Members of the Women's Army Auxiliary Corps (WAAC) preparing vegetables in an infantry camp in Rouen. (IWM Q5741)

Developments had moved very quickly and several hundred women had already been sent overseas before the publication in July of a comprehensive ACI codifying numerous aspects to do with the new organization.[80] The Corps' purpose was 'to effect substitution of women for soldiers in certain employments throughout units, formations and offices administered by the Army Council … at Home, and at the Bases and on the Lines of Communication Overseas'. Such substitution was to be based on clear, if unflattering, guidelines: four women clerks or four technical women for the RFC and ASC Motor Transport would be considered respectively as equivalent to three soldier clerks or three technical soldiers. A certain number of women would be required for clerical and domestic duties, and a scale was laid down for the employment of the latter in military messes and cookhouses. It was also specifically stipulated that no woman would be employed unless her employment relieved a soldier for other purposes. There followed detailed instructions on administration, hierarchy, pay and allowances, uniform, discipline and accommodation.

The main effort initially was the provision of women for overseas but it was noted that the Military Cookery and the Motor Transport sections of the Women's Legion could be gradually

80 War Office, *Statistics of the British Military Effort,* p. 205 and TNA 293/7 ACI 1069 of 7 July 1917 – Women's Army Auxiliary Corps.

Members of the WAAC sorting spare parts at an advanced motor transport store at Abbeville, 15 September 1917. (IWM Q5955)

absorbed into the WAAC. Existing contracts would be honoured but any Women's Legion member who wished and passed the medical standard could enrol in the WAAC. At home the substitution of servicewomen for soldiers was initially very slow: only 815 in September but then rising to 15,696 in December. The number of women in France grew steadily: by September there would be 2,280 and 4,105 in December.[81] Although this equated to a few battalions' worth of men, it was still well short of Lawson's anticipated 12,000. The problem was that women were not coming forward in anything like the numbers anticipated, mainly because of the many other job opportunities that had opened up for them in the absence of men serving abroad. The munitions industries, for example, were booming and an unskilled worker could earn far more there than doing domestic work with the Army. As a result, WAAC domestic trades were to prove surprisingly difficult to fill. Clerks proved easier to recruit as the work offered encouraged them to make use of their skills, gain different types of clerical experience and retain their job status. The most likely recruits were young unmarried women with no domestic commitments

81 Ibid., p. 206.

Clerks of the WAAC working at an advanced motor transport depot at Abbeville, 15 September 1917. (IWM Q 5950)

at home; married women could volunteer but were not eligible for overseas service if they had husbands serving in France. It was a big step, however, for a young woman to enrol and it was probably not surprising that recruiting was slow.

Formation of Labour Corps

The WAAC was not the only new Corps to be formed in early 1917. In April, the Labour Corps was formed to rationalise the use of men employed as labour.[82] Existing ASC Labour Companies and Infantry Labour battalions were absorbed into the new Corps and men of lesser fitness categories were transferred into it.[83] The men of the new Corps were generally older or

82 TNA WO 293/6: ACI 611 of 13 April 1917.
83 For example, the Cheshire Regiment had provided five Labour battalions in France: 18th, 19th, 20th, 21st and 22nd (Labour) Battalions. In April 1917, these were split up to form 56th-65th Labour

of lower medical categories than infantrymen at the Front, although every Labour Corps soldier was medically re-examined each month to see if they were fit enough to be upgraded. They were organized in Employment companies, of which there were two types: Labour companies (450 men under 5 officers) and Area companies (2 officers and 270 men). Men of Divisional Employment Companies could be employed as Brigade clerks, loaders for divisional trains, on salvage duties and in the divisional canteens, in each case to replace men who were fit for active duty.[84] In July, GHQ could report that some 7,000 unfit men from England had been formed into Divisional Employment Companies, and that Area Employment Companies for Army and Corps HQs were also now arriving.[85]

Allocation of Recruits

Despite the decline in numbers, the Army was still obtaining recruits but greater care was now being taken over their allocation to their future employment. On being enlisted, recruits were categorized according to their level of physical fitness by Recruiting Medical Boards and were then allocated to Arms and Services according to monthly instructions issued by the Army Council.[86] As many 'A' men as possible would be sent to the Infantry Regimental Reserves: (Reserve, Extra Reserve and TF Reserve Battalions) and the Training Reserve. Those not destined for the Infantry were allocated elsewhere according to the current monthly requirements. In March 1917, for example, 11,000 'A' men were to go to the Artillery and 100 to the Mounted Military Police (MMP). Allocations were distributed by Commands: Western Command was to provide 2,440 of the 11,100 Artillerymen. Men in the lower fitness categories, B(i), B(ii), C(i) and C(ii) were allotted to other arms, such as the ASC, as appropriate to their fitness levels.

One side effect of the political resistance to universal compulsion was that it remained possible to volunteer for service before being called up and many continued to do so. In early February William Tonkyn, a 23-year old civil servant, who as such could have remained exempt, requested permission from his Government Department to enlist.[87] The young Ivor Hanson had attested four days before his 18th birthday in November 1916. He could then have waited to be called up on reaching 18 years 8 months but instead enlisted in early January 1917. On the suggestion that he had already been called up, he rather curtly informed the hapless enquirer: 'That's not true, for I shall not be of military age until about nine months' time, but I am enlisting as a

Companies respectively.

84 TNA WO 95/1519: 5th Division A&Q Branch War Diary entry for 23 May 1917.

85 TNA WO 32/5093: GHQ letter O.B/1070 dated 16 July 1917.

86 TNA WO 293/5: ACI 2418 of 24 December 1916; WO 293/6 ACI 158 of 26 January 1917, ACI 358 of 1 March 1917; ACI 536 of 28 March 1917; ACI 688 of 26 April 1917; all entitled 'Posting recruits who are called up from Class B, Army Reserve, or who come forward for service before being called up, on or after 1 [month] 1917'. ACI 865 of 27 May onwards: 'Arrangements for posting men to the Army who present themselves for service during the month of (June) 1917'. See Appendix IV re medical categories.

87 IWM: Con. Shelf Letters of W.D. Tonkyn. NB This individual is cited as a conscript in I. R. Bet-El *Conscripts* (Stroud: Sutton Publishing Ltd, 2003 edition) pp. 29 and 32 as a conscript bur it is quite clear from his diary that he applied for permission to enlist.

volunteer'.[88] Some 34,936 men are shown as having enlisted voluntarily between October 1916 and 30 September 1917 but hidden within other overall figures for enlistments for the Regular Army and TF between 1916 and 1918 are hundreds of thousands of 'Derby' men who continued to think of themselves as volunteers and not conscripts.[89]

The monthly Recruit Posting ACIs emphasized that recruits should be posted to units in which they wished to serve, provided they were suitable for them. Allocations to each corps or unit were to include men who had originally volunteered to serve in a particular one unless there were no vacancies, in which case he should be posted to other units, Regular or Territorial, raised in the same county or district.[90] William Tonkyn naturally asked to join the Civil Service Rifles. Two weeks later he learned that he had been accepted and that he would be released from Government service so long as he passed the medical examination. Pronounced fit, he was posted to the Civil Service Rifles on 1 March and arrived at Hazeley Down Camp a week later to join 3/15th London Regt (Civil Service Rifles).[91]

The emphasis on meeting recruits' preferences continued throughout the year. At the end of May the message was clear:

> The fullest consideration must be given to recruits' preference for … their own national or even local corps. Advantage must be taken of everything that tends in any way to foster *esprit de corps* and these national and local sentiments are a valuable asset which must be kept in view … In the case of Infantry of the Line, recruits who have any such preference should be posted, wherever possible, to their own local regiments.[92]

In September it was stated that volunteers were to be posted to their chosen corps irrespective of the numbers allotted, providing they were physically and technically suited. It was again confirmed that any man over 18 years 8 months wishing, with good reason, to be posted to a particular Infantry Regiment should have his request granted by the posting officer:

> [T]he fullest consideration must be given to the men's preference for what they regard as their own national or even local corps provided that they are suitable as regards Medical Categories etc. Advantage must be taken of everything that leads in any way to [their] *esprit de corps* and these national and local sentiments are a valuable asset which must be kept in view.

Lads under 18 years 8 months, who expressed a preference for a particular regiment, should not be posted 'indiscriminately' to a TRB in the Command in which they presented themselves for service but were to be posted to a TR Brigade affiliated to the same District as their chosen

88 J.I. Hanson & A. Wakefield, *Plough and Scatter* (Yeovil: Haynes, 2009), pp. 48, 56–57, 67. In mid-January 1917, he joined the RFA and was posted to Bettisfield Park Camp in Shropshire.
89 War Office, *General Annual Reports on the British Army 1913 – 1919*(London: HMSO, 1921), p. 60.
90 TNA WO 293/6: ACI 158 of 26 January 1917.
91 IWM: Con Shelf Diary of W. D. Tonkyn. 535391 Pte W D Tonkyn 12B Pl C Coy, 3/15th London Regt (Civil Service Rifles), Hazeley Down Camp, Winchester.
92 TNA WO 293/6: ACI 865 of 27 May 1917.

Regiment; their documents were to be endorsed showing this choice. [93] It seems that, despite the pressures on recruiting, the value of *esprit de corps* gained by keeping soldiers with others from the same locality continued to be recognized throughout 1917.[94] The operative phrase, however, was 'wherever possible'.

Infantry Recruit Training

Adult recruits for the Infantry continued to be allocated in the first place to the Regimental Reserves and only once these had been filled to the TR battalions. Their training continued to follow a fourteen weeks' syllabus designed to produce men able to march and shoot to a standard where they could take their place in a rifle section.[95] No one was supposed to be sent overseas unless he was 'up to the standard required for the particular draft concerned, both as regards training and physical fitness'.[96] For various reasons, however, not all men did complete their training before being drafted. In early 1917, 3rd TRB consisted of six companies: three for recruits, two for returned BEF men and one containing unfit men and permanent staff.[97] The Battalion noted bitterly that in December 1916 over half their Category 'A' NCOs had been required for overseas reinforcements, thus reducing the number of instructors by about 40. Furthermore, after February no officer, WO or NCO fit for General Service should be retained in a TRB for more than six months, which meant that potentially two thirds of the instructional staff of NCOs could be sent overseas at any moment. There were also difficulties in conducting training. The scale of SMLE rifles and bayonets for TR battalions was set at just 25 percent of the establishment which meant that, however carefully training was organized, units found it impossible to ensure that each man used the same rifle continuously throughout his musketry course, with consequent problems for zeroing the weapon and successful completion of the marksmanship tests.[98] As a result of the training problems, all 415 drafts sent to France by 3rd TRB in the first six months of 1917 were shown as partially trained.[99] Such men were categorized as 'A(ii)' (recruits who should be fit for 'A(i)' as soon as trained) and the nominal roll for such a draft was to be headed 'SPECIAL'. If it was the full musketry course that had not been completed, a note was also to be placed against each man's name: 'Fired only parts … GMC'.[100] It was expected that training would be completed on arrival at the Base(s) overseas.

New instructions for the organization and roles of men within a platoon, culled from lessons learned on the Somme, had been issued in February, and aspects of these were introduced into

93 TNA WO 293/7: ACI 1329 of 29 August Arrangements for posting men to the Army who present themselves for service during the month of September 1917.
94 This would appear to contradict Captain Dunn's reported conversation with Major Roger Poore concerning an 'inspector's comment': 'I suppose this is another piece of your esprit de corps. Well, there's to be no more of it'. NB: Poore was not attached to 2nd RWF until early 1917 so would have been with 2nd Wiltshire Yeomanry at the time of the alleged comment. See Dunn, *The War the Infantry Knew*, p. 246.
95 TNA WO 293/5: ACI 1968 of September 1916.
96 TNA WO 293/6: ACI 431 and 432 of 11 March 1917 and 533 of 28 March 1917.
97 TNA WO 95/5460: 3rd TRB War Diary. NB 'Employed men' were the Permanent Staff of the unit.
98 TNA WO 293/6: ACIs 313, 986 and 987 of 1917.
99 TNA WO 95/5460: 3rd TRB War Diary.
100 TNA WO 293/6: ACI 431 and 432 of 11 March 1917 and 533 of 28 March 1917.

recruit training as soon as possible, although initially it is unlikely that many of the recruit training instructors would have had the necessary experience for this training.[101] It would not be until August, however, that Infantry recruit training syllabi would be specifically amended to ensure that not only would every man be 'sufficiently trained to take his place in his platoon overseas, but also that the training of Infantry drafts [met] the requirements of SS143 Instructions for the Training of Platoons for Offensive Action, 1917'.[102]

Training of Young Recruits

In January, the War Cabinet had agreed to lower the call-up age for youths from 18 years 7 months to 18 years.[103] Up to then, young recruits had been posted to the normal reserve units with others of all ages, although the youths were trained in separate squads until turning 18 years and 8 months, when they would be posted to the draft-producing companies of their unit.[104]

Robertson and Macready were unhappy with this approach, and from February onwards changes to the training of young soldiers were gradually introduced, starting with the announcement that all future 'A(iv)' recruits under 18 years 8 months were to be posted to selected TR battalions for their training.[105] There was of necessity a transition period: on 26 February 4th TRB became an 'A(iv)' battalion to train recruits aged under 19, whilst 2nd TRB followed on 6 April and 5th on 1 May.[106] For young recruits already in the system, the changes could have long-term effects. Clyde Hulme, from Burslem in Staffordshire, volunteered on 22 January 1917, a month before his 18th birthday. Mobilized on 2 April 1917, he reported to the local Depot. His age meant that he was destined for a YS battalion and he should have been posted to one serving his local district, No 6. The process of re-designation of TRBs, however, threw up anomalies and although Clyde was posted fairly locally, to Rugeley, it was to 8th TRB, serving No 5 District. Both these Districts belonged to Northern Command but this initial posting placed Clyde, now TR/5/31291 Pte Hulme, with recruits from elsewhere in the Command and his future postings would be to units of No 5 District.[107]

Further rationalization of young soldiers' training came during May.[108] Under the 'General Scheme' all youths enlisting under 18 years and 8 months, except those allocated elsewhere under the monthly recruit disposal ACI, were to be posted to selected TR battalions. On completion of four months' training they would be transferred to Infantry battalions to continue training until they turned 19; non-Infantrymen would continue their TR training or be transferred to other arms. The June posting ACI confirmed the new approach but the whole recruit training

101 General Staff instructions: SS 143 Instructions for the Training of Platoons for Offensive Action, 1917 and SS 144 The Normal Formation for the Attack, both issued in February 1917; TNA WO 293/6 ACI 322 of 22 February 1917.
102 TNA WO 293/7: ACI 1230 of 6 August 1917 Training of Infantry Recruits.
103 TNA CAB 23/1/39: Appendix II to Minutes of 39th War Cabinet Meeting of 19 January 1917.
104 TNA WO 293/5: ACI 2418 dated 24 December 1916 and WO 293/6 ACI 158 of 26 January 1917.
105 Robertson, *From Private to Field-Marshal*, p. 304 and TNA WO 293/6: ACI 358 of 1 March 1917, ACI 536 of 28 March 1917 and ACI 688 of 26 April 1917.
106 TNA WO 95/5459: 1st TR Brigade War Diary.
107 <www.ancestry.com> Service Record for 64802 Pte Clyde Hulme DLI.
108 TNA WO 293/6: ACI 803 of 17 May 1917 'Posting and Training of Men under 19 Years of Age'.

organization was now so complicated that a chart was included.[109] An abbreviated version is given in Table 6.

Category	<18y8m	> 18y 8m & < 25y	25y & < 30y	30y and over
A	TR	Regimental Reserves, TR, Foot Guards, monthly allotments to other Arms		
B (i)	TR	RH, RFA and RGA according to allotments in monthly posting ACI; surplus to TR		Arms other than Infantry, according to allotments; TR
B (ii)	TR	TR	Arms other than Infantry: as allotted; Labour Units, Employment Companies	Arms other than Infantry: as allotted; Labour Units, Employment Companies; ASC MT learners
B (iii)	TR	TR	Clerks – or to Reserve 'B'	Clerks – or to Reserve 'B'
C (i)	TR	RFC, RFA and RGA according to allotments; and TR	RFC, RFA and RGA as allotted; and TR	Arms other than Infantry: as allotted; RFC, TR, ASC MT Learners
C (ii)	TR	TR	Arms other than Infantry: as allotted; Labour Units, Employment Companies	Arms other than Infantry: as allotted; Labour Units, Employment Companies
C (iii)	TR	TR	Clerks – or to Reserve 'B'	Clerks – or to Reserve 'B'

Table 6. Posting of recruits enlisted from 1 June 1917.

This was further amplified a few days later by specific instructions allocating Infantry recruits by age and medical categories as shown in Table 7.[110]

Units	Age of Recruits	
Young Soldiers Battalions	18 years 1 month	A (iv) B (i) C (i)
Junior Training Reserve Battalions	Under 18 years 8 Months	A (iv) B (i) C (i) (not required for the YS bns) B(ii), B(iii), C(ii), or C(iii)

109 TNA WO 293/6: ACI 865 of 27 May 1917 'Arrangements for posting men to the Army who present themselves for service during the month of June 1917'.

110 TNA WO 293/6: ACI 873 of 31 May 1917: Disposal of Recruits Allotted to Infantry in Monthly ACI for Posting of Recruits.

Regimental Reserves (Reserve, Extra Reserve, TF Res Bns)	Over 18 years 8 months	A (ii)
Senior Trg Res Bns	Over 18 years 8 months	B (i), B(ii), B(iii), C (i), C(ii), and C(iii)
NB. After six weeks training men in the lowest medical categories considered unlikely ever to be upgraded to Categories A, B(i) or C(i) would be transferred to other arms or the Labour Corps.		

Table 7. Allocation of Infantry recruits by age and medical category wef 1 June 1917.

The new instructions had placed the youngest recruits in Young Soldiers (YS) battalions for the first four months of their training but were then vague about what happened afterwards. This was remedied a few days later by the creation of Graduated Battalions, which were to be affiliated in pairs to each YS battalion.[111] The youngest recruits, those aged 18 years 1 month, in Categories 'A(iv)', 'B(i)' and 'C(i)' would complete four months' training in a YS battalion before being posted to a Graduated battalion. Companies in both YS and Graduated battalions were organized specifically by age: for example, the 3rd Company of a YS battalion would contain lads aged 18 years 3 months. On reaching 18 years 5 months they would move as a formed company, 250 strong, to an affiliated Graduated battalion which they would also move through by age.[112] The YS training continued to follow the ACI 322 syllabus up to the eighth fortnight, with the proviso that the recruits were to have fired the GMC on the SMLE rifle during this period.[113] On joining the Graduated battalions, those selected as bombers, Lewis gunners and signalers would begin specialized training. Before leaving the Graduated battalions, all recruits would be put through a refresher course on the SMLE rifle, including live firing. Allowing two weeks for inoculations and a further two weeks for leave, the time spent in the YS and Graduated battalions would take recruits up to the age of 19, when they could be drafted overseas.

Those slightly older youths who were posted to Junior TRBs would receive six months' training. It was recognized that these recruits were still developing physically so any categorized below 'B(i)' and 'C(i)' were initially to undergo six weeks' fitness training. After that, those unlikely ever to become 'A', 'B(i)' or 'C(i)' would be transferred to other units whilst any who might be upgraded could start their six months' recruit training as soon as considered fit. The training syllabus was organized in fortnightly blocks; after the eighth fortnight, some of the hours allotted to 'field work', 'field engineering' and 'bombing' would train the recruit to take his place in a platoon organized in accordance with SS143.[114] On completion of six months' training, the recruit would be transferred as required.

As a result of the organizational changes, there was a period of flux for the TR Brigades, as their battalions were converted to the new organization: 28 Graduated battalions would be linked in pairs to 14 designated YS battalions whilst the remaining 60 TR battalions would

111 TNA WO 293/6: ACI 925 of 12 June 1917: Training of Junior Training Reserve Battalions, Young Soldiers Battalions and Graduated Battalions.
112 Ibid., ACI 986 of 21 June 1917.
113 Ibid., ACI 322 of 22 February 1917: Training of Category A(iv) Infantry Recruits Under 18 Years 8 Months. The Training Syllabus was broken up into 12 fortnightly periods.
114 General Staff, *Instructions for the Training of Platoons for Offensive Action 1917* (London: HMSO, 1917).

consist of Junior and Senior TRBs. In the continuing search for re-deployable manpower it was soon realized that Graduated battalions could be used for Home Defence. With five companies each they could send a company abroad every two months and still have four companies containing youths at various stages of training.[115] From July onwards Graduated battalions would gradually replace Second Line and HS Garrison battalions in the 71st, 72nd and 73rd home-service Divisions.[116] The battalions replaced were thus freed up to provide replacements ready for drafting or substitutes for other men released for service overseas.

Although serving their purpose, the TR in general remained unpopular in an Army used to Regimental links for the Infantry.[117] Harold Mellersh found his posting to the 5th TR Battalion at Rugely during September 1917:

> [E]ntirely impersonal. The men did not know each other nor have anything in common. … In belonging to the 5th TRB one belonged to nothing. … And the conscripts did not want to be there any more than I did.

It is not clear how much this view was due to Mellersh's own antipathy to 'another home-service job' or to misplaced hindsight: at that time 5th TRB was a YS battalion taking recruits aged 18 years 1 month, some of whom will have been conscripted but others will have volunteered before being called up. Mellersh may simply have been echoing the Regimental officer's prevailing view of the TRBs.

For adult Infantry recruits who spent only fourteen weeks in training the lack of Regimental links seems to have been seen as a lesser problem but for the youths who would spend almost a year in the system some change was deemed necessary. In late October a further nine YS and eighteen Graduated battalions were added to the existing fourteen YS and twenty-eight Graduated battalions and were all allotted to twenty-three Infantry Regiments. The Graduated battalions became the 51st and 52nd battalions of each regiment with the YS becoming the 53rd battalions. Scant regard was paid to the provenance of the original Reserve battalions, although usually the new battalions had originated in the same recruiting District; nine, however, changed recruiting districts but remained within the same command. The new 51st Cheshire had started life as 13th SWB, both in District 4, but the 225th Graduated Battalion, formerly 50th TRB and originally 14th (Reserve) Cheshire, would become 51st Manchester, thus moving from District 4 to District 3 albeit remaining within Western Command.

115 Robertson, *From Private to Field*-Marshal, p. 305.

116 In mid-July, 4th TRB left 1st TR Brigade for Ipswich becoming 258th (Graduated) Battalion in 215th Brigade, 72nd Division. In mid-August all but one of 1st TR Brigade's battalions were re-designated: 2nd and 5th became YS battalions and 3rd and a new 4th became Graduated battalions. The subsequent departure of 3rd TRB to Surrey and 4th TRB to Stockton on Tees as the 276th and 273rd (Graduated) Infantry Battalions respectively and the arrival of 12th and 13th YS battalions meant that by October the 1st TR Brigade became solely a YS Brigade.

117 H.E.L. Mellersh, *Schoolboy into War* (London: William Kimber, 1978), p. 125.

Posting, Drafting and Transfers

Demands for replacements for the BEF continued to be made by DAG 3rd Echelon to the War Office, which then issued orders to the appropriate Commands for the preparation and despatch of the necessary drafts. Men selected for drafts were to be 'A(i)', unless destined for garrison or labour units or designated 'special' drafts requiring completion of their training on arrival overseas. Men who had previously been returned sick or wounded would be available for drafting as soon as they were 'A(i)' again.[118]

The increased flexibility over postings and the frequency of transfer had led to administrative difficulties in keeping track of soldiers. This was particularly the case for the TF in which each battalion had historically issued its own series of regimental numbers. This meant that each time a TF soldier was posted between units even of the same Regiment he had to be allocated a new number. The increasing frequency with which men were now being transferred to different units on arrival at the Bases had meant increased clerical labour with the consequent risk of errors. In late 1916 it was therefore decided that, in order to make it easier to keep track of TF Infantry soldiers, new TF Regimental numbers were to be allocated by March 1917. Each Infantry Regiment was allocated a block of six figure numbers starting at 200001, which were then broken down into blocks for each TF battalion.[119] Each TF soldier was allocated a new number from his battalion's particular block which he would retain as long as he continued to serve in the same regiment, irrespective of whether he was posted to a TF or Regular battalion. Only on posting to a new regiment would he receive a new number.[120] The same ACI also confirmed that after 1 March the only men who could become TF infantry soldiers in future would be those directly enlisting into a TF unit or existing TF soldiers from other arms who were transferred to TF Infantry. The only other category of men who would in future receive TF numbers were those who, on being called up from Army Reserve Class B, were posted to TF units as their first unit. The change also applied to Regular soldiers in that they would in future retain their regular numbers even when posted to a TF unit of their own regiment.

The increasing need to transfer men between cap-badges had thrown up certain anomalies, and by August it became necessary for the War Office to issue amended instructions on the procedures for posting and transferring all soldiers.[121] The extent of the problem may be seen by it being thought necessary to confirm that, irrespective of whether he had a Regular or TF Regimental number, a man serving on a Regular attestation or record of service paper was a Regular soldier whilst a man serving on a TF attestation was a TF soldier. In future a recruit called up under the MSAs or who enlisted voluntarily was to be allotted a Regular number irrespective of whether his first posting was to a Regular or a TF unit. The only exception to

118 TNA WO 293/6: ACI 432 of 11 March 1917 Despatch of Cavalry, Yeomanry and Infantry Drafts to units serving with the Expeditionary Force.

119 TNA WO 293/5: ACI 2414 of 23 December 1916: Infantry of the TF – Re-Numbering of Personnel and Alterations in Administrative Arrangements. For example, 4th Cheshire was allocated 200001 – 240000, 5th Cheshire 240001 to 265000 and 6th Cheshire 265001 – 290000.

120 On being transferred to a different Regiment, a TF Infantry soldier would be posted initially to a TF unit of that Regiment and allocated an appropriate number which he would then keep on being posted to a Regular battalion of that Regiment.

121 TNA WO 293/7: ACI 1245 of 11 August 1917. Procedure on Transfer and Posting of Regular and Territorial Force Soldiers. Amended Instructions.

this would be if he was posted to units of corps without any regular unit, such as the Honourable Artillery Company (HAC). For ease of reference a chart (reproduced in Table 8) was contained in the ACI to make the transfer procedures absolutely clear:

A. Description of Corps in which a Regular soldier is required to serve	Transfer	Posting	Re-numbering
Any Corps (except HAC etc)	He will be transferred to the Corps in which he is required to serve.	He will then be posted to a Regular or TF unit of the new Corps as required.	The Officer i/c Regular Records of the new Corps will allot the soldier a Regular number
B. Description of corps in which a TF Soldier is required to serve on transfer	**Transfer**	**Posting**	**Re-numbering**
A corps containing one or more TF units	He will be transferred to the Corps in which he is required to serve	He will then be posted to a regular or TF unit of the new corps as required.	The Officer i/c TF Records of the new Corps will allot the soldier a TF number from the series assigned to the TF unit or units of the new corps.
A Corps including both Regular and TF soldiers but not containing a TF unit.	He will be transferred to the corps in which he is required to serve	He will then be posted to a unit of the new corps as required	The Officer ic Records of the new corps will allot the soldier a regular number.
A corps not containing a TF unit and not including TF soldiers He will be enlisted on a regular attestation, posted to a unit of the corps in which he is required to serve and discharged automatically from his former corps under para 144 of TF Regulations.			The Officer ic Records of the new corps will allot the soldier a regular number.

Table 8. Amended instructions for the transfer and posting of Regular and TF soldiers.

It was also decided in mid-August to make a subtle change concerning the provision of Infantry drafts.[122] In future the onus would be on Reserve units to telegraph the War Office as soon as they anticipated that they would have drafts completely ready for despatch. The telegram was to show the numbers available, their state of training and when they would be ready for

122 Ibid., ACI 1301 of 21 August 1917 Despatch of Infantry Drafts to Units serving with the Expeditionary Forces.

despatch. The War Office would then inform the Reserve unit for which theatre and regiment (or unit) the draft should be prepared, or whether it was to be allocated on arrival overseas. Lists of drafts available would be sent daily from the War Office to the Commands concerned for calling forward as required. It was a simple change but designed to speed up the despatch of appropriate drafts to the overseas Commands.

Overview

Throughout 1917 the provision of manpower had been a predominant issue, both politically and for the Army. There seems little evidence that men had been deliberately withheld; instead it appears to have been a systemic problem, with the Government simply unable rather than unwilling to force the Departments of State to release manpower for service with the Army. Although a step towards universal compulsion appeared to have been taken at the end of 1916, it was recoiled from and even the introduction of National Service remained firmly based on the voluntary principle. It would not be until later in the year with the appointment as DGNS of Geddes, with his understanding of national manpower issues, that any real co-ordination of the nation's manpower might become possible.

Within the Army, the shortage of recruits had forced greater attention to be focused on the better use of the manpower it already had. Lawson's evidence that there were 'A' men not being used to best advantage in France had prompted positive action and the 'combing out', at home and overseas, of men who were fit to fight. The revising of the medical categories had also enabled better use of manpower, particularly in the newly created Labour Corps, and the arrival of women for service with the Army, although not in the numbers as hoped for, had also played a part in freeing up fit men to fight.

The allocation of recruits to appropriate parts of the Army with the monthly posting ACIs had been rigorously controlled and Infantry recruit training had been streamlined, particularly for the youngest recruits, with the introduction of new units. Training had continued to follow the fourteen-week syllabus laid down the previous year.

The test of the measures put in place during 1917 would be whether sufficient manpower would be available to replace the Infantry losses during the year.

6

Attrition on the Western Front

Much has been written on the offensives of 1917 on the Western Front, but this chapter approaches them from the perspective of manpower, both for the BEF as a whole and for the Marcher battalions of Western Command. All the offensives would prove costly, requiring large numbers of replacements which, as has been seen in the last chapter, were proving difficult to find. It closes with the end of the Third Battle of Ypres since in manpower terms the fall-out from the subsequent Battle of Cambrai would last into early 1918.

Winter 1916–17

It had been agreed at Chantilly during the preceding November that current operations would continue over the winter. Co-ordinated offensives would recommence in the spring with attacks by the French between the Oise and the Somme, and by the British between Bapaume and Arras. Haig felt he could, if necessary, launch attacks by 1 February but would have preferred to wait until May when it was anticipated that the BEF would be in a better position. The actual choice of date had to be a joint decision with the French, however, so agreement was reached that they would be ready for action by the first fortnight of February but that if the enemy remained contained they might delay the offensives until a more favourable date.[1]

The winter of 1916/17 was a period of consolidation and rebuilding after the battles of 1916. Reinforcements were arriving: between 21 November and 31 December 171,802 were despatched to France with a further 35,738 under orders to move.[2] It had been decided that all Infantry battalions should be increased to 100 men above establishment and that the training of untrained men should be completed at the Front.[3] It would prove difficult, however, to

1 *BOH 1917 Vol. 1* pp. 9-10.

2 NA: WO 162/28 AG2 document dated 1 January 1917 Drafts despatched 21 November – 31 December 1916. The grand total of those despatched to all Theatres was 205,188. Of those despatched to France, the total included 146,700 Infantry (114,408 British plus 32,292 Colonial) with 35,680 British and 58 Colonial under orders.

3 TNA WO 95/26: AG GHQ War Diary entry 19 December 1916.

maintain the Scottish, Welsh and Irish Regiments at full strength whilst retaining their national characteristics. A War Office letter in late January gave authority for English troops to be posted to these units if necessary but stipulated that Scots, Welsh and Irish were 'on no account ... to be transferred to any regiment other than those of their own nationality'.[4]

At the same time as reinforcements were being sent from England, there was also an increased recognition of the need to take care of the battle-hardened men they already had: a Fourth Army Routine Order on Wastage Returns exhorted:

> The replacement of trained men is a very costly business, and it is difficult to place any limit to the value to our country of the trained man who has been through the experience of the Somme Battle. His loss from bad man mastership [sic] is, therefore, a reflection on his Officer of the most serious nature. Every effort should be made by all officers to keep the men in good health, good spirits, and training. Care and forethought are necessary in arranging duties and work, so that the men may be spared the unnecessary fatigue entailed by waiting, falling in too soon etc etc.[5]

The intention was good, but many soldiers would have been surprised by the last sentence.

The BEF now contained 56 Infantry divisions, divided between five Armies, and more TF divisions were due to arrive during February and March. The 42nd (East Lancashire) Division arrived from Egypt in late February and a further four second line TF divisions, the 57th, 58th, 59th and 62nd, from England. Such was the degree of movement that it was requested that all leave be stopped from the BEF between 8 February-15 March in order to release shipping for the new divisions. As was by now normal practice, they would be introduced into the line: gradually; in mid-February 64 officers and 178 men from the 66th (Second East Lancashire) Division were attached to the 5th Division for familiarization purposes.[6]

The events of the first few months of 1917 were described by the *Official History* as: winter fighting on the Somme battlefield, the pursuit of the enemy as he withdrew to the Hindenburg Line during February and March and the capture of outposts in front of that line. The 'short-range enterprises' of the winter fighting were 'almost all successful and frequently at small cost', but even so the BEF's overall casualty figures for January were 12,535.[7] More alarming were the 'sick wastage' figures: 41,543 in January, 41,302 in February and 54,950 in March were suffering from various illnesses, undoubtedly due to the atrocious weather conditions of the winter.[8] Reinforcements continued to arrive but in declining numbers: 82,165 in January and 62,672 in February (both exclusive of RE, RA and RFC), but it is difficult to draw comparisons since in March the way in which the reinforcement figures were presented was changed to show only those sent to the divisions: 58,860 Cavalry and Infantry had been despatched.[9]

4 TNA WO 95/26: AG GHQ War Diary entry for 27 January 1917.
5 TNA WO 95/441: Fourth Army A & Q War Diary December 1916.
6 TNA WO 95/26: AG GHQ War Diary for February 1917 and WO 95/1519 5th Division A & Q Diary for 14 February 1917.
7 *BOH 1917 Vol. 1*, p. 543.
8 TNA WO 95/26: AG GHQ War Diary figures for January-March 1917.
9 There is a difficulty in playing with figures since those in the AG's War Diaries accord with neither those in the *Statistics of the Military Effort* nor in the *Medical Services: Casualties and Medical Statistics*

During the winter, 'troops of all arms showed an intelligence and adaptability ... which was the fruit of hard-won experience and training'.[10] Once the Germans withdrew to the Hindenburg Line, however, it became a different kind of warfare with rising casualty figures: 21,023 and 22,361 respectively for February and March. The *Official History* would subsequently note:

> Our inexperienced young soldiers seemed quite at sea when they got into the open, and enterprising young leaders were non-existent through lack of training in open warfare.

The urgent need to send out replacements for the losses of 1916 appears also to have meant that initial training had in some cases been curtailed:

> [M]any men come out quite untrained - sometimes only nine weeks after enlistment ... It will be realized that the art of movement so as to gain every inch of advantageous ground can only be learnt by careful training ...[11]

Arrangements for completing the training of untrained drafts seem to have varied according to the formation concerned. In 2nd Division, 1st KRRC complained that a draft of 128 untrained men was received on 19 March and that 'close order drill, and the handling of arms, at both of which the untrained Draft are particularly slow' required great attention.[12] In the 5th Division, however, it had been decided as early as January that untrained drafts would be sent to Brigade Training Centres on arrival; on 3 March 1st Cheshire noted the arrival of 40 reinforcements that had come from the 15th Brigade Training Depot and there is no mention of the need for any further training.[13] There would inevitably continue to be general comments made about men arriving untrained but occasionally these were recognized as perceptions rather than actual reality: a May 1917 poem, apparently circulated by GHQ, described the 'Lads who have scarcely been out a year ... are to Alf but as untrained boys', Alf being the old soldier who had been out since 1914.[14]

New drafts needed time to be absorbed by units and the larger the draft the longer this might take. However, as the Cheshires had found in 1916, 'given the opportunity to get the Battalion together in a rest area, these men soon became one with the unit'.[15] Training helped weld a unit together and the publication in early 1917 of two General Staff pamphlets based on lessons learned in 1916, SS 135, *Instructions for the Training of Divisions for Offensive Action* and SS 143, *Instructions for the Training of Platoons for Offensive Action,* meant that there was plenty to be done before the anticipated spring battles. In SS 135 there was growing emphasis on the

of the Great War. This was highlighted in the *Official History 1917 Vol. 1* p. 557. I have chosen to use the AG's figures as these were compiled from the information available at the time for those fighting the war and would be the basis on which reinforcements would be requested.

10 *BOH 1917 Vol. 1*, p. 543.

11 Ibid.,quoting an un-named GSO2 and Maj Gen C.E. Pereira, GOC 2nd Division, pp. 544 and 555.

12 TNA WO 95/1371: 1st KRRC War Diary 19 March and 1 April 1917.

13 TNA WO 95/1519: 5th Division A & Q Branch War Diary entries for 2 and 4 January 1917 and WO 95/1571 1st Cheshire War Diary for 3 March 1917.

14 C.H. Dudley Ward, *Regimental Records of the Royal Welch Fusiliers Vol. III 1914-1918* (Uckfield: Naval & Military Press, 2005), p. 307.

15 Crookenden, *The History of the Cheshire Regiment in the Great War*, p. 77.

need for both careful preparations before any action and the co-ordination of different types of weapon into a coherent whole, whilst in SS 143, the platoon was treated as a self-contained unit with four fighting sections. All men were riflemen and bayonet fighters but each section had its own specialty: a section of picked shots and bayonet fighters, and scouts; the bombing section; the rifle bombers; and the Lewis gun team.[16] For trench-to-trench attacks, the concept was now that platoons would attack in two waves: the first wave would be the assault team of riflemen and bombers, and the second wave the fire team with rifle grenades and the Lewis gun.

The collective training necessary to disseminate the new organization and tactics was started at once. The 13th Cheshire spent the afternoon of 16 February re-organizing its companies, platoons and sections 'under the scheme set out in GHQ letter No OB 1919 dated 7 February'.[17] The 1st Cheshire's War Diary shows training being carried out whenever the battalion was out of the line. From 23 January onwards, training is shown daily for nine days, including time in early February on the Divisional Range at Le Quesnoy where 40 men from each company fired 100 yards grouping, 200 yards application and 200 yards rapid fire. After a spell in the trenches, training continued through late March and into April. On 27 March the battalion practised an attack in wave formation, from 9:00-10:45 am with specialist training after that whilst on 4 April they spent the day on a 'Brigade manoeuvre'.[18] Similarly, the 7th KSLI in 3rd Division was heavily involved in training from January onwards. Their training through February is described as 'progressive' and, after a spell working on the fortification of the caves under Arras, they moved back with their Brigade on 21 March to Liencourt for training in open warfare; further practice attacks were held daily until 30 March, when the battalion returned to Arras to take over a section of the trenches opposite Tilloy.[19] The examples of these two battalions, one from First and the other from Third Army, indicate the type of detailed training and preparation now incorporated into the build-up for the forthcoming offensives.

The anticipated spring offensive would start in April and GHQ had been moving Corps and Divisions between Armies in order to create the attacking force required in First and Third Armies. It was another period of organizational change: letters on the 'Distribution of Corps and Divisions to Armies' were sent on 26 January and 7 February, with a forecast being issued on 21 February of the 'Movements to be carried out between Armies before the commencement of operations'. In order to ensure that the attacking divisions would be up to strength AG's staffs were notified of those, such as 24th and 34th Divisions, requiring immediate priority for reinforcements.[20]

16 SS 135, *Instructions for the Training of Divisions for Offensive Action* issued by the General Staff December 1916 and SS 143 *Instructions for the Training of Platoons for Offensive Action 1917*, issued by the General Staff February 1917.
17 TNA WO 95/2246/3: 13th Cheshire War Diary for February 1917.
18 TNA WO 95/1571: 1st Cheshire War Diary 1917.
19 Major W. de B. Wood, *History of the King's Shropshire Light Infantry* (London: The Medici Society, 1925; Uckfield: Naval & Military Press, 2003), pp. 234-36. The main excitement on 3 April was a raid in order to capture a prisoner for identification purposes; the ground was thick with snow and there was a nearly full moon but the men, dressed in sheets and ladies' nightdresses purchased in Arras, entered the enemy trenches and returned with a prisoner, having not suffered any casualties themselves.
20 TNA WO 95/11: GHQ GS War Diaries for January and February 1917.

The effectiveness of the casualty reporting procedures had been reviewed and, in late March, Fowke confirmed that the system of reporting approximate Cavalry and Infantry casualty numbers by telegram during heavy fighting would continue. A couple of minor adjustments were made: divisions in which any battalions had suffered 50 or more casualties were to wire the numbers by battalions by 6 pm daily to AG GHQ and the DAG, 3rd Echelon. Should further casualties in excess of 50 occur during the night another wire would be sent the next morning as soon as the total numbers for the Battalion could be estimated. The main change, however was that in future casualties would be reported by phases, the duration of which would vary according to the fighting and the number of casualties suffered. Effectively a running total was kept as each wire was to begin with: 'Total estimated casualties from … (date of commencement of phase inserted)'. A further change was that battalions were to be represented by letters of the alphabet and the terms 'officers' and 'other ranks' were not to be used. As an example, under the new system the message: 'Total estimated casualties from 10th March, B 5 and 315 …' indicated that since 10 March the 2/4th North Lancashire had lost 5 officers and 315 other ranks. As before accurate casualty reports were still to follow the estimated reports.[21] The rapid transmission of approximate numbers indicated as quickly as possible the numbers of reinforcements that would be needed, whilst the introduction of codes for sometimes lengthy battalion titles saved on signal traffic and to an extent would also hide the identities of the battalions concerned.

The Armies were also making their own arrangements for the handling of reinforcements during the offensive. Only Third Army, however, is specifically mentioned as having gained approval from GHQ for the formation of a reinforcement camp in each Corps where the personnel not taking part in an attack would assemble, and where reinforcements would be held on arrival. These would not replace casualties from day to day but would be kept there to reconstitute units at a definite point.[22]

Spring Offensive April – May 1917

The offensive of early 1917 was launched in support of a larger French offensive on the Chemin des Dames. The British action is often referred to as the Battle of Arras but was in fact a series of battles during April and May, which started on 9 April with the attack on Vimy Ridge and the first battle of the Scarpe, continued with a further two battles on the Scarpe and culminated at Bullecourt in May.[23] Twenty-six Infantry divisions, four of which were Canadian, took part altogether and nine Marcher battalions were in action. Of these, 7th KSLI took part in all three Battles of the Scarpe, whilst 1st Cheshire was in support to the Canadians for the attack on Vimy and during the Second Battle of the Scarpe. These battalions have been selected for closer examination.

21 TNA WO 95/26: AG GHQ War Diary for 28 March 1917 and Appendix I for that month.
22 Ibid., AG GHQ War Diary for 11 March 1917.
23 9-14 April First Battle of the Scarpe and Battle of Vimy Ridge; 23-24 April Second Battle of the Scarpe; 28–29 April Battle of Arleux; 3-4 May Third Battle of the Scarpe with capture of Fresnoy; 3-17 May Battle of Bullecourt, fought after a first unsuccessful attack on 11 April.

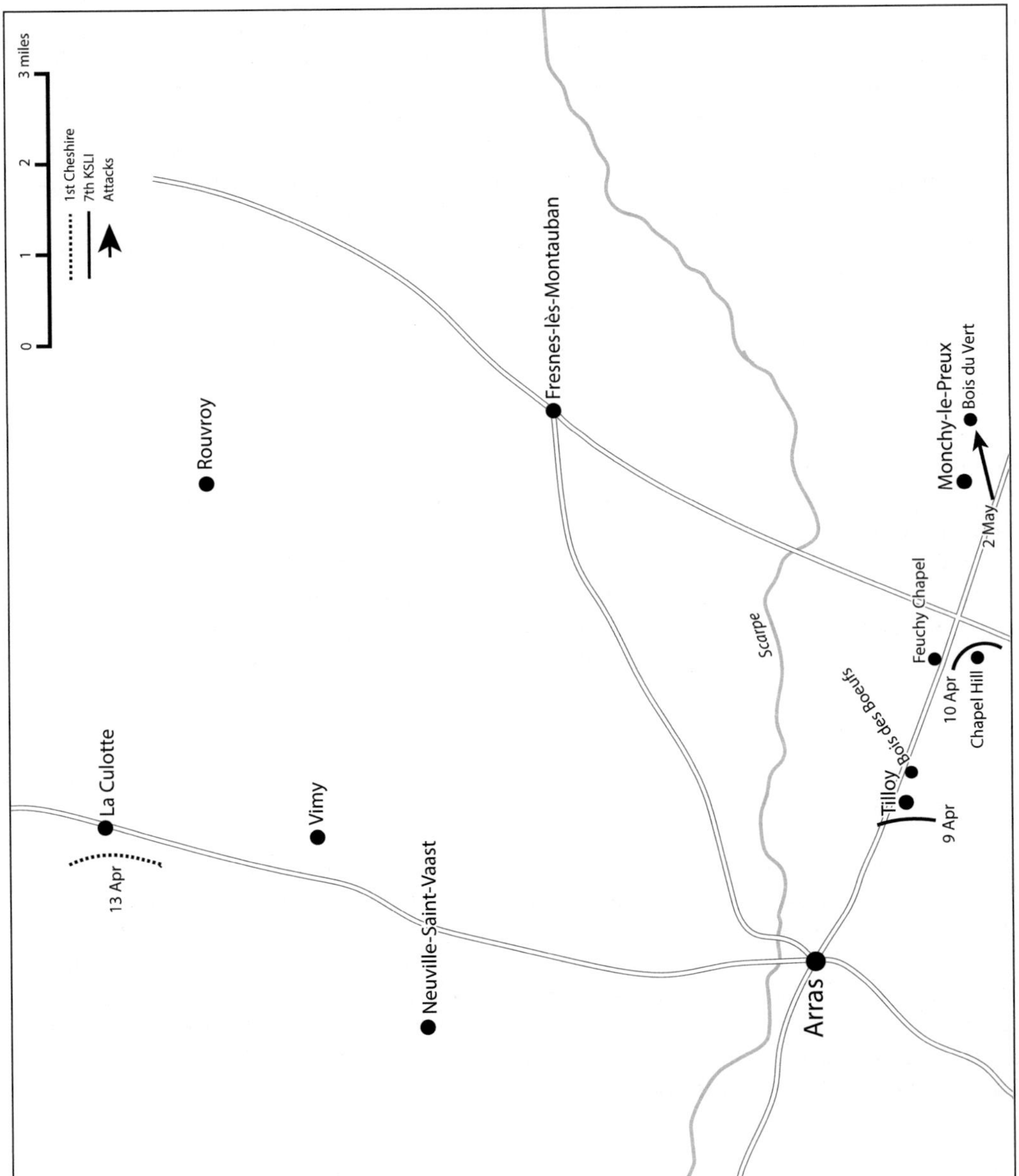

Map 5: Battles of the Scarpe and Vimy Ridge, April-May 1917: 7th KSLI and 1st Cheshire

On Easter Monday, 9 April, the three Brigades of the 3rd Division took part in the First Battle of the Scarpe with the German first, second and third lines as their objectives. The 7th KSLI, in 8th Brigade, was to take part in the final assault to capture the enemy's third line and secure the high ground immediately south of Feuchy Chapel, known as Chapel Hill. At 8:50 am the Brigade advanced but on reaching Tilloy in the second line found that the village had not yet been cleared. The KSLI left-front company decided to move around the village's northern flank and capture the Bois des Boeufs. Having fought off a German party sent to assist the garrison in the wood, they proceeded to clear it and then continued towards the third line but at about 2:30 pm were stopped by intense rifle and machine gun fire from the flanks. They had also found very strong uncut wire in front of the position. A bombardment to cut the wire was ordered at 5:30 pm, to be followed by a further infantry attack at 7:00 pm. Both were unsuccessful. The KSLI dug themselves in overnight about 600 yards from the enemy in readiness for a subsequent bombardment and attack the following morning, which proved successful. During their attack they had advanced over 5,000 yards and captured 156 prisoners. Their own casualties amounted to 167: one officer killed and eight wounded, and 22 other ranks killed, 131 wounded and 5 missing.[24] They would hold their newly captured sector of the enemy line until being relieved on the night of 13/14 April. They returned to billets in Arras, where their training was continued on the Arras racecourse. Ten days later, 23 April, they returned to the trenches for the Second Battle of the Scarpe, during which they suffered a further 29 casualties: 8 killed, 20 wounded and 1 missing.[25]

A return from Third Army giving the strengths of its divisions as at 6 pm on 1 May shows the 3rd Division as having 399 officers and 11034 men, plus a further 33 officers and 401 men in the Corps Depots. Although it had suffered estimated casualties of 139 officers and 3027 men, the Division was still considered fit for fighting.[26] Some 39 officers and 2142 men had been sent to units as reinforcements during April.[27] Not only was this 885 fewer than the number of casualties incurred but some battalions were receiving nothing like the replacements they needed: only 17 men reached 7th KSLI during April, with a further 16 at the Corps Depot, against a total casualty toll of 187. The 7th KSLI would be in action again in early May, advancing at 4:45 am on 2 May in support of an attack on the Bois du Vert. During their advance the battalion captured three enemy machine guns. The attack was checked by further machine-gun fire and the battalion dug themselves in about 8:00 am. No further advance was possible, so they were employed in consolidating the ground gained until they were relieved on 7 May, by which time they had suffered 5 officer and 98 soldier casualties. They returned to

24 Wood, *History of the King's Shropshire Light Infantry*, pp. 237-8; TNA: WO 95/1384 3rd Division A & Q War Diary note dated 16 April shows KSLI OR casualties 9-13 Apr as 22 killed, 129 wounded and 16 missing; SDGW shows 34 deaths for the same period, of which 30 were KIA. This highlights the difficulty of obtaining accurate figures.

25 TNA WO 95/1384: 3rd Division A & Q War Diary note dated 30 April 1917 showing casualties 23-27 April.

26 TNA WO 158/20: State of Divisions in Third Army as at 1 May 1917. NB Other Divisions were less fit: eg 31st and 33rd would be fit for fighting in about seven days but the 34th was tired and needed three or four weeks rest; the 29th Division was 'weak and has had hard fighting but spirit very good'; whilst the 12th Division was fit for fighting and the 18th Division had yet to be used and was 'Fresh and fit for fighting'.

27 TNA WO 95/1384: 3rd Division A & Q War Diary for April 1917.

the front line between 10-15 May, during which period they suffered a further 2 officer and 40 soldier casualties.

The 3rd Division War Diary shows that between 9 April-16 May 7th KSLI suffered 383 soldier casualties, of whom 46 had been killed, 307 wounded and 30 missing. *SDGW* shows 107 deaths for the same period which includes many of the missing plus those who would die of wounds. The 7th KSLI was a Service battalion formed in September 1914, as part of the Third New Army, and had arrived in France a year later, joining the 3rd Division in October 1915. It had fought on the Somme and by now might have been expected to be showing a serious change in its composition. Analysis shows, however, that two thirds of the 107 who died had enlisted in the Shropshires' recruiting area, with a further 18 percent having joined in No 4 District, mainly from the neighbouring areas of Cheshire and North Wales. Altogether 96 percent had enlisted in Western Command, with many of those enlisting in No 3 District having come from southern Lancashire. Of the men who died, 96 had enlisted as KSLI soldiers, although not all had started out in 7th KSLI. The exceptions were five each from the Shropshire Yeomanry and the Cheshire Regiment, plus one from the Somerset Light Infantry. Just under one third had arrived in France in 1915; at the other end of the scale eight appear to have been mobilized in the second half of 1916 (although whether they were 'Derby men' or conscripts is unknown due to the dearth of Service Records) and would have arrived with the battalion in early 1917.[28] The fact that 90 percent were original KSLI soldiers, albeit from various battalions, appears to confirm that even on transfer men were continuing to be posted to their parent regiment.

The 1st Cheshire, in 15th Brigade of 5th Division, would play a less active part in the battles of April/May. With the exception of 13th Brigade which was in action on 9 April, the 5th Division had been in reserve for the Canadians and it would not be until 13 April that it moved up to relieve the 4th Canadian Division. At dusk 1st Cheshire deployed in former German trenches but as contact with the enemy had been lost it was decided to push forward to a line of outposts towards La Culotte. This had just been done when a peremptory order from 15th Brigade HQ instructed the Battalion to withdraw to the line they had left. By the time this had been done, fresh orders were received that the battalion was to act as advance guard to the Brigade as it went forward. As the Cheshire Regimental History notes: 'Practically none of the officers had any experience of this form of manoeuvre and only after very strenuous work by the Battalion staff was the unit ready to advance at the appointed time.' On nearing La Culotte they came across a formidable entrenched position, protected by three deep belts of barbed wire and fully manned. The houses, mine buildings and factory had also been strengthened, fortified and occupied by machine gun posts. No further advance was possible. To make matters worse, a party from a neighbouring battalion, on approaching from the rear, mistook the Cheshire Battalion HQ for the enemy and opened fire, killing A/RSM Eldridge who had arrived from England less than three weeks earlier.

Taking the same dates as for 7th KSLI, 40 soldiers of 1st Cheshire lost their lives between 9 April-14 May. Fortunately, far more Service Records have survived for this group. Half were TF soldiers who had joined the battalion in August and September 1916, having been transferred under the authority of AO 204 and ACI 1499 of 1916, and five men were from a

28 SDGW and <www.ancestry.com>; there are very few KSLI Service Records available. I am grateful to Annette Burgoyne for some of the information on 7th KSLI soldiers.

draft of over 100 from 2/1st Denbigh Yeomanry which was sent to France and transferred to 1st Cheshire in early October 1916. Virtually all the previously TF soldiers had joined in 1914 and 1915 and their transfer to a Regular battalion had been made possible by MSA(2) of 1916. Of the rest of those killed, eleven were pre-war soldiers recalled in 1914, a couple were 'Derby' men and just one, the 34-year old Alexander Tydd, was definitely a conscript who had been called up in March 1916. The most unfortunate were eight men who had joined the battalion only in February 1917, one of whom, Sydney Goodier, was killed a month before his nineteenth birthday. Some 70 percent had enlisted in Cheshire with a further 10 percent from North Wales and Shropshire; altogether 88 percent had enlisted in Western Command. Despite the losses of the Somme, the great majority of men in 1st Cheshire thus continued to have a connection with its traditional recruiting areas.

It is difficult to be sure how well-trained the reinforcements were that arrived at units during this period. For the GHQ Manning staff it was often a balance between the need for reinforcements to reach units as quickly as possible against time spent at the Base to familiarise them with conditions in France. It also depended on the availability of trained reinforcements to meet the specific requirement. On 11 April, it had been decided that:

> Owing to the necessity of rapidly bringing up to establishment Divisions which have been temporarily withdrawn from the line for training and refitting …in certain cases it might be necessary to send reinforcements up to Divisions from the Base before completing their 9 days Base Training.[29]

What is not absolutely clear, however, is how this dovetailed in with the arrangements preferred by the different formations: 5th Division had their Brigade Training Battalions; Third Army had its Corps Reinforcement Camps and the XIII Corps of First Army had the following arrangements in place by early May:

> Railhead for reinforcements is at Pernes. From there drafts are brought under Corps arrangements to Ecoivres, where they are met by Divisional Guides and conducted to transport lines of units. Privates who have not previously served in this country, on arrival at Pernes, are sent to a Corps Training Depot at Floringhem for purpose of completing their training.[30]

In many cases, reinforcements continued to be men returning after having been wounded, who would need little or no training. In mid-May 5th Division noted that 'Since April 9th 1,147 ORs have joined as reinforcements. These are composed chiefly of men returning from hospital.'[31]

The *Official History* gives the total losses for First, Third and Fifth Armies for April and May as 158,660, of whom 29,505 had been killed.[32] The ferocity of the fighting had been such that the daily rate of casualties had been higher than encountered during the Somme in 1916

29 TNA WO 95/26: AG GHQ War Diary April 1917.
30 TNA WO 95/1519: 5th Division A&Q Branch War Diary of 6 May 1917.
31 Ibid., 5th Division A&Q War Diary for 14 May 1917.
32 *BOH 1917 Vol. 1*, p. 558.

or would be sustained in the future during Third Ypres or the Hundred Days.[33] Some 150,733 Cavalry and Infantry reinforcements were despatched to divisions during April and May but most of these were directed to the divisions preparing for the next offensive, plans for which were already nearing fruition.[34] It was against this background that Macready produced his memorandum on recruiting for submission to the War Cabinet.[35]

On 7 May, Haig had informed the Army Commanders that he hoped to capture the Messines Ridge in a month's time. The battle was to be prefaced by the explosion at zero hour of nineteen mines underneath the German lines and then Second Army would attack with twelve divisions which had not fought in the Arras area. Prior to the battle, training areas had been laid out to the rear of each corps sector on ground resembling that to be crossed during the assault and marked with tapes and coloured flags showing the various farms, woods, strongpoints and objectives. The assaulting brigades carried out several rehearsals with the men wearing full kit and practising every detail.[36]

Other preparations were being made. Although AG GHQ's Branch had remained at Montreuil during the Battle of Arras it seems to have been decided to revert to the operation of an AG Advanced HQ for the next offensives. On 3 June it was opened up at Blendecques, near St Omer, with 8 officers and 18 clerks, in preparation for the forthcoming battle. It would remain there until late September, returning with GHQ Advanced HQ to Montreuil for the winter.

At 3:10 am on 7 June the attack on the Messines Ridge went in as planned and was a 'stunning success', due to much careful planning and preparation beforehand.[37] There were comparatively few casualties during the assault itself but many more were caused by subsequent heavy and accurate German shelling of the newly-gained lines. Altogether 24,562 casualties were incurred by the Second Army between 1-12 June. By 14 June the battle was over with all objectives having been gained.

Had the Messines casualties been the total for the month of June, life would have been a lot easier for the Manning staffs both at home and in France but the overall number of soldier casualties for the BEF for that month was 64,962, which with a 'sick wastage' figure of 38,925 made a total of 103,925 all arms. The Cavalry and Infantry reinforcements despatched to Divisions could number only 83,134. The War Office had suggested in mid-May that, due to the difficulties in maintaining the BEF in both horses and men, a Cavalry Division should be dismounted and formed into four Infantry battalions but GHQ requested that this measure be delayed since the Cavalry Corps was then in the process of taking over a considerable portion of the front line and any alteration would seriously affect current plans.[38] In late June, the necessary action was finally taken in order to release men to be transferred to the Infantry, when the War Office sanctioned the dismounting of twelve Corps Cavalry Regiments instead

33 J. Nicholls, *Cheerful Sacrifice, The Battle of Arras 1917* (Barnsley: Pen & Sword (reprint), 2013), p. 210.
34 TNA WO 95/26: AG GHQ War Diary end of month returns for April and May 1917 and *BO H 1917 Vol. 1*, p. 508.
35 TNA CAB 24/15/66: Army Council Memorandum by the Adjutant General Regarding the Position and Prospects of Recruiting dated 31 May 1917.
36 *BOH 1917 Vol. 2*, p. 34.
37 J.M. Bourne, *Britain and the Great War 1914–1918* (London: Edward Arnold, 1989), p. 72.
38 TNA WO 95/26: AG GHQ War Diary entries for 12 and 14 May 1917.

of a Cavalry Division. GHQ responded within two days with the names of six Corps Cavalry regiments which could be disbanded and the number of men that would be gained.[39]

Arrival of New Units and Re-Organization of Divisions

Insufficient replacements meant that in extreme cases battalions had to be withdrawn from the line and replaced by new ones, or else amalgamated. After the 9th Division's actions in the First and Third Battles of the Scarpe it appeared unlikely that there would be sufficient reinforcements for its South African Brigade until late September. Consequently, three third line TF battalions were sent out to replace it: 3/4th Royal West Surrey, 3/4th Royal West Kent and 3/10th Middlesex landed at Le Havre in early June. Sufficient replacements for the South African Brigade appear to have been found from somewhere, however, since it was again able to take its place in 9th Division within a few weeks. The three TF battalions were now spare and AG GHQ requested advice from the War Office on their disposal. The response, ten days later, stated that they should be used to replace three battalions to be taken from regiments which had 'too many battalions in the field', namely the Royal Irish Rifles, the Royal Inniskilling Fusiliers, the Royal Irish Fusiliers or the Northumberland Fusiliers, the implication being that it was proving too difficult to find reinforcements for them. The final decisions as to which battalions to amalgamate were left to GHQ and involved yet another merry-go-round of units:

- 3/4th Royal West Surrey was to join 21st Division. On its arrival 12th and 13th Northumberland Fusiliers were to be amalgamated to form 12/13th Northumberland Fusiliers.
- 3/4th Royal West Kent was to join 17th Division, replacing 9th Northumberland Fusiliers, which would be posted to 103rd Brigade of 34th Division to replace two existing battalions selected for amalgamation. (The 24th and 27th Northumberland Fusiliers were subsequently amalgamated to form 24th/27th Northumberland Fusiliers.)
- 3/10th Middlesex was to join 4th Division, replacing 1st Royal Irish Fusiliers which would move to 36th (Ulster) Division and enable the amalgamation at the end of August of 8th and 9th Royal Irish Rifles.[40]

It is symptomatic of the reinforcement problems facing these units that such moves had to be undertaken at the start of the Third Battle of Ypres. Both 36th and 34th Divisions would be in action during August but the 4th, 17th and 21st Divisions were more fortunate in having until October to settle down.[41] A further series of moves, which would again bolster an Irish division, was enabled by the arrival of 1/4th KSLI from Hong Kong.[42] They were to join 63rd Division, enabling the departure of 10th Dublin Fusiliers to 16th (Irish) Division, where the 7th and 8th Inniskilling Fusiliers would be amalgamated to make room.

39 TNA WO 95/26: AG GHQ War Diary entries for 26 and 28 June 1917.
40 Ibid., AG GHQ War Diary entries for 25 May, 17, 27 and 30 July and 1, 3 and 21 August 1917.
41 TNA WO 158/20: Third Ypres: Divisions Taking Part in Attacks 31 July-12 October 1917.
42 TNA WO 95/26: AH GHQ War Diary entry for 29 July 1917.

Minor Amendments to Casualty Reporting Procedures

In mid-July Casualty Reporting procedures were further refined in the light of recent experience. In future when an Infantry battalion had lost 50 or more men missing in any single day a footnote was to be added to the Daily Casualty list stating the probable number that had been taken prisoner. At the end of each week a separate return was to be submitted showing the total missing by Divisions, plus the numbers included in the totals thought to have been taken prisoner alive.[43]

Third Battle of Ypres

The Third Battle of Ypres would start on 31 July. Again, as before the Battle of the Somme, training of the assaulting battalions had had to be fitted in around the need to provide working parties for the preparation of the front. The main attack would be launched by Fifth Army and during the preceding weeks models had been constructed in Corps training areas showing the lie of the ground to be crossed. Lectures and practical demonstrations had been given on how to deal with various possible situations and each Infantry Brigade had thoroughly rehearsed its task over ground on which were shown the outlines of the trenches and strongpoints to be attacked. Particular attention was paid to attacks on pillboxes with parties of bombers, supported by Lewis gun fire and rifle grenades. The numbers for the initial objective had been calculated on one man for every three yards of front plus half or a whole platoon for the capture of each group of farm buildings in the intermediate area. The *Official History* notes that battalions taking part in the offensive had been brought up to strength, averaging 35 officers and 925 ORs, but only some 16 officers and about 660 ORs were to go into action leaving the rest behind in order to provide a nucleus of reinforcements.[44] In reality, the strengths of many of the battalions were lower: 13th, 14th, 15th and 16th RWF in 38th Division would go into battle with 551, 294, 420 and 456 ORs respectively.[45]

At 3:50 am on 31 July, the Second and Fifth Armies attacked. The Second Army managed to extend its line in many places, but further progress was dependent on the Fifth Army's progress along the high ground of the main Ypres Ridge towards Gheluvelt. Unfortunately, despite a good start, Fifth Army met with mixed fortunes. On the left and in the centre two German lines had been over-run and the line advanced about 3,000 yards with the capture of the Pilckem Ridge. On the right, however, II Corps had been less successful in assaulting the Gheluvelt Plateau, although they had captured the German front line and advanced about 1,000 yards beyond. The estimated casualties reported to AG GHQ by the 14 divisions actively engaged on 31 July were 592 officers and 17,022 ORs and for the 1-3 August amounted to 481 officers plus 12,925 men.[46] These numbers were fewer than those of 1 July 1916, but the nine leading divisions of Fifth Army had already lost 30-60 percent of their fighting strength.[47]

43 Ibid., AG GHQ War Diary entry dated 14 July 1917.
44 *BOH 1917 Vol. 2*, p. 147 and fn 2.
45 Ward, *Regimental Records of the Royal Welch Fusiliers Vol. III 1914-1918*, p.328.
46 TNA WO 95/26: AG GHQ War Diary for 31 July and 1, 2, 3 August 1917.
47 *BOH 1917 Vol. 2*, pp. 178 and 179. The divisional losses, which include field artillery and machine gun companies, show 39th Division with the highest loss of men: 3,871.

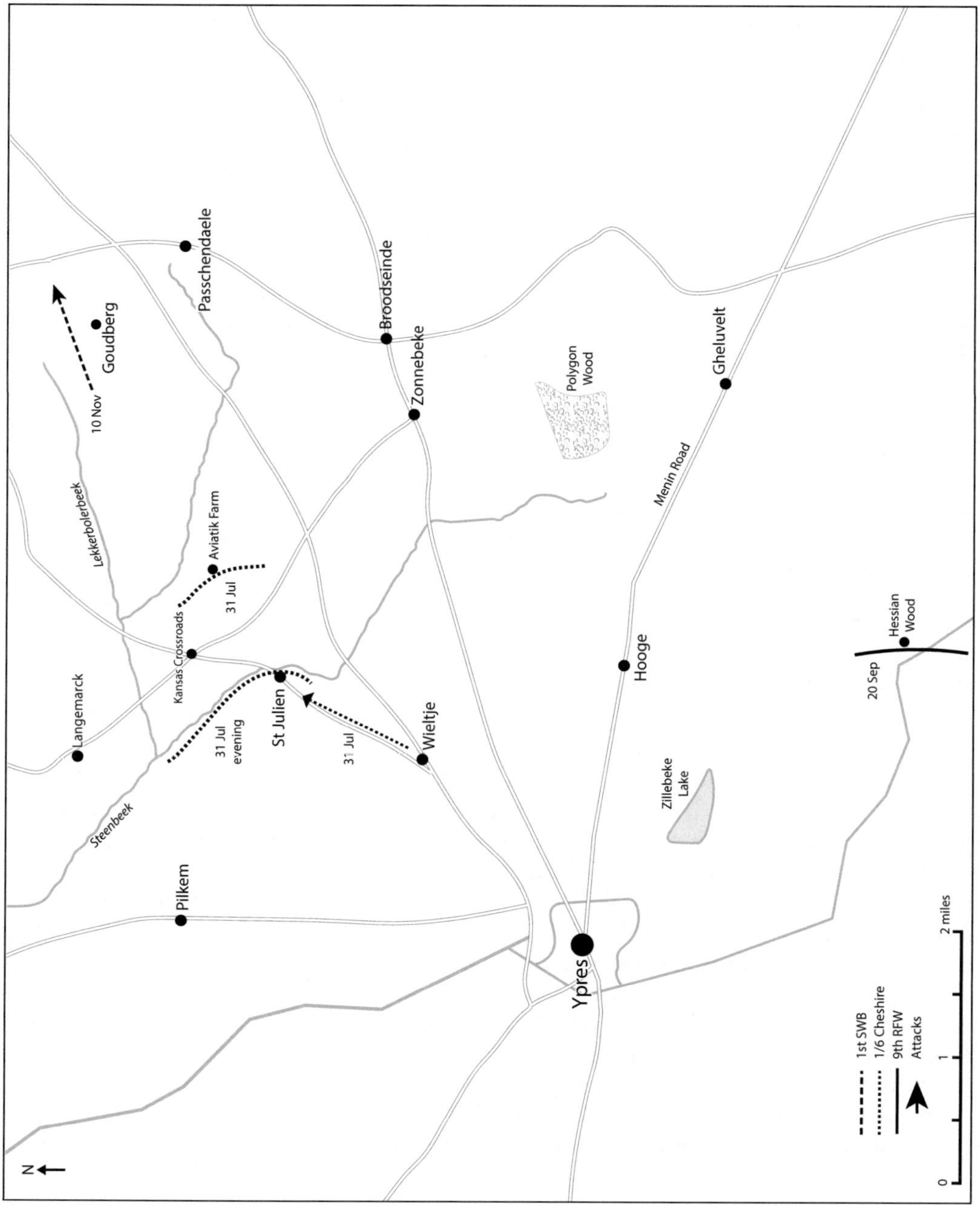

Map 6: Third Battle of Ypres: 1/6th Cheshire, 9th RWF and 1st SWB.

Sixteen Marcher battalions were involved, although not all would take part in the initial attack. At about 10:00 am, 1/6th Cheshire, in 118th Brigade of 39th Division, moved forward to connect the left of the main attack with the defensive front along the Steenbeek. They advanced steadily from near Wieltje through pouring rain, passed through St Julien and captured the final objective, the German Third Line west of Aviatik Farm, some 1,100 yards north-east of St Julien. Unfortunately, the troops on the right had been held up short of St Julien and the Cheshire's right flank became exposed. The Germans spotted this and attacked, causing many casualties. Fierce fighting ensued, and a heavy German barrage then compounded the situation. Eventually the Cheshires were able to withdraw and the whole line fell back to the east bank of the Steenbeek – where yet more casualties were caused by the British guns shelling them during the evening.[48] During the day 1/6th Cheshire had lost approximately 500 men, killed, wounded or missing; by the time they were relieved during the evening of 1 August their strength had been reduced to 3 officers and 57 ORs. Some returning stragglers turned up so the next day when they returned to garrison the captured trenches with 3 officers and 121 ORs. By the time they were relieved on 5 August, the total casualties would be 3 officers and 193 men killed or missing with a further 12 officers and 269 men wounded.[49]

The Cheshires moved back to rest and reorganise, and were rejoined by the men who had been left out of the action. A period of feverish activity now ensued for the Battalion clerks, one of whom was Walter Williamson, and whose diary gives a clear account of the work necessary to identify casualties after a battalion had been in action. In this instance, the difficulty of obtaining accurate information had been compounded by a shell having taken out the 1/6th Cheshire's Orderly Room dugout, causing the loss of the companies' records, so it was very difficult to sort out details of the casualties.

Williamson recounts how a fresh nominal roll of the Battalion was obtained from the 3rd Echelon at the Base, which the Battalion clerks used to work out who was still present with the unit. Details were then obtained of those men who were known to have been killed and this information was then further checked against lists received from officers in charge of burial parties. Daily lists were also coming in from Casualty Clearing Stations, but a long roll still remained of men unaccounted for. These would be reported as 'Missing' for the time being until such time as evidence came though that they were officially notified as Prisoners of War. Those that still remained unaccounted for and were reported as missing would, after a statutory period be shown in the casualty lists as 'No … Reported Missing July 31st 1917 now presumed Killed in Action'.[50]

A total of 114 1/6th Cheshire men are shown in *SDGW* as having been killed on 31 July. Unfortunately, very few of their Service Records have survived but examination of available information indicates a battalion still predominantly made up of Cheshire soldiers. Over 90 of those killed had enlisted in Cheshire, many in the battalion's home town of Stockport, with a further 13 from neighbouring counties. Over a third (45) had been with the battalion since 1915, 18 of whom had arrived in France with it in November 1914. The loss of so many 'originals' must have hit the battalion hard. Of those arriving after 1915, 19 were shown as

48 *BOH 1917 Vol. 2*, p. 168 and Crookenden, *Cheshire Regiment in the Great War*, p. 113.
49 TNA WO 95/2590: 1/6 Cheshire War Diary 31 July-5 August 1917.
50 Walter Williamson, *A Tommy at Ypres – Walter's War*, p. 155.

Typical Infantry battalion Orderly Room clerks: 11th Cheshire Orderly Room staff in 1915. Left to right: LCpl Jones, Sgt Hornby, Cpl Hayes and CSgt Butler. (Cheshire Regimental Archives)

already belonging to 1/6th Cheshire on arrival at the IBD and appear to have been drafted from the Reserve battalion as replacements during the latter part of 1916. Some 16 of the rest had seen previous service in other Cheshire battalions, both Regular and TF, but it is likely that many of the late 1916 arrivals shown on arrival at the IBD as unallocated Cheshire soldiers were Derbyites like Walter Williamson who had attested in late 1915. He had been called up in June 1916 and had been posted to 3rd Cheshire, with the number 44170. In December 1916 he had been posted to France, arriving at No 4 IBD in Rouen where he was allocated to 1/6th Cheshire, with a new number 15362. He joined the battalion as part of a draft of 283 which arrived on 12 December.[51] Of the men who died on 1 July, only 8 had regimental numbers in the five-figure 15xxx range which were higher than Williamson's; they may not have been part of the same draft but it is safe to assume that they had arrived with the battalion between December 1916 and 1 March 1917, when the new 6-figure numbers were allocated to TF soldiers; Williamson's number then changed to 268163. However, without the Service Records, it remains impossible to identify how many might have been conscripts rather than volunteers. Geographically, of the total who died only 18 had not originally enlisted in the Cheshires and 12 of these had already been transferred to the Regiment prior to arriving in France. In late July 1917, therefore, the

51 Ibid and TNA WO 95/95/2590: 1/6th Cheshire War Diary entry for 12 December 1916.

1/6th Cheshire remained predominantly a Cheshire battalion, which had been able to replace previous losses from within Regimental resources.[52]

Overall, however, the manpower situation for the BEF as a whole was becoming increasingly serious. Correspondence passed rapidly between London and GHQ as the two AG Branches sought to obtain men. In early August the War Office warned GHQ that the estimated minimum number of Infantry reinforcements available for France during the months of August, September and October would be 123,000 British and 34,250 Overseas Contingents.[53] Although it was noted as a minimum, it was unlikely that there would be many more to replace the anticipated further losses of the offensive. A General Staff Memorandum on 11 August showed the infantry to be 85,000 men deficient, an average of 1,650 men short in each division. On 17 August the situation was made even clearer in a letter from Robertson to GHQ warning that probably less than 8,000 men would arrive as drafts during September.[54] As a special measure it was decided temporarily to deplete certain arms (unspecified) of the Service at home in order to provide drafts for Infantry units in France. This would free up an additional 20,000 Infantry Reinforcements for August, September and October.[55] Haig held a Manpower Conference on 21 August at which he warned the Army Commanders that British divisions in France would probably be 100,000 men below establishment by the end of October, and emphasized the necessity for 'A' men to be released for the Infantry whenever possible.[56] The same day he directed that immediate steps should be taken to examine all Directorates and departments and to send to the Base Depots 'all personnel, trained and untrained whose services can be dispensed with temporarily'. Daily reports were to be forwarded of the numbers despatched to Base Depots and a roll of the men sent to HQ 3rd Echelon stating to which Base Depot they had been sent.[57]

AG Branch GHQ continued to seek more men from other sources already in theatre. Any possible source of manpower was being considered. In early August the disbandment of all except four of the ten Entrenching Battalions was proposed. Instructions were subsequently given for the disbandment of all Entrenching Battalions except Number 7, which received Guards and reinforcements from Rouen and Le Havre, and Number 10, which received reinforcements from Étaples and Calais.[58] Later in the month Infantry attached to the RE Tunneling Companies were also withdrawn to be used as ordinary reinforcements.[59] Attention had also returned to the Cavalry and on 4 August it was decided that twelve Corps Cavalry Regiments were to be dismounted and the men thus released withdrawn to the Base for training as Infantry. It was also decided that since only 2000 reinforcements were to be maintained in theatre for the various branches of the MGC, only 100 were necessary for the Cavalry Brigade MGC, thus releasing a further 400 for Infantry reinforcements.

52 *SDGW* deaths for 1/6th Cheshire on 31 July 1917 plus Medal Rolls and Service Records on <www.ancestry.com>
53 TNA WO 95/26: AG GHQ War Diary entry 7 August 1917.
54 *BOH 1917 Vol. 2*, p.234 and fn. 2.
55 TNA WO 95/26: AG GHQ War Diary entry 22 August: War Office letter 121/Drafts/7509 (AG1).
56 Ibid., AG GHQ War Diary entry 21 August 1917.
57 Ibid., AG GHQ War Diary entry 21 August 1917 – C in C letter C/408/1 to QMG, DGMS, E in C, DGT, GOC L of C Area.
58 Ibid., AG GHQ War Diary entries dated 3, 6, 11, 25 and 27 August 1917.
59 Ibid., AG War Diary entry for 21 August 1917.

The level of training of reinforcements remained variable. Drafts continued to arrive in France requiring completion of their training but time at the Base for these men was now reduced still further to five days.[60] The drafts were certainly needed at the front as soon as possible but in late August, Divisional commanders protested to Fifth Army that divisions now needed at least four weeks, and preferably six, to replace casualties and train up new drafts before being sent back into action.[61] Training capacity at the Bases, however, was also now required to turn fit men 'combed out' at the Base and from the L of C into Infantry, which seems to have taken about six weeks. In early September the War Office offered to despatch 10,000 'B1' men to be substituted for a similar number of 'A1' men so long as the latter could be made available as reinforcements before 1 October. GHQ appears to have responded that the 'A1' men thus released could not be retrained and made ready for use as reinforcements before 1 November since the War Office offer was withdrawn on the grounds that the men could be better used for substitution at home.[62] Time was also needed to turn Cavalrymen into Infantry soldiers. They had been dismounted in August but it would be October before the 16th Warwickshire would receive a draft 'for the most part fellows of good physique; mostly cavalrymen from the base drafted into the infantry'.[63]

The *Official History* shows the number of casualties for the period 31 July-28 August as 3,424 officers and 64,586 ORs but the August figures for the BEF as a whole were 5,096 officers and 103,998 ORs. The total Cavalry and Infantry reinforcements despatched to divisions had been 4,111 officers and 90,844 men.[64] It was a massive shortfall, although the bulk of the reinforcements would have gone to those divisions engaged in the offensive. Some 22 British divisions had been in action on the Fifth Army front, 14 of which had been withdrawn for replenishment and, despite the nucleus of officers and men held back from the battle, would not be fit for action again for some weeks.

A further indication of the seriousness of the manpower situation is visible in the dwindling recruiting figures. Drafts arriving in France during August would have had to have started their training in April. That month the number of 'A' men required had been 267,494 but only 55,857 were actually recruited, of whom 18,660 were lads who could not be posted abroad until they turned 19.[65]

Some battalions were more fortunate than others. The 1/6th Cheshire received several drafts during September, many of whom were returned casualties from their own and other Cheshire battalions. The question of the absorption of these drafts was always a consideration but Walter Williamson felt that:

> The CO had a thoughtful way of dealing with these. He would call all men out who had been with the battalion previously and put them in the companies that they wished for,

60 Ibid., AG War Diary entry dated 22 August 1917.
61 *BOH 1917 Vol. 2* p. 192 fn1.
62 TNA WO 95/26: AG GHQ War Diary entries 1 and 11 September 1917.
63 J. Cooksey & D. Griffiths, *Harry's War* (London: Ebury Press, 2013), p. 264, Wednesday 17 October 1917.
64 *BOH 1917 Vol. 2*, p. 209 and TNA 95/26 AG War Diary figures for August 1917.
65 War Office, *Statistics of the Military Effort*, p. 369.

> so that they could get amongst their old friends again. The remainder were then divided amongst the four companies to bring them as near as possible to equal strength.

Altogether, between 9-17 September 33 men rejoined and 216 reinforcements arrived.[66]

During the second week of September a disturbance occurred at the huge Base Depot in Étaples that, if it had escalated, could have seriously affected the supply of reinforcements for divisions preparing for the next offensive. Étaples at that time was the largest Base Depot, catering for some 50,000 reinforcements, and also contained the biggest base hospital complex. The training regime there had acquired a reputation for being particularly harsh, that does not seem to have been shared by those at other Base Depots such as Rouen and Calais. George Culpitt, for example, arrived at the Rouen Base on 14 September on his return from sick leave in England. There he stayed for seven days 'engaged in the various exasperating manoeuvres with which these rotten camps were infested'. Similarly, Geoffrey Husbands had arrived back at the Calais Base on 11 September after a spell at home. His draft was to be put through a general course of training in all activities: musketry, bayonet fighting, assault practices, gas tests and bombing. He refers to the 'Base Wallah' instructors' 'old tricks, trying to be as regimental as they could' and the consequent 'feud' between them and the BEF drafts. The chief grouse seemed to be that parades and training were badly timetabled 'with irritating delays and waste of time at one stage and then being conducted in a frantic hustle at the next'.[67] There were no major incidents at Rouen and Calais, however, just the soldier's perennial irritation at being 'messed around'. The difficulties at Étaples appear to have arisen from an excessively harsh training regime, that nonetheless allowed the men a great deal of free time. The camp police also seem to have been particularly officious.

The men passing through Étaples in September were a complex mixture of reinforcements newly arrived from England, men who had been 'combed out' from units at the Base and those returning from hospitals and convalescent depots. Even the reinforcements from England were not simple to categorize as they would have included men returning from convalescence at home and newly trained recruits, both volunteers and conscripted men. Some of the latter would undoubtedly have been amongst those called up after having been re-examined under the unpopular Review of Exceptions Act, who would by now have completed their fourteen weeks' training. There were also Canadian and New Zealand troops in the camp, the Canadian IBD having exchanged places with that of the Australians in mid-1917. Altogether it was a volatile mix requiring careful handling, particularly given the large numbers passing through each day; on 8 September, for example, some 3871 men arrived from England, including a huge draft of 1519 New Zealanders, and 353 from other Base areas.[68]

The disturbance started during the afternoon of Sunday 9 September when a New Zealander, Gunner Healy, was arrested by the camp police as he returned from the town of Étaples. The reason for his arrest is not entirely clear and he was soon released. The arrest had been witnessed by other groups of men, however, and an angry crowd began to arrive which was soon swelled by men leaving the afternoon performance at the nearby camp cinema. Attempts were made to

66 Walter Williamson, *A Tommy at Ypres*, p. 171 and TNA: WO 95/2590 1/6th Cheshire War Diary.
67 <www.culpitt-war-diary.org.uk/index.htm> George Culpitt's diart entries for September 1917 and J. M. Bourne & Bob Bushaway (eds.) *Joffrey's War* (Nottingham: Salient Books, 2011), p. 469.
68 TNA WO 95/4027/5: Étaples War Diary entry for 8 September 1917.

rush the police post with stones being thrown by a crowd now numbering about 3-4,000 and containing many New Zealanders and also Scots. One of the camp police, Pte Reeve, seems to have panicked and, having snatched a pistol, fired shots over the heads of the crowd, one of which hit and killed Cpl Wood, a Gordon Highlander, who had been standing on the edge of the crowd. The crowd was now so incensed and threatening towards the camp police that the latter rapidly took cover. The Camp Adjutant, Captain V. C Guinness, was informed of the shooting and reported the incident to the OC Reinforcements, Colonel Nason, who immediately ordered the New Zealand IBD to provide a picquet of one officer and fifty men. Two further picquets, each of 100 men, were ordered from No 19 IBD (Argyll and Sutherland Highlanders and Cameron Highlanders) and No 25 IBD (Border and Loyal North Lancashire Regiments) and a further officer and fifteen men were detailed from No 18 IBD (Royal Highlanders, Gordon Highlanders and Seaforth Highlanders). Rifles and bayonets were carried but no ammunition issued. With the assistance of officers from other IBDS the disturbance was quietened down, the men were gradually got back to camp and by about 10:00 pm all was quiet. The crowd's antagonism seems to have been aimed solely at the camp police and the use of officers and picquets from the parent IBDs of the New Zealanders and the Scottish soldiers seemed to have assisted in calming the situation.[69] The use of men from these IBDs indicates no apparent disquiet on the part of the military authorities concerning these particular units.

Over the next few days what followed was a very strange kind of 'mutiny', with no one else killed and no ammunition, although issued, used in its dispersal. Hundreds of reinforcements continued to arrive daily at the camp and drafts departed for the front as normal: some 628 men were despatched to various divisions on 10 September and a further 900 on 11 September. The thousands of men remaining in the camp continued to carry on with routine training and activities during the working day and it was only after these had finished that further disturbances occurred as crowds of men attempted to get into Étaples. The main problem appears to have been that the camp police had become increasingly unpopular through over-exerting their authority. The shooting of Cpl Wood was the final straw and they were now under serious threat. They were immediately extracted, their places being taken by officers and picquets from the IBDs. Although there were some 'noisy meetings', the crowd continued to be generally good-humoured and order was restored to both the town and camp by about 10:00 pm each night. It was obvious, however, that the situation could not be allowed to continue and by 11 September it was agreed that troops from elsewhere were urgently needed. The following day, all reinforcements were confined to camp but, perhaps inevitably, further break-outs occurred. Mid-afternoon about 1,000 men marched themselves to Paris Plage but then returned, having caused no disturbance or damage. Around 6:30 pm outside troops arrived in the form of some 384 men of 1st HAC, and their Commanding Officer took over command of the camp and the guards and picquets. The disturbance now gradually subsided. On 13 September only about 100 men left camp in the afternoon and a further 200 that evening but almost all were back in camp by 9:00 pm. By now, however, GHQ had decided to send the 1st RWF and 22nd Manchester, from 7th Division, to Étaples. The 1st RWF arrived about midnight and found the situation 'well in hand'. The following day one company mounted guard over the Field Prisoners

69 Ibid., Étaples War Diary entry for 9 September 1917.

Compound whilst the rest of the battalion stood to.[70] The display of discipline had the desired effect and by Saturday 15 September order had been fully restored and the reinforcements were again allowed to leave camp to enjoy Étaples. The camp police had been replaced by an entirely new group of men, all the original police having been dispersed elsewhere.[71] The 1st RWF, having enjoyed a breath of sea air and a swim in sea-water departed for the front again on 17 September. Altogether fifty-four men from the camp were subsequently court martialled for various offences arising from the disturbances, but only four, deemed to have been ringleaders, were charged with and found guilty of mutiny. Of these, only one was executed.

There is no mention of the disturbance in AG GHQ War Diary but Haig noted in a brief part of his diary entry for Wednesday 12 September that Fowke had mentioned 'some disturbances' to him 'due to some men of new drafts with revolutionary ideas who produced red flags and refused to obey orders'.[72] There is no mention of red flags in the Étaples War Diary and witnesses at the courts martial were unclear as to whether they had seen flags or simply red, and other coloured, handkerchiefs. There is some evidence that it was the suggestion of socialist tendencies amongst the mutineers that prompted Haig to move the training of Infantry reinforcements away from the Bases to Corps Reinforcement Camps, ostensibly to remove them from the influence of Republican elements amongst the dockers, but whether this was in fact the prime reason is unsubstantiated.[73] Suffice it to say that in his summary for September the Étaples Camp Commandant noted that training at 1 and 2 Training Camps had virtually closed down on 24 September as Infantry reinforcements were now going to the front to complete their training. In future reinforcements would pass swiftly through the Bases for processing before being sent forward.

In the meantime, planning was continuing for the next stage of the offensive. The lead had now passed to Second Army and Plumer produced a plan based on a series of steps, each with a strictly limited objective, culminating in gaining the Gheluvelt plateau. On 20 September, Second and Fifth Armies attacked with 11 divisions at the start of the Battle of the Menin Road Ridge. It was a complete success. There were of course casualties: those for the Infantry on the first day were estimated at 450 officers and 13,028 ORs.[74] In 19th Division, 9th RWF was in reserve but was hurried up to hold the line at Hessian Wood, arriving in time to ward off a German counter-attack but coming under heavy shell-fire. Over 20-21September they suffered 109 casualties: 3 officers wounded, 21 ORs killed (including 7 died of wounds), 73 wounded and 12 missing.[75] Analysis of the 21 men killed shows that one third had not originally enlisted in the RWF, although all except two had enlisted within Western Command. The other two-thirds had all served previously in 9th RWF or other RWF battalions but the effect of the 'combing out' activities of earlier in the summer is clearly visible: four men had come from being attached to Tunnelling Companies, two had been in 4th (Garrison) RWF and two had been

70 Ward *Regimental Recrods of the Royal Welch Fusiliers Vol. III*, p. 353.
71 TNA WO 95/4027/5: Étaples War Diary for September 1917 and Putkowski, J. *British Army Mutineers 1914-1922* (London: Francis Boutle Publishers, 1998), pp. 2 26.
72 Sheffield, G. & Bourne, J. *Douglas Haig War Diaries and Letters 1914-1918* (London: Weidenfeld & Nicolson, 2005), p. 325.
73 TNA WO 256/22: Haig's diary entry for 23 September 1917 cited in C. Messenger, *Call to Arms* (London: Cassell Military Paperbacks, 2006), p. 404.
74 TNA WO 95/26: AG GHQ War Diary entry for 20 September 1917.
75 TNA WO 95/2092-1: 9th RWF War Diary 20-21 September 1917.

in the 19th Division Cyclist Company. However, the fact that two thirds of those killed had previous RWF service would appear to indicate that even during 'combing out' some attention was paid to regimental affiliations.

The second 'step', the Battle of Polygon Wood, began on 26 September with an attack by Second and Fifth Armies across the Gheluvelt plateau. The main attack, by I Anzac Corps of Second Army, was intended to gain the whole of Polygon Wood and the southern part of the village of Zonnebeke. The X Corps was to cover the ANZAC's right and attack with two divisions either side of the Menin Road whilst on the Second Army's left the Fifth Army was to reach a line between Zonnebeke Station and Kansas Crossroads. Four Marcher battalions would be involved, 2nd and 10th RWF, 1/6th Cheshire and 7th KSLI, although none would take part in the first assault. The 10th RWF and 7th KSLI of 3rd Division had arrived in the Salient about a week earlier whilst 2nd RWF in 33rd Division had been moved south from the coast, arriving in the line on 23 September. The newly arrived divisions had trained as much as they could: the 10th RWF had spent ten days training before they left their previous location, whilst the 3rd Division's Brigades had practised assembling at night on taped positions and by day attacking strong-points with rifle and rifle grenade.[76] What they brought to the forthcoming attack were fresh troops in units that were up to strength: 7th KSLI's strength was 44 officers and 957 ORs.[77]

At 5:50 am on 26 September the Second and Fifth Armies attacked with seven divisions. The estimated Infantry casualties reported during the first day were 161 officers and 4,969 men but by the end of the period 26 September-3 October the 'all arms' casualty figures had risen to 681 officers and 14,694 OR.[78] For the four Marcher battalions the casualties totalled 1046 ORs, although it is difficult to draw exact comparisons as the War Diary figures for each battalion cover slightly different periods.[79]

Battalion	Brigade/Division	In Action	Killed	Wounded	Missing	Total Cas
2nd RWF	19th Bde, 33rd Div	26-27 Sep	31	121	37	189
10th RWF	76th Bde, 3rd Div	26-29 Sep	39	202	38	279
7th KSLI	8th Bde, 3rd Div	26-30 Sep	36	237	27	300
1/6th Cheshire	118th Bde, 39th Div	20-27 Sep	60	167	51	278
			166	**727**	**153**	**1046**

Table 9. Casualty figures for 2nd and 10th RWF, 7th KSLI and 1/6th Cheshire between 20-30 September 1917.

76 Ward, *Regimental Records of the Royal Welch Fusiliers Vol. III*, p. 348.
77 Wood, *King's Shropshire Light Infantry*, p. 243.
78 TNA WO 95/26: AG GHQ War Diary entry for 26 September 1917 and *BOH 1917 Vol. 2*, p. 293.
79 TNA WO 95/2423-1: War Diary of 2nd RWF for 26/27 September 1917; WO 95/1436-2: War Diary of 10th RWF for 26/29 September; WO 95/2590-3: War Diary of 1/6th Cheshire casualty figures for 20-27 September; Wood, *King's Shropshire Light Infantry*, p. 244.

All the battalions had lost a large proportion of their fighting strength; although 2nd RWF's total casualties look to be the least, Dr James Dunn considered that they were one-third of the trench strength with which they had gone into action.[80]

The BEF's OR losses for the whole of September were 101,253 (total casualties all arms 59,201 and 'sick wastage' of 42,052). The number of Cavalry and Infantry reinforcements sent to the Divisions, 116,982, was the highest of the whole year, presumably as a result of the 'combing out' measures taken in August.[81] As ever, however, the availability of specific reinforcements was patchy. The Welsh battalions seem to have had the greatest difficulty in getting speedy reinforcements. It would not be until 5 November that 2nd RWF received 168 ORs from the Base, whilst 10th RWF received 'penny packets' of 8 ORS during October and a further 179 by 22 November.[82] On 3 October 7th KSLI showed a strength of 670 ORs but drafts amounting to only 53 were received during that month and a further 14 during November.[83] In contrast, the first draft for 1/6th Cheshire arrived on 29 September; by the end of October 62 men had rejoined and 410 reinforcements had been received.[84] It is difficult to draw specific conclusions about the availability of reinforcements, however, since it is apparent that the War Diary writers did not all have the same priorities: both 2nd and 10th RWF War Diaries are meticulous in mentioning anything that happened to every single officer but ORs appear rather as an afterthought, whilst 1/6th Cheshire's separates out those ORs rejoining the battalion and those newly arriving from the Base. It was not just a problem of numbers, though, as however many reinforcements arrived, they could not replace the loss of experience gained in battle: of those who had been killed, both 2nd RWF and 7th KSLI had lost Company Sergeant-Majors, 1/6th Cheshire had lost five Sergeants whilst 2nd and 10th RWF had each lost four, and between the four battalions some 21 Junior NCOs had been lost. Although men would be promoted into their vacancies, it takes time to grow into a more senior rank and the different responsibilities devolving upon it.

The 3rd and 33rd Divisions had taken part in only one attack, Polygon Wood, but would play no further part in Third Ypres.[85] The 33rd Division, to 2nd RWF's disgust, was now moved south to an 'inactive' Corps, near Messines.[86] The 3rd Division moved to Third Army and arrived in the St Omer area. It would be involved in a subsidiary attack near Bullecourt in November but as far as 7th KSLI was concerned it was a quiet period; the battalion's total casualties for November were 2 officers and 9 ORs wounded and 3 ORs killed.[87] The 39th Division had taken part in three battles, Pilckem Ridge, Menin Road and Polygon Wood, but remained in the area, presumably because sufficient TF reinforcements were available to bring it rapidly back to strength. It did not take part in any further attacks although 1/6th Cheshire

80 Dunn, *The War the Infantry Knew*, pp. 404-5. NB. Dunn states that more than 60 were dead.
81 TNA WO 95/26: AG GHQ War Diary figures for September 1917.
82 TNA WO 95/2423-1: War Diary of 2nd RWF for 26 September-5 November 1917; WO 95/1436-2 War Diary of 10th RWF for 26 September-22 November 1917.
83 Wood, *King's Shropshire Light Infantry*, pp. 243-4.
84 TNA WO 95/2590-3: 1/6th Cheshire War Diary for September-October 1917.
85 TNA WO 158-20: Items 737 and 738 Divisions taking part in attacks 31 July-12 October 1917, Ypres.
86 Dunn, *The War the Infantry Knew*, pp. 406-8.
87 Wood, *King's Shropshire Light Infantry*, pp. 244-5.

would have an uncomfortable time during the Battle of Poelcappelle supplying working parties at Hell Fire Corner, just outside Ypres, from 5:00 am to 5:00 pm for five days.[88]

Battle of Poelcappelle. Walking wounded coming down and reinforcements going up a duckboard trench near Langemarck (Langemark-Poelkapelle), 11 October 1917. IWM Q 3006

The success of the 'steps' achieved so far encouraged GHQ to attempt a third: to capture the eastern edge of the Gheluvelt Plateau and the village of Broodseinde on a frontage of 14,000 yards with twelve divisions, half of which had not previously taken part in Third Ypres.[89] The attack started on 4 October and the main objectives were rapidly gained, although there were more difficulties on the flanks. Very few Marcher battalions were involved. For 1st Cheshire, it was the first time the Fifth Division had taken part in Third Ypres. In the event, the Cheshires, although moved up into the front line on 5 October, spent their time under heavy German shellfire at a cost of 36 men killed and about 150 wounded. Some 53 replacements arrived on 15 October.[90] The total Second Army losses for 4-8 October were 12,498, of which 10,862 were Infantry, whilst between 4-6 October the four assaulting divisions of the Fifth Army lost

88 Crookenden, *Cheshire Regiment in the Great War*, p. 123.
89 WO 158/20: Third Ypres Divisions taking part in attacks 31 July-12 October 1917.
90 TNA 95/1571: 1st Cheshire War Diary October 1917.

4,283.[91] It was a further successful step, with the line having been advanced about 1,000 yards closer to the Passchendaele Ridge and almost all the Gheluvelt Plateau gained.

The battles of Poelcappelle, and then First Passchendaele, followed in quick succession but there would be little Marcher involvement until Second Passchendaele which started on 26 October and lasted officially until 10 November. By now it had been raining continuously since 4 October and conditions had become atrocious. The Canadian Corps put in the main attack but on the right X Corps made a third attempt to capture the Gheluvelt and Polderhoek spurs. Later in the battle the 1st Division, including 1st SWB, would play their first and only part in Third Ypres, having spent the previous months some miles west of Dunkirk preparing to land on the Belgian coast once the anticipated gains of the Ypres battle had been exploited. There their training had been limited to embarkation and disembarkation, and scaling replicas of the high walls of the German coastal defences. They were brought south in late October and at 5:00 am on 10 November 1st SWB attacked north-eastwards beyond Goudberg. They came up against fierce opposition and by early afternoon were forced to fall back from the line they had reached. They had suffered heavy losses with 372 OR casualties, well over two thirds of those who had gone into action.[92] On 12 November they were withdrawn from the line and the next few days were spent in trying to clean off the Flanders mud from themselves and their equipment. A draft of 83 arrived on 23 November but it would be January 1918 before the battalion would be fully brought back up to strength.

On 20 November Haig finally closed down the Ypres campaign. The total all ranks casualties for Third Ypres, between 31 July-10 November, were 238,313, of which the Infantry casualties amounted to 170,534. Some 33,713 ORs had been killed plus a further 29,036 were missing, many of whom would never be found.[93] The overall figures for the BEF in France were much higher: between 1 August and 31 October the total losses were 404,629 (276,674 casualties and 127,955 'sick wastage'). Although 116,982 Infantry and Cavalry OR reinforcements had been found to send to divisions in September, in October the figure had dropped to 78,233 men and in November to 59,205.[94] The manning situation was becoming ever worse.

The size of Haig's force had also been diminished by his being required towards the end of the year to despatch five British Divisions to the Italian front. These included the 5th and 7th Divisions so 1st Cheshire and 1st RWF were now away from the Western Front. It would be April before 1st Cheshire would return.

91 *BOH 1917 Vol. 2*, pp. 311, 315.
92 Atkinson, *History of the South Wales* Borderers, pp. 345-9 and TNA: WO 95/1280/3 1st South Wales Borderers War Diary for November and December 1917 and January 1918.
93 *BOH 1917 Vol. 2*, p.360 and fn 2; p.361, 364-5.
94 TNA WO 95/26: Figures from AG GHQ War Diary for August-December 1917. NB the War Diary does not contain the overall figures for November 1917.

Detailed Analysis of Selected Battalions

The selected Battalions, apart from 1/4th KSLI which had not arrived on the Western Front until mid-August, had been in action throughout 1917.[95] It would be expected by now that analysis of those who had died would begin to show a lesser ability to reinforce from within the traditional sources for the Marcher Regiments, particularly for those battalions recruited in Wales. As Tables 10.1 and 10.2 show, this is true to an extent but not as much in every case as might have been anticipated.

Enlistment Location	1st Cheshire		9th Cheshire		1st KSLI		1/6th KSLI	
Regimental Area	70	59%	62	67%	43	53%	104	*73%*
Elsewhere in No 4 District - England	1				10		10	
Elsewhere in No 4 District - Wales	14		1		11		7	
Total enlisted in No 4 District	85	72%	63	68%	64	79%	121	85%
Enlisted in No 3 District	9		11		5		8	
• Liverpool/Manchester	8		4		2		6	
Total Enlisted in Western Command	**102**	**86%**	**78**	**85%**	**71**	**88%**	**135**	**94%**
Northern Command	9		7		4		3	
Southern Command	3		4		2		1	
• Birmingham	0		1		1			
Eastern	1		2				4	
London District	2				3			
Scotland/Ireland	1							
Overseas	0							
Total Other Commands	**16**		**14**		**10**		**8**	
Total Deaths	**118**		**92**		**81**		**143**	

Table 10.1. Enlistment locations of soldiers of selected English Regular battalions who were killed/died between 1 July-30 November 1917.

The Cheshire Regiment's ability to reinforce its Regular battalions with men enlisted within the Regimental area of Cheshire has dropped for 1st Cheshire from 71 percent in 1916 to 59 percent but has remained steady for 9th Cheshire at 67 percent. The KSLI enlistments in their

95 1/4th KSLI had been in Far East since February 1915; landed at Le Havre 29 July 1917 and joined 190th Brigade, 63rd Division on 18 August 1917.

Regimental area have also dropped from the 1916 figures: 1st KSLI is down by 18 percent to 53 percent whilst 6th KSLI has fallen 9 percent to 73 percent. Turning the figures round, however, in the second half of 1917 about two-thirds of 1st and 9th Cheshire had still been enlisted within the Regimental area whilst the KSLI varied between just over half for 1st KSLI and almost three-quarters for 6th KSLI. The ability of the two English county regiments to make up their numbers from within No 4 District remains visible with, at the lowest, 9th Cheshire showing 68 percent and, at the highest, 6th KSLI at 85 percent enlistments in that area. Looking at the figures for enlistments in Western Command as whole, the figures have fallen since 1916 but still stand at 85 percent for both Cheshire battalions and 88 and 94 percent for 1st and 6th KSLI respectively having been enlisted within their Home Command. It is thus apparent that even by the second half of 1917, the Cheshire and the KSLI Regular battalions are still able to draw to a large extent on men from their traditional recruiting areas.

Enlistment Location	2nd RWF		9th RWF		1st SWB		10th SWB	
Regimental Area	39	28%	11	14%	45	31%	39	*45%*
Elsewhere in No 4 District - England	20		4		8		6	
Elsewhere in No 4 District - Wales	26		15		33	23%	7	
Total enlisted in No 4 District	85	61%	30	38%	86	60%	52	60%
Enlisted in No 3 District	16		16	20%	3		2	
• Liverpool/Manchester	13		14	18%	9		4	
Total Enlisted in Western Command	**114**	**81%**	**60**	**76%**	**98**	**67%**	**58**	**67%**
Northern Command	6		5		10		1	
Southern Command	3		2		2		5	
• Birmingham	2				3		1	
Eastern	5		7		11	8%	16	*18%*
London District	8		5		18	13%	6	*7%*
Scotland/Ireland	2				1			
Overseas								
Total Other Commands	**26**		**19**		**45**		**29**	
Total Deaths	**140**		**79**		**143**		**87**	

Table 10.2. Enlistment locations of soldiers of selected Welsh Regular battalions who were killed/died between 1 July-30 November 1917.

Turning to the RWF and the SWB, the picture is more varied. Only 28 and 14 percent respectively were enlisted into the 2nd and 9th RWF in their Regimental area. Traditionally, however, their recruits had come from throughout Wales and neighbouring English counties, so the figures for No 4 District rise to 61 percent for 2nd RWF but reach only 38 percent for 9th RWF. The influence of Lancashire, and particularly Liverpool and Manchester, can be seen, however, within the figures of 81 percent and 76 percent enlistments in Western Command. The Birmingham influence on 2nd RWF has virtually disappeared now with only two men out of 140 having enlisted in that city. The SWB show greater numbers having enlisted in the Regimental area, with an increase of 5 percent over 1916 for 1st SWB although there is a serious drop of 45 percent for 10th SWB. For both SWB battalions 60 percent had enlisted in No 4 District, rising to 67 percent for both from Western Command.

Birth location	**1st Cheshire**		**9th Cheshire**		**1st KSLI**		**6th KSLI**	
Regimental Area	47	40%	43	47%	39	48%	80	*56%*
Elsewhere in No 4 District – England	4				10		10	
Elsewhere in No 4 District - Wales	5		2		2		6	
Total born in No 4 District	56	47%	45	49%	51	63%	96	67%
Born in No 3 District	17		15		6		8	
• Liverpool/Manchester	8		3		0		5	
Total Born in Western Command	**81**	**67%**	**63**	**68%**	**57**	**70%**	**109**	**76%**
Northern Command	15		11		4		11	
Southern Command	2		6		4		5	
• Birmingham	0		1		1		1	
Eastern	2		1		3		6	
London District	4		1		3		1	
Scotland/Ireland	1		1		2			
Overseas	0							
Total Other Commands	**24**		**21**		**17**		**24**	
Location of Birth Unknown	13		8		7		10	
Total Deaths	**118**		**92**		**81**		**143**	

Table 10.3. Birth locations of soldiers of selected English Regular battalions who were killed/died between 1 July-30 November 1917.

A growing spread of birth locations across all sample battalions is visible in Tables 10.3. and 10.4. For the English battalions, the numbers of those born within the respective Regimental areas has fallen slightly. The figures for those born in Cheshire have dropped but only by four and five percent respectively for the 1st and 9th battalions. For 1st KSLI, the number of those born in Shropshire, Herefordshire or Radnorshire has fallen by just 2 percent, although the drop for 6th KSLI is 12 percent. For all four battalions, however, the numbers of those born within Western Command remains above two thirds of the whole.

For the Welsh battalions, less than a quarter of those who had died during the period were born in the Regimental areas of their respective battalions. Even when the numbers of those born in Wales are added, the percentages for all battalions are still well below 50 percent. Overall, they are lower, but not markedly so, than the 1916 figures. Conversely, the figures for those born in Western Command are slightly higher for 2nd RWF and within 1 percent for 9th RWF and 1st SWB. Only 10th SWB shows a fall of 10 percent in the number having been born within Western Command; in part, however, this may be explained by the men who had been born just across the Welsh border in Gloucestershire and Somerset, thus being shown against Southern Command, but had moved to the South Wales coalfields for work and where they had subsequently enlisted.

Birth location	2nd RWF		9th RWF		1st SWB		10th SWB	
Regimental Area	30	21%	12	15%	26	18%	21	*24%*
Elsewhere in No 4 District – England	21		4		11		10	
Elsewhere in No 4 District - Wales	24		10		32	22%	10	
Total born in No 4 District	75	54%	26	33%	69	48%	41	47%
Born in No 3 District	17		13	16%	6		3	
• Liverpool/Manchester	6		10	13%	7		2	
Total Born in Western Command	**98**	**70%**	**49**	**62%**	**82**	**57%**	**46**	**53%**
Northern Command	12		9		11		2	
Southern Command	7		3		9		17	
• Birmingham					3		1	
Eastern	6		3		8		13	
London District	6		5		18		4	
Scotland/Ireland	2		3		3			
Overseas			1					
Total Other Commands	**33**		**24**		**52**		**37**	
Location of Birth Unknown	9		6		9		4	
Total Deaths	**140**		**79**		**143**		**87**	

Table 10.4. Birth locations of soldiers of selected Welsh Regular battalions who were killed/died between 1 July-30 November 1917.

The figures for enlistments in the TF battalions (see Table 10.5 below) reflect even greater continuing homogeneity, although for 1/5th Cheshire, 1/4th RWF and 1/4th KSLI, the totals are small and consequently skew their percentages. It is clear from the figures for 1/6th Cheshire and 1/2nd Monmouthshire that they were continuing to be able to replace largely from within their own Regimental areas. When enlistments in No 4 Area are considered 80 percent of 1/6th Cheshire and 86 percent of 1/2nd Monmouthshire had enlisted there, rising to 89 percent and 99 percent respectively for Western Command. It seems likely that these higher figures reflect both the number of original TF HS soldiers that had become available for posting overseas as a result of the 1916 MSAs and also the number of Derby men who had enlisted in the TF.

Enlistment Location	1/5th Cheshire		1/6th Cheshire		1/4th KSLI		1 /4th RWF		1/2nd Monmouths	
Regimental Area	7	*88%*	188	*77%*	36	*97%*	9	*50%*	59	*66%*
Elsewhere in No 4 District - England			6		1		1		8	
Elsewhere in No 4 District - Wales							4		11	
Total enlisted in No 4 District	7	88%	194	80%	37	100%	14	78%	78	86%
Enlisted in No 3 District			15				2		6	
• Liverpool/Manchester	1		9						4	
Total Enlisted in Western Command	**8**	**100%**	**218**	**89%**	**37**	**100%**	**16**	**89%**	**88**	**99%**
Northern Command			15				1			
Southern Command			1						1	
• Birmingham			1							
Eastern			3				1			
London District			4							
Scotland/Ireland			2							
Overseas										
Total Other Commands			**26**				**2**		**1**	
Total Deaths	**8**		**244**		**37**		**18**		**89**	

Table 10.5. Enlistment locations of soldiers of selected TF battalions who were killed/died between 1 July – 30 November 1917.

Birth location	1/5th Cheshire		1/6th Cheshire		1/4th KSLI		1/4th RWF		1/2nd Monmouths	
Regimental Area	6	75%	121	50%	28	76%	4	22%	31	35%
Elsewhere in No 4 District – England			9						11	
Elsewhere in No 4 District - Wales			2		3		1		14	
Total born in No 4 District	6		132	54%	31	84%	5	28%	56	63%
Born in No 3 District	1		22				1		4	
• Liverpool/Manchester			10				1		3	
Total Born in Western Command	**7**	**88%**	**164**	**67%**	**31**	**84%**	**7**	**39%**	**63**	**71%**
Northern Command	1		22				1		1	
Southern Command			2		2				6	
Birmingham										
Eastern			9				1		2	
London District			3		3				1	
Scotland/Ireland			4							
Overseas			1							
Total Other Commands	**1**		**41**		**5**		**2**		**10**	
Location of Birth Unknown			39		1		9		16	
Total Deaths	**8**		**244**		**37**		**18**		**89**	

Table 10.6. Birth locations of soldiers of selected TF battalions who were killed/died between 1 July – 30 November 1917.

The TF birth locations (Table 10.6. above) appear to show an ever-widening gap between those of the English and the Welsh, particularly 1/4th RWF, battalions. As with enlistments, however, the small number of deaths skew the percentages.

Overall, the analysis shows that for the Regular battalions of the English and Welsh Marches the majority of those who had died had enlisted in Western Command. For the TF, the figures are even higher, presumably since many of their numbers had not become available for use as reinforcements until late 1916. It continues to appear that the pre-war plans for the provision of reinforcements from local and Command areas were still proving effective, at least for the Marcher Regiments, to a greater extent than might have been anticipated by this stage in the war.

Overview

The procedures for reporting casualties and obtaining replacements remained, with only minor tweaks, those that had been tried and tested during the Battle of the Somme and earlier. The draft system continued to function appropriately but by the end of the year was becoming increasingly affected by the shortage of manpower available to be recruited, as is evident from the fall in the number of reinforcements received in France.

Adoption of the new doctrine for Infantry tactics contained in SS135 and SS143 had been embodied in training, both for units in France and recruits at home. Inevitably, however, comments continued to be made during 1917 on how poorly trained the new drafts for the BEF were but such comments had been being made since late 1914. The recruits and drafts of 1917 were continuing to follow the training programmes laid down earlier in the war and the youths who had come through the new training units for under 19s were in fact better trained than their predecessors. The key factor, however, was that no amount of training could ever equate to hard-won experience gained in combat. Moreover, the real problem was the continued losses of the experienced NCOs and soldiers that the BEF needed in battle.

Although difficulties in obtaining replacements were undoubtedly being encountered by some Regiments, analysis of the deaths suffered by selected Marcher battalions shows that the majority of men had been enlisted in the traditional recruiting areas and the parent Command of the battalions concerned. Despite gloomy predictions to the contrary it still remained possible for a man to choose to serve in his local regiment and the value of *esprit de corps* continued to be recognised.

7

Manpower Crisis

By 1917 the demands of the Army had increasingly to be balanced with those of the whole nation. The supply of manpower was finite and other areas which were heavily involved in the war effort, such as ship-building, munitions, mining, railways and agriculture, could no longer be placed in jeopardy by the withdrawal for the Army of excessive numbers of men. Recruiting had declined in the face of the conflicting demands from these other areas and enlistments during the year had numbered 820,646 men for the Regular Army and the Territorial Force. Not all those obtained, however, were necessarily fit enough for Active Service immediately or old enough to be sent overseas.

The decline in inflow was worsened by the continuing outflow of casualties. Although Third Ypres had been halted in November, the offensives of 1917 continued with the Battle of Cambrai, 20 November-7 December. It was initially successful with the German front being penetrated to a maximum depth of 7000 yards and many prisoners being taken. Celebrations of what appeared to have been a great victory were premature, however, as the momentum of the attack was not maintained, and no breakthrough achieved. On 30 November the Germans counter-attacked, driving the British back and gaining more ground than they had earlier lost. Whilst the total casualty figures for the first day had been about 4,000, by 8 December the total number of OR casualties for the battle had reached 41,817, of whom 4,666 had been killed, 26,774 wounded and 10,377 missing.[1] By the end of 1917, the total British casualties in France and Flanders for that year had risen to some 640,000 of whom 144,448 had been killed or had died of wounds or disease.[2] It had become a constant battle to balance the equation and provide the BEF in France with the replacements required to maintain its operational capability.

By late 1917 the situation was serious. As the year had progressed the shortfall in numbers of men obtained against the Army's stated requirement had grown to the extent that by October

1 *BOH 1917 Vol. 3* pp. 88 and 382.

2 War Office *Statistics of the British Military Effort of the British Empire during the Great War*, pp. 260-265, 364. NB. The casualty figures shown do not include the casualties sustained by the Royal Naval Division (RND) which would be replaced by men from within the Navy's allocation.

the deficit of Category A men suitable for the Infantry stood at 361,105.[3] The effect of this was that it was already anticipated that by the following March the BEF's Infantry would be approximately 250,000, or about 40 percent, below establishment.[4] Without urgent action of some kind, the long-term prospects for later in 1918 would be increasingly poor and the short term deficit would cause mounting problems for the BEF in France.

This chapter considers the manning problems encountered and the attempts to resolve them during late 1917 and early 1918.

Re-organization of Army Recruiting by the MNS

Army recruiting had been reorganized in the Autumn of 1917 following the decision that the War Office was to hand over the role to the MNS. This took time to effect and it was not until 1 November that the MNS formally assumed responsibility for 'recruiting, enlistment, the call up of men of the Reserve Forces individually and otherwise in relation to the provision of men for the Army'.[5] At midnight on 31 October the Army's recruiting organization was subsumed into a new regionally-based structure, with the former Regimental Area Commanders becoming 'Assistant Directors of Recruiting', answering now to the appropriate civilian Regional Director of Recruiting for the 'efficient working and organization of their Areas'. There were to be ten Regions, which geographically differed slightly from the Army's Home Commands. For example, for recruiting purposes the Regimental Areas of the Cheshire and the South Lancashire Regiments now became part of North Western Region, whilst the KSLI's recruiting area became part of the West Midlands. Wales now formed a region on its own. The monthly number of recruits required for Military Service would be allotted proportionately among the regions.[6]

The effect of these changes on the Army, however, was not as fundamental as might appear, since the Military authorities retained the right of final approval of recruits thus obtained and their subsequent posting. The MNS Recruiting Areas within the new Regions remained the old Regimental Areas and once a recruit had been enlisted for the Infantry he was sent to the appropriate Infantry Depot for the Area, now known as the 'Reception Depot', for posting. It remained possible for men to volunteer for service in the regiment or corps of their choice, either before being sent a calling up notice or through what was termed 'Direct' enlistment, which applied when an individual was not liable for Military Service under the MSAs, usually because of his age. Such voluntary enlistments might be conditional on the man being posted to the corps of his choice, so long as he met the physical or technical standard required. If he could not meet those standards, and declined to be posted to any other corps, he could return to civilian life. In the case of the Infantry, irrespective of whether he was a volunteer or not, full consideration was still to be given to the individual's preference for regiment provided he was of the right medical category: 'if a man over 18 years and physically suited desires to be posted to

3 War Office, *Statistics of the Military Effort of the British Empire During the Great War*, p. 370.
4 *BOH 1918 Vol. I*, Appendix 4 Letter from Field Marshal Sir Douglas Haig to the War Office dated 24 November 1917.
5 TNA NATS 1/859: Press release of 1 November 1917.
6 IWM: *Ministry of National Service Instructions Issued During November and December 1917, Numbers 1–47 (inclusive) of 1917* (London: HMSO, 1919).

a particular infantry regiment with good reason, his request should be granted by the Posting Officer, and no other authority is necessary'.[7]

The MNS also introduced its own medical grading system for military recruits.[8] These were:

Grade 1	Fit for general service
Grade II	Likely to improve with training
Grade III	Only fit for labouring duties or sedentary work
Grade IV	Permanently and totally unfit to any form of military service

These were very general categories used solely to describe the fitness of the man at the point of recruitment. The Army continued to apply its more specific criteria as these related to the fitness standards necessary for the various different Arms. The distinction between categories 'B' and 'C' was finally abolished with effect from 1 November.[9]

Later in November a Recruit Distribution Battalion was created in each Command in order to post all 'B(2)' and 'B(3)' recruits received from the MNS.[10] Any of these recruits whom it was thought might become fit enough to be upgraded to 'A' or 'B1' after a three-months course of physical training were to be retained until the end of this period. At that point they would be brought before a medical board for re-assessment and posted according to the outcome. Those thought unlikely to benefit from the physical training course, or who had failed to be upgraded, would be posted to other corps as dictated by the continuing monthly posting ACIs. Men in categories lower than 'A' who were likely to be sent overseas would in future be selected on the basis of a special medical examination at the time they were required to depart abroad. There seem to have been a few disparities over the standards applied by the various medical boards, however, as in December it was dictated that in future the Medical Officer inspecting every draft was to note his comments as to the man's fitness for service 'in his own handwriting against each man's name on the nominal roll of the draft' and personally to sign the roll.[11]

The organization responsible for the administration of recruiting might have changed but the length of time from being called-up to emerging from Infantry recruit training and ready for drafting remained about four to five months. Thus, a man called up in November 1917 and enlisted in December would still not be ready for posting until about April 1918 at the earliest. The fundamental problem remained the lack of men available for call-up.

7 TNA WO 293/7: ACI 1621 of 29 October 1917: Arrangements for posting to the Army men who present themselves for service during the month of November 1917 and ACI 1731 of 28 November 1917: Arrangements for Posting to the Army men accepted for service during the month of December 1917.

8 IWM: *Ministry of National Service Instructions Issued During November and December 1917, No 13 of 1917: Medical Grades of the National Service Boards.*

9 TNA WO 293/7: ACI 1606 of 25 October 1917: Alteration of Classification of Men by Categories. Details of the categories are at Appendix IV.

10 Ibid., ACI 1702 of 20 November 1917: Organization of Recruit Distribution Battalions, Training Reserve, for the reception and disposal of Category 'B(2)' and 'B(3)' Recruits.

11 Ibid., ACI 1829 of 16 December 1917: Regulations for ensuring fitness of men sent to join Expeditionary Forces, and fixing responsibility for same.

Manpower Situation at the end of 1917

At the end of 1917, Haig's short-term need was for fully trained men to return the BEF to full strength as soon as possible, whilst in the longer term the requirement was for provision to be made for further drafts throughout 1918 and potentially into 1919. The passing of responsibility for recruiting from the military to the MNS in November did not of itself enable the raising of greater numbers of men. Some 36,543 men of all fitness categories had been recruited in October, of whom 23,372 would be old enough and sufficiently trained to be drafted by about February 1918, but by December 1917 the overall figure obtained had fallen to 24,923. Within this figure, only 13,730 were classified as Grade 1, and of these only 5,781 were over 19 and thus available for drafting as soon as they were trained.[12]

In early November, the AG's Branch in London informed Haig that it was anticipated that only 418,000 Infantrymen would be available for the BEF during the year ending 31 October 1918. As the wastage over this period was estimated to be about 782,000 and a further 75,000 men were already required to bring the divisions back up to strength, the total requirement for Infantrymen for the year would be 857,000. There was thus an anticipated deficit of 439,000 but this would be reduced to some extent by 180,000 sick and wounded becoming fit to return to duty to around 259,000 men.[13] It was expected that at least 140,000 men could be sent to France by 1 April 1918 and these would be augmented by an estimated 15,000 per month returning to duty from hospitals in France, thus making a total of 215,000 by that date. Every effort would be made to increase these figures by cutting out non-essential men at Home, but the letter ended, on a slightly confrontational note: 'a process which must be continued with vigour throughout the Force under your Command'.[14] Haig's response inevitably reminded the Army Council of 'the very serious situation which is likely to arise in regard to manpower' in the British units in France by 31 March, when the BEF's Infantry would be approximately 40 per cent below establishment. This would not only paralyze the BEF's offensive power but also reduce the amount of line that it could hold. Unless more men could urgently be made available, he suggested that it would be necessary to break up 15 British divisions and redistribute the men in order to bring 31 divisions up to full Infantry strength. He needed decisions urgently so that plans could be made for holding the line and the distribution and training of troops over the winter.[15]

The Army Council was only too aware of the situation and was conducting its own battles with the Government. On 15 November, the DGNS, Geddes, had submitted a paper on the 'Problem of the Maintenance of the Armed Forces' for consideration by the War Cabinet. It contained a detailed review of the nation's manpower and sought decisions from the War Cabinet on the priorities to be given to the demands for additional labour for both military service and civil

12 War Office, SME, pp. 364, 370.

13 *BOH 1918 Vol. I*, Appendix 3 War Office letter from AG2 (signed Corcoran) to Haig dated 3 Nov 17. (Extract at Appendix 6).

14 Ibid.

15 Ibid., Appendix 4 Letter from Field Marshal Sir Douglas Haig to the War Office dated 24 November 1917.

industries.[16] In examining the availability of Army manpower at home, Geddes had identified 490,000 Category A men who would at some point be available for drafting.[17] It was noted that this figure included 113,000 men engaged in munitions, skilled trades, dock and transport battalions and Home Service Units and 40,000 who were skilled tradesmen and thus not available for Infantry drafts. A further 90,000 were said by the War Office to be unavailable for various reasons; Geddes urged that at least a third of these, plus 4,000 in the dock and transport battalions and 18,000 of the 30,000 Category A men in Home Service units should be released. This would yield a total of 429,000 Category A men and to this Geddes added a credit of 20,000, having decided that the War Office figure of 10 per cent wastage at home was too high, thus making a total of 449,000 available for Infantry drafts worldwide within the next few months. A note from Haig was attached as an appendix to Geddes' memorandum which indicated that 355,100 men would be needed to make good deficiencies and meet the estimated wastage in order to bring the BEF's British Infantry up to establishment by 31 March.[18] It thus appeared that, contrary to the Army Council's position, the BEF's immediate requirement could be covered by the end of March from within existing Army resources and that the issue requiring attention was the means by which the necessary recruits could be obtained for later in 1918.

The Army had submitted a requirement to the MNS for 600,000 Category 'A' recruits plus 320,000 of lower categories to be obtained between December 1917 and June 1918. The Navy required 90,000 and industries such as munitions, ship-building and agriculture also needed large numbers of men. The Ministry of Munitions, for example, had submitted a demand for approximately 80,500 men up to the end of October 1918. Having closely scrutinized all the demands, Geddes had concluded that it would be impossible to meet in full the demands of both the Navy and Army under the existing Military Service legislation and trade agreements. He proposed that priority be given to the Navy, with only a proportion, namely 200,000, of the Army's demand being met. Furthermore, he had calculated that only 150,000 Category 'A' men could be recruited from those men of military age still in civil life and that 90,000 of these should be allocated to the Navy. This meant that only 60,000 remained available for the Army, thus causing a deficit of 140,000 on the already reduced proportion that had been suggested. The only way more men could be obtained for the Army would be through new legislation to introduce the following:

- Lowering of the age for overseas service.[19]
- Lowering the Military Age to 17.
- Raising the Military Age to 45, with further power to raise it to 50 by Order in Council.
- Abolishing the period of grace automatically given on the expiry or withdrawal of exemptions.

16 TNA CAB 24/4/24: G.174 Problem of the Maintenance of the Armed Forces dated 15 November 1917.

17 Ibid. The numbers were broken down as follows: A1: 192,000 who should be immediately available; A2: 124,000 recruits now in training who should be available within three or four months; and A4: 174,000 youths in training who would be available at some point before 30 September 1918

18 TNA CAB/24/4: G. 174 Problem of the Maintenance of the Armed Forces dated 15 November 1917: Appendix II Letter from Haig to the War Office dated 2 November 1917.

19 Legislation was not strictly necessary as MSA 2 (1916) had stated only that as far as possible men would not be sent abroad until they were 19.

- Limiting the power of tribunals.
- Cancelling Occupational exemptions.
- Extending Compulsory Service to Ireland.

Inevitably, Geddes' figure of 449,000 available for drafting within the next few months was disputed by the War Office, which claimed that over half were youths under 19 in Home Service Divisions and that others were Army Service Corps (ASC) and Royal Flying Corps (RFC) tradesman and so unsuitable for the Infantry.[20] According to the Army Council, therefore, Geddes' figures for available drafts were over-inflated. However, the same War Officc minute also stated that the deficiency on War Establishment in all theatres of war was 75,500 Infantry and 16,000 Labour. Given such constantly differing figures from the Army, the figure of 449,000 available in the short term for drafting stood.

Geddes' detailed analysis of the need for additional labour for both civil industries and military service had placed action firmly in the War Cabinet's domain and his Memorandum formed the basis for their future discussions. Predictably, on 3 December, the War Cabinet's immediate reaction to his paper was that the proposed legislation was impossible. Further discussions, however, served only to highlight the gravity of the national manpower situation and on 6 December it was proposed that a Cabinet Committee be created to address the issue and to produce proposals to resolve the crisis that the Government could present to Parliament.[21] This new Manpower Committee would be chaired by Lloyd George himself and contain four other Cabinet members: Lord Curzon, the Leader of the House of Lords and a member of the War Policy Committee; George Barnes, the Minister of Pensions; Sir Edward Carson, Minister Without Portfolio; and General Smuts, Cabinet Member and Member of the War Policy Committee. It was a high-powered committee and needed to be in view of the gravity of the situation which was defined by the War Cabinet's Secretary, Maurice Hankey:

> The economic crisis instead of being a danger to be guarded against, is actually present; and, second: that the seriousness of the military man-power crisis is not merely that we shall not smash the enemy if the men are not forthcoming, but that the enemy may smash us. The problem that confronts the Committee, therefore, is to avert a military catastrophe without plunging us into an economic catastrophe equally fatal to the cause of the Allies.[22]

The Manpower Committee (MPC) would take evidence from the various Government departments. Although not formally a member, Geddes' growing importance is evident in that he attended all its main meetings in his capacity as DGNS. Despite his previous role as Director of Army Recruiting, he had already succeeded in establishing himself as an 'honest broker' and was now viewed as an expert advisor on the nation's manpower requirements as a whole, playing a key part in providing information and analysis for the MPC. In addition to his previously recommended legislative changes, he now proposed the revision of the Schedule

20 TNA CAB/24/33: Note on Recruiting for the Army submitted to the War Cabinet by the Secretary of State for War on 24 November 1917.

21 TNA CAB 23/4: War Cabinet Meetings WC 289 of 3 December 1917 and 293 of 6 December 1917.

22 TNA CAB 27/14: Manpower Committee (MPC) 2 Note by Secretary 8 December 1917.

of Protected Employments. This would require detailed negotiations with the Trades Unions, but the urgency of the situation was such that on 20 December Lloyd George paved the way by alerting Parliament to the impending revisions.

There is some evidence in the Minutes of the MPC meetings that Lloyd George, far from preventing men being sent to France, actually tried to persuade the War Office to take the necessary action. In the meeting of 15 December 1917, he suggested that as many men as could be spared from Home Defence, including from the Division in Ireland, should be sent to France. The response of the Adjutant General, was that 'there was great difficulty in carrying out this proposal' as most of these men were of a lower category. Some 8,000 had gone but GHQ was reluctant to find employment for more than 11,000. There were also 7,800 Category 'A' men in the 65th Division in Ireland and Lloyd George suggested that if they could be sent to France then they might be replaced by the withdrawal of a Cavalry Division.[23] The response of the CGS Home Forces, Shaw, who was also present at the meeting was that 'The question of cutting down the Home Army was one for the War Office to decide, in consultation with the Admiralty'. The reaction of the military authorities must have been intensely frustrating for the MPC. The Army Council continued to hold out for new men to be called up from the rapidly dwindling civilian workforce, but the impression given to the War Cabinet was of a reluctance to make best use of those already serving.

The MPC's draft report was circulated at the beginning of January and discussed by the War Cabinet on 9 January, when the accuracy of some figures was queried, and then again on 22 January when a subsidiary question was raised relating to labour for the shipyards.[24] In fact the report was never fully signed off but became effectively a working document with decisions being taken on its initial findings and further negotiations being conducted with the Trades Unions.[25]

In reaching its conclusions, the Committee's underlying premise had been the need to safeguard the 'staying power' of the Allies until sufficient American forces would arrive in France and restore the balance of numbers on the Western Front in the Allies favour. That staying power was considered to involve not only that of the fighting forces but of the Allied nations as a whole. Consequently, the draft warned that if the number of men withdrawn for military service from industry or production was so great that it impaired 'our power of maintaining our Allies during the coming year the war might be lost, and already our powers in this respect are severely taxed'. The MPC had therefore 'carefully considered and balanced the requirements of the fighting forces and of the nation and of the Allies' in recommending the following priorities for distributing the nation's manpower:

1. The fighting personnel requirements of the Royal Navy and the Air Services.
2. Shipbuilding, and then the construction of aeroplanes and tanks.
3. Food production, timber felling and the provision of food storage accommodation.[26]

23 TNA CAB 27/14: Minutes of the Cabinet Committee on Manpower of 15 December 1917.
24 TNA CAB 23/5/11: Minutes of 319th Meeting of War Cabinet on 9 January 1918 and CAB 23/5/30 338th War Cabinet Meeting of 22 January 1918.
25 TNA CAB 24/4/36: Final Revise of Draft Report of the Cabinet Committee on Manpower (Paper G.185) dated 2 April 1918.
26 Ibid., pp. 27-8.

To the Army Council's dismay, the priority to be given to the Army's requirements was not specifically stated. Instead the MPC made various recommendations for finding manpower for the Army based on the, soon to be proved false, assumption that the Americans would allow their battalions to be incorporated in British Brigades and the equally spurious view that the adoption of a defensive posture on the Western Front would 'avoid wastage of manpower by the adoption of suitable strategy and tactics, and by the development of fortifications'. More specific recommendations concerned the redistribution of existing Army manpower, including reduction in the number of battalions per division from twelve to nine and in the number of British cavalry on the Western Front, and for a review of the force allocated to Home Defence. In short, the MPC had accepted Geddes' figures and the Army was to find manpower from within its own resources for its immediate needs.

The MPC's recommendations, however, were not all to the detriment of the Army. Although it had accepted neither the proposed alterations to the upper and lower age limits for military service nor the extension of compulsory military service to Ireland, it had agreed some of Geddes' proposals for further legislation to free up men for the Army. With the intention of creating 'an easily understood system of clear cuts by age, by occupation' a two-clause Military Service Bill was introduced in the Commons on 14 January 1918.[27] It was designed to reduce to two weeks the period of grace automatically added to exemptions for military service and to enable the DGNS to cancel existing occupational exemptions; the latter provision was required to complement the proposed revision of the Schedule of Protected Occupations. There was some opposition from the Labour Party, but the Government decided to press ahead in view of the urgency of the manpower situation. The new Military Service (No 1) Act 1918 received Royal Assent on 6 February whilst the revised Schedule of Protected Occupations had already been issued on 1 February.[28] Recruiting began to increase slightly with, for example, the number of munition workers released rising from 3,700 in the third week of March to 9,000 in the second week of April.[29] Consequently, Geddes made no immediate use of the power to cancel existing exemptions. Although there was some immediate improvement in numbers obtained, the problem as ever was the conflict between the Army's immediate and longer-term needs. Men of military age obtained in April would not be trained and ready for drafting until late summer.

Manning Issues in France Over the Winter of 1917/18

Haig's plans for 1918 had had to be produced against what must have been a frustrating set of unknowns for GHQ: the future availability of manpower, the organization of divisions in France and continuing French requests for the British to take over more of the line. At the same time, there was the increasing likelihood of a German attack in the spring. The messages reaching him from London were not hopeful and the decline in numbers was reflected in the number of reinforcements reaching the BEF. In December 1917 some 60,534 reinforcements,

27 Hansard HC Debate 14 January 1918 vol 101 cc 58-134.
28 TNA MH 47/142/3: M.M. 130 (Revised) Schedule of Protected Occupations for men employed on Admiralty, War Office or Munitions Work or in Railway Workshops.
29 *History of the Ministry of Munitions VI Part 2* (London: HMSO, 1922), pp. 49-50 cited in K. Grieves, *The Politics of Manpower, 1914-18* (Manchester: Manchester University Press, 1988), p. 192.

both Cavalry and Infantry, were despatched to divisions but the overall all Arms losses in the BEF for that month had been 102,109 (47,581 casualties and 54,528 sick).[30]

As far as GHQ was concerned, the men they needed were in England and should be released immediately. There were indeed trained soldiers at Home, but it proved hard to identify how many could be released for service overseas. The note submitted by Lord Derby to the War Cabinet on 24 November 1917 had explained that the number of 'A' men serving at Home included men in units already preparing for overseas, draft-finding units, Home Service men and those in depots and administrative units.[31] It subsequently became apparent, however, that the Army Council's figures of November had been somewhat disingenuous. A note produced by Robertson in January 1918 on the number of troops required to be retained at Home for defence purposes indicated that there were in fact 1,420,000 men on the strength of the Army at home, although only 410,000 of these were actually allocated to Home Defence, against an establishment of 400,979 that had been previously authorised by the War Cabinet.[32] The balance was made up by men employed by different War Office departments: some 80,000 belonged to the RFC; close to 50,000 were in the Medical Corps; some 90,000 belonged to the Army Service Corps (ASC); others to the Army Ordnance Corps (AOC) and the Army Pay Corps (APC); and there were nearly 200,000 employed by the Labour Corps. Some 46,000 soldiers were also employed under the Ministry of Munitions, in agriculture, and on dock and transport work. Finally, there could be between 300,000 - 400,000 sick and wounded at home at any one time. It was alleged that, after deducting these figures from the whole, less than a third were potential drafts for overseas service once they were sufficiently trained and old enough to go to the front.[33] Robertson would subsequently admit in his memoirs, however, that the number of men retained at Home in early 1918 was much greater than it should have been, but that he had failed on many occasions to get it reduced. Each department of the War Office retained men for its own purposes, and responsibility for reducing the numbers lay with their representatives on the Army Council. Rather weakly, he claimed that the 'General Staff could do nothing except try to bring about a reduction'.[34] It would appear, therefore, that Geddes and the War Cabinet were right to query the figures provided by the War Office for the number of men retained on duties at Home.

Lack of manpower for the foreseeable future was not the only reason that the BEF's plans for the Western Front in 1918 were on hold: in early November the British, French and Italian Prime Ministers had agreed to form a Supreme War Council, to be composed of the Prime Minister and a Member of the Government of each of the countries whose Armies were fighting on the Western Front. Its overall aim was the creation of:

> a central body charged with the duty of continuously surveying the field of operations as a whole and, by the light of information derived from all fronts and from all Governments

30 TNA WO 95/26: AG GHQ War Diary figures for December 1917.
31 TNA CAB/24/33: Note on Recruiting for the Army submitted to the War Cabinet by the Secretary of State for War on 24 November 1917.
32 TNA CAB/24/38: Troops Required for Home Defence dated 3 January 1918.
33 Robertson, *From Private to Field-Marshal*, pp. 342-3.
34 Ibid.

> and Staffs, of coordinating the plans prepared by the different General Staffs, and, if necessary, of making proposals of their own for the better conduct of the War.[35]

The Council would be based at Versailles where its members would be assisted by 'Permanent Military Representatives' acting as technical military advisers but without executive roles. At the second meeting in early December the Military Representatives were instructed to examine the military situation and make recommendations on plans for future operations. This was much too late and meant that there could be no decisions on future military policy for the foreseeable future.

In the meantime, however, Haig had to position the BEF as best he could. On 4 December, the War Cabinet had approved his proposal to take up a 'somewhat withdrawn defensive position'. In response to Robertson's confirmation of this decision, Haig warned that although he now had fresh divisions on the Cambrai front, his forces were 'none too strong' on the Western Front as a whole should any German attacks be made. Consequently, he could not take over any more of the French line at present and needed as many trained drafts as possible in order to refill his divisions which were very weak and would have to do 'heavy work on the construction of roads and railways as well as to fight'. He also submitted that no more troops should be sent to Italy.[36]

On 7 December Haig advised his Army Commanders that it would be necessary to adopt a defensive posture for the next few months since Russia's withdrawal from the war meant that Germany could move some 30 more divisions to the Western Front.[37] The inference drawn was that Germany could and probably would mount an offensive in the spring. Over the preceding two years the BEF had concentrated on offensives and, if the anticipated German offensive was to be withstood, now urgently needed training in defence together with the necessary logistic preparations. Detailed instructions on defensive measures were consequently issued by GHQ on 14 December.[38] Preparations were initiated immediately and progressed as quickly as labour, weather and other conditions allowed. They were conducted, however, against a period of organizational flux in the BEF.

In late 1917 it had been decided to re-organize the drafting and training organization in France. This was probably due to a desire to avoid a reoccurrence of the disturbance that had taken place at the huge Étaples Base in September but may also have been a wish to familiarize and train newly arrived drafts closer to the front line. Lack of training had been the perennial claim made after offensives, most recently after the Battle of Cambrai and also the action at Westroosebeke on the Passchendaele ridge in early December. Under the new organization, the IBDs would act simply as receiving units for processing drafts before passing them on for further in-country training. As the time spent at the Base would be much shorter, fewer IBDs were required and in December they were reduced to just thirteen, designated by letter A to M. The twenty former IBDs at Étaples, for example, were replaced by just five (E, F, G, H, J), plus a Medical Board Depot through which all hospital discharges were to pass.[39] There is some evidence of continued links to the Home Commands and Districts; reinforcements for the

35 HC Deb 14 November 1917 vol 99 cc389-91 Statement by the Prime Minister.
36 TNA CAB 23/4/66: Minutes of War Cabinet Meeting No 292 of 5 December 1917.
37 Sheffield & Bourne, *Douglas Haig, War Diaries and Letters*, p. 358.
38 *BOH 1918 Vol. 1*, p. 39.
39 TNA WO 95/4027: Etaples Base War Diary entry dated 15 December 1917.

Cheshire Regiment and the KSLI passed through 'C' IBD at Rouen whilst those for Southern Command Regiments seem to have passed through 'D' IBD.[40]

In future Infantry drafts would receive their in-theatre training at Corps Reinforcement Camps and on arrival at their units. The roles of these Camps were now: to train Infantry drafts and 'combed-out' men who had been transferred to the Infantry; and to act as holding locations both for trained Infantry reinforcements awaiting despatch to their units and for personnel not taken into action by their units. Once sufficiently trained, men could be sent immediately to their units so long as these were not in action and would have seven clear days in which to absorb the draft. The revised organizations were formalized in the January 1918 revised edition of *SS 152 Instructions for the Training of the British Armies in France*.[41]

The new Reinforcement Camps were organized in Divisional Wings for the Corps concerned, although these were sometimes referred to as Divisional Depot Battalions. The VII Corps Reinforcement Training Camp, for example, contained 'Wings' for 16th (Irish), 39th, 21st and 9th Divisions.[42] The reorganization had started in mid-December but would not be completed until the last new Corps Reinforcement Camp was in place, which was not until early February.[43] There was thus an inevitable period of flux in the training of drafts arriving during December and January. This was not helped by the need for the receiving units to conduct defensive training whilst making the necessary logistic preparations. The volatility of the situation was further compounded by the long anticipated re-organization of divisions.

In early 1917 the Cabinet had asked the War Office to consider the possibility of reducing the number of battalions in a division.[44] The Army Council had responded that no such reorganization should be made until it had become clearly impossible 'to obtain the number of men required to maintain divisions at their present establishment'.[45] That moment had now arrived and the MPC firmly recommended reduction of the number of battalions in British divisions on the Western Front from twelve to nine.

GHQ had for some months anticipated that at some point it would be forced to re-organize the BEF's divisions due to the lack of reinforcements arriving. In both August and November 1917 the GS Staff had analysed alternative organizational permutations, concentrating in the end on two options: breaking up divisions or reducing the number of battalions per division.[46] The first option would create least dislocation, both organizationally and tactically, reduce the number of trained commanders and staffs to be found and could also 'afford an opportunity of breaking up certain divisions who do not, perhaps, quite pull their weight.' There would, however, be strong political resistance to this option in view of the likely reaction of the French

40 TNA WO 95/4186: 'D' IBD War Diary for 1918.
41 General Staff, *SS 152 Instructions for the Training of the British Armies in France* (London: HMSO, January 1918).
42 TNA WO 95/521: Fifth Army GS Box containing VII Corps Reinforcement Training Camp diary for 21-29 March 1918.
43 TNA WO 95/26: AG GHQ War Diary entry for 4 February 1918.
44 TNA CAB 23/1/55: Minutes of 55th Meeting of War Cabinet on 5 February 1917.
45 TNA CAB 24/19/97 and WO 163/22: Army Council Memorandum of 10 February 1917 cited in Precis No 855 prepared for Army Council 204th Meeting of 6 March 1917.
46 TNA WO 158/20: GHQ Item 139: Notes dated 11 August 1917 and G.S Note Reduction of number of divisions or Reduction of number of battalions in each division dated 28 November 1917.

since a reduced number of divisions would affect the length of the British front line. The alternative of reducing the number of battalions would mean far more widespread dislocation, the revision of current and familiar tactical doctrine, the reorganization of all supporting arms within divisions and would also fail to address the shortage of trained staff officers. However, both France and Germany had reduced the number of battalions in their divisions and it was recognized that concentrations were easier with larger numbers of small formations than with smaller numbers of large ones. It was also admitted that there were:

> [S]entimental objections to reducing the number of battalions and any such decrease would be unpopular, at any rate to start with. Experience shows, however, that the feeling soon disappears and all amalgamations carried out heretofore have been a success.[47]

Logically, it would have been preferable to break up divisions, but the decision was in the end to be political. There were some positive outcomes, however, as Geoffrey Husbands observed:

> We welcomed the draft that joined us with open arms, for it was not only a matter of increase in numbers but of tried and experienced troops …[48]

The Army Council appears to have decided to forestall a direct order from Cabinet, following the MPC recommendation, and on 5 January warned GHQ that divisions in France were to be re-organized. The order was subsequently confirmed by War Office letter on 10 January.[49] Divisions were to be reduced in strength from twelve to nine battalions, plus a pioneer battalion, and a list of 145 battalions was sent to GHQ from which those to be disbanded were to be chosen. Care was to be taken 'to break up battalions with the shortest service to their credit, and to preserve as far as possible Regular battalions, first line Territorial battalions, and the earlier units of the New Army'.[50]

It took an enormous amount of hurried staff work but GHQ's plans were notified to the War Office by 18 January. Rather than leave some divisions untouched it was decided to reduce all British divisions in France between 29 January and 15 February.[51] On 23 January GHQ issued Corps with details of the organizational changes required. These were then amplified by AG GHQ with instructions concerning the disposal of men of battalions selected for disbandment or amalgamation: they were to be posted to other battalions of their own Regiment or withdrawn to a general pool of reinforcements for subsequent posting. As far as possible groups of men posted to new units were to be composed of those who had served in the same sub-units.[52] Once

47 Ibid.
48 Bourne & Bushaway, *Joffrey's War*, p. 530.
49 TNA WO 95/26: AG GHQ War diary entry of 5 January 1918. Confirmation was subsequently received in War Office letter 121/Drafts/8579 dated 10 January 1918.
50 Macready, *Annals of an Active Life*, p. 283.
51 *BOH 1918 Vol. 1*, pp. 54 -5.
52 TNA WO 95/2056: 19th Division GS War Diary and WO 95/2058: 19th Division A&Q War Diary, both for January 1918. The A & Q War Diary contains copies of relevant letters from GHQ, Third Army and Third Echelon.

all postings had been carried out as instructed any surplus personnel were to be withdrawn to Corps Reinforcement Camps or to newly reformed Entrenching battalions.[53]

The 19th Division was notified that all four battalions of 56th Brigade (7th King's Own, 7th East Lancashire, 7th South Lancashire and 7th North Lancashire) were to be disbanded on 4 February. The Brigade would then be reconstituted by the movement within the Division of 9th Cheshire and 8th North Staffordshire, from 58th and 57th Brigades respectively, and with the arrival of 1/4th KSLI from 63rd Division. Instructions for postings of all men of disbanded battalions were sent from the DAG 3rd Echelon's office: for example, ten officers and 202 men from 7th East Lancashire were to be sent to 1st East Lancashire whilst the 9th RWF, remaining in 58th Brigade, received five officers and 147 men from 10th RWF, disbanded in the 3rd Division.[54] Drafts from both 10th RWF and 19th RWF, were also sent to other battalions of the RWF; the remainder were amalgamated to form the 8th Entrenching Battalion.[55] The 38th (Welsh) Division was ordered to disband four locally raised battalions, distributing the officers and men amongst other battalions of the Division, but in return received 2nd RWF from the 33rd Division.[56] The overall impact on battalions of the Marcher Regiments may be seen at Appendix IX, which confirms that wherever possible men had been posted to battalions of their parent regiments.

Some divisions escaped. The British divisions in Italy retained their 12-battalion structure, as did the Dominion divisions in France, although some re-organization of the latter was necessary to ensure a continued supply of drafts. The 4th New Zealand Brigade in England had already received instructions that it was to be disbanded in order to provide reinforcements for the rest of the New Zealand Brigades. This was completed by 15 February.[57] Similarly the 5th Canadian Division was broken up in order to provide 100 men over establishment for each Canadian battalion in France. The five Australian Divisions still had sufficient drafts, for the time being, to maintain twelve battalions in each.

The MPC draft report had suggested that it might be possible to bring the reduced British divisions back up to strength by incorporating newly-arrived American battalions but by the end of January it had become clear that the Americans would not agree to this. In any case, their numbers in France were increasing only gradually. On 1 December 130,000 men were in France but this gave a false picture: on 9 January the War Cabinet was informed that the actual American fighting force numbered just 58,000 rifles and machine guns, the equivalent of four American divisions.[58]

The GHQ timetable for re-organizing the British divisions proved wildly optimistic and the reorganization was not completed until 4 March. By then 115 British battalions in France had been disbanded, 38 had been amalgamated to form 19 units and seven had been converted to

53 TNA WO 95/26: AG GHQ War Diary entry for 12 February 1918.

54 TNA WO 95/2058: 19th Division A&Q War Diary entry dated 20 February 1918.

55 Ward, *Regimental Records of the Royal Welsh Fusiliers Vol. III 1914–1918*, p. 378.

56 Lt Col J. E. Munby, *A History of the 38th (Welsh) Division* (London: Rees, 1920; Uckfield: Naval & Military Press, 2003), pp. 31-2. The battalions disbanded were: 15th (London Welsh) RWF, 113th Bde; 10th (1st Rhondda) Welsh, 114th Bde; 11th (2nd Gwent) SWB and 16th (Cardiff City) Welsh, both of 115th Bde.

57 TNA WO 95/26: AG GHQ War Diary entries for 15 December 1917 and 15 February 1918 and *BOH 1918 Vol. I*, p. 55.

58 Ibid., p. 35 and TNA: CAB 23/5 War Cabinet Meeting No 319 of 9 January 1918.

Pioneers.[59] It had been a period of both heartache and great organizational flux and, although battalions were again at or near full strength, 'it would have been less detrimental to efficiency if the change could have been spread over a long period'.[60] As it was, the reorganization was finally completed just 17 days before the start of the German Spring Offensive.

To compound the organizational turmoil caused by the reorganization of the drafting and training organization and the composition of divisions, in late January the BEF had, on instructions from the Supreme War Council, taken over more of the front line from the French. Haig had resisted as long as possible on the grounds of his lack of manpower but by early February the front occupied by the BEF had been extended by 30 percent, from 95 to 123 miles. The British line now stretched from north to south: Fourth Army from north of Ypres to north of Armentières; First Army from north of Armentières to Gavrelle, six miles north-east of Arras; Third Army from Gavrelle to Gouzeaucourt; and Fifth Army from Gouzeaucourt to the Barisis-St Gobain railway.[61] Arrangements had been agreed in principle for co-operation between the French and British Armies. By March these had been firmed up: relief was to be asked for only in the event of the British being engaged in a battle on another part of their front, whilst intervention might be requested in the event of a serious and sustained German offensive against any part of the British front making it difficult for the British to find sufficient reserves to continue the fight.[62]

It had long been anticipated that the Germans would mount an offensive early in 1918. The collapse of Russia in 1917 had enabled the movement of large numbers of German divisions from the Eastern to the Western Front, whilst for the German High Command the continuing build-up of American troops meant that any offensive must be undertaken sooner rather than later. It was a period of great tension for the BEF. In his dispatches, Haig later wrote:

> Towards the middle of February 1918, it became evident that the enemy was preparing for a big offensive on the Western Front … By the end of February 1918 these preparations had become very marked opposite the front held by the Third and Fifth British Armies … As the 21st March approached it became certain that an attack on this sector was imminent.[63]

Overview

There is a prevailing myth, given credence by a comment in the *Official History*, that the Government, and by implication the Prime Minister, Lloyd George, could have brought the BEF up to full establishment before 21 March 1918 had they so willed.[64] In reality, the issues

59 *BOH 1918 Vol. I*, p. 55.
60 Macready, *Annals of an Active Life*, p. 283.
61 *BOH 1918 Vol. 1*, p.115. Fourth Army reverted to being called Second Army when it was taken over again by Plumer on his return from Italy.
62 Ibid., pp. 48, 101-2.
63 E. Wyrall, *The Nineteenth Division 1914-1918* (London: Edward Arnold, 1932; Uckfield: Naval & Military Press, 1999), p. 132.
64 Brigadier-General J. E. Edmonds, *British Military Operations France and Belgium 1918 Vol. 1* (BOH Vol.1), p. 52, fn. 1.

surrounding manpower at that time were wider than the simply political, relating not just to availability but also to provision and suitability. There seems little evidence that the Government had wilfully withheld men from the Army. The lack of manpower was more a systemic problem within the nation itself with the Government simply unable rather than unwilling to force the Departments of State to release their manpower. Although an attempt had been made towards universal compulsion, fear of opposition from the Labour movement meant that the voluntary approach was maintained much longer than it should have been. It was not until later in 1917 and into early 1918 that the issue began to be addressed with the creation of the Ministry of National Service, the revision of the Schedule of Protected Occupations and legislation to reduce occupational exemptions. By then, however, political and economic considerations for the nation were such that the Army could not be accorded top priority to meet its manpower demands from within the civilian workforce.

8

The German Offensives of 1918

---

21 March – 5 April: The First Battles of the Somme 1918

The German attack opened at 4:40 am on 21 March with a terrific bombardment on the whole of the Fifth Army's front, on three-quarters of that of the Third and stretching as far north as Armentières. It was the first act of an offensive that would last into April and consist of six distinct phases.[1] The subsequent Infantry attack followed some five hours later in thick mist. The BEF's casualties mounted rapidly but the chaos and confusion were such that it became impossible to produce reliable casualty returns until later and then they would cover a period of several days.[2] The first estimated casualties shown in the AG GHQ War Diary are for the period up to 23 March and show 1861 officers and 53,691 ORs. Emergency steps to find reinforcements had been taken in theatre: all leave had been stopped as had the sending home of officers on courses; the 3rd Echelon had been instructed on the policy concerning reinforcement of divisions and transfer of personnel; and the DGMS had been ordered to 'comb out drastically' the convalescent depots in order to obtain 5,000 'A' men at once and 500 more in a few days. A cipher telegram was sent to the War Office explaining the situation and asking what reinforcements could be provided as an emergency measure. The response was that 2,000 Infantry drafts would be sent daily and that number would be increased.[3]

1 Battles of: St Quentin, 21-23 March; First Battle of Bapaume, 24-25 March; Rosières, 26-27 March; First Battle of Arras, 28 March; the Avre, 4 April; and the Ancre, 5 April 1918. NB There was a subsequent action at Villers Bretonneux in late April.
2 *BOH 1918 Vol. I*, p. 216.
3 TNA WO 95/26: AG GHQ War Diary entry for 23 March 1918.

The Rush to Find More Men

The need to find additional reinforcements for the BEF dominated the War Cabinet's discussions on 23 March.[4] The CIGS, now General Sir Henry Wilson, informed the Cabinet that the Executive War Board in Versailles had decided that two French divisions and one British should be brought back from Italy. Whether British divisions should be brought from Palestine and Mesopotamia was also discussed but no decisions reached; moving divisions from Salonika was ruled out, at least for the time being, since although up to strength numerically they were weakened by malaria. Discussions then turned to resources available nearer to home. There were some 30,000 drafts already in depots in France, and Major General Hutchinson, Director of Organization in the War Office, had identified a total of 231,000 from which drafts could be produced. Not all these men were in fact available immediately, however, since it would be necessary to examine the impact of calling up 16,000 trained soldiers working on munitions plus 45,000 from agriculture. The remaining 170,000 men could be sent, including 88,000 currently on leave from the BEF, 5,000 men on commissioning courses and 50,000 boys aged over 18½ but under 19 who had completed their training. The release of this last group required a Cabinet decision since it had previously been pledged that boys under 19 should not be sent abroad except in national emergency. It was reluctantly decided that that time had come and that 18½ year olds who had completed their training should be sent. The limiting factor to the number to be sent daily was transport. It was thought possible to move about 8,000 men a day but this would take up the whole of the cross-Channel transport capacity during the next three weeks.

The GHQ staff would have been relieved at the arrival of a War Office telegram on 24 March advising that, once men returning from leave had been sent, some 10,000 reinforcements (all arms) would be sent daily. In the meantime, the GHQ staff were putting in place their own ad hoc and longer-term arrangements. It was recognized that this might not be the only German onslaught and instructions were given that divisions in First and Second Armies, as yet unscathed, were to be kept up to strength.[5] Men belonging to these Armies and also VI and XVII Corps of Third Army who returned from leave and hospital were to proceed to their units but all others, except for staff officers, were to be detained at Base Camps until further orders. When a division that had been under attack was definitely pulled out of the line, 3rd Echelon was to be informed and battalions brought up to 800 ORs as soon as possible; initially the 6th and 34th Divisions were placed on the priority list for reinforcements.[6]

On 25 March Lord Derby informed the War Cabinet that the number of men available for immediate drafting to France was 106,000, of whom 95,400 were Infantry.[7] Together with the 88,000 on leave at Home and a further 18,000 trained men who would be available as drafts by 20 April, a total of 212,000 men would be available for France within the next month. What

4 TNA CAB 23/5: Minutes of War Cabinet Meeting 371 of 23 March 1918.
5 Fourth Army had been retitled Second Army on the return of Plumer from Italy on 17 March and the departure of Rawlinson for Versailles.
6 TNA GHQ AG: War Diary entry for 24 March 1918. NB. The instruction that Infantry drafts, casuals or returned leave men should be sent to VI or XVII Corps was countermanded on 26 March.
7 TNA CAB 23/5: Minutes of War Cabinet Meeting 372 of 25 March 1918.

was needed was more shipping so that 20,000-25,000 might be sent daily and the First Sea Lord and the Minister of Shipping undertook to address this.

Having confirmed the immediate availability of reinforcements, the War Cabinet now turned its attention to further sources of manpower. Some actions could be taken immediately such as authorizing Geddes to cut the 'calling up' notice period from 14 to 7 days and to reduce the size of Medical Boards so that more might be created and thus speed up the rate of recruit examinations to approximately 90,000 a week. Macready also announced that a new, less stringent eye-test was to be introduced that should gain more 'A' men for the Army. The perennial topic of the withdrawal of men from the munitions industry, coal mines and dockyards was discussed together with the stopping of recruiting for the Navy and even the recall of wounded men who had been discharged. It was recognized that the immediately available measures, however, were only short-term. The main topics under consideration for the longer-term were Geddes' earlier proposals to raise the upper age limit for recruiting to 55 and to extend conscription to Ireland. The War Cabinet at last decided that he should produce further proposals for increasing the number of men available for military service; it was opportunistically noted that the present military situation could enable previously insurmountable political difficulties to be overcome. Geddes was now tasked to produce a short bill for consideration.[8]

Reinforcements for France

On 25 March, the War Office had notified GHQ that available shipping capacity limited drafts to 12,000 a day but asked whether more could be 'digested in France' if that number could be increased. In response, GHQ requested as many as possible be sent, at least for the next ten days. Drafts were currently unable to reach units on the battle front but GHQ would notify the War Office if congestion at the Bases made a pause necessary. It appears from the AG GHQ War Diary entries to have taken time for the number of reinforcements to build up as on 27 March 3,969 arrived at Boulogne with a further 6,280 due the following day. On 29 March a further 4,720 arrived there and 2,098 via Calais. On 30 March 7,886 were due to embark for France. These figures, however, seem to be minus those for returning leave men; the *Official History* shows 39,384, including leave men, being sent over between 24-28 March. Fortunately, sufficient accommodation was available at the different Bases for the retention of the men flooding in as by now operational considerations were beginning to affect their onward movement. On 30 March it was noted that drafts arriving at Boulogne and Calais were no longer to be sent to Bases at Rouen or Le Havre but were to be retained at Étaples and Calais and sent from there when required. On 31 March it was warned that railway traffic from the south and south-west of Amiens was to be kept to a minimum but that every effort was to be made to get through reinforcements who were waiting at Rouen and Le Havre.[9]

The arrival rate of reinforcements rapidly increased and during the first week of April 73,618 men landed in France.[10] The 1st TR Brigade noted that its battalions had been 'practically denuded'; on 6 April a draft of 123 boys, aged between 18½ and 18¾, with four months

8 TNA CAB 23/5: Minutes of War Cabinet Meeting No. 372 of 25 March 1918.
9 TNA GHQ AG: War Diary entries for 25, 27, 29, 30 and 31 March 1918.
10 *BOH 1918 Vol. 2*, p. 11.

training, was despatched, without the normal pre-draft leave.[11] Against this, however, casualty numbers had continued to rise: the estimated running total reported to GHQ by 31 March was 4,477 officers and 119,985 ORs. By 5 April this had risen to 8,344 officers and 169,145, but as the *Official History* points out, these are gross, uncorrected figures. When figures for the approximate number of missing who later returned are applied, it seems that the total casualties were about 160,000, of whom about 22,000 were probably killed, 96,000 wounded or gassed and 42,000 unwounded taken prisoner.[12] The Germans had also lost heavily but by the end of 5 April had advanced some 40 miles and had come within reach of the vital railway junctions at Amiens.

Several Marcher battalions had suffered under the German onslaught, although there were only three in Fifth Army, which bore the main brunt of the German attack.[13] On 21 March the 39th Division was in Reserve to the north of Péronne but was released at noon and placed at the disposal of VII Corps. Its 118th Brigade, containing 1/6th Cheshire, 1/1st Cambridgeshire and 4/5th Black Watch, was ordered forward at 5:00 pm to construct a switch line from Tincourt Wood to Saulcourt. The next day the 118th and 117th Brigades occupied the new trench and, as other units retired through them, became 'the front line as far as active resistance was concerned' until 7:00 pm when they received orders to retire.[14] The following morning they retired again, and occupied a trench on Mont St Quentin, to the north of Péronne, facing south-east. The enemy attacked at about 4:00 pm and 1/6th Cheshire was withdrawn only just in time to avoid being entirely captured: 'there was no chance of getting any of the wounded away and a certain number of men must have fallen into [the enemy's] hands'.[15] By nightfall 118th Brigade had crossed the Somme and was in position opposite Cléry. The following two days seem to have been relatively quiet but on 27 March the enemy attacked in force, and 118th Brigade was forced to retire, having suffered a number of casualties from machine gun fire. Further retirements followed during that day with units and men becoming scattered; late on 6th Cheshire found only 3 officers and 35 men. The following day composite battalions were formed from the remains of all units, the 118th Brigade Composite Battalion taking the place of its former individual battalions.[16] Further withdrawal followed to the area of Aubercourt before a very depleted 39th Division was relieved on 31 March and withdrawn to south-east of Amiens. By now its total all ranks strength was 4538. It had suffered 3941 casualties but had received 801 reinforcements.[17]

The 1/6th Cheshire War Diary shows a total of 332 soldier casualties for the period 21-30 March: 20 dead, 139 wounded and 162 missing; whilst *SDGW* shows 51 deaths for the battalion

11 TNA WO 95/5459: 1st Training Reserve Brigade Diary entries 31 March and 6 April 1918.
12 TNA WO 95/26: for 51 March and OH p. 489-490.
13 Fifth Army: 6th KSLI in 20th Division, 15th Cheshire in 35th Division and 1/6th Cheshire in 39th Division.
14 E. Riddell & M.V. Clayton, *The Cambridgeshires 1914 to 1919* (Cambridge: Bowes & Bowes, 1934; Uckfield: Naval & Military Press, 2004), p. 156 and TNA WO 95/2590/3: War Diary of 1/6th Cheshire March 1918.
15 TNA WO 95/2590/3: 1/6th Cheshire War Diary entry for 23 March 1918.
16 Ibid., 1/6th Cheshire War Diary entry for 28 March 1918.
17 TNA WO 95/26: AG GHQ War Diary figures for March 1918.

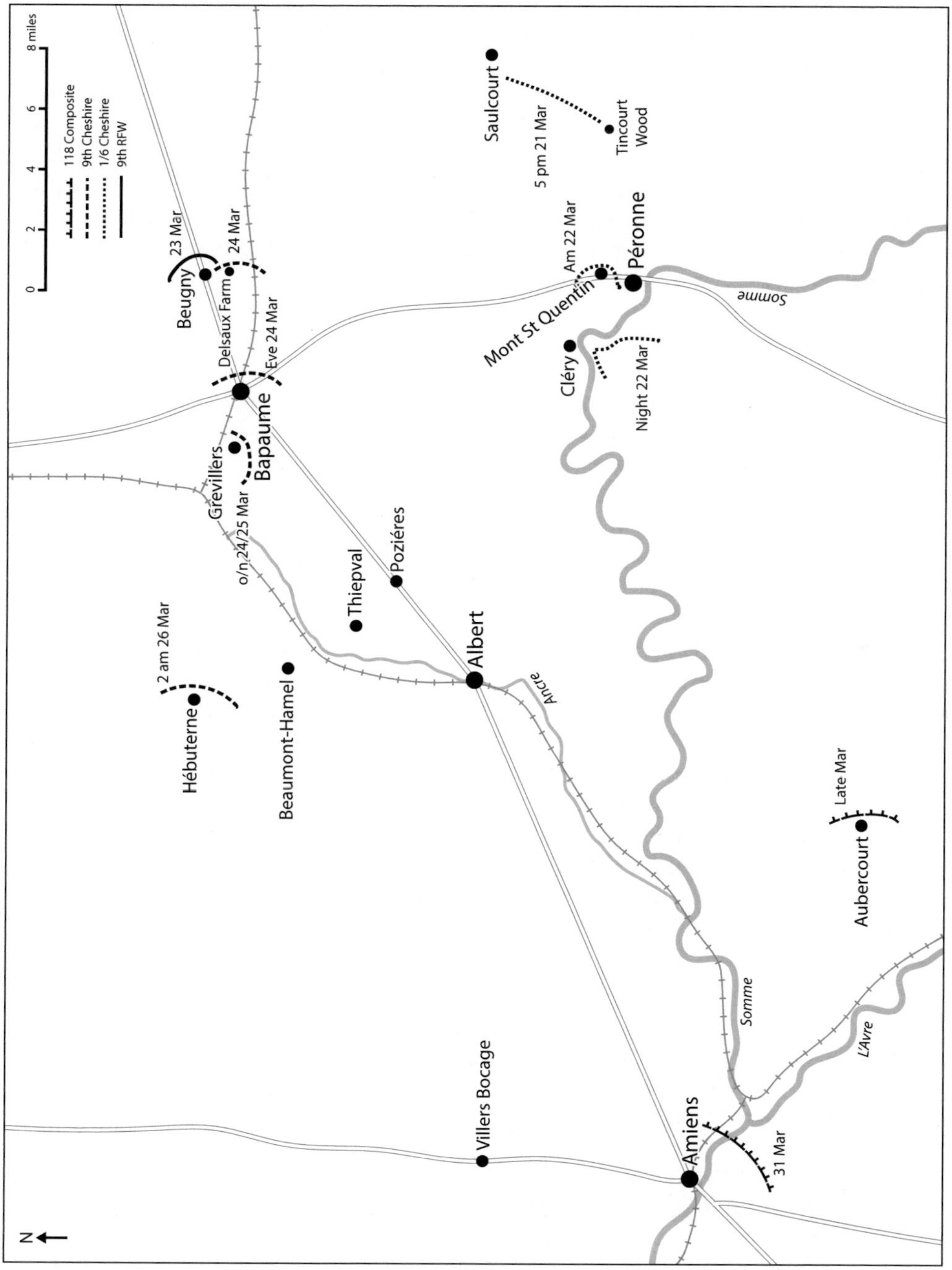

Map 7: Battle of the Somme 1918: 1/6th Cheshire, 9th Cheshire, 9th RWF, and 1/4th KSLI.

up to 31 March.[18] The discrepancy may be explained by the confusion of the retreat and the number of those shown as missing whose deaths were later assumed. Analysis of the available details for the individuals shown in *SDGW* gives a cross-section of the battalion in early 1918. It still consisted predominantly of Cheshire Regiment men, with some 76 percent having arrived in France as Cheshire soldiers, both Regular and TF. Despite its being a TF battalion, however, the available Service Records show that only 18 were original TF soldiers. Even at this late stage of the war over half of those who died (30) had attested in 1914 and 1915, although 8 of these were Derby men mobilized after mid-1916. Twelve were attested after mid-1916, five of whom were volunteers and seven conscripted. Their experience of service in France varied, with 22 having arrived before the end of Third Ypres. Some 18 men had joined the battalion in 1918, six of whom had been part of the draft of 100 men from 16th Cheshire on the latter's disbandment.

The Marcher battalions in Third Army were encountering much the same difficulties as those of Fifth Army.[19] The 19th (Western) Division, which contained 9th Cheshire and 1/4th KSLI in 56th Brigade and 9th RWF in 58th Brigade, with 5th SWB as its Pioneer battalion, had been in the rear zone, east of Bapaume and to the south of the Bapaume-Cambrai road, during most of March. Once the German attack started orders were given for the Division to move forward to assembly positions but there was much changing of instructions during 21 March and by evening the marching and counter-marching had 'caused great fatigue to all ranks'.[20] However, the 19th Division had not so far been attacked, other than by shellfire. It was involved in some fighting, and more movement, on 22 March, but it would not be until 23 March that the German blow would really fall.

After a quiet night which had enabled rations to be brought up to units which by now had none left and were also very short of water, the morning of 23 March saw fierce fighting along the fronts held by 57th and 58th Brigades. They were under heavy artillery and machine gun fire and by late morning 58th Brigade HQ sent orders that 9th RWF, together with 6th Wiltshire, were to withdraw to the outskirts of Beugny. By the time the orders arrived at 2:30 pm however, the whole line was heavily engaged in desperate fighting and the battalions could not withdraw because the 41st Division on their left had not received similar orders. Eventually, at 5:00 pm they prepared to get away as best they could. When the remnants of 9th RWF finally reached the Green Line at about 6:30 pm they numbered about 9 officers with 60 ORs.[21]

The 24 March saw heavy artillery fire from both sides as soon as it was light. In 56th Brigade, 9th Cheshire were holding the front line at Delsaux Farm, which was slightly in advance of the

18 TNA WO 95/2590/3: Appendix 1 to 1/6th Cheshire War Diary for March 1918 and SDGW deaths for 1/6th Cheshire 21-31 March 1918.

19 Marcher battalions in Third Army: 3rd Division: 7th KSLI; 6th Division: 1st KSLI; 19th Division: 9th Cheshire, 9th RWF, 1/4th KSLI and 5th SWB (Pioneers); 25th Division: 10th Cheshire, 11th Cheshire and 6th SWB; and 47th Division: 1/4th RWF.

20 Wyrall, *The Nineteenth Division,* p. 140.

21 Ibid., pp. 145 and 158. NB. The part of the Green Line held by 19th Division was as follows: on the right 56th Brigade held from just south of the Lebucquière – Fremicourt road to the Bapaume-Cambrai road just west of Beugny with 58th Brigade on left to the north of the Bapaume-Cambrai road. The 57th Brigade was to the west of Fremicourt prior to moving into Red Line which ran approximately north and south east of Bancourt and thence in a north-westerly direction to a point north-east of Achiet-le-Grand.

general line. Between 9:00 am and 10:45 am the enemy subjected them to a heavy barrage and then mounted a massive attack which forced the Cheshires out of part of the front line trenches. The men were quickly re-organized, however, and within 30 minutes had mounted a successful counter-attack and retaken the lost trench. This counter attack was subsequently described by the Divisional historian as 'the most brilliant piece of fighting' carried out on 24 March.[22]

About mid-day, 9th Cheshire received preparatory orders to fall back if the 2nd Division Brigade on its right gave ground. When that Brigade subsequently withdrew about 2:00 pm, the Cheshires could not be warned and so hung on until the large numbers of enemy attacking their now exposed right flank forced them to fall back. Fighting all the way, they retired firstly to a line in front of Bapaume, and then at 5:30 pm a further move was ordered before finally they moved overnight to positions south of Grevillers, in support of 1/4th KSLI.

By 2:00 am on 25 March, the total rifle strength of 19th Division had been reduced to about 2,200 and it now held a line some 5 kilometres back from its position just two days earlier. During the day, the brigades continued to fall back in the face of heavy attacks and units became totally disorganized. At nightfall, 56th Brigade was ordered to withdraw and concentrate on Hébuterne, an order which it carried out with difficulty as it was not known where its units had halted for the night. 'As many men as possible were collected and two weak battalions were formed: practically the whole of the 9th Cheshire Regiment was unaccounted for.' The 58th Brigade was in the same state: by 4:00 pm when it reached the Irles area it was just thirty strong with four officers. The 9th RWF had begun the day with a strength of only 80 rifles and now contained only eight plus one officer. The Brigade fell back to Hébuterne, arriving about 2:00 am on 26 March. Once there, it reorganized itself as a battalion, with each of its former battalions now forming one company of between one and three platoons.

The 19th Division was now ordered to concentrate on Hébuterne, which it found very difficult to do in the dark and with new reinforcements arriving, many without proper badges or distinguishing marks. Some 500 stragglers were also returned, having been collected by straggler posts formed the previous day by Divisional staff officers. The Division's rifle strength had fallen to approximately 1,800: 56th Brigade 800, 57th Brigade 600 and 58th Brigade 400. The casualties for 56th and 58th Brigades between 21-26 March had been 970 1434 all ranks, respectively.[23] Losses for 9th Cheshire were 369 whilst 9th RWF had lost 460.[24] Late on 26 March a much depleted 19th Division was relieved by 4th Australian Brigade and a few days later it was moved north to the quiet Messines sector to recuperate.[25]

During the five days from 23-28 March some 70 soldiers of 9th Cheshire were killed in action. A brief analysis of their records gives an idea of the composition of the battalion before the German offensive and provides a basis for later comparison with the reinforcements that

22 Ibid., pp. 158–161. It was the initial loss of the trenches which was described in the 17th Royal Fusiliers War Diary entry for 24 March 1918 (TNA: WO 95/1363) as the Cheshires 'bolting'. This seems to have been an exaggeration. It is possible that one company of 9th Cheshire withdrew hastily but the trenches were speedily retaken by the successful counter-attack mounted by that same unit.

23 Ibid., pp. 166-7, 173.

24 Crookenden, *The Cheshire Regiment in the Great War*, p. 131 and Ward, *Royal Welsh Fusiliers Vol. III 1914–1918*, p. 406.

25 *BOH 1918 Vol. 1*, p. 524 and TNA WO 95/2079/1: 9th Cheshire War Diary for 29 March 1918.

were immediately rushed out to replace them.[26] Some seven of those who died were original 9th Cheshire soldiers who had arrived in France with the battalion in mid-1915 and had served with it ever since. Of the total fatalities, even at this late stage of the war most (57) had been volunteers, judging by the dates of their enlistments and their previous service. Some 23 were former TF soldiers who had been posted to France in late 1916 as a result of the second MSA which had enabled them to be posted overseas and transferred to a Regular battalion. The remaining 16 fatalities were probably conscripted. The vast majority (59) had served with various Cheshire battalions in France and many had previously been wounded at least once, if not twice. Of the others, most had previously served in Yeomanry regiments and only 4 appear to have come straight from TR battalions.

The ages and types of enlistment may be charted:

Ages	Number	Comments
18	0	
19	8	three definite volunteers; one possibly a volunteer; four conscripts
20	8	At least five were TF volunteers going by the dates of their enlistment; Three later enlistments were possibly conscripted.
21-28	29	26 volunteers, including 12 former TF soldiers and some 'Derby' men; Three likely conscripts going by the probable date of their enlistment.
29	5	Three volunteers; two probably conscripts
30s	23	18 volunteers; five probably conscripts
40s	0	

Table 11. Age and types of enlistment of 9th Cheshire soldiers killed between 23 – 28 March 1918.

Finally, 55 percent (40) had enlisted in Cheshire and a further ten elsewhere in No 4 District. Together with a further seven from No 3 District that makes a total of 78 percent from the Battalion's parent Home Command. Of those who did not enlist within Western Command, several had nonetheless enlisted specifically for service in the Cheshire Regiment. It would seem, therefore, that even at this stage of the war the composition of 9th Cheshire remained much the same as in earlier years.

On 1 April, amongst Haig's 58 divisions, excluding Cavalry and Portuguese, were nine 'used' divisions, each having drafts posted, arrived or en route so would shortly be made up to 800 Infantry, seven 'used' divisions in the course of being refilled, three 'exhausted' divisions which could not be refilled at present, and fifteen 'exhausted' divisions still in or near the line. Fresh divisions were sent south to reinforce the Third and Fifth Armies whilst some of the most battered divisions, including the 19th and 25th, were now sent north to Second Army, to be

26 *SDGW* and ww.ancestry.com. Only 32 Service Records are available but by extrapolating from the Regimental numbers, the War Gratuities paid and the previous units in which the man served it is possible to make some assumptions about their military service.

placed in a 'quiet' area behind the Lys front for reorganization, including assimilation of the newly arrived drafts, and rest.[27]

Reinforcements were gradually arriving. In 19th Division, 9th Cheshire received 477 ORs between 3-8 April, and by 10 April, when the battalion moved north to Nieppe, it numbered 12 officers and 752 men, some 63 percent of the latter having arrived during the previous week. The 9th RWF had received some 400 men, although it was noted that very few had any previous battle experience.[28] Some of those arriving with the battalions were returning wounded: Major Clayton of 1/1st Cambridgeshire rejoined the 39th Division with 'a large draft, many still in bandages, picked up on the railway linc at Calais'.[29] Even under the trying circumstances at the time, however, it is evident that it remained possible for returning wounded to rejoin their own battalions, or at least their parent Regiment.

The 25th Division had also lost heavily during the recent battle, suffering 3,357 all ranks casualties.[30] It was now in the Ploegsteert sector where reinforcements were rapidly arriving, and its battalions were practically up to strength. The Divisional History notes that many reinforcements were aged 19 and were 'most excellent' material but that the absence of older men suitable for promotion to NCO rank was, in some units, a serious disadvantage. Like the other divisions, the 25th now needed several weeks of hard training to enable officers to get to know their men, to absorb reinforcements and to become a useful fighting force again. With this in mind it had been placed with other divisions in the same state 'in what was supposed would be a quiet sector for at least an appreciable time'.[31]

The Military Service Act (No 2), 1918

Without further legislation there was no possibility of obtaining more men for the Army for later in the year. This was at last recognized and, as requested by the War Cabinet on 25 March, Geddes produced a draft bill for their consideration. The contents were far-reaching, perhaps in anticipation of their being toned down. Geddes proposed that the age limit for military service should be lowered to 17 and raised to 55 for male British and Irish subjects, albeit with the proviso that under 18s and over 50s would not be called up so long as they served with the Volunteer Force at Home; existing exemptions would be withdrawn and the power to grant exemptions would be abolished; and the tribunal system should be abolished and replaced by Military Service Advisory Committees to consider priorities for conscription.[32] After several Cabinet discussions it was agreed that, whilst some of the proposals were feasible, the lowering

27 *BOH 1918 Vol. 2,* pp. 113-4. 'Used' divisions, now refilled: 3rd, 6th, 17th, 19th, 25th, 34th, 56th, 59th and 63rd. 'Used' divisions in the process of being refilled: Guards, 9th, 21st, 31st, 40th, 41st and 51st. 'Exhausted' divisions for whom insufficient replacements available: 30th, 36th and 50th. "Exhausted' divisions still in or near the line: 8th, 12th, 14th, 16th, 18th, 20th, 24th, 35th, 39th, 42nd, 47th, 58th, 61st, 62nd and 66th.

28 TNA WO 95/2079: 9th Cheshire War Diary April 1918 and Ward, *Records of the Royal Welsh Fusiliers*, p. 410.

29 Riddell & Clayton, *The Cambridgeshires 1914 to 1919*, p. 156.

30 *Official History, 1918 Vol. 2* p. 492.

31 M. Kincaid-Smith, *The 25th Division in France and Flanders*, (Uckfield: Naval & Military Press, 2001), pp. 193-4.

32 TNA CAB 24/46/37: NSR 32 dated 26 March 1918.

of the recruiting age to 17 would be impracticable and that the imposition of service in the Volunteer Force at home would cause opposition as well as a loss to industry. As far as the introduction of conscription in Ireland was concerned, it was decided that the furthest they could go towards it, until such time as it ultimately became necessary and the benefits appeared to outweigh the risks of further rebellion, would be to place a provision in the Bill giving the Government the power to introduce it by Order in Council at a future date. The Cabinet was also uncomfortable with the abolition of the existing Tribunal system.[33] So it was a somewhat watered-down draft Bill that was approved on 6 April for submission to Parliament. By then, the provision concerning the abolition of Tribunals had been lightened to enable the remodeling of existing Tribunals rather than disturbing the whole system. There were still some reservations over the extension of the age limit to 55 and opposition to this was expected in the Commons. The Prime Minister himself stated, however, that

> The main object of this Bill was to get in readiness an army for next year, and that it was most essential, in view of the certainty that the Germans would, during the autumn, use all their reserves available, that we should maintain our reserves at full strength.[34]

The Bill was introduced to Parliament on 9 April. It did not have an easy ride but was passed on 18 April as the Military Service (No 2) Act, 1918. In its final form it raised the upper age limit for conscription to 50, which could be extended to 55 by Order in Council if necessary in the future, it made possible the future extension of conscription to Ireland by Order in Council, enabled the closer regulation of Appeals Tribunals and granted power by proclamation to withdraw certificates of exemption in case of national emergency.[35]

The new legislation had been passed but any more recruits now made available would not be ready for drafting until the Autumn at the earliest. In the meantime, Germany launched the next offensive.

9-29 April: Battle of the Lys

The next German offensive, Operation Georgette, was aimed at strategic targets just behind the British lines in Flanders: Hazebrouck with its rail network linking the British lines to the Channel ports; and the high ground around Mont Kemmel over-looking Ypres. The plan was to attack south of the River Lys, heading towards Hazebrouck, with a second attack on the following day between the Lys and Ypres. If successful, the British occupation of the Ypres Salient would become untenable.

The area to be attacked was roughly bisected by the River Lys with the British First Army holding the southern part of the line and Plumer's Second Army north of the river. It had been a relatively quiet area since 1915 and five of the divisions that would face the attack had been sent there to recuperate after the March offensive. Second Army's IX Corps' section of

33 TNA CAB 23/5/68: Minutes of War Cabinet Meeting 376 of 28 March, CAB 23/5/69 Meeting 377 of 29 March and CAB 23/6/5 Meeting 383 of 5 April.

34 TNA CAB 23/6/6: War Cabinet Meeting 384 of 6 April 1918.

35 *Public General Acts, 8&9 Geo 5* (London: Eyre & Spottiswoode, 1918), pp. 5-12.

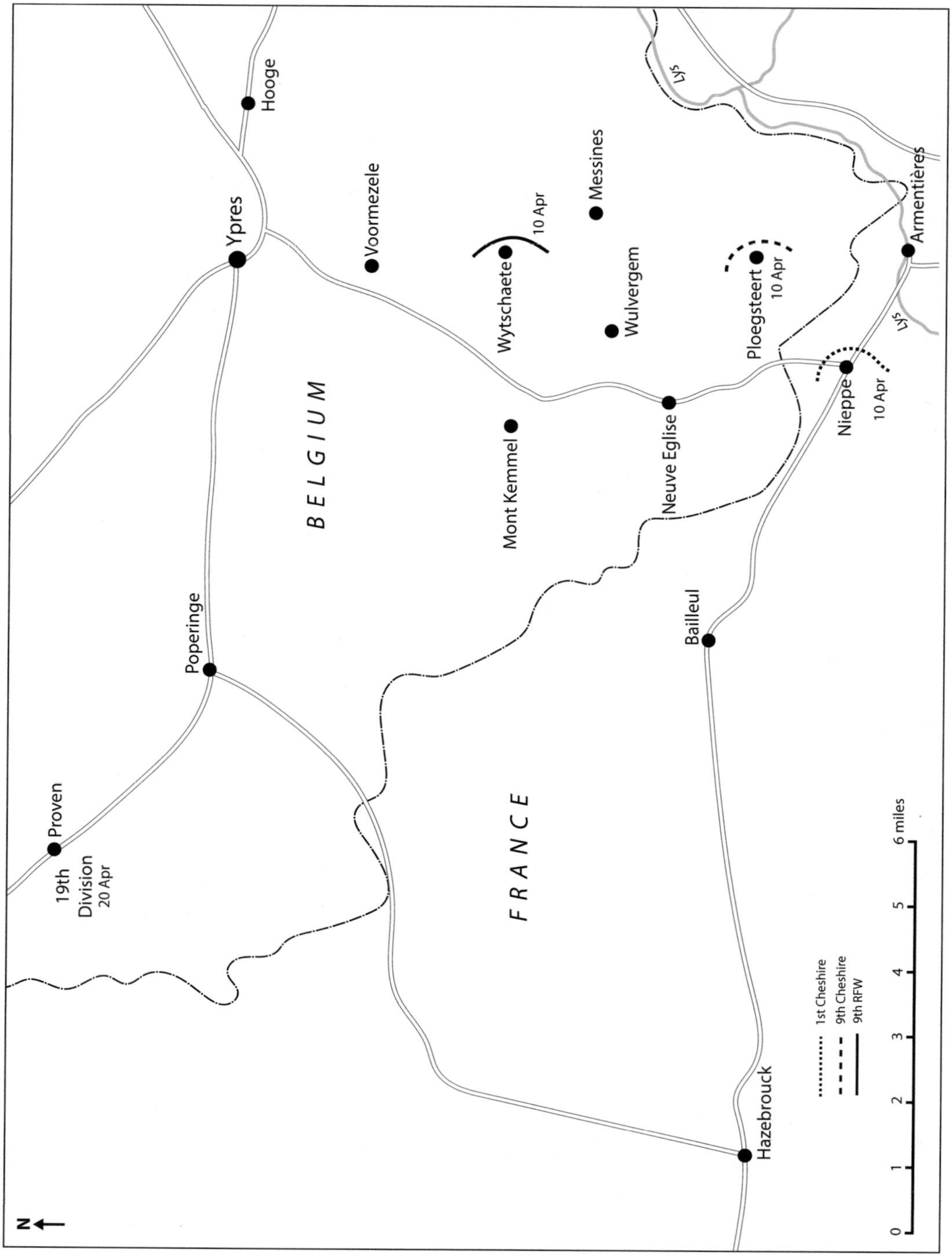

Map 8: Battle of the Lys, April 1918: 9th Cheshire, 9th RWF, 1/4th KSLI and 1st Cheshire

the line ran from a mile north of Ypres, included the Messines Ridge and ended just north of Armentières. From left to right its divisions were the 9th, 19th and 25th, all of which were still refitting. The last thing they needed after their losses on the Somme the previous month was another German offensive.

The Germans attacked on 9 April and there was to be fierce fighting over the next three weeks with a succession of battles.[36] The British line was relentlessly pushed back until the German advance was halted within sight of Ypres. They had failed both to take Hazebrouck and to oust the British from Ypres. In repelling them, however, the British had lost 82,040 casualties.

The Marcher battalions of 19th and 25th Divisions that had been involved in the March offensive had again been mauled. Amongst the Reserves hurried into line had also been 2nd SWB of 29th Division and 1st Cheshire of the 5th Division, the latter division having only newly returned from Italy. The experiences of March were repeated, with battalions being moved between brigades and divisions, and their companies becoming separated. As early as 10 April 9th Cheshire had in the space of a few hours been transferred from 19th to 34th and then to 25th Division, being joined in the latter division by 1/4th KSLI.[37] Further north near Wytschaete, the 9th RWF, with 58th Brigade, had been placed under command of 9th Division on its left. By the evening HQ 9th RWF had to send out patrols to discover where its companies were. Two were found but the front and support line companies, A and D, had lost heavily and there were only vague rumours of small parties holding out.[38] By 12 April IX Corps' line, extending from Nieppe, across the forward slopes of the Neuve Eglise rise, to the slopes of the Wulverghem spur and almost to Wytschaete, was held by a mixture of brigades and units of five different divisions.[39] Even the Pioneer battalions of 19th and 25th Divisions, the 5th and 6th SWB, had been pressed into use to defend the line. What was effectively crisis management continued as the line continued to fall back. Finally, overnight on 18 April 19th Division was relieved by the 28th French Division, more slowly than usual owing to 'difficulties of interpretation'.[40] 'Very tired and much reduced in numbers,' the troops rested during 19-20 April and then moved to the Proven area for a further rest and refit. On 20 April, 53 officers and 2626 ORs arrived from the 19th Divisional Wing of the IX Corps Reinforcement Camp for distribution to units; 9th Cheshire received 156 reinforcements over the next couple of days.[41]

The 25th Division's casualties between 9-30 April were 7,584; between 9 April-4 May its three Marches battalions lost:

36 Battles of the Lys: Estaires 9-11 April (XI and XV Corps, First Army), Messines 10-11 April (IX Corps, Second Army), Hazebrouck 12-15 April (First Army), Bailleul 13-15 April (IX Corps), Kemmel 17-19 and 25-26 April and Scherpenberg 29 April 1918.

37 Wyrall, *The Nineteenth Division 1914-1918*, p. 177; Crookenden, *The Cheshire Regiment in the Great War*, p. 136.

38 Ward, *Royal Welsh Fusiliers Vol. III 1914-1918*, p. 412.

39 *BOH 1918 Vol. 2*, p. 272.

40 TNA WO 95/2079-1: 9th Cheshire War Diary entry 18/19 April 1918.

41 TNA WO 95/2058: 19th Division A&Q War Diary entry 20 April and WO 95/2079 9th Cheshire War Diary entries 22 and 24 April.

ORs	Killed	Wounded	Missing	Total
10th Cheshire	32	295	336	663
11th Cheshire	32	305	532	869
6th SWB	32	293	82	407

Although replacements had been found in a hurry after the March offensives, their quality had been variable:

> It had been abundantly proved during the recent battle that the units with their abnormal proportion of boys under 20 years of age and older men over 35 were not up to the previous standard. The scarcity of men of the best fighting ages between 21 and 28 was most noticeable in every unit. The older men, largely men combed out from administrative employment and past the best fighting age, proved the fallacy of the theory that it is possible to make a fighting soldier of the man of 35 equal to the continental soldier of the same age who has performed military service in his youth.[42]

Between 28 March-8 April, 9th Cheshire received some 554 OR reinforcements and when it went into action on 10 April was again up to strength with 12 officers and 752 OR, plus a further 144 men who had been left out of action. It was to lose a further 80 men killed in action during the period 10-29 April.[43] Analysis of their details gives a general picture of the composition of a battalion that had been largely refilled following the earlier German attack. It might have been expected by this stage that most men would be conscripts but overall 61 percent of those killed (49, including 7 'Derby-men') were volunteers, 21 were Conscripts and 10 unknown.[44] Over half of the men had seen previous Cheshire Regiment service in various battalions and at least eight had come to France originally with 9th Cheshire in mid-1915. Finally, the available enlistment details show that 24 had enlisted in Cheshire and a further 21 in Wales, making a total of 45 from No 4 District. Together with a further 20 from No 3 District, this makes a total of 65, or 81 percent of those killed, who had been enlisted in Western Command.

Amongst the 80 who were killed, the available Service records show that 34 had been amongst the draft that arrived between late March and early April and a further 3 had joined on 22 April as part of a draft of 148.[45] Although these 37 equate only to about 5 percent of the reinforcements received between 28 March-24 April, analysis of their details indicates the composition of the drafts that had been rushed out to 9th Cheshire. Even now they were still predominantly volunteers, 24, including four 'Derby' men, as against 13 who had been

42 *BOH 1918 Vol. 2,* p. 493 and Kincaid-Smith, *The 25th Division in France and Flanders*, pp. 243, 251-2.
43 *SDGW* records for soldiers of 9th Cheshire 10-29 April 1918 and <www.ancestry.co.uk>. Most unusually almost all the Service Records of these men have survived, thus enabling detailed analysis. NB. Some 54 soldiers died between 10-18 April, but a longer period has been analysed to give greater evidence of the composition of the battalion.
44 The Record of Service/Enrolment Forms have been used to analyse the types of engagement. Army Form B 2513 was used to attest conscripts.
45 The battalion remained close to the line and was subjected to heavy shelling on 26, 27 and 29 April. Drafts were received: 22 April 148 and 24 April 8.

conscripted. Just on a third of the 37 had seen previous Cheshire Regiment service in various battalions and at least eight of these had served in France for more than a year. Of the rest, 11 (RWF five and SWB six) had come from other Regiments in No 4 District thus making a total of 26 from the Cheshire's home district. The rest were more varied and included four from the London Regiment, two 'combed out' men from the Army Veterinary Corps (AVC) and three from the Devonshire Regiment. Overall, however, 30 out of the 34 who had arrived with the drafts of late March/early April had enlisted in Western Command. Although rushed out in haste, the drafts still predominantly contained men from the same Home Command.

The age profile of the group may be charted:

Age	Numbers	Comments
18	4	All aged over 18½; one conscripted.
19	18	Seven conscripted.
20	2	
21-28	6	'Best fighting ages'. One conscripted.
29	1	Wounded in August 1917 and posted to 9th Cheshire on return to France in April 1918.
30s	5	Four conscripted; three called up in late 1917 so just four months training.
40s	1	Volunteered in 1915 aged 40 and joined AVC

Table 12. Age profile of 9th Cheshire soldiers killed between 10-29 April 1918.

As might have been expected, by far the largest proportion was made up of 19-year olds, of whom just over a third had been conscripted. Many of them had been in the training system for nearly a year and thus had received longer initial training than the adults. Even the four 18-year olds had all received over five months training, a month more than the adults. In comparison, the number of men aged 21-28 is surprisingly low and, despite the views of the 25th Division's historian on the 'best fighting age', they were not necessarily the best specimens. Of the six men in this age bracket, five had previously been evacuated to the UK for treatment for wounds or ailments such as trench foot and diarrhoea and had been 'combed out' in late March from their recuperation at the Western Command Depot. Two other men, the 24-year old LCpl Robert Newcomb and the 43-year old Pte Harry King, had previously served in the AVC in France and had been 'combed out' during in 1917 to be trained as Infantrymen.

In comparison with the men lost during March 1918, it can be confirmed that the majority of their replacements were definitely younger, although the 19-year olds were already of an age to be posted overseas and hardly qualified for the terms 'beardless youths' or boys. They were products of the fresh 'crop' of recruits enlisted when they turned 18, before they were sucked into industrial work, and would almost certainly have been of better quality than the returning older men or the 30-year olds being called up.

Cadreization of Divisions and New Arrivals

The 39th Division, having lost 4,588 casualties between 21 March-5 April, had moved back to Le Tréport for refitting and training. On 10 April orders were received to organize a strong Composite Brigade of four battalions and move hurriedly to Hill 60, near Ypres. No 4 Battalion contained men of 1/1st Cambridgeshire, 4/5th Black Watch and 1/6th Cheshire and was allotted the defences in and around Voormezeele. At Watten, with 39th Division's spare transport, Major Clayton of the Cambridgeshires was endeavouring:

> to teach musketry and fire tactics to transport-drivers and cooks. This was a hair-raising job; 'England's last hope', as the force was irreverently called, had unorthodox views regarding the safety of firearms, and it was just as well they did not go into action![46]

The manning situation continued to worsen and on 20 April GHQ decided to reduce the 14th, 16th, 30th, 34th, 39th, 40th and 66th Divisions to cadres. This usually meant reducing infantry battalions to 10 officers and 45 ORs, with the surplus being sent to the Base Depots for re-posting. In this instance, however, the battalion training staffs from 16th, 30th, 39th and 66th Divisions were to be used to train the arriving Americans, whilst the depleted battalions were left in place and continued to receive reinforcements.[47] The 1/6th Cheshire sent 3 officers and 14 men 'to join the 77th Division American Army as specialist instructors' but the battalion continued to exist, receiving 2 officers and 85 men from the Base and 40 men from hospital. It was now effectively in three parts, with further men remaining with the 39th Division's Composite units.[48]

Reinforcements also began arriving from other theatres, with 'divisions and brigades turning up of whose existence the troops in France had never before heard'.[49] The 52nd and 74th Divisions began to arrive from Egypt and more shipping was made available for the transportation of the American Armies. Slowly numbers began to improve and at the end of April, AG GHQ reported on an improvement in Infantry and Cavalry strengths[50]:

	Officers	Men
Strength beginning of April	21,652	482,817
Battle casualties	4,112	108,286
Reinforcements	6,490	179,668
Strength at end of April	23,550	538,334

46 Riddell & Clayton, *The Cambridgeshires 1914 to 1919*, pp. 167-8.
47 TNA WO 95/26: AG GHQ War Diary entry for 20 April 1918 and *BOH 1918 Vol.* 3, p. 5.
48 C. Smith, *War History of the 6th Battalion, The Cheshire Regiment (TF)* (Chester: 6th Cheshire, 1932), p. 3.
49 Robertson, *From Private to Field Marshal*, p. 337.
50 TNA WO 95/26: AG GHQ War Diary entries 22, 28 April and 6 May 1918.

The powers granted in MSA (No 1) of 1918, enabling the withdrawal of exemption certificates granted on occupational grounds, had remained unused but under the new MSA (No 2) of 1918 this could be done by Proclamation. The first of these, withdrawing exemption from men under 23 who were fit for general service, was issued on 20 April. Recruiting for the Army began to increase, rising from 30,197 in March, to 78,298 in April; 84,019 in May and peaking at 88,950 in June.[51] It could not continue at that rate, however, without serious damage to the nation's economy. In the Army Council's eyes, the new legislation was too little too late since the earliest the new recruits would be available after the minimum of training would be September. Moreover, almost a third of the recruits obtained were under 19 and would therefore be unavailable until even later.

The Maurice Debate

On 6 May AG GHQ reported that the total casualties between 21 March-30 April had been 9,704 officers and 230,089 men.[52] Inevitably, the quest was now on to apportion blame for the losses and for the BEF's performance and both the Government and the military authorities were under attack. The Army's feeling of grievance would come to a head in May with the actions of Major-General Frederick Maurice.

In introducing the draft Bill to Parliament on 9 April, Lloyd George had made two statements that subsequently proved to have been inaccurate: namely, that the Army in France had been stronger on 1 January 1918 than on 1 January 1917 and that there were only three 'white' (ie British) divisions in Palestine and Egypt. The figures were queried in some newspapers and on 18 April a question was raised in Parliament as to whether the January 1918 numbers given by Lloyd George included labour units and non-combatants. It emerged that they had included these numbers. It is clear from the subsequent response that not only had there been a misunderstanding over the composition of the figures but also that the War Office had provided incorrect figures for France and Flanders, having included 86,000 troops based in Italy.[53] A subsequent Parliamentary statement on 23 April by Andrew Bonar Law, the Chancellor of the Exchequer, further suggested that the extension of the British line in January 1918 had been an arrangement made solely by the British and French military authorities. The implications of the statements made were that on 21 March 1918 the British had indeed had more fighting troops on the Western Front than the Germans and had not been weakened by any action of the Government.

Matters came to a head on 7 May with the publication in *The Times* and other newspapers of letters by Major-General Frederick Maurice, the former War Office Director of Military Operations. It was a brave move which put him in breach of military discipline and cost him his career. He charged that the Government had deliberately misled the House of Commons over the decision to extend the front, the strength of the Army in France on 1 January 1918 and the number of British Infantry divisions in Egypt and Palestine. His aim appears to have been to prompt a public inquiry into his allegations.

51 War Office, *Statistics of the Military Effort*, pp. 371-2.
52 TNA WO 95/26: AG GHQ War Diary entry May 1918.
53 *HC Deb* 18 April 1918 vol 105 c563.

In fact, Maurice's allegations were correct as the statements made to Parliament had been inaccurate: the extension of the line had been decided by the Supreme War Council and was thus a political decision; at the date of Lloyd George's speech there were six British divisions in Egypt; and labour and non-combatant figures had been erroneously included in the figures for the Army in France. The latter error might have been a genuine mistake, albeit never admitted as such by Lloyd George, particularly as the War Office continued to provide conflicting and inaccurate figures.[54] Maurice was not to get a public inquiry, however. Instead the issue was raised in Parliament and turned by the Government into what was effectively a vote of confidence in the country's war leadership. Lloyd George made a powerful speech, if based on somewhat doubtful material, refuting all Maurice's charges.[55] The Government did not fall, but yet further mistrust had been sown between it and the military authorities.

Reinforcements for France

In early May the War Office warned GHQ that the maximum number of British Infantry reinforcements that could be expected from England by the end of August was 93,000.[56] In the meantime, battalions and divisions were being brought back from the Middle East but there was a long lead time between notification of their departure and their actual arrival. The 74th Division, formed in early 1917 from dismounted Yeomanry regiments, had left Egypt in April but did not complete disembarkation at Marseilles until 11 May. Word also came that a further 23 Infantry battalions were being released from Egypt but would not arrive in France until June.[57] Other sources were tapped: seven former TF battalions, including 23rd Cheshire, arrived from UK at the end of May to become Garrison Guard battalions.[58]

Changes to the BEF's Reinforcement Organisation

It was decided in late May to abolish Corps Reinforcement Camps, perhaps because their forward positions had meant that too many of them had been caught up in the fighting of March and April and had consequently proved unable to send reinforcements forward. Instead, Reception Camps were to be established for each Army, Corps and Division and two new Reinforcement Training Camps were to be established back near the Bases for 'combed out' men and those requiring training. By mid-June the new organization was in place. Army Reception Camps had been formed: Second Army's at Watten, First and Fifth Army sharing a camp at Auvin, Third Army's at Doullens and Fourth Army's at Longpré. Corps Reception Camps had been formed for all Corps, apart from the IXth, and Divisional Reception Camps for all divisions

54 TNA WO 32/10085: Minute from Colonel Kirke, Colonel GS, to DMO dated 10 May 1918 cited in N. Maurice, *The Maurice Case* (London: Leo Cooper, 1972), p.140.
55 *HC Deb* 9 May 1918 vol 105 cc2355-2405.
56 TNA WO 95/26: AG GHQ War Diary entry for 8 May 1918: War Office letter 121/Drafts/9946 (AG2b) dated 8 May 1915: May 20,000; June 23,000; July 22,000 and August 28,000.
57 Ibid., AG GHQ War Diary entries for 9 and 11 May and 30 June 1918.
58 Ibid., AG GHQ War Diary entry for 30 May 1918. The seven arrivals were: 25th Liverpool; 15th Essex; 2/6th DLI; 11th Somerset LI; 11th R Scots Fusiliers; 36th Northumberland Fusiliers; and 23rd Cheshire.

except those previously cadreized. No 1 Reinforcement Training Camp had been completed at Audresselles and orders issued for No 2 Camp to be prepared at Ste Marguerite.[59] The purpose behind the changes would appear to have been to streamline the organisation.

Re-organization and Rebuilding

The divisions that had been reduced to cadre continued to limp along. In early May it was planned that the 30th and 34th Divisions would be reconstituted as first-line divisions with battalions arriving from Egypt and Palestine and that 40th and 59th Divisions would be refilled with 'B' men as garrison divisions. The 14th and 16th Divisions were to be sent to England in mid-June to be reconstituted with Infantry battalions of 'B1' personnel and would then return to France.[60]

The 39th Division remained as a cadre for training American troops, but its battalions were beginning to be dispersed. Both 1/6th Cheshire and 1/1st Cambridgeshire were sent to join divisions with largely the same Home Command affiliations. On 25 May 1/6th Cheshire moved south to join the 25th Division, where it joined 10th and 11th Cheshire. Earlier in May 1/1st Cambridgeshire had joined 12th (Eastern) Division, absorbing 11 officers and 408 men from 7th Suffolk, thus making it effectively an amalgamation of three battalions as the 7th Suffolk had already absorbed the 8th Suffolk in February. It had also received drafts and was now up to strength again with experienced NCOs and men, mainly 'slightly wounded men returned to duty after the Spring battles'.[61] Training was now the Cambridgeshires' main activity in order to weld the battalion into 'an effective fighting weapon and give it the essential qualities of self-confidence and *esprit de corps*'.[62]

There was a pause in German attacks during the first three weeks of May, but the line still had to be held. All along it were divisions in various states of rebuilding but there were still others that had been uninvolved in the earlier German offensives. The 38th (Welsh) Division was one of these, having been moved south to the area of the Somme in early April to make way for the battered divisions being sent north. On the night of 11/12 April, it had relieved the 12th Division in the line near Albert. Orders were received to capture the high ground near Aveluy and the subsequent attack on 22 April was made by 113th Brigade, containing the 13th, 14th and 16th RWF, and 2nd RWF of 115th Brigade. Although it failed to drive the enemy completely off the plateau, the operation moved the line forward some 250 yards, pushing the Germans from most of the high ground so they could no longer observe the British positions. It was a costly attack, however, with some of the companies involved being reduced to 30 men. The 13th RWF had been on the right and, although the most successful of the battalions taking part, had sustained the greatest number of casualties: eight officers and 262 ORs, of whom 79 of the latter had been killed or subsequently died of wounds. The battalion had been particularly unlucky as the 2nd RWF had lost only 18 dead. The Germans twice counter-attacked the next day but were repulsed and made another determined attack on the 9 May but the Welsh retained

59 Ibid., AG GHQ War Diary entries for 25 May, 15 and 21 June 1918.
60 *BOH 1918 Vol.* 3, pp. 5-6 and TNA: WO 95/26 AG GHQ War Diary entries of 17 and 18 June.
61 Riddell & Clayton, *The Cambridgeshires 1914 to 1919*, pp. 178–181.
62 Ibid.

their hold of the high ground they had gained. The enemy, however, retained possession of the crest of the ridge running parallel to the River Ancre. It was consequently decided that troops of the 38th Division should attack from the north on 10 May but the preparatory artillery barrage suddenly and accidentally fell short, causing loss and disorganization and the attack was abandoned. The 38th Division remained in the line, subsequently carrying out a successful raid with the 14th and 16th RWF, before being withdrawn for a fortnight's rest on 20 May. During this period 'considerable drafts' were received so the time was spent largely on musketry training, culminating in a rifle meeting held on the day before the Division went back into the line. During June all three battalions of 318th American Infantry Regiment would be attached to 38th Division for instruction, but life for the Welsh during this period remained relatively quiet.[63]

The same could not be said for other divisions. It had been agreed with the French in April that four, possibly five, 'tired' divisions should be sent to a quiet French sector, the Chemin des Dames, to recuperate and refit whilst releasing French divisions for a General Reserve. Four divisions, 8th, 21st, 25th and 50th, would be sent with IX Corps to French Sixth Army on the Aisne front, west of Reims, and the 19th Division would join VIII Corps with the French Fourth Army near Chalons sur Marne.[64] HQ IX Corps had arrived on 26 April and its divisions had followed over the next couple of weeks. The 19th Division arrived later, on 18-19 May; on arrival 9th Cheshire found their new location at La Chaussée very comfortable with 'exceedingly good' billets. The surrounding countryside 'was very fine and the canal offered good facilities for bathing, which was much enjoyed by all during the hot weather that followed'.[65] It was a peaceful existence for the battalions of these divisions, which between the 19th and 25th Divisions included eight from the Marcher Regiments.

On 26 May warning was received of a German plan to attack the Chemin des Dames either the next day or the day after, and the IX Corps divisions were moved into the front line by the French Sixth Army Commander, General Duchêne. On 27 May the German opening bombardment on the front and support lines, headquarters and other vulnerable points, was 'generally agreed to have been the heaviest, most terrible and most destructive of the war'.[66] The assault that followed it up was swift and brutal. By the end of the day the Germans had crossed the Rivers Aisne and Vesle, had driven a salient 25 miles wide at the base and nearly 12 miles deep into the Allied line.[67] The British divisions in the line had been virtually destroyed for a third time:

> [I]n their exhausted, untrained and unwelded state, both out-numbered, ungunned and practically unprovided with aeroplanes [they] were totally unable to withstand the shock of the German assaults and successfully defend the sector of the line assigned to them along the Aisne.[68]

63 Munby, *A History of the 38th (Welsh) Division*, pp. 41-7.
64 *BOH 1918 Vol. 3*, pp. 12, 30-1.
65 TNA WO 95/2079: 9th Cheshire War Diary entry 18 May 1918.
66 Crookenden, *The Cheshire Regiment in the Great War*, p. 142.
67 *BOH 1918 Vol. 3*, p. 8.
68 Kincaid-Smith, *The 25th Division in France and Flanders*, p. 25.

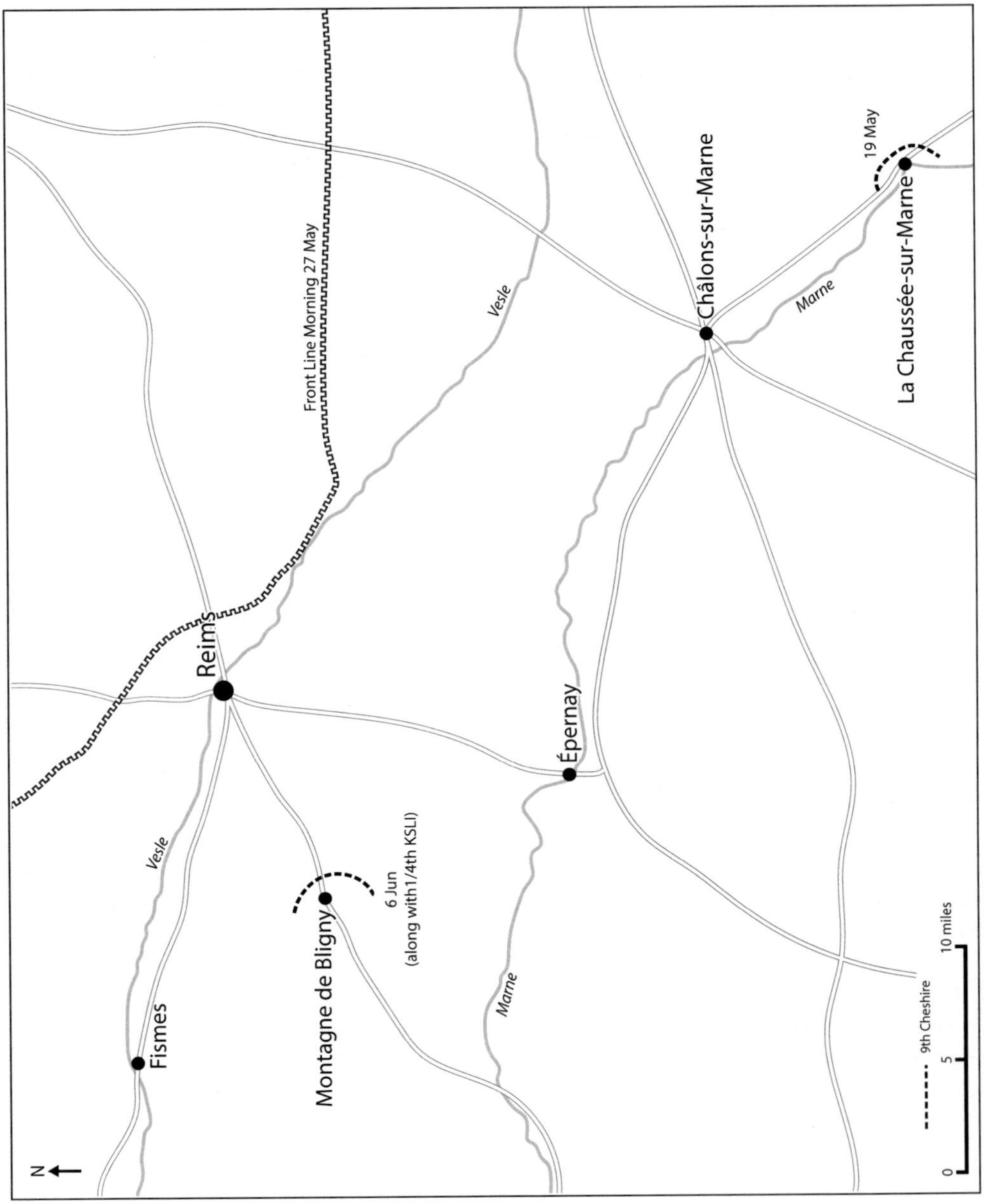

Map 9: Battle of the Aisne May 1918: 9th Cheshire, 9th RWF and 1/4th KSLI.

Over the next four days the Allies gradually fell back before the onslaught and it became a similar tale to the previous German offensives with changes of command within divisions and composite units being formed. On 29 May the much-depleted divisions of IX Corps were joined by 19th Division from VIII Corps and the following day about 500 all ranks in small parties from 8th, 25th and 50th Divisions were temporarily absorbed by the 19th Division battalions. During further heavy fighting during the day practically the whole of 9th RWF and 9th Welsh became surrounded and were killed or captured, and the following morning the remnants were organized into a composite company and placed under command of 9th Cheshire.[69] On 1 June the remains of 74th Brigade of 25th Division were withdrawn to reorganize; it would now be composed of two composite battalions of 25th Division and two of 8th Division.[70] The fighting finally began to die down and 25th Division noted no further enemy attacks between 2-5 June apart from heavy shellfire. There was a further flurry of activity on 6 June when the enemy launched a big attack against the Montagne de Bligny. The 58th Composite battalion, formed of remnants of 2nd Wiltshire, 9th RWF and 9th Welsh, left their trenches and fought off the enemy with bayonets. A further attack was made mid-morning against which a 9th Cheshire counter-attack failed but 1/4th KSLI was brought up from reserve and staged a further counter-attack, going forward 'with great dash, the remnants of 9th Cheshire being carried forward (for the second time) by the magnificent dash and spirit of their comrades'. The enemy was taken by surprise and by 12:15 the Montagne de Bligny was again in British hands. It was not without cost, however. The 19th Division OR casualty figures for 1-8 June show totals of 25 killed, 298 wounded and 378 missing with a note that the majority had occurred on 6 June.[71] Overall, the IX Corps casualties between 27 May-19 June were 1,298 officers and 27,405 ORs.[72]

Further Reorganization and Re-building

The process of rebuilding continued. The CIGS, Sir Henry Wilson, had promised a further 70,000 shortly but admitted that almost all would be 'B' men, obtained by reducing the number of Home Service Divisions to four.[73] GHQ's plan for rebuilding both the cadreized divisions and those that had been mauled on the Aisne was outlined by Haig in a letter to Foch on 10 June, which clearly shows the shortage of completely fit men.[74] The 8th, 21st and 19th Divisions were to be withdrawn and refilled with 'A' men; the 30th, 34th and either the 25th or 50th Divisions were to be reconstituted with battalions from Palestine and Salonika; the 40th and 59th Divisions would be refilled by 'B' men already in France whilst the cadres of 14th and 16th Divisions, together with that of either the 25th or 50th Divisions, would be sent to England to be refilled with 'B' men before returning to France. The 39th and 66th Divisions would remain as training cadres for the five American Divisions in the British zone.

69 Wyrall, *The Nineteenth Division 1914-1918*, p. 203.
70 Kincaid-Smith, *The 25th Division in France and Flanders*, pp. 267–8.
71 Wyrall, *The Nineteenth Division 1914-1918*, pp. 207-8 and TNA WO 95/2058: 19th Division A & Q Branch War Diary for June 1918.
72 *BOH 1918 Vol. 3*, p. 159. The totals for the 19th Division were 151 officers and 3,460 ORs and for 25th Division were 201 officers and 4,137 ORs.
73 General Sir Henry Wilson had replaced General Sir 'Wullie' Robertson as CIGS in February 1918.
74 *BOH 1918 Vol. 3*, pp. 168-9.

1/4th KSLI: '[A] few of those left in A Company' after the Battle of Bligny, 6 June 1918. (Shropshire Regimental Museum)

The 25th Division had learned on 9 June that it was to be broken up and its battalions used as reinforcements for other units. Wherever possible the policy of retaining Regular, TF and the earlier Service battalions continued. On 8 July 1/6th Cheshire moved to 30th Division where it was joined by the 25th Division's Pioneer battalion, 6th SWB. Both 10th and 11th Cheshire had lost heavily on the Aisne and were now effectively disbanded. Men from the 10th were absorbed by 9th Cheshire of 19th Division, whilst 11th Cheshire, which had lost over half its number in casualties on the Aisne, sent 16 officers and 492 men to be absorbed by 1/6th Cheshire. The latter battalion was highly relieved as it had feared that it might be the other way round![75] The 25th Divisional cadre left for England where some doubt was expressed about the quality of the replacements provided for it. In the end it would be refilled with nine battalions from British divisions from the Italian front.

In mid-June, after a period of uncertainty as to its future, 40th Division learned that it was to become a 'semi-mobile' division of 'garrison' battalions.[76] Some of these had been formed from 'B1' men collected from various labour companies which were now given regimental titles: 8th Garrison Battalion, for example, became 13th (Garrison) East Lancashire. Others were 'Garrison Guard' battalions formed from TF Home Service battalions that had arrived

75 Walter Williamson, *A Tommy at Ypres – Walter's War, The Diary and Letters of Walter Williamson*, p. 281.
76 F.E. Whitton, *History of the 40th Division* (Aldershot: Gale & Polden, nd), p. 274.

in France during May, one of which was 23rd Cheshire. The Brigade Commander of 119th Brigade, Frank Crozier, was dismayed to see the quality of the men arriving for his Brigade and instructed the Regimental Medical Officers of his new battalions to comb out any 'old fellows whom they consider beyond hope of physical redemption'. The process was repeated with fresh drafts and eventually Crozier had three battalions and a trench mortar battery.[77] Intensive training was needed to get the men fit, together with musketry training as many of the men had done no military training for a very long time and some had never fired a rifle. Almost equally as important was the need to develop self-confidence and *esprit de corps*. The title 'Garrison' was quietly dropped from the battalions during July.

The remains of the 19th Division were relieved on 19 June by the 8th Italian Division and withdrawn for rest and refit. It still contained many men from other divisions who had been temporarily attached to it and these were now sorted and returned. The 3rd Worcestershire was transferred from 25th Division and reinforcements arrived from the 19th Divisional Wing. On 30 June the Division began moving back to the British zone where it was to be held in GHQ Reserve.[78] It would spend July resting and training the new drafts before moving back into the line at Locon and Hinges in early August. It would be in and out of the line from then on but would not take part in a major operation until the Battle of the Selle in mid-October.[79]

Sickness and Postings

Officially, it had remained policy throughout the war that men returning from having been wounded or sick should whenever possible be sent back to their own battalions. That this did not always happen is apparent from various anecdotal accounts, but it does seem that efforts continued to be made at least to post men to their own regiments. A case in point is that of Pte James Riley of the King's Own Yorkshire Light Infantry (KOYLI). A 'Derby' man, he had been called up in October 1916 and posted to 2/5th KOYLI which arrived in France in January 1917. He was wounded in his left arm during the Second Battle of Bullecourt and, once recovered, was subsequently posted to 1/4th KOYLI. Wounded again in October 1917, he was evacuated to Scotland for treatment but by late November had recovered sufficiently to be posted back to France, this time joining 10th KOYLI. On the disbandment of that battalion in February 1918 Pte Riley was transferred to 2nd KOYLI. In early 1918 he was wounded again, in the ankle, but returned to the 2nd KOYLI, serving with it until the end of the war.[80]

That such a policy of returning men to their battalion had continued to exist is confirmed by the fact that in late May it became necessary for GHQ to warn that there was to be an amendment. This had become necessary since the combination of reinforcements from home and returning convalescents was causing the size of some battalions to become unbalanced. A letter was sent to the HQs of all Armies informing them that:

77 F. Crozier, *A Brass Hat in No Man's Land* (London: Jonathan Cape, 1930), p. 215.
78 TNA WO 95/2038: 19th Division A & Q War Diary for June 1918 and TNA WO 95/26: AG GHQ War Diary entry for 30 June 1918.
79 Wyrall, *The Nineteenth Division 1914-1918*, pp. 210-11.
80 I am grateful to Chris Preston for the information about his grandfather Pte James William Riley.

> In order that the best use may be made of our available resources, it is regretted that it will be necessary to depart from the procedure hitherto in force under which NCOs and men of British Infantry rejoined their Battalions on discharge from hospitals or convalescent hospitals in France.
>
> As far as possible this will be carried out, but it is of primary importance that the strength of Battalions should be maintained at the same level, so casuals will be posted to the Battalion of their own Regiment in which they are most required.
>
> The necessity for this stop has been exemplified during the recent operations, and certain battalions which had been brought up to establishment continued to increase in strength owing to the return of casuals whilst others of the same regiment remained weak.[81]

The situation had been exacerbated by outbreaks of a mild but highly infectious type of influenza amongst units of First Army during May and June. Patients usually returned to duty after a week or ten days, but the numbers affected were such that 3,000 beds made available at Étaples for these cases on 21 June were filled within three days. It was yet another factor to be taken into account in the use of divisions: on 20 June an attack by 29th Division against La Becque had to be postponed.[82]

There must have been times when the hard-pressed staff of 'A' Branch in GHQ felt the odds had been stacked against them. On 30 June it was discovered that men of the various battalions that had arrived from Salonika and Palestine had malaria and would need medical treatment and two months' isolation before being posted to divisions. These battalions, which included 4th and 7th Cheshire and 1/1st Herefordshire, were earmarked to reconstitute the 30th and 34th Divisions but in the meantime had to be sent to a separate camp in Serqueux where they would be administered by the now cadreized 50th Division. Perhaps more in hope than expectation, GHQ suggested to the War Office that 9,000 reinforcements from England should be earmarked for malarial battalions but there is no indication of their response.[83]

Manpower Outlook for the Rest of the Year

In mid-July Geddes submitted a paper to the War Cabinet seeking decisions on recruiting priorities for the rest of the year. Since 1 January 1918, over 450,000 men had been raised for the Armed Forces but the Admiralty was now owed 37,500 to meet its original demand, the Army Council had requested 551,000 recruits for July-August, with more demands anticipated later in the year, and the Air Ministry wanted 196,000 men for the period up to 31 May 1919. These demands could not be met in full since Geddes forecasted that the total recruitment for 1918 could not much exceed 700,000 men 'without shattering industry and severely crippling our whole war effort.[84]

81 TNA WO 95/2890: War Diary of 52 (Lowland) Division A&Q Branch: 'A' Summary No 2 of 8 June 1918 which publicised AG GHQ letter No AG/37 (P) of 31 May 1918.
82 Macpherson, *Medical Services General History Vol. III*, pp. 258-9.
83 TNA WO 95/26: AG GHQ War Diary entries for 30 June and 16 July 1918.
84 TNA CAB 24/58: War Cabinet Paper GT 5127 Memorandum by the Minister of National Service on the Manpower Situation Second Half of 1918 dated 16 July 1918.

Manpower was discussed by the War Cabinet on 19 July.[85] The Prime Minister, having taken advice from four Departments other than the War Office and also other unspecified 'first-class' experts, queried again whether the Army was making the best use of its manpower in France. The main issue under discussion, however, was the wider one of manpower in the nation as a whole, where the strain on industry was proving too great and output was being seriously affected. The Minister of Munitions, Winston Churchill, stated that it would be impossible for him to release more men except slowly through dilution. As examples of the effects of releases already made he cited that the output of aeroplane engines was running at 55 percent of the level previously arranged, the output of tanks had fallen by half and it was impossible to meet the War Office's demands for breach mechanisms. Auckland Geddes commented that almost two thirds of the total number of men available at the start of the war had been recruited, which gave an idea of the strain on the country. The physical standard of the men left was very low and that, apart from boys coming of age, only older men were available who were 'difficult to get and not worth much'. Nearly 500,000 men had been obtained this year, but this had caused a severe strain on industries. 'Even if recruits were urgently necessary, Sir Auckland Geddes said that they could not be got at the present time'. Both the First Lord of the Admiralty, Sir Eric Geddes, and the Minister of Labour, Mr Roberts, endorsed the previous comments. All Milner could say, on behalf of the War Office, was that whilst he could not dispute the facts being put forward, the War Cabinet must realise that the effect would be a smaller army in 1919 than this year.; they would be passing from 'an army of big to one of moderate dimensions'. In summing up, Lloyd George noted that the manpower question was bound up with those of the country's future war policy and the part to be played by the Americans the next year. Until decisions had been reached on these questions, the Cabinet could not adopt any formal resolution. Instead, it should be left to Geddes' discretion 'as to how far, having regard to the manpower at his disposal, it would be possible to meet the total demands put forward by the three fighting services'.

Whatever Geddes' decisions, however, men recruited during the rest of the year would not be available for drafting until December 1918. In the meantime, the Army would have to make do with what it had.

Overview

The manpower crisis of early 1918 had been coming since 1914 but the German Spring Offensive threw the manpower shortage into stark relief and forced long overdue actions to be taken. Many of those rushed out initially were not new men but were already in the Army, having been retained at Home by different War Office Departments and for the purposes of Home defence. The General Staff had long been urging a reduction in their numbers and this was now forced upon them.[86] Inevitably some of these men were not of the highest physical robustness; many had been previously wounded more than once and others had been ill with successive minor ailments. Macready subsequently doubted whether

85 TNA CAB 23/7: Minutes of the War Cabinet Meeting WC 449 of 19 July 1918.
86 Robertson, *From Private to Field-Marshal*, p. 342-3.

> the Government would have cared for the fierce light of publicity to have been thrown on the methods which had to be employed, or indeed, in thousands of cases, on the class of men who had to be sent, men who were in reality not fit in any capacity for the theatre of war.[87]

Whilst no doubt true in a number of cases, the comment can hardly be applied to the Government's decision to send out youths of over 18½ who had finished their training. Many of these young soldiers proved to be excellent material; they had received longer initial training than the adults and, in common with recruits of earlier in the war, had gained in physical fitness and maturity during the process. There were, of course, those that were classed as 'immatures' and these were retained in the camps that had been established.

The main problem concerning the reinforcements who were rushed out to stem the German onslaughts was not that they were all useless, narrow-chested unfit conscripts. It was the lack of time available for them to gain experience of the Western Front before being thrust into action.

87 Macready, *Annals of an Active Life, Vol. 1*, p. 287.

9

The 100 Days: Just Enough

In late July, the three Allied Commanders-in-Chief on the Western Front, Field Marshal Haig and Generals Pétain for the French and Pershing for the Americans, were present at a conference summoned by General Foch to consider counter-offensives against the Germans. The general plan for the following few weeks was that the Allied Armies should regain the initiative and launch limited objective attacks to clear the main railway lines in preparation for further operations.[1] It was still not anticipated, however, that there would be an early end to the war and the question of the number of reserves that would be available for the following year remained a key topic of discussion.

Any men called up from mid-1918 onwards would effectively be unavailable for drafting until the end of the year. Consequently, the BEF would have to fight any offensives initiated in August and the next few months with men already serving. Recruits already enlisted would become available for drafting once trained and old enough whilst other Category 'A' men would continue to be 'combed out' from wherever they might be found. Requirements for men of lower medical categories were to be met from the Home Army.

In the event, the operations that started in early August 1918 would gather momentum and the next 100 days would see the Allies making such rapid and successful progress that the Germans would sign an Armistice in November. As the men who would be involved in the events of August onwards were already in the Army, this final chapter touches only briefly on political aspects and then concentrates on events on the Western Front during the last months of the war. The battles of the '100 Days' are not examined in detail, other than to place in context the involvement and consequent effects on the Marcher battalions taking part.

Continuing Pressure on the British Government

The Government's continuing struggle was to balance the conflicting demands of different sectors of the nation's economy within the prevailing political climate. As an example, it was

1 Sheffield & Bourne, (eds.) *Douglas Haig, War Diaries and Letters 1914–1918*, p. 434.

intended in August to temporarily release 20,000 men from within the Army to assist with the harvest. These would be in addition to those fit enough to be sent from the Command Depots. The Secretary of State for Scotland wished to go further and sought the release of 1,400 men who had recently been called up from agriculture in Scotland. His request was refused since these were Category 'A' men, but he was at least promised that half of the 20,000 should be made available for harvest work in Scotland.[2] The Government's dilemma was, perhaps, felt most acutely in the coal mining industry. Miners were essential to the war economy, but they also made excellent soldiers. Throughout 1918 the Government, and especially Lloyd George, 'flip-flopped' over conscripting miners and releasing them back to the Home Front.[3] It was not just those retained at home who were called upon; in August, for example, GHQ received a demand for 500 'B' miners to be returned home.[4]

The new men raised by the changes in recruiting since March were now about to be ready for drafting but the Government continued to be the target of repeated attacks in the Press over the supply of reinforcements and whether enough men had been sent to France earlier in the year. An article on the subject in the *Daily Chronicle* of 10 September prompted discussions in the War Cabinet as to whether the actual figures of those sent to France should be published. The Prime Minister had been provided with more figures: between January and 21 March 167,000 fighting men had been sent to France and a further 535,000, including returning wounded, had been sent since. It was pointed out during the discussion that the criticism continued to be that the troops had not been sent before 21 March to which the Prime Minister responded that the Government had raised the troops and it was for the General Staff to settle whether the men should be in France or in England. In the end it was agreed that the figures should be published 'in order that the people at home and our Allies should have a clearer conception of the magnitude of our effort'.[5] The damage had been done, however, and the Government would fail to live down the charge that it had starved the BEF of men in early 1918.

There were also external pressures from the French Government, which persisted in believing that its British counterpart was failing to release as many men for the Army as it could; they questioned in particular why the large reserve existing in Ireland could not be tapped. In June permission had been given for the French to send an officer, Colonel Roure, to London to examine the War Office's figures. He visited twice, forcing the War Office and Macready to spend time they could ill-afford in explaining the reasons for the 1,248,000 men on the strength of the Home Army[6]. Roure professed himself satisfied but the French Government remained unconvinced by his report. The matter rumbled on and was discussed by Lord Derby, now the British Ambassador in Paris, with Clemenceau, the French Prime Minister, at the end of August. His account of the meeting was discussed by the War Cabinet on 30 August when Colonel Roure was described as a junior officer and not really competent to examine such difficult questions as

2 TNA CAB 23/7/18: Minutes of War Cabinet Meeting 455 of 7 August 1918.
3 See David Stevenson, *With Our Backs to the Wall: Victory and Defeat in 1918* (London: Allen Lane, 2011), p. 386. For the problems of coal mining during the war, see Barry Supple, *The History of the British Coal Industry Vol. 4: 1913–46 The Political Economy of Decline*, (Oxford: Oxford University press, 2004), pp. 43-116.
4 TNA WO 95/26: AG GHQ War Diary entry for 30 August 1918.
5 TNA CAB 23/7: Minutes of War Cabinet Meetings 471 of 10 September and 472 of 13 September 1918.
6 Macready, *Annals of an Active Life*, Vol. 1, pp. 294–7.

to whether the British were retaining too many men of military age in munitions or recruiting too extensively for the Fleet. It was decided that the British Government's response should take the form of a letter, to be handed personally to the French Prime Minister, Clemenceau, inviting two French Cabinet Ministers to be sent to England, accompanied by any experts they wished, to discuss the whole question of British manpower with the British Government before the next meeting of the Supreme War Council.[7] Clemenceau does not appear to have taken up the invitation but the matter remained in the background with both sides niggling away at each other. It was not helped by articles such as a mischievous one written by the war correspondent of the *Morning Post*, Charles á Court Repington, which appeared on 11 September and claimed that 'England was not playing her part and the French knew it'.[8]

Fortunately, the succession of victories during the next four months would focus attention in a different direction.

August – September 1918

The period between 8 August and 3 September heralded a turn in the tide. Foch's plan of limited attacks started with the highly successful one on Amiens. The next stage would be a series of coordinated attacks by six British and French Armies between 20-26 August on a 75-mile front from Arras to Soissons. The British Third Army held the line between Arras and Albert and would attack on 21 August. No Marcher battalions had been in action at Amiens, but several would take part in this attack which would become known as the Battle of Albert. It is not intended to consider this or the following Battle of Bapaume, 31 August-3 September, in great detail but the experiences of three Marcher battalions now in Third Army, namely 2nd RWF in 38th Division, 1st Cheshire in 5th Division and 7th KSLI in 3rd Division, enable comparisons to be made as to their composition at this stage of the war. The 38th (Welsh) Division was already part of Third Army's V Corps. The 3rd and 5th Divisions, together with the 63rd and the 17th Divisions, had been placed at Third Army's disposal for this period and joined VI and IV Corps respectively.

The 38th (Welsh) Division now contained the largest single concentration of Marcher battalions: eight locally raised Welsh battalions plus 2nd RWF. The latter battalion had joined 115th Brigade during the re-organization of divisions in February. There seems to have been a certain amount of ambivalence about the move, at least amongst the officers who considered they would be joining a division 'begotten in Welsh parish politics' which had 'been in GHQ's bad books since the Mametz muddle'.[9] The feeling does not appear to have persisted for long, however, once the reorganization had taken place.

Having been moved in late March from the Armentieres area and arriving on the Somme in early April, the Division had escaped being on the receiving end of the German Spring offensives. It had since seen some action but still remained comparatively unscathed. On 5 August, following a period of rest, it went back into the line to the north and south of Aveluy Wood, to the west of the River Ancre.

7 TNA CAB 23/14: Minutes of War Cabinet Meeting No 466A held on 30 August 1918.
8 TNA CAB 23/7: Minutes of War Cabinet Meeting 472 of 13 September 1918.
9 Dunn, *The War the Infantry Knew*, p. 440.

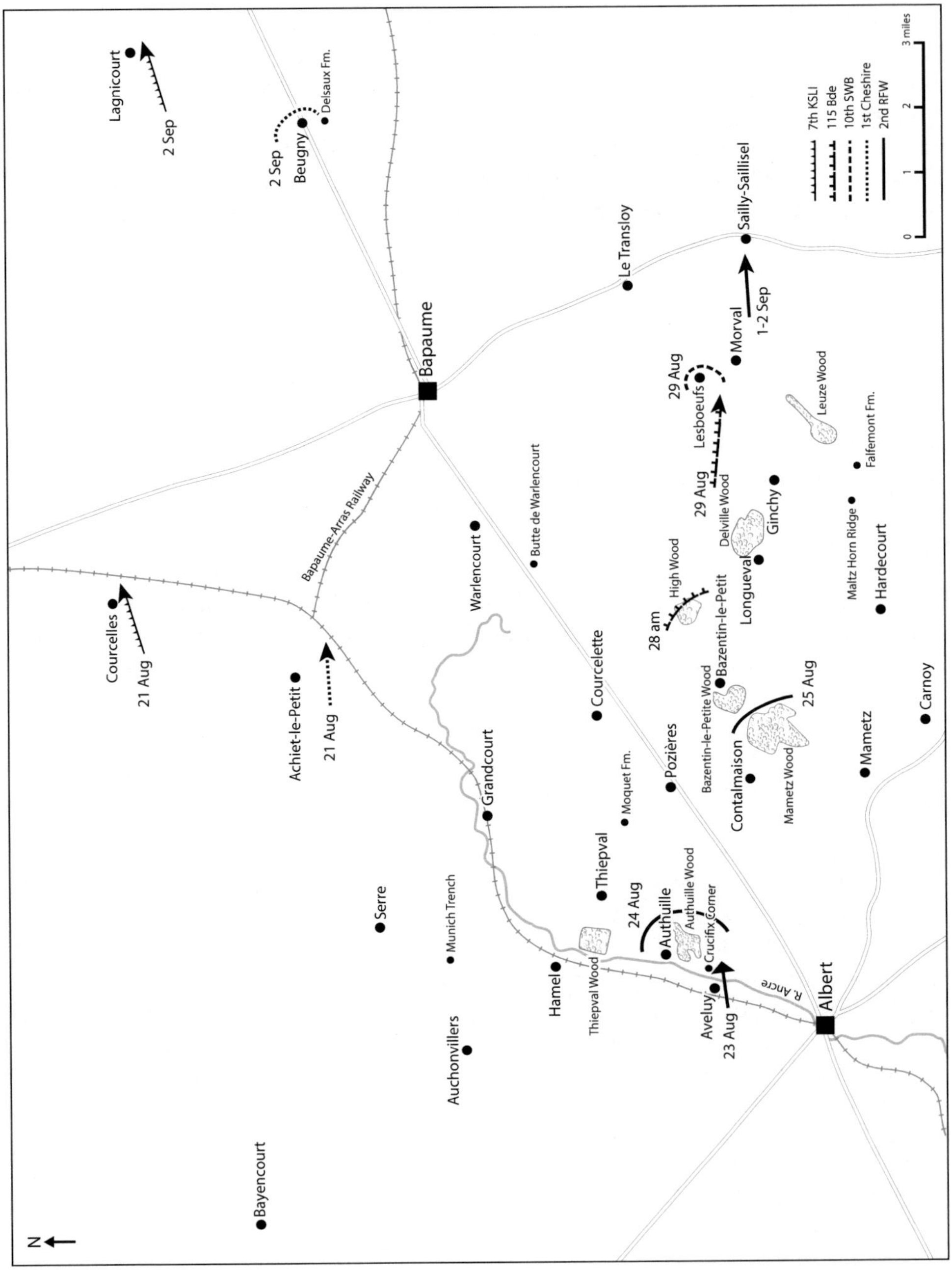

Map 10: Battles of Albert and Bapaume, August-September 1918: 1st Cheshire, 2nd RWF and 7th KSLI.

The V Corps was the southernmost of Third Army's three Corps and would have to cross the old Somme battlefield in the forthcoming attack. The initial plan for 38th Division on 21 August was that it should cross the River Ancre between Hamel and Albert and then press on towards Pozières. A crossing near Hamel was achieved overnight on 21/22 but the one in Albert was not managed until the following night, and it was 23 August before 115th Brigade, including 2nd RWF, managed to cross at Aveluy. From then on, fighting was more or less continuous as Third Army's overall task was extended eastwards. On 24 August 2nd RWF succeeded in clearing the Triangle, the area around Crucifix Corner, Authuille Wood and the village of Authuille, before continuing towards Pozières and Contalmaison which were taken on 25 August. The battalion consolidated its position NW of Mametz Wood whilst one company pushed towards Bazentin-le-Petit where it met violent opposition and was forced back. At this point, 2nd RWF was attached to 113th Brigade to act as reserve for a dawn attack the next day on Bazentin-le-Grand and Longueval. They were coming under heavy fire at this point and 'casualties in Bn [sic] rather heavy'.[10] Longueval and Ginchy were attacked the following day and the 2nd RWF moved to rejoin 115th Brigade during the morning, establishing itself in trenches south of High Wood. There it was subjected to heavy shelling but remained in the same position the next day. On 29 August, 115th Brigade attacked eastwards, moving on Morval and Lesboeufs with 2nd RWF in support. The first objective, the railway south west of Lesboeufs was taken without opposition, but then they came under heavy fire from the Lesbouefs-Morval Ridge. The 10th SWB succeeded in penetrating Lesboeufs but was held up there, together with supporting companies of 2nd RWF, for the next three days under heavy shelling the whole time. On 1 September 2nd RWF was the left assaulting battalion in an attack on Sailly-Saillisel. Again, they came under an intense enemy barrage and the village was not cleared until the night of 2/3 September. The advance continued but by 4 September 2nd RWF had been reduced to one company of 4 platoons with a strength of about 90 ORs. Finally, on 5 September, the battalion was relieved and moved back to huts and bivouacs south of Lesboeufs where it could rest and reorganize itself.[11]

Between 21August-5 September some 86 men of 2nd RWF had been killed or had died of their wounds. As the battalion had escaped involvement in the earlier German offensives, examination of the details of those who had died during this period gives an indication of the composition of a battalion which had been refilled after the actions of 1917 but had since suffered only normal wastage. Unfortunately, only 16 Service Records appear to be available but analysis of the Service numbers of all those who died, together with their Medal Index cards, Medal Roll entries and the size of their War Gratuities, provides at least an outline picture of these individuals. Going by the likely dates of enlistment as shown by their Service numbers, some 34 had volunteered for service before the introduction of compulsion. There may have been more volunteers amongst the others but without the Service Records it is impossible to say how many of the later enlistments might also have enlisted voluntarily by pre-empting their call up. Some 26 men appear to have enlisted in early 1917. Allowing for their four months' training, they should have been ready for drafting in the summer and had possibly arrived with the battalion during July 1917 when drafts totalling 326 had been received. These were followed

10 TNA WO 95/2561: 2nd RWF War Diary entry for 25 August 1918.
11 Ibid., 2nd RWF War Diary for the period 21 August-5 September 1918.

by successive drafts: 90 in August, 46 in September and 169 in early November.[12] Nearly 90 percent (76) of those killed had thus served with the battalion since late 1917. The other ten men, six of whom were aged 20 or under, had had less than 12 months' total service but it is not clear when they had arrived with the battalion as references to the arrival of OR drafts are sparse in the 1918 War Diary.[13]

Although not all those killed had seen previous RWF service, it is apparent that 2nd RWF had been refilled over time with men predominantly from Wales; out of the twelve men who had previously served in France with other cap-badges, six had come from the Welsh Regiment. Similarly, although only 17 of the fatalities had enlisted in the Regimental area, altogether some 36 men, or 43 percent, had enlisted in Wales. A further five had enlisted in the English areas of No 4 District so almost half of those killed had enlisted in the battalion's parent District. Of the rest, some 31 were from Lancashire and, as many of these enlistments were from early 1917 onwards, this may be an indication of growing difficulties in recruiting in Wales; it is likely that these men had been sent from a No 3 District TR battalion. Historically, however, RWF soldiers had often enlisted just across the border in Cheshire and Lancashire. Combining the enlistment figures for No 3 and No 4 District, some 88 percent of those killed had enlisted in Western Command. This shows a very high percentage still being drawn from the parent Command in late 1918.

Another Marcher battalion, 1st Cheshire, had returned from Italy with the rest of 5th Division in April and had taken part in the Battle of the Lys. Since then it had remained in the Forêt de Nieppe area where further attacks were constantly expected but none actually materialised. In mid-August the 5th Division was moved south, arriving in Bayencourt on 19 August where it joined Third Army's IV Corps. The 1st Cheshire was in action on 21 August, when its objective was the railway line south-east of Achiet-le-Petit. Having first captured the village, the Cheshires pressed on and took their portion of the railway line, only to find that, together with the 16th Warwickshire on their right, they were now some 500 yards ahead of any other troops and needed to retire to a trench running along the face of the hill they had just come up, before being relieved during the evening. They had gone into action 600 strong but had lost 300 casualties during the day, of whom 37 had been killed. They would next be in action in early September when the plan was for a dawn attack on 2 September to capture the village of Beugny and then to advance about two miles to Delsaux Farm, where 9th Cheshire had been during the previous March. They moved forward to the frontline during the night of 1 September but whilst waiting to start the attack:

> at 5 am the enemy guns opened on our trench and in less time than it takes to write this had just about blown us to hell. Great big shells fell right into the trench, causing at least 50 per cent casualties before we started. We also got sneezing gas, and liquid fire was mixed up with the HE.[14]

12 TNA WO 95/2423: 2nd RWF War Diary for 1917.
13 TNA WO 95/2561: 2nd RWF for 1918.
14 Crookenden, *History of the Cheshire Regiment in the Great War*, p. 158. Extract from diary of Captain L.I.L. Ferguson, Cheshire.

The Cheshires tried to press on with the attack but got only as far as the village of Beugny. Again, the losses had been heavy; many of the casualties were men of a large draft which had joined the battalion on 29 August and had moved forward to take part in the attack. Between 21 August-4 September, the estimated number of casualties for the battalion was 20 officers and 600 men.[15] Some 94 ORs were waiting in the Reinforcement Camp, with another 7 expected from the Base, and a further 98 were 'dumped' personnel.

Of 1st Cheshire's estimated casualties, 110 men had been killed or subsequently died of wounds sustained in the recent encounters. About two-thirds of the Service Records for these men are available and from these, together with the Regimental numbers and the sizes of the War Gratuities paid out, it is possible to deduce that at least 66 men had enlisted before the introduction of conscription. Of those enlisting afterwards, and for whom records are available, at least 11 had volunteered for service before reaching the age of 18 years 1 month. Of the ten 18-year olds killed during the period in question seven were conscripts, one a volunteer and the status of the other two is unknown. The high level of volunteers from earlier in the war, however, does not necessarily indicate lengthy overseas service and experience. Many were former TF HS soldiers who had been made available for overseas service only by MSA (2) of 1916 and others seem to have been retained at home for long periods, either due to wounds or sickness, or just lack of fitness. Several men had been obtained at the end of April 1918 from the Command Depot at Prescot where they had been recuperating and rushed out in drafts; at least two had tried to abscond on the way, with the result that they did not actually arrive with the battalion until August.

The majority of those who died had had former service with the Cheshire Regiment, either with the 1st Battalion or with other battalions such as the 11th and 16th, now disbanded. Even the seventeen men who had arrived straight from the Training Reserve had, with one exception, arrived from battalions affiliated to No 4 District and twelve had come from the Graduated Battalions of the Cheshire Regiment. Some men, namely three former RFA and eight ASC soldiers, were the products of the 'combing out' exercises of late 1917 who had joined 1st Cheshire in October and November 1917 respectively. Altogether, some 33 men had had previous active service in France before being transferred to the Cheshires; in addition to the RFA and ASC men, this number includes 12 from 5th North Staffordshire who had had the misfortune to arrive in a large draft on 29 August 1918.

Some 49 men had enlisted in Cheshire with a further nine from elsewhere in No 4 District, making a total of 58 from the Cheshire Regiment's Home District. A further 29 men had enlisted in No 3 District making a total of 86 or 78 percent from Western Command. Although the MNS had been responsible for recruiting since late 1917, it is difficult to draw any conclusions as yet. Of the twelve men who had enlisted after 1 November 1917, three were from Lancashire whilst eight were from No 4 District; the other one had been born in Denbighshire but had enlisted in Ireland. Overall, therefore, in late summer 1918 1st Cheshire still remained very definitely a Cheshire battalion.

The other Marcher battalion to be considered for this period, 7th KSLI, was in 8th Brigade of 3rd Division, now in VI Corps. In March the Division had been driven back in the Arras area

15 TNA WO 95/1520: 5th Division A & Q War Diary: Fighting Strength Return as at 4 September 1918.

and had then been moved north to recuperate only to find itself caught up in the Battle of the Lys. It was refilled after this and in mid-August moved south again, having been transferred to Third Army Reserve. On 19 August 7th KSLI arrived at Monchy and bivouacked in the caves there, ready for an attack near Courcelles on the 8th Brigade's objective, the Bapaume- Arras railway, to the east of Courcelles. The intention was that the 99th Brigade of 2nd Division would capture the enemy's front line and the 8th Brigade would then pass through to continue the advance and capture the railway.

The 7th KSLI was one of the two leading battalions when 8th Brigade attacked the railway line early on the morning of 21 August. By 7:30 am they had reached the strongly held railway embankment and the final assault was made with the bayonet. The objective was gained successfully, and the position consolidated. The following day the enemy attempted two strong counter-attacks, but both were successfully repulsed. On 23 August 7th KSLI continued its advance, gaining its second objective, before being withdrawn into Corps Reserve with the rest of 3rd Division on 24 August. By then some 232 ORs had been killed or wounded during the recent attacks. Fortunately, some 301 OR reinforcements had been received during August.[16]

On 2 September 8th Brigade was again in action with 7th KSLI on its right as it advanced towards the high ground around Lagnicourt, which was very strongly defended by the enemy. Although 62nd Division on 7th KSLI's right failed to progress and the 2nd Royal Scots and 1st Royal Scots Fusiliers were checked on its left, the Shropshires made a continuous advance of 4,000 yards, noted in the Regimental History as having been 'a stiff test at the present standard of individual training'.[17] They had suffered heavily though and by the time Lagnicourt had been captured the following day the fighting strength of the battalion was returned as 4 officers and 201 ORs; the total OR casualties were 248. The battalion now withdrew to bivouac near the railway by Hamelincourt.

The total deaths for 7th KSLI between 21 August and 3 September numbered 93. It has not been possible to find any Service Records, so analysis has been based on the Medal Index Cards and Rolls and the size of the War Gratuity paid to each man. Some 38 men, including 11 with TF numbers, had enlisted before March 1916 so may be said with certainty to have been volunteers. Only 15 of these, however, had seen service in France prior to the end of 1915 and only two had originally arrived with 7th KSLI in September 1915. A quarter of the total had seen previous KSLI service in various battalions, including the 7th, but the number of times many of them are shown as having passed through the IBD would indicate wounds or continuing bouts of sickness. The majority (52) of the rest had been posted or diverted to 7th KSLI on first arriving at the Base. Of the latter, 21 had come from a No 4 District TR battalion whilst six had come from a Southern Command TR battalion based in No 8 District. It is possible, but cannot be substantiated without the Service Records, that these six men had been destined for the Wiltshire Regiment but had become surplus to requirements, possibly when 6th Wiltshire was reduced to a cadre in May 1918 and returned to England with 14th Division in June for reconstitution. Similarly, two men had arrived from 7th and 16th Rifle Brigades respectively, both of which battalions had been cadreized earlier in 1918, and nine men had seen service with Sherwood Forester battalions which had since been either reduced

16 Wood, *King's Shropshire Light Infantry in the Greta War* p. 259.
17 Ibid., p. 260.

or disbanded. Overall, the battalion appears somewhat mixed, which is probably what gave rise to the comment about its state of training. Nonetheless, 68, or 73 percent, of those killed had enlisted in Western Command. These figures are made up of 19 enlisted in Shropshire or Herefordshire, the Regimental recruiting area, 24 enlisted elsewhere in No 4 District and 25 in No 3 District. This was a battalion which had been refilled after the German Spring offensive and again after the battalion of the Lys. Its composition reflects this.

All three battalions analysed had shown a number of teenagers amongst those killed. Indeed, in mid-August the perception in Third Army was that 50 percent of the Infantry in its thirteen divisions were 'boys'.[18] The implication was that these were 18-year olds rushed out in the wake of the German offensives but the term itself is unclear. In January 1918, 1st SWB had noted that a draft of 102 ORs had arrived, 'mostly boys' and about 20 men recovering from wounds received in November 1917.[19] As official agreement for the drafting of under 19-year olds had not been given at that stage it seems the term is more likely to apply to any who were still aged under 20, and indeed the *BOH* refers to 'the eighteen and nineteen year-old boys who filled the ranks'.[20] The validity of Third Army's perception may be tested to some extent by analysing the ages of those killed in 2nd RWF, 1st Cheshire and 7th KSLI during the actions of 21 August-3 September. Overall, a total of 289 had been killed between the three battalions.[21]

Battalion	**2nd RWF (38th Div)**	**%**	**1st Cheshire (5th Div)**	**%**	**7th KSLI (3rd Div)**	**%**
Total deaths 21 August-3 September 1918	86		110		93	
Known ages	83		103		87	
18	2		10		16	
19	12		20		19	
Total aged 18 and 19	14	17%	30	29%	35	40%
20	10		9		5	
Total aged 18-20	24	29%	39	38%	40	46%
Total aged 21-29; best fighting age in terms of physical strength and maturity	42	51%	48	47%	33	38%
30s and 40s	17	20%	16	15%	14	16%
Average age of those known	25		24		23	

Table 13. Age profiles of soldiers of 2nd RWF, 1st Cheshire and 7th KSLI killed between 21 August-3 September 1918.

18 *BOH 1918 Vol. 4*, p. 181.
19 TNA WO 95/1280-3: 1st SWB War Diary entry for 13 January 1918.
20 *BOH 1918 Vol. 4*, p. 184.
21 The data has been extracted primarily from CWGC and then by using Census records and BMD on <www.ancestry.com> for the 'unknowns'. Where there has been any doubt, or the name is too common to search, the age has been left as unknown. The percentages are against the known ages.

The earlier losses sustained by each battalion during 1918 with their consequent replacements were reflected in the composition of each battalion by early September but are even more clearly visible in the average ages of those killed. Of the three battalions, 7th KSLI was the one which had been involved in the German attacks of March and April and had had to be refilled after both. Unsurprisingly, that battalion shows the highest number of 18 and 19-year olds: 40 percent (34) of the known ages. In 1st Cheshire, which had been involved solely in the Battle of the Lys, the figure drops to 29 percent whilst it is only 17 percent in 2nd RWF which had not been involved in any of the earlier German offensives.[22] Even when twenty-year olds are included, the proportion of those who might be termed 'boys' remains less than 50 percent in any of the battalions. The perception of the extreme youth of Third Army battalions thus does not appear to have been universally accurate, depending to a large extent on how heavily particular battalions had been used during the preceding months.

How the 'boys' performed in action is rarely noted in battalion War Diaries, but some references appear in Battalion Histories. The 1/1st Cambridgeshire, now in 12th Division, had received drafts amounting to 350 in late August.[23] About 50 were experienced men but the rest were 'boys', called up in the spring and with an average length of service of about 15 weeks. Although they had fired their musketry course, they knew nothing about Lewis guns and, having come straight from the Base, had never been under fire. In early September, when the battalion was in action around Nurlu, the CO was impressed by the newly-arrived youngsters' performance, noting that 'as long as they had leaders they kept steadily on'. It was only when the officers and platoon sergeants became casualties that 'they quickly lost cohesion and were scattered in depth, to become victims of their inexperience in how to make use of ground and cover'. Once out of the line again, the battalion had time for a week's intensive training and 'the youngsters daily grew more like hardened veterans.[24]

Overall, there were mixed views in units on the usefulness of 18-year olds. Many 'were most excellent material', having received longer training at home than adult recruits, but a proportion were insufficiently developed and had had to be held back at the Base.

> Owing to age and physique some of these immature boys were quite incapable of carrying the weight and doing the work required of an infantry soldier in the line: their presence in the ranks rendered them a danger to their units. To use them at the time was only a waste of those who might later on, with proper training and physical development, have become valuable reinforcements for the Army.[25]

The number of those found insufficiently developed was such that the existing 'Under-age Battalion', which had been created in early 1917 at Étaples and had moved to Cayeux in early

22 Captain Dunn believed that all but twenty of the drafts received by 2nd RWF in early November 1917 were eighteen-year olds. Dunn, *The War the Infantry Knew*, p. 414. It is impossible to test the validity of this.

23 Riddell & Clayton, *The Cambridgeshires 1914-1919*, p. 194. In August the 1/1st Cambridgeshire, which had moved from the 39th Division to 12th Division, received a 'large draft of men, mainly Cambridgeshires and Suffolks – a good useful lot, but many had spent too long under Base Depot conditions, and were not looking as hard and bronzed as the remainder of the Battalion'.

24 Ibid., pp. 216, 228-9, 231.

25 Kincaid-Smith, *The 25th Division in France and Flanders*, pp. 193-4.

1918, was augmented during September by two 'Young Soldiers' (YS) battalions. The training staff for these 'immatures' was provided by the battalion training staffs of 9th Suffolk and 17th King's Royal Rifle Corps (KRRC). A third such YS battalion would be formed at the end of October.[26]

There was also concern at home about using up future capital through the early deployment of youths who would be of more effect once they had matured.

E Coy. 52nd (Grad) Bn. Cheshire: Winners of the Shield, July and August 1918 (Cheshire Regimental Archives)

The matter was discussed by the War Cabinet in early August when it was concluded that the national emergency had now passed and that no more lads under 19 were to be sent abroad. The War Office would have preferred 1 October as the effective date for implementation of this decision since by then the full effect of the increased recruiting in May and June would have begun to be felt. Haig's view that lads of under 19 were not fit to carry packs for any distance

26 TNA WO 95/26: AG GHQ War Diary for September and October 1918.

E Coy. 52nd (Grad) Bn. Cheshire: Winners of Physical Training Competition - July and August 1918 (Cheshire Regimental Archives)

was quoted, however, and the Cabinet's decision was that no more youths aged under 19 were to be sent on active service after 31 August.[27]

By the end of the first week of September, the Third Army had advanced roughly fifteen miles since the start of the Battle of Albert and had forced the Germans back to the line they had held before 21 March, and into the Hindenburg Line. The successes had come at a heavy cost, however, since casualties had been high. Although replacements continued to arrive they were often too few to bring the divisions that had been involved in the recent fighting completely back to strength. For the 3rd, 5th and 38th Divisions the August strengths for Infantry and Cavalry ORs were as follows:[28]

27 TNA CAB 23/7: Minutes of War Cabinet Meeting WC 455 of 7 August 1918 and WO 95/26 AG GHQ War Diary entry for 16 August 1918.

28 TNA WO 95/26: AG GHQ War Diary AG GHQ War Diary Monthly Statement of Casualties, Reinforcements and Strength by Divisions, Infantry and Cavalry only, for August 1918.

	Beginning of month	Battle casualties	Reinforcements	End of month
3rd Div	9,333	2,919	2,149	7,898
5th Div	12,184	3,093	2,356	10,621
38th Div	9,162	1,965	1,375	7,494

Table 14. Infantry and Cavalry OR strengths for 3rd, 5th and 38th Divisions, August 1918.

NB. No explanation is given for the apparent discrepancies in the figures, which should have been higher at the end of the month given the reinforcements received. It might be because they do not include the wastage figures for the sick during the month. For example, the numbers of sick for just the week ending Saturday 31 August were as follows: 3rd Division 188, 5th Division 127 and 38th Division 257.[29]

The OR strength returns for 1 and 8 September show the following available fighting strengths for the three battalions analysed earlier:[30]

	1 September 1918	8 September 1918
7th KSLI (3rd Div)	837	608 + 54 reinforcements en route
1st Cheshire (5th Div)	779	670 + 70 " " "
2nd RWF (38th Div)	714	483

Table 15. Available fighting strengths 1-8 September 1918 for 7th KSLI, 1st Cheshire and 2nd RWF.

It should be noted that all these figures are very fluid, both because of the difficulty in ascertaining final casualty figures and because of the arrival of reinforcements, returning sick and wounded and also, in some cases, the reappearance of stragglers. For the BEF, the overall strength of its British Infantry and Cavalry rose slightly during August from 417,994 to 418,764. Their battle casualties had been 67,021 and 66,551 reinforcements had been received.[31]

September – October – The Hindenburg Line

By the end of the first week of September, the Third Army had reached the new German positions. The continuing momentum of the advance meant that reinforcements had continually to be moved forward to catch up with the fighting divisions. On 3 September the 38th Division established

29 TNA WO 95/380: Third Army War Diary - Wastage return for Week Ending Saturday 31 August 1918.
30 Ibid., Third Army War Diary - Strength returns for 1 and 8 September 1918.
31 TNA WO 95/26: AG GHQ War Diary Monthly Statement of Casualties, Reinforcements and Strength by Divisions, Infantry and Cavalry only, for August 1918. NB The number of reinforcements is fewer than the number of casualties but the slight increase overall may presumably be explained by the return to duty of those who had been only slightly wounded.

a temporary Reinforcement Staging Camp at Contalmaison which three days later had to move to Beaulencourt, where the following day the Division's Reception Camp arrived to take over.[32]

Although fighting had continued, the Army Commander, General Sir Julian Byng, had ordered on 4 September that:

> Troops would, as far as possible, be rested, our resources conserved, and our communications improved with a view to a resumption of a vigorous offensive in the near future. As many Divisions as possible would at once be withdrawn by Corps into reserve for rest and training.[33]

The 7th KSLI had already been withdrawn and was now bivouacked near Hamlincourt. Although the time was spent in training there was also significant movement as it moved forward through Gommiecourt and Beugny. The 1st Cheshire was withdrawn on 4 September and spent the time out of the line in training, which included practising attacks. Neither of these two battalions would take part in another attack until 27 September. The 2nd RWF was withdrawn on 5 September to Lesboeufs for a short rest. The 38th Division had been continuously in action for more than a fortnight, fighting hard and driving the enemy back 15 miles. It had suffered 3,614 casualties.[34]

The progress made at Amiens, Albert and Bapaume, appears to have convinced Haig that the character of the war had changed and that an early conclusion might be possible, although quite what he meant by this is not clear. During a meeting in London with Lord Milner, Secretary of State for War, on 10 September, he urged that 'all yeomanry, cyclists etc now kept for civil defence should be sent to France *at once*' so that the recent successes could be exploited to the full, urging that 'if we act with energy now, a decision can be obtained in the very near future'. Somewhat detracting from this optimistic position, however, he continued to demand that all units should be brought up to strength by 1 April 1919, if necessary by reducing reserves of ammunition and aeroplanes, in order to set men free for the Army and that men already earmarked for the Navy should be sent to the Army for the next six months. Given all that had gone before, this proposed side-lining of other industries and Services necessary for the war effort, was naïve of Haig. Milner certainly seems to have thought so as nothing was actually changed.[35] Indeed, some eleven days later on a visit to GHQ, Milner told Haig that recruiting was bad and warned him very clearly that if the British Army was used up now there would not be one in 1919. Haig's reaction was that the situation was most satisfactory, and every available man should be used at once.[36] The commander on the ground and the politician were poles apart, neither understanding the other's position.

The next 'vigorous offensive' anticipated by Byng for Third Army would be participation in the sequence of battles which would become known as the Battles of the Hindenburg Line: Havrincourt, Epéhy, Canal du Nord, St Quentin Canal, Beaurevoir and Cambrai 1918. The first of these, at Havrincourt, was to be a Third Army attack whilst at Epéhy its V Corps would be in support for Fourth Army. The subsequent Third and Fourth Army offensives to break the

32 TNA WO 95/2541: 38th Division A & Q War Diary for September 1918.
33 TNA WO 95/393: Third Army GS War Diary entry for 4 September 1918.
34 Munby (ed.) *A History of the 38th (Welsh) Division* p. 60.
35 Sheffield & Bourne, *Douglas Haig, War Diaries and Letters 1914 – 1918* pp. 458-9.
36 Ibid., p. 463.

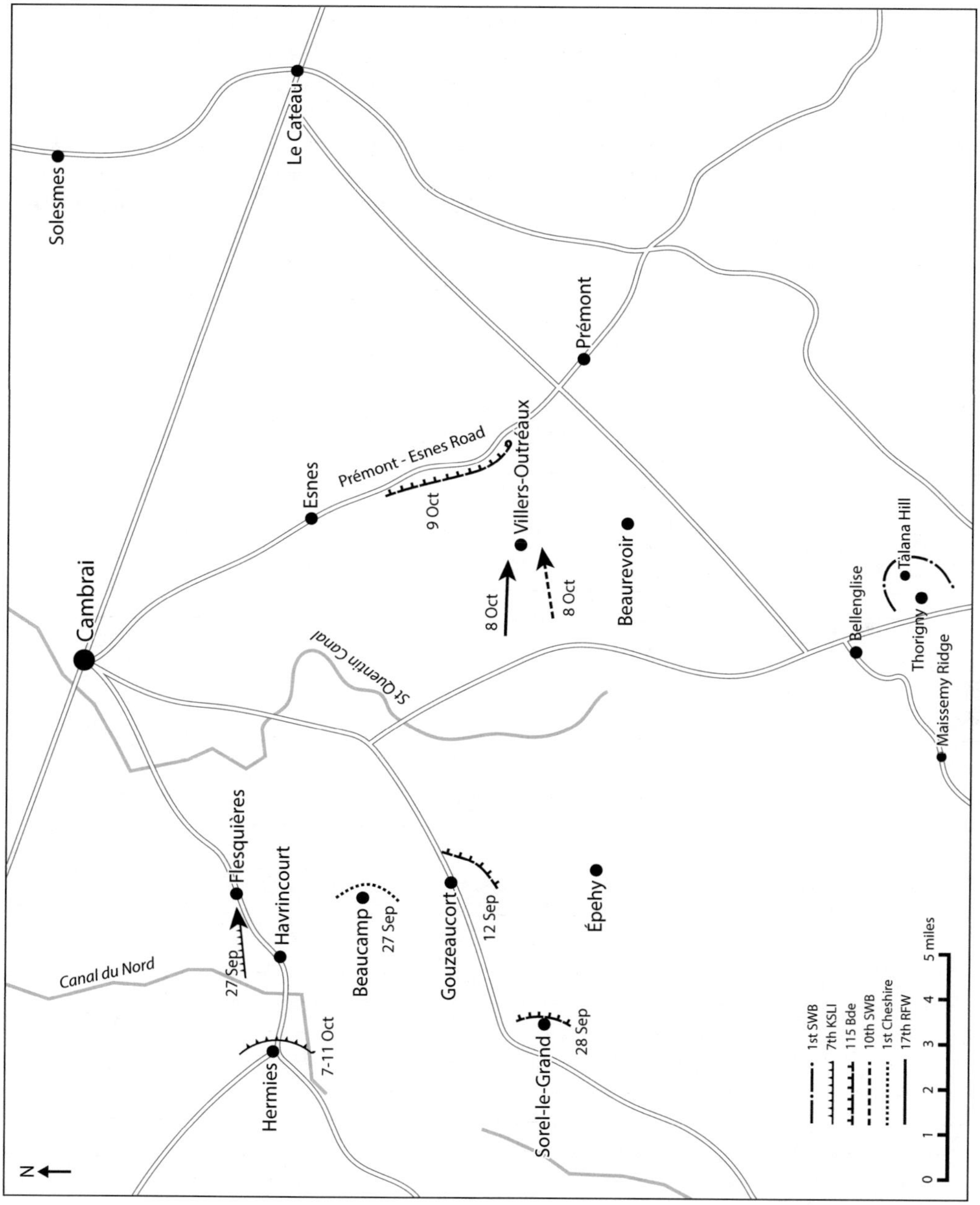

Map 11: Battles of the Hindenburg Line, September–October 1918.

Hindenburg Line would be part of a plan of coordinated attacks from 26 September onwards along the Western Front. The French and the Americans would attack in the South on 26 September, whilst the following day the British First and Third Armies would attack across the Hindenburg Line towards Cambrai. Two days later, on 28 September the French, the Belgians and the British Second Army would launch an attack in Flanders and on 29 September the Fourth Army would attack the Hindenburg Line in its sector. Finally, for this sequence, the Battle of Cambrai would take place in early October.

In addition to the Marcher battalions in Third Army, there were four in Fourth Army: 1st SWB in 1st Division, 1st KSLI in 6th Division and the former Yeomanry battalions, 25th RWF and 10th KSLI, in 74th Division. From the table below, it is evident that, as in earlier years and offensives, a form of divisional rotation was in operation within Corps, with brigades also being rotated within their divisions. This meant that although a division might have taken part in an attack, not all its battalions would necessarily have been involved. Much depended on the state of the formation and units concerned after its previous actions.

Havrincourt 12 Sep	**Epéhy 18 Sep**	**Canal du Nord 27 Sep-1 Oct**	**St Quentin Canal 29 Sep-2 Oct**	**Beaurevoir 3-5 Oct**	**Cambrai 1918 8-9 Oct**
		Third Army			
		3rd Div			**3rd Div**
		8th Bde			
		7th KSLI			
	5th Div	**5th Div**			
		15th Bde			
		1st Cheshire			
38th Div	**38th Div**				**38th Div**
115th Bde	*113th Bde*				*115th Bde*
2nd RWF	13th RWF				2nd RWF
17th RWF	14th RWF				17th RWF
10th SWB	16th RWF				10th SWB
					113th Bde
					13th RWF
					14th RWF
					16th RWF
		Fourth Army			
	1st Div		**1st Div**	**1st Div**	
			3rd Bde		
			1st SWB		
	6th Div		**6th Div**	**6th Div**	**6th Div**
	16th Bde				16th Bde
	1st KSLI				1st KSLI
	74th Div				
	231st Bde				
	25th RWF				
	10th KSLI				

Table 16. Marcher battalions in attacks during the Battles of the Hindenburg Line.[37]

37 James, *Record of the Battles and Engagement of the British Armies in France and Flanders, 1914–1918*, pp. 35-37.

The only division containing Marcher battalions shown as having been in action at the Battle of Havrincourt was the 38th Division. In fact, that Division was only on the fringe of the main action as its 115th Brigade was holding the front line, in front of Gouzeaucourt, to the right of the main attack. It came under heavy shellfire on 12 September, during which the 2nd RWF suffered some 20 casualties with a further 13 being killed the following day when the enemy counter-attacked. The Brigade was relieved by 113th and 114th Brigades on 16 September.

The next battle, around Epéhy, was primarily a Fourth Army action but the only Fourth Army Marcher battalions that took part were 1st KSLI in the 6th Division and two former Yeomanry battalions in 74th Division, 25th RWF and 10th KSLI. The 1st SWB in 1st Division had been drawn back into reserve and did no more than occupy a support position on Maissemy Ridge until the night of 21/22 September. The V Corps of Third Army was in support of Fourth Army for Epéhy. The 38th Division was in action, but its presence was limited to the 113th and 114th Brigades, the former containing 13th, 14th and 16th RWF. The 2nd RWF and the rest of 115th Brigade would not be involved. Similarly, the 5th Division's involvement in protecting 38th Division's left flank, did not include 1st Cheshire or the rest of its 15th Brigade.

By 22 September, the strengths of the Third Army divisions containing Marcher battalions were: 3rd Division 7840; 5th Division 8958 and 38th Division 5292. Although the 3rd Division's strength had dropped by only 58 since the end of August, that of 5th Division was lower by 1,663 whilst that of 38th Division had fallen by 2,202.[38] Reinforcements had continued to arrive but the quantity for each unit varied. On 15 September some 13 men for 1st Cheshire and 103 for 7th KSLI were shown as being en route, whilst there were none for the 38th Division units. The following week, 8 and 10 men respectively were allocated to 1st Cheshire and 7th KSLI, whilst 112 were destined for 16th RWF.

The intention was to get drafts, few as they often were, to the battalions as soon as possible. The 5th Division, for example, laid down clear instructions that reinforcements, together with men returning from leave and 'casuals' (usually those returning individually from hospitals or courses), were to be sent up automatically each day whenever its Brigades were in Support or Reserve; if necessary, they could also be sent up if demanded by Brigades when they were actually in the Line. 'Dumped' personnel, the nucleus left behind when battalions went into action, would rejoin their Brigades, if demanded, when Brigades were withdrawn into Divisional Reserve.[39]

The battles of Havrincourt and Epéhy had brought Third Army to good jumping-off positions for its next main offensive on 27 September, the assault on the Canal du Nord. Its orders were

> to operate in the direction of the general line Le Cateau-Solesmes … and to press forward to secure the passage of the Canal de L'Escaut, so as to be in a position to co-operate closely with the Fourth Army on [29 September].[40]

The Corps taking part would be, from left to right, the XVII, the VI (7th KSLI in 3rd Division) and the IV (1st Cheshire in 5th Division). The attack started early on the morning of 27 September, but progress was varied and nowhere was the final objective, the St Quentin Canal,

38 TNA WO 95/380: Third Army A & Q War Diary : Strength Returns for 15 and 22 September 1918.
39 TNA WO 95/1520-3: 5th Division Standing Administrative Instructions for Battle dated 23 September 1918.
40 *BOH Vol. 5:* p. 15. NB The Canal de L'Escaut is also known as the St Quentin Canal.

reached. The 7th KSLI took part in the initial attack at 05:20 am 'with magnificent dash in spite of severe opposition'.[41] They gained their objective, the capture of Flesquières, but 37 ORs were killed and 127 wounded. Only one company of 1st Cheshire was to take part in the 5th Division attack; its role would be to 'mop up' the village of Beaucamp once it had been taken. Both Marcher battalions achieved their objectives but overall less ground had been gained by Third Army than anticipated, despite having advanced 'over deliberately planned defences, which would have been hailed as a great victory in 1916 at the Somme'.[42] The offensive continued the following day when better progress was made, with Third Army reaching the St. Quentin Canal from Marcoing northwards.

The next offensive, the crossing of the St Quentin Canal, would be led by Fourth Army on 29 September. On this occasion, 1st KSLI in 6th Division was not in action, having been fighting almost continuously against strong opposition from 18 September to the night of 24/25 September. During this time, it had sustained some 242 casualties and it consequently made sense for it to be rested, albeit only briefly.[43] The 1st Division was in action, however, and 1st SWB, which had not taken part in the Epéhy battle, now had two very successful days, achieving all its objectives in taking the village of Thorigny and Talana Hill. Its losses were 4 ORs killed and 31 wounded.[44]

The fighting during September, whilst enabling successful advances, had come with heavy costs. By the end of the month, the overall strength of the BEF's Infantry and Cavalry was 510,822, a drop of 16,788. Some 78,943 reinforcements had been received but the battle casualties had been 103,900. The end of September figures for the divisions containing Marcher battalions which had been in action in the battles on the Hindenburg Line were as follows:

	Beginning of month	Battle casualties	Reinforcements	End of month
1st Div	9464	2531	1165	7399
3rd Div	7552	2844	2107	6996
5th Div	10677	2877	1553	9240
6th Div	9285	3036	2751	7882
38th Div	7501	2407	2744	7272
74th Div	8873	2829	1292	6975

Table 17. Battle casualties and reinforcements for September 1918 for divisions containing Marcher battalions.

Reinforcements had arrived, but in every case, with the exception of 38th Division, they were fewer than the number of battle casualties.[45]

41 Wood, *King's Shropshire Light Infantry* p. 261.
42 *BOH Vol. 5,* p. 45.
43 Wood, *History of the King's Shropshire Light Infantry 1914–1918* pp. 57-60.
44 TNA WO 95/1280: 1st SWB War Diary for 29 amd 30 September 1918.
45 TNA WO 95/26: AG GHQ War Diary for September 1918. NB The 74th Division entrained for

Although elements of the Third Army had been fighting almost continuously between 27 September-5 October, the 38th Division had remained in Corps support and had not been called upon. It would not go into action again until the Third Army was virtually through the Hindenburg defences when it would take part in the battle around Cambrai in early October. The 3rd Division would also take part in this battle but not the 7th KSLI, which spent the period 7-11 October in rest at Hermies. The 5th Division would not take part either as it was only now in the process of being reduced from 12 to 9 battalions, having been in Italy during the February reorganisation.

During the days preceding the next attack, the battalions of 115th Brigade of 38th Division had been resting, refitting and training. The 2nd RWF had concentrated on Lewis gun instruction and firing and had also practised trench to trench attacks. On 27 September, the officers had attended a class on compass work whilst the NCOs were instructed in map-reading. The following day, the Brigade moved to Sorel-le-Grand where training continued. Both 17th RWF and 10th SWB practised throwing German stick bombs, rifle grenade firing and trench to trench attacks. There remained time for physical recreation, however, which was mentioned more by 17th RWF, although 2nd RWF played a rugby match on 2 October against 10th SWB. Neither side mentions who won, however. Although they knew they were preparing for their next action, the men seem to have been in good heart; the 10th SWB War Diary notes particularly on 30 September that 'The victories from all fronts are raising the moral [sic] of the men to a very high degree'.[46]

For the 38th Division, Cambrai 1918, where its task was to advance over five thousand yards through a very strong German position at Villers-Outreaux, is described as perhaps its 'stiffest fighting of the whole advance'.[47] Two battalions of 115th Brigade, 10th SWB and 17th RWF, were to attack by the south and north of Villers Outreaux respectively at 1:00 am on 8 October whilst 2nd RWF, as the weakest of the three battalions at this point, remained in Brigade Reserve to deal with the village itself at daybreak. The 16th and 13th RWF of 113th Brigade were also to attack and advance through Mortho Wood. The objective of both these attacks was a trench line running north and south just to the east of the village. The 115th Brigade failed in its first attempt, the 10th SWB having been delayed by thick and uncut wire and machine-gun fire whilst to the north of the main road the 17th RWF was also encountering 'wire which was under a murderous fire from machine guns in the trench beyond'; its first two companies had already lost 120 men. Both battalions withdrew and reorganized, and 115th Brigade's second attack was a complete success. The arrival of 2nd RWF at dawn enabled a further move forward and the taking of the enemy's trench. By the afternoon the final objective, the line of the Premont – Esnes road, had been reached. The 114th Brigade held it overnight with the RWF battalions of 113th Brigade in support whilst 115th Brigade went into billets in Villers-Outreaux: the first time they had seen a habitable house since 4 August. Losses had been heavy: whilst 2nd RWF had escaped comparatively unscathed with 2 ORs wounded and 1 missing,

Fifth Army at the end of September.

46 TNA WO 95/2561: 2nd RWF and 17th RWF War Diaries for September and October 1918 and WO 95/2562: 10th SWB War Diary for September and October 1918.

47 Munby, *History of the 38th (Welsh) Division*, p.66-71.

the 17th RWF had suffered 117 OR casualties whilst the 10th SWB had lost 189 men.[48] There was some difficulty in getting the Division fed in its new positions, however, as the railhead had reached only as far as Fins and the Divisional Train was near Epéhy.[49] No mention is made of the arrival of reinforcements.

The available fighting strengths of the 115th Brigade battalions when they went into action were: 2nd RWF 502, 17th RWF 588 and 10th SWB 647. None of the battalions' War Diaries makes any mention of the recent arrival of reinforcements, the last entries for 10th SWB showed 120 arriving on 30 August, but Third Army A&Q Diary indicates that some were available. The numbers were small, however: between 22-29 September there were 15 for 2nd RWF, 18 for 17th RWF and 41 for 10th SWB. Presumably having been held back until after the attack were a further 23 for 2nd RWF, 17 for 17th RWF and 74 for 10th SWB who were shown on 6 October as being *en route* from the Base.[50]

Overall, and once the casualty figures had been reconciled, some 89 men of 115th Brigade had died: 38 in 17th RWF, 35 in 10th SWB and 16 in 2nd RWF. The ages are known of 83 of these men.

Battalions in 115th Brigade	**2nd RWF**	**%**	**17th RWF**	**%**	**10th SWB**	**%**
Total deaths 8-9 Oct 18	16		38		35	
Known ages	12		38		33	
18	0		1		0	
19	2		6		5	
20	3		3		4	
Total aged 18-20	5	36%	10	26%	9	27%
Total aged 21-29: best fighting age in terms of physical strength and maturity	6	55%	24	63%	18	54%
30s and 40s	1		4		6	
Average age of those known	24		24		25	

Table 18. Age profiles of soldiers of 115th Brigade, 38th (Welsh) Division killed 8-9 October 1918.

None of these battalions had been in action during the German Spring Offensives, so it is not surprising that fewer than 30 percent of the 17th RWF (ten) and 10th SWB (nine) men should

48 TNA WO 95//2541: 38th Division A & Q War Diary for 1918. The Estimated casualties for the Division are carefully noted for each day throughout the advance as are the names of all officer casualties and reinforcements, but the diary makes absolutely no mention of OR reinforcements. It does, however, note occurrences such as the departure on 27 September of the OC 38th Division MT Company on 7 days Special leave to England to purchase for the Division a new Cinema engine and soda-water plant!

49 Munby, *History of the 38th (Welsh) Division*, p.66-71.

50 TNA WO 95/380: Third Army A&Q War Diary Strength Return for weeks ending 22, 29 September and 6 October 1918.

be aged 20 or under. The percentage of 2nd RWF is skewed by the smaller overall numbers involved: five out of 12. All three battalions show an average age of around 24 (24.8 for 10th SWB) and in each battalion over half of those killed were in the age group 21-29. In terms of age, therefore, all three battalions reflect a reasonable distribution of ages with most men falling within the 'best fighting age' range.

In the absence of Service Records for these men it is difficult to be sure what type of engagement they were serving on and how many had been conscripted. For 2nd RWF, two TF soldiers had joined in 1914 and four men, presumably Short Service volunteers, in 1915. Some 38 percent of those killed had thus been volunteers. Only five men had been in the Army for less than 12 months and as these were all over 20 it is likely that they had been conscripted. The total number of 2nd RWF men killed is too small, however, for more meaningful analysis.

The 17th RWF lost three of its original men who had crossed to France with it in December 1915, together with a further three who had originally belonged to 15th RWF; it is likely that they had been transferred to 17th RWF in February 1918 as part of drafts totalling about 142 that were received when 15th RWF was disbanded. The dates of enlistments show that some 11 men, including two TF soldiers, had enlisted as volunteers. At the other end of the scale, some eleven men received only £5 War Gratuity indicating that they had had less than 12 months service. Three of the Service Records of these men exist, however, which indicate a slightly different picture:

- John and Lewis James (unrelated) were both 'Derby' men:
    - John James had enlisted on 19 February 1916, aged 19. His occupation was shown as 'Driver Underground' which is presumably why he was not mobilised until 18 April 1918, when he was posted to the SWB.
    - Lewis James enlisted on 25 February 1916, aged 18. His occupation was 'Colliery lamp man' and he was not mobilised until 23 April 1918, when he was posted to 3rd SWB.
- George James Powis had volunteered for service in early 1917, aged 17 years 220 days, and was mobilised on 2 July 1917 when he was 18 years 1 month. He passed through 57th TRB and 51st (Graduated) Battalion SWB.

All three of these men were sent to France in September 1918, arriving with 17th RWF at the end of the month as part of a large draft of men from the SWB. They had been with 17th RWF for just a week when they were killed.

For 10th SWB it had also been a sad day as five of those killed had originally crossed to France with the battalion on 3 December 1915. A further 2 had been original 11th SWB men. Overall, all except nine men had served with the SWB from their arrival in France, if not in 10th SWB then in the 11th or 12th battalions, both of which had been disbanded in February 1918. Of the other nine men, one was a 'combed out' ASC driver and another a former cavalryman. Others had commenced their training in various Regiments from within Western Command, with the exception of one from the Gloucesters, one from the Bedfords and a Sapper. The 17th RWF shows a similar picture. Those indicated as having joined from outside the RWF again came predominantly from other Western Command Regiments: nine were former South Wales Borderers, two were ex-Cheshires, and two were from the Welsh Regiment. Only two were from outside the Command, namely a Hussar and a former London Regiment man.

Looking at the areas in which the men had enlisted, not many of the RWF men had enlisted in the Regiment's recruiting area but over half had enlisted in Wales. Some 57 percent of those from 10th SWB had enlisted in the SWB's home recruiting area of Monmouthshire and Brecknockshire. For each of the battalions, however, and despite this late stage in the war, over three quarters of those killed had enlisted in Western Command.

October 1918

Reinforcements were continuing to arrive in France from other parts of the world but were not always of the quality or quantity required. A further 12,000 malarial cases were due to arrive from Salonika during October and it became necessary to provide some sort of organization to administer them. Consequently, 197th Infantry Brigade was withdrawn from 66th Division to administer all Infantry reinforcements suffering from malaria. Its place in that division was taken by the South African Brigade, which had been refilled but was now re-organized into three battalions due to lack of reinforcements. Even the Australians were now running short of men and it was now proposed that their divisions should be reduced to ten battalions per division.[51] In the event, the Australian divisions prevaricated and the threatened reduction was postponed.

Battle of the Selle 17-25 October

The great advance continued. The Hindenburg Line had been breached and further north the British Second Army had taken part in yet another battle around Ypres and was now pressing eastwards towards Courtrai, where a further battle would take place between 14-19 October. The main thrust, however, continued to be further south, in Artois and Picardy. By 10 October, the Germans had been forced to retreat along almost the whole of the Front held by the British First, Third and Fourth Armies and was now firmly established on the eastern bank of the River Selle. This river was not particularly large, although in places it was too deep to scramble through, but it lay in a valley beyond which were a railway embankment and a ridge. It offered the Germans a good defensive position and crossing it would require a full-scale assault.

The Battle of the Selle took place over the period 17-25 October and involved First, Third and Fourth Armies. On 17 October Fourth Army attacked on a ten-mile front south of Le Cateau but made slow progress. Although its centre and left forced crossings over the river against strong opposition, most progress was made on the right where Le Cateau was taken by nightfall. Fighting continued over the next two days by which time Fourth Army had advanced over five miles, pushing the Germans back towards the Sambre-Oise Canal. The First Army had joined in on 19 October and by that evening had fought its way into a position from where it could attack to the north of Le Cateau. Early the following day, a surprise attack was made by both First and Third Armies during which the latter succeeded in taking the high ground east of the Selle. Three days later, on 23 October, a combined assault was made by all three Armies, First,

51 TNA WO 95/26: AG GHQ War Diary for September 1918. Much to their disgust, the Fifth Division, which had escaped reorganization whilst in Italy, would also lose battalions in early October. TNA WO 95/1520/3: Fifth Division War Diary entry for 1 October 1918.

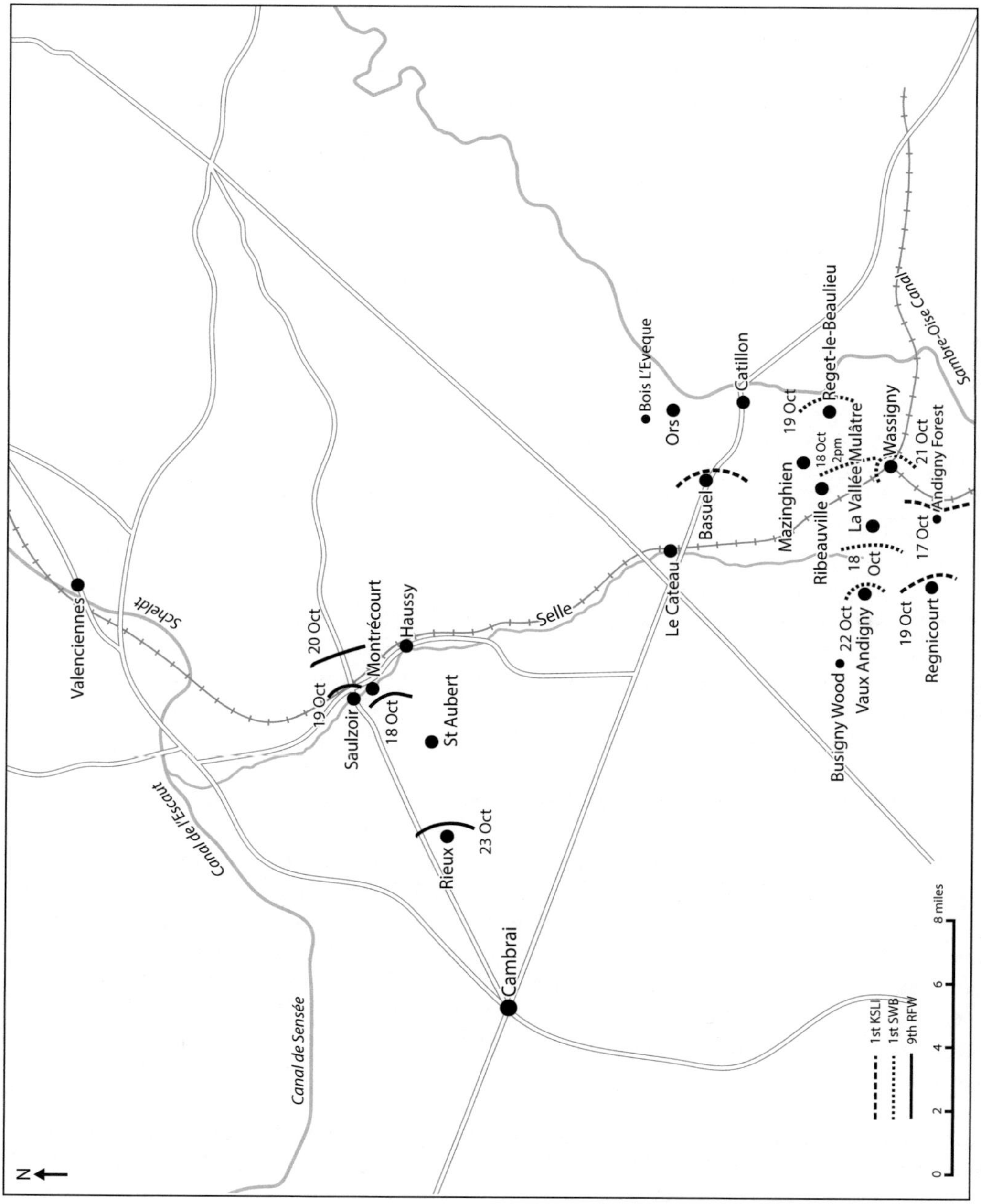

Map 12: Battle of the Selle, 17-25 October 1918: 1st SWB, 9th RWF and 7th KSLI.

Third and Fourth, which advanced six miles in two days. The Germans withdrew and formed another new line between Valenciennes and the River Sambre.

Amongst the Fourth Army battalions which took part in the battle were the 1st SWB in 3rd Brigade of the 1st Division and 1st KSLI in 16th Brigade of the 6th Division. Both these divisions formed part of IX Corps which was to attack on a front of 7,000 yards running from Vaux-Andigny southwards to the junction with the French. The 6th Division, together with the 46th, was to take the first objective along the northern and western edges of Andigny Forest. The 1st Division was then to pass through them and take the final objective, which included the villages of La Vallée Mulâtre and Wassigny.

The 1st KSLI had been in action three times during the second half of September during which period it had suffered some 362 casualties. These were partially replaced by the arrival in early October of a draft of 209 ORs from two TF battalions: 10th KSLI and 2/5th Gloucestershire. There was little time to assimilate them as 1st KSLI was in action on 9 October but fortunately the Shropshires were able to gain their objective without meeting much opposition. They then enjoyed a brief period of rest whilst 16th Brigade was in Divisional Reserve between 10-16 October.[52]

The 1st KSLI's next objective, on 17 October, was a line of new enemy trenches along the railway to the east of Vaux Andigny station. The other two battalions of 16th Brigade, 1st Buffs and 2nd York and Lancaster, were then to pass through the Shropshires to the next objective. The 1st KSLI attacked at dawn from the south-east corner of Busigny Wood and immediately came up against practically uncut wire. The enemy appeared to be holding the line almost entirely with machine guns posts as many were captured by the advancing Shropshires. There was also thick fog which made direction finding difficult and hampered contact with the flanking units. Nonetheless they reached their objective on time but had suffered 25 percent casualties, of whom some 21 men had been killed or would subsequently die of their wounds.[53] The following day, the KSLI remained in the trenches they had taken the previous day ready to support the 1st Division which was to continue the attack. They were not called upon, however, and on 19 October were withdrawn to billets at Regnicourt where they would stay for the next two days. Fourteen subalterns were noted as having joined the Battalion, but no mention is made of the arrival of any ORs.

The 1st SWB had moved to the area west of Vaux Andigny on 17 October where they remained in support with the rest of 3rd Brigade whilst 1st and 2nd Brigades took over the attack from the 6th Division. The following day they followed up the previous day's advance, moving to an area just west of La Vallée Mulâtre. The morning was again foggy which hampered their planned reconnaissance of the line. At 10:30 am 1st SWB moved forward to their assembly positions under cover of a smoke barrage but it was not quite thick enough and D Company came under heavy fire from machine guns to their front. At 11:00 am A and D Companies advanced; some of the machine gun crews in front surrendered but a party of about 30 held out so D Company went in with their bayonets, killing 12 and taking the rest prisoner. By 2:00 pm the SWB had taken their final objective of the day, the road between Ribeauville and Wassigny. The battalion was reorganized and consolidated ready for a further attack the following day. The new objective

52 Wood, *King's Shropshire Light Infantry in the Great War*, pp. 57–62.
53 TNA WO 95/1609: 1st KSLI War Diary for October 1918 and *SDGW* for 1st KSLI 17-18 October 1918.

was the village of Reget-le-Beaulieu and the high ground to the west of it. No opposition was encountered until they reached the village where a machine gun crew was captured. The village was taken, and patrols were then pushed forward to the high ground to the east of it and an outpost line was established about 200 yards in front of the main road running through the village. Efforts were made to push patrols forward to the Sambre-Oise Canal but the machine gun opposition was too great. The SWB casualties during 18/19 October had been high with nine ORs having been killed and 60 wounded. For the next couple of days, they remained in the same position, where they were subjected to intermittent shelling before being relieved on 21 October and moving back to comfortable billets in Wassigny.[54]

The 1st KSLI had moved from Regnicourt on 21 October to billets in St Martin Riviere. The 16th Brigade would be in Reserve for Fourth Army's next action on 23 October but late that afternoon 1st KSLI was warned that, together with the 2nd York and Lancaster, they would be renewing the attack in the Mazinghien sector the next day. They moved up to the line during the night, taking up positions along the road running north-east through Bois L'Eveque. In the early morning they moved forward to assemble for the attack but D Company on the extreme left encountered some difficulty from an enemy machine gun post which required neutralizing before they could make progress. At 09:30 am 1st KSLI attacked under cover of a creeping barrage and reached their objective on the right. On their left, however, the right flank of 25th Division had not made sufficient progress. The KSLI continued to try to gain their objective on the left but could make little progress due to the 'lack of co-operation from 25th Division'. Late that evening the Shropshires were relieved and moved back to billets in Basuel, two miles south-east of Le Cateau, having suffered 30 OR casualties, of whom nine had been killed.[55]

The 1st SWB was also not allowed to rest for long before being moved forward during the night of 22 October to support the 2nd Welsh who were to attack the following day. The SWB's D Company was attached to the Welsh for this attack during which it was caught by the German barrage and suffered heavy casualties: five ORs were killed and 19 wounded. The attack was successful overall, however, and 1st Division had now reached the outskirts of Ors and Catillon. On completion of the action, the 1st SWB returned to Wassigny and then back to Vaux Andigny the following day.[56]

Meanwhile, the Third Army, to the north of Fourth Army, had launched a successful attack on 20 October, taking all its objectives, but logistical problems then forced it to wait until 23 October to exploit its success. It had been joined in early October by a 'fresh' division which had been brought south to join XVII Corps: the 19th Division, containing 9th Cheshire, 9th RWF, 1/4th KSLI and 5th (Pioneers) SWB. This Division had been mauled and rebuilt on three occasions earlier in the year and since then had seen action in Flanders during August and early September. It would now take part in the Battle of the Selle.

It was initially placed in Corps Reserve around Cambrai where it was warned on 14 October that it was to take over the front held by 24th Division on the night of 17/18 October. Further orders from HQ XVII Corps the following day warned 19th Division to be prepared to attack in a north-easterly direction and capture high ground to the east of the River Selle, between

54 TNA WO 95/1280: 1st SWB War Diary for October 1918.
55 TNA WO 95/1609: 1st KSLI War Diary for October 1918 and *SDGW* for 1st KSLI 24 October 1918.
56 TNA WO 95/1280: 1st SWB War Diary for 22-24 October 1918.

Saulzoir and Haussy. The river here was unfordable and temporary bridges previously erected by the 24th Division had been destroyed. Before any attack could begin it would be necessary for the RE, assisted by 19th Division's Pioneers, 5th SWB, to place infantry bridges across the river during the opening barrage.

On 18 October the 9th RWF moved into assembly positions near St Aubert and Montrecourt, where they remained for the whole of the following day. The Battalion War Diary is a little terse on what happened, but the Regimental History gives more detail. During the afternoon of 19 October, 9th RWF sent out patrols to try and secure a foothold across the river and on the railway embankment beyond. A patrol succeeded in crossing at Saulzoir and driving out the enemy there. It then set about clearing the enemy machine gun posts along the embankment by enfilading them from Saulzoir. The rest of the companies were then able to cross the river and take up positions from which to launch the main attack, thus making their task the following day much easier. At 2:00 am on 20 October they attacked and gained their appointed objectives on the high ground east of the Selle with little opposition. They remained in the line for the next three days before being relieved and returning to Rieux on the evening of 23 October. The casualties had been high: 19 ORs killed and 61 wounded.[57]

Many of the wounded in the 1st SWB, 1st KSLI and 9th RWF during the Battle of the Selle would die from their wounds; between 17 and 25 October, the total number of deaths across the three battalions was 85, the ages of 83 of whom are known.

Battalion	1st SWB	%	1st KSLI	%	9th RWF	%
Total deaths 17-25 October 1918	24		31		30	
Known ages	23		31		29	
18			2		2	
19	4	19%	6	19%	6	28%
20	4		4		5	
Total aged 18-20	8	38%	12	38%	13	45%
Total aged 21-29: best fighting age in terms of physical strength and maturity	9	43%	13	43%	10	34%
30s and 40s	4	19%	6	19%	6	21%
Average age of those known	24		24		24	

Table 19. Age profiles of 1st SWB, 1st KSLI and 9th RWF soldiers killed 17-25 October 1918.

By now, 'boys' who had been rushed out six months earlier would have turned 19 so the two eighteen-year-olds apiece in 1st KSLI and 9th RWF must have been later arrivals sent out before the tap was turned off at the end of August. The average age of those who died in all three battalions was again 24 but all now show a greater number of youngsters amongst the

57 TNA WO 95/2092: 9th RWF War Diary for October 1918 and Dudley Ward *Regimental Records of the Royal Welch Fusiliers* pp. 485-488.

dead, with 9th RWF showing 45 percent aged 20 and below. The average ages of each battalion would have been lower had they not contained a proportion of men over thirty, but these were not necessarily men who had been conscripted late; many were former TF soldiers, such as 39-year-old Pte David Hughes of 9th RWF who had first arrived in France in November 1914 with 1/4th RWF.

Of the 31 who died in 1st KSLI, ten had enlisted before the end of 1915 and five of these had first arrived in France during that year. At the other end of the scale, some thirteen had served for less than a year and at least one, the 19-year old Pte Albert Semmens, had been part of a draft which had arrived in France on 29 September. His Platoon Officer's letter to his parents referred to his having done extremely well in two previous attacks so it seems likely that he had joined the battalion with the draft that arrived on 2 October.[58] Five of those killed had served in other KSLI battalions and had been transferred across in early 1918 when these battalions had been disbanded. Of the rest, however, nine had not started out in Shropshire battalions but had been transferred in, mainly from Southern Command; five of these were former Gloucester TF soldiers who had also arrived in 2 October draft. The impression given is that although it continued to function well, 1st KSLI was by now a bit of a mixed battalion in terms of experience and composition.

The 1st SWB presents a slightly different picture. Ten of those killed had enlisted before the end of 1915 although only three of these had arrived in France during that year. Only one man appears to have had less than 12 months service, with the majority of the rest (eight) having enlisted during the first half of 1917. All except six had arrived at the IBD as SWB soldiers and had served in various SWB battalions, including the 11th and 12th, both of which had been disbanded in February 1918. The others were two from the TR, two former Cheshires, one Herefordshire and one RWF.

The 9th RWF shows yet another mix of men. Some 15 had enlisted early enough to be volunteers. One of these had landed in France with 4th RWF at the end of 1914 whilst five had arrived in there in 1915; three of these were original 9th RWF soldiers who landed on 19 July 1915. A further man had served with the SWB in Gallipoli before being posted to the RWF. Some ten men were TF, almost entirely from 4th RWF plus two from 23rd RWF. Two, for whom the Service Records have survived, had been 'Derby' men; one appears to have volunteered aged 17 whilst the other had signed up for Home Service only. These two men had spent their entire service at home until they were sent to France in June 1918. Of the more recent enlistments, only one man had less than a year's service but a further nine had enlisted in 1917, most having had only just over a year's service when they died. Thus, there was a mix of some men with extensive overseas experience, others who had lengthy service but almost all of it at home and those who had arrived within the preceding eighteen months.

Of the 85 men who had died across the three battalions, at least 35 may definitely be said to have been volunteers since analysis of the combination of their Service Numbers, the amount of the War Gratuity that was paid to their beneficiaries and even their Medal Index Cards (MIC) indicate that they had enlisted before the end of 1915. The lack of Service Records makes it impossible to say with any certainty how many other men had volunteered before March 1916 or later in the war. Taking the known figures, however, at least 41 percent of those who died in

58 <www.ancestry.co.uk> *De Ruvigny* Vol. 5 p. 149.

these three battalions at the Battle of the Selle had enlisted voluntarily. So, in the same way that it is not sustainable to say that the army was made up of boys at that time it also appears that to refer to it as a 'conscript' army is too much of a generalization to be factually correct.

The October offensives had been successful but not without further cost in terms of casualties. By the end of October, the British Infantry and Cavalry strength had fallen to 380,825 from 407,045 at the start of the month. The Battle casualties had numbered 69,449 whilst 73,041 reinforcements had been received but it is not clear who the extra 3,592 were intended to replace.[59] It is possible they were to replace the sick, since the extracts below from the Third Army Wastage Returns show that a large number of men fell into this category at any one time.[60]

Division	5 October		19 October		26 October	
	Sick	Wounded	Sick	Wounded	Sick	Wounded
3rd	241	630	181	38	131	803
5th	100	611	148	96	100	473
38th	172	93	276	383	233	465

Table 20. Wastage Returns for 3rd, 5th and 38th Divisions for October 1918.

Many of the sick were probably suffering from influenza since the Third Army Routine Orders for Wednesday 30 October warned that:

> During the present incidence of influenza, and with a view to lessening the risk of infection, no cinema shows or concert parties will be held in any building, and church parade services should take place in the open air.[61]

In the 6th Division, 1st KSLI had been drawn back into Brigade Reserve on 25 October where it spent its time reorganizing and refitting. Training was carried out, including elementary schemes, and time was found for baths for all the men. On 28 October the battalion returned to the line and sent patrols out along the bank of the Ors Canal, locating three strongly situated enemy posts on the west bank. Very early on the morning of 30 October three fighting patrols were sent out to deal with these posts, two of which were vacated by the enemy whilst the crew of the third was killed. Later that day, the 6th Division was relieved and 1st KSLI moved back to Fresnoy-le-Grand where it would spend the last few days of the war in training and assimilating a draft of 269 ORs which joined the battalion on 1 November.[62]

In Third Army, the 19th Division had been relieved overnight on 23/24 October, having lost 111 killed, 603 wounded and 25 missing during the battle of the Selle. It now had a few days

59 TNA WO 95/26: AG GHQ War Diary Infantry and Cavalry Strength Return for October 1918.
60 TNA WO 95/380: Third Army A & Q Wastage Returns for October 1918. NB The return for 12 October is missing.
61 Ibid., Third Army A & Q War Diary, General Routine Order issued 30 October 1918: 1840 Influenza Epidemic.
62 TNA WO 95/1609: 1st KSLI War Diary for October/November 1918.

rest during which a large number of reinforcements arrived, mostly young soldiers without any previous experience of the war.

> Time was short in which to prepare them for the next battle, but training in open warfare began at once and it was surprising to see how quickly they grasped the principles; they were taught by instructors who were by now seasoned warriors.[63]

Reinforcements continued to arrive but in 'penny-packets' rather than large drafts. Between 20-30 October 9th Cheshire, which had been in reserve for the Selle, had received 19 ORs.

November 1918

The First Army's successful attack at Valenciennes on 1 November gave the BEF a line running almost north to south from east of Valenciennes to east of Le Cateau, but the country over which the next advance was to take place would be difficult. To the north the fortified line of Le Quesnoy had to be breached; in the centre lay the Forêt de Mormal; whilst in the south the River Sambre had to be crossed. A full-scale attack was to be made on 4 November by First, Third and Fourth Armies on a thirty-mile front from Valenciennes to the Sambre, north of Oisy.

In Fourth Army, the 1st SWB had moved back to Vaux Andigny on 24 October where it spent the next few days resting and training. It took over the line in front of Catillon in preparation for the 1st Division's attempt on 4 November to cross the Sambre et Oise Canal, which here was 20 yards wide with swampy ground on its banks. The battalion was to attack Catillon from the west which it achieved without difficulty. The Regimental History described it as 'a neat and most successful operation, especially satisfactory because success was so cheaply achieved, only five men being killed, … and 15 men wounded'.[64] This would be 1st SWB's last action of the war as the 1st Division was relieved that night and sent back into reserve.

The Third Army's sector covered 10 miles and included the Forêt de Mormal, the fortress of Le Quesnoy and difficult countryside made up of towns and villages and several small rivers which would have to be crossed. It was in this latter area that the 19th Division would attack, being confronted by numerous reasonably sized villages, railways, roads, hills and valleys and four small streams or rivers.[65] The 19th Division, having come late to Third Army, would now be in action almost to the end: the Sambre on 4 November and the Passage of the Grande Honnelle 5-7 November. By now the average strength of the BEF's British Divisions was about 7,200 Infantry and Cavalry ORs. The 19th Division's strength remained over a thousand higher with 8377 ORs so it was a prime candidate to carry on the momentum of the attacks.[66]

Since being withdrawn from the line on 24 October, the Division's battalions had continued to train for further advances; on 31 October 9th Cheshire and 1/4th KSLI took part in 56th

63 Wyrall, *The Nineteenth Division 1914-1918*, p. 222.
64 Atkinson, *History of the South Wales Borderers 1914-1918*, pp. 474-5.
65 Wyrall, *The Nineteenth Division 1914-1918* pp. 222-3.
66 TNA WO 95/26: AG GHQ War Diary Strength of Infantry and Cavalry as at 1 November 1918.

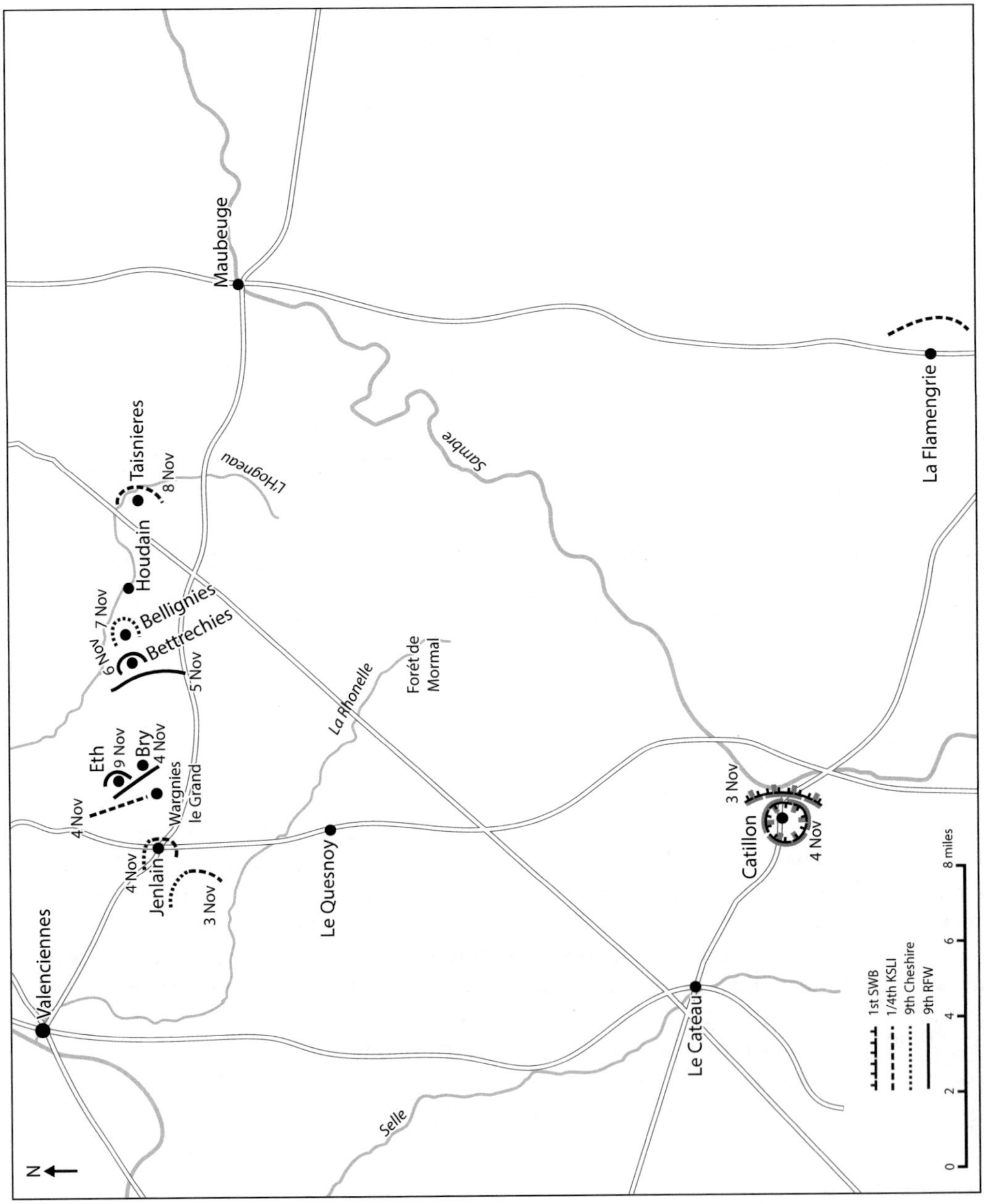

Map 13: Battle of the Sambre and the Passage of the Grande Honnelle, 4-7 November 1918: 1st SWB, 9th Cheshire, 9th RWF and 1/4th KSLI.

Brigade's practise scheme of attack.[67] That evening, 56th and 58th Brigades were informed that they were to lead the Division's attack on 4 November. When further orders were issued on 2 November, the plan had been finalised: 56th Brigade was to capture the first objective, the high ground just west of the village of Jenlain, whilst the second objective, to be taken by 58th Brigade on the left and 57th Brigade on the right, was the spur west of and overlooking the villages of Bry and Eth.

On the morning of 3 November it appeared that the enemy had withdrawn and 56th Brigade was ordered to send out patrols to find them. Both 9th Cheshire and 1/4th KSLI sent out companies to regain contact, neither encountering much opposition until they reached the high ground south west of Jenlain when they came under heavy shell and machine gun fire. The Cheshires continued to push forward and a platoon managed to get into the northern side of the village. The Cheshires left company was then able to establish itself beyond the northern edge of the village whilst the right company reached the railway which ran towards the village. By late afternoon the enemy had already been driven from the high ground that had been set as the first objective for the following day, so plans had hastily to be changed and the 57th and 58th Brigades were brought further forward for the start of their respective attacks.

Early on 4 November 9th Cheshire and 1/4th KSLI resumed the attack through Jenlain from the west under a heavy barrage, but successfully clearing the whole village by mid-morning. By the time the Shropshires had moved through the village they had sustained 110 casualties whilst 9th Cheshire had taken casualties from both the enemy's and the British barrage, the latter falling very far short. They were later placed in reserve whilst 1/4th KSLI consolidated on a line running north from Wargnies le Grand railway station, ready to continue the advance the following day. The other Marcher battalion, 9th RWF, in 58th Brigade Reserve, saw little action on 4 November, and simply followed the two attacking battalions, 9th Welsh and 2nd Wiltshire, arriving at the west bank of the Petit Aunelle river and later to the west of the villages of Bry and Eth.

On 5 November the 1/4th KSLI resumed the attack towards Le Calotin, sustaining slight casualties before consolidating on high ground east of La Flamengrie. Further advance was impossible due to heavy fire from the high ground west of the Hogneau River. The 9th RWF now received orders to pass through 58th Brigade's attacking battalions and continue the advance. They attacked in the afternoon, encountering little opposition until the high ground west of Bettrechies. All attempts to push on over the crest, however, were stopped by heavy machine gun fire from a spur south west of the village. The following day, in conjunction with 56th Brigade on the right, 9th RWF succeeded in occupying Bettrechies. Two patrols managed to cross the River Hogneau but were pushed back by enemy machine gun fire. The following day, 7 November, 9th Cheshire was lent to 57th Brigade to assist in an attack across the River Hogneau to capture Bellignies. All objectives were gained, although from the Cheshires' comments this would appear again to have been no thanks to the British barrage. By now the troops were exhausted and Divisional HQ gave orders that there would be no further advance that day so that they might have a chance to rest. It was not to be, however, as at 7:00 pm Corps HQ ordered a further advance for the following morning. The 1/4th KSLI commented on its movements on 8 November: 'owing to the exigencies of the situation caused by the rapid

67 TNA WO 95/2079: 9th Cheshire War Diary entry for 31 October 1918.

retirement of the enemy, the Battalion was compelled to march to Taisnieres via La Flamengrie and Houdain. The men were very footsore and weary …'.

By the night of 8/9 November 57th Brigade held the line of the Mauberge-Mons railway along the whole Divisional front, 58th Brigade was in Houdain and Breaugies and 56th Brigade in Taisnieres. The CO of 9th RWF, Lt Col Smeathman, noted that:

All troops were sopped [sic] to the skin and tired out, having come approximately 14 miles since the 3rd November. They had consolidated no less than eight different lines, and had practically no hot food during the entire period.

On 9 November, 19th Division became the Corps reserve and its war effectively ended. During its final advance its OR casualties were 126 killed, 784 wounded and 46 missing. The OR casualties shown in the Marcher battalions' respective War Diaries were: 9th Cheshire 12 killed and 132 wounded; 9th RWF 8 killed and 51 wounded; and 1/4th KSLI 2 killed and about 118 wounded.[68] The casualties suffered by battalions were now appreciably fewer than might have been expected for what had been a sustained period of fighting, although whether this is due to the different style of warfare, the reduced size of the battalions themselves or simply the dwindling opposition is difficult to say.

The final figures of those who died in these three battalions during the period 3 – 9 November are higher than those shown above as they include those who later died of their wounds and also several who succumbed to sickness, almost certainly influenza. Analysis of their details in Table 20 shows that the composition of these Marcher battalions of 19th Division remained predominantly drawn from Western Command but that there are differences within those figures. Despite everything that had happened to the battalion over its time in France, and particularly during 1918, over half of those members of 9th Cheshire who died in this last phase had been enlisted in the Cheshire's recruiting area. A further two had enlisted in Wales plus four from No 3 District making a total of 22, or 75 percent, from Western Command. The proportion of men in 9th RWF who had enlisted in the RWF recruiting area was lower than for the Cheshires, but then it always had been throughout the war with men from all over Wales wishing to join the Regiment. There had also been the active policy of posting Welsh soldiers to their native battalions. Altogether 13 men (72 percent) had enlisted in Wales; a further four from No 3 District brings the total drawn from Western Command to 94 percent. The small number of 1/4th KSLI men enlisted in the Shropshires' recruiting area is surprising given that this was a TF battalion but since its arrival in France in late July 1917 it had been well used. Other men had enlisted in No 4 District, but the total was still low and required a further 14 from No 3 District to bring the number from Western Command up to 87 percent. The composition of 1/4th KSLI was thus more diverse at this point than the other two battalions, but it had nonetheless continued to be refilled by men drawn from the traditional sources of reinforcement in its parent Home Command.

68 TNA WO 95/2078: 1/4th KSLI War Diary for November 1918, WO 95/2079 9th Cheshire After Action Report Z546 3-10 November, WO 95/2092: 9th RWF War Diary After Action Report for 3-9 November 1918 and Wyrall, *The Nineteenth Division 1914-1918* pp. 223-230. NB It is clear from careful reading of the KSLI and Cheshire War Diaries that the Divisional History is incorrect in stating that it was the 1/4th KSLI that gained the northern edge of Jenlain on 3 November. It was a platoon from 9th Cheshire.

3-9 November 1918	9th Cheshire	9th RWF	1/4th KSLI
Total Deaths	28	18	31
Enlisted Regimental Area	16	5	6
Elsewhere in No 4 District – England			4
Elsewhere in No 4 District - Wales	2	8	3
Total enlisted in No 4 District	18	13	13
Enlisted in No 3 District	1	3	9
• Plus Liverpool/Manchester	3	1	5
Total Enlisted in Western Command	**22**	**17**	**27**
Northern Command	4	1	1
Southern Command	2		1
• Plus Birmingham			
Eastern			1
London District			
Scotland/Ireland			
Overseas			1
Total Other Commands	**6**	**1**	**4**

Table 21. Enlistment locations of soldiers of 9th Cheshire, 9th RWF and 1/4th KSLI who died between 3-9 November 1918.

The Armistice was signed on 11 November. At the start of the 100 Days, the total OR strength of the Infantry and Cavalry of the BEF's British Divisions had been 417,994; on 11 November it was in the region of 381,000, despite 198,578 reinforcements having been sent out during the period up to 31 October.[69] The reinforcement tap had thus not been entirely turned off although the men available were appreciably fewer than they had been earlier in the war.

AG Organisation

Throughout the war the work of the AG Branches both at GHQ and at the Base had increased exponentially. The expansion this had necessitated at GHQ may be seen by comparing the photographs of AG's Branch in 1914 with that of 1918. The latter shows only officers and none of the number of clerks who would have been supporting them.

The actual administration of the reinforcements arriving in France had been the work of the unsung staff of the 3rd Echelon at the Base. This organisation was responsible for all the

69 TNA WO 95/26: AG GHQ War Diary August to November 1918.

Adjutant General and staff, France 1918. Lieutenant General George Fowke, the Adjutant-General of the British Expeditionary Force, and his Staff (unnamed), Montreuil, 1918. IWM Q 9943

documentation for the soldiers in the field so that casualties could be quickly and accurately traced and reported to the War Office. It was also responsible for taking on strength all reinforcements as they arrived and for their subsequent despatch to replace casualties in the field. At the start of the war it had numbered about 200 personnel but by the end there were close on 4,000, most of whom were officers and men who had been incapacitated on active service. Since 1917 women clerks had also played their part.[70]

Detailed Analysis of Selected Battalions for 1918

As with previous years, a more detailed analysis of selected battalions of English/Welsh Marcher Regiments has been produced in order to examine changes in their composition.[71]

70 Macready, *Annals of an Active Life* p. 201.
71 For ease of comparison and to include soldiers who died immediately post the Armistice the date period has been kept the same as that of previous years.

Inevitably, the dwindling availability of manpower had had some effect and by 1918 the numbers originally enlisting in the respective Regimental areas had decreased for the Regular battalions of the Cheshire Regiment, KSLI and SWB, (Table 20.1) although those for the RWF remained the same as in 1914: around 25 per cent (Table 20.2). The percentages for those enlisted in No 4 District had also decreased by 1918 but nonetheless remained above 50 percent for all the Regular battalions and had actually risen for the RWF which had become more Welsh. The pattern continued for those enlisted in Western Command where, despite a fall from 1914 levels, 73 percent and above had been enlisted in that Command.

Enlistment Location	**1st Cheshire**		**9th Cheshire**		**1st KSLI**		**6th KSLI**	
Regimental Area	95	39%	35	50%	55	35%	14	39%
Elsewhere in No 4 District - England	8				14		3	
Elsewhere in No 4 District - Wales	17		6		28		6	
Total enlisted in No 4 District	120	50%	41	59%	97	61%	23	64%
Enlisted in No 3 District	30		7		21		5	
• Liverpool/Manchester	25		5		12		2	
Total Enlisted in Western Command	**175**	**73%**	**53**	**76%**	**130**	**82%**	**30**	**83%**
Northern Command	31		7		2		1	
Southern Command	8		3		17		3	
• Birmingham	3				2		1	
Eastern	11		2		5		1	
London District	7		4		1			
Scotland/Ireland	6		1					
Overseas					2			
Total Other Commands	**66**		**17**		**29**		**6**	
Total Deaths	**241**		**70**		**159**		**36**	

Table 22.1. Enlistment locations of soldiers of selected English Regular battalions who were killed/ died between 1 July-30 November 1918.

Enlistment Location	2nd RWF		9th RWF		1st SWB		10th SWB	
Regimental Area	49	*25%*	19	*19%*	22	*22%*	63	36%
Elsewhere in No 4 District - England	14		6		9		10	
Elsewhere in No 4 District - Wales	55		32		23		39	
Total enlisted in No 4 District	118	60%	57	58%	54	54%	112	64%
Enlisted in No 3 District	28		15		15		23	
• Liverpool/Manchester	19		8		10		5	
Total Enlisted in Western Command	**165**	**84%**	**80**	**81%**	**79**	**79%**	**140**	**80%**
Northern Command	10		4		4		5	
Southern Command	3		1		2		6	
• Birmingham	5		1				3	
Eastern	2		3		5		11	
London District	10		9		10		9	
Scotland/Ireland			1				1	
Overseas	1							
Total Other Commands	**31**		**19**		**21**		**35**	
Total Deaths	**196**		**99**		**100**		**175**	

Table 22.2. Enlistment locations of soldiers of selected Welsh Regular battalions who were killed/died between 1 July-30 November 1918.

The existence of Lancashire, with the conurbations of Liverpool and Manchester, in the other District of Western Command had undoubtedly helped retain the homogeneity of the battalions surveyed, as it always had done in previous decades. Although the transfer of recruiting to the MNS in late 1917 had redrawn the regional boundaries for actual recruiting any impact arising from this would only become apparent in men drafted after around April 1918. Some change may be seen amongst the enlistment locations of those who died in late 1918 but overall, around three-quarters of those killed in the Regular battalions of the Marches had continued to come from the traditional recruiting areas of Western Command.

The 1918 birth locations (see Tables 20.3 and 20.4) do not show such a great difference from those of 1914.

Birth location	1st Cheshire		9th Cheshire		1st KSLI		6th KSLI	
Regimental Area	69	29%	26	37%	49	41%	8	22%
Elsewhere in No 4 District-England	6				14		3	
Elsewhere in No 4 District-Wales	14		5		21		4	
Total born in No 4 District	89	37%	31	44%	84	53%	15	42%
Born in No 3 District	38		11		24		4	
• Liverpool/Manchester	20		8		5		4	
Total Born in Western Command	**147**	***61%***	**50**	***71%***	**113**	***71%***	**23**	***64%***
Northern Command	35		7		9		3	
Southern Command	7		3		20		4	
• Birmingham	2				3		1	
Eastern	10		3		6		2	
London District	10		2					
Scotland/Ireland	7		1					
Overseas			1		2			
Total Other Commands	**71**		**17**		**38**		**10**	
Location of Birth Unknown	23		3		8		3	
Total Deaths	**241**		**70**		**159**		**36**	

Table 22.3. Birth locations of soldiers of selected English Regular battalions who were killed/died between 1 July-30 November 1918.

Birth location	2nd RWF		9th RWF		1st SWB		10th SWB	
Regimental Area	37	19%	17	17%	11	11%	38	22%
Elsewhere in No 4 District-England	11		8		6		10	
Elsewhere in No 4 District Wales	39		21		19		40	
Total born in No 4 District	87	44%	46	46%	36	36%	88	50%
Born in No 3 District	32		11		17		23	
• Liverpool/Manchester	14		5		8		3	
Total Born in Western Command	**133**	**68%**	**62**	**63%**	**61**	**61%**	**114**	**65%**
Northern Command	15		3		9		7	
Southern Command	11		6		6		17	
• Birmingham	4				1			
Eastern	3		5		4		12	
London District	7		8		9		11	
Scotland/Ireland	1		2		2		3	
Overseas	2						2	
Total Other Commands	**43**		**24**		**31**		**52**	
Location of Birth Unknown	20		11		8		9	
Total Deaths	**196**		**99**		**100**		**175**	

Table 22.4. Birth locations of soldiers of selected Welsh Regular battalions who were killed/died between 1 July-30 November 1918.

The greatest fall in birth locations had been for 1st Cheshire, from 55 percent in 1914 having been born in Cheshire to 29 percent in 1918. In 1st KSLI and 1st SWB, the drop had been just 8 percent whilst for 2nd RWF the number of those born within its recruiting area had risen by 8 per cent. This is likely to have been caused by the policy of posting Welsh soldiers to Welsh units. Whilst the figures for the Cheshire soldiers born within Western Command had fallen from 1914 levels, for the other battalions, both English and Welsh, the numbers of those born within the Command remained above 60 percent.

The smaller numbers of TF deaths in 1918, except for those for 1/6th Cheshire and 1/4th KSLI, slightly skew the percentages. However, although the localized recruiting for TF battalions had inevitably been eroded, Table 20.5 shows that over 77 percent continued to be drawn from Western Command.

Enlistment Locations	**1/5th Cheshire**		**1/6th Cheshire**		**1/4th KSLI**		**1/4th RWF**		**1/2nd Monmouths**	
Regimental Area	13	81%	30	53%	20	24%	14	42%	10	59%
Elsewhere in No 4 District-England					14		5		2	
Elsewhere in No 4 District-Wales			1		5		4		1	
Total enlisted in No 4 District	13	81%	31	54%	39	46%	23	70%	13	76%
Enlisted in No 3 District	2		7		16		2			
• Liverpool/Manchester			6		10		2		2	
Total Enlisted in Western Command	**15**	**94%**	**44**	**77%**	**65**	**77%**	**27**	**82%**	**15**	**88%**
Northern Command			4		3		4			
Southern Command			4		8					
• Birmingham							1			
Eastern	1		4		3		1		1	
London District			1		4				1	
Scotland/Ireland										
Overseas					1					
Total Other Commands	**1**		**13**		**19**		**6**		**2**	
Total Deaths	**16**		**57**		**84**		**33**		**17**	

Table 22.5. Enlistment locations of soldiers of selected TF battalions who were killed/died between 1 July-30 November 1918.

Birth Locations	1/5th Cheshire		1/6th Cheshire		1/4th KSLI		1/4th RWF		1/2nd Monmouths	
Regimental Area	11	67%	19	33%	17	20%	9	27%	4	24%
Elsewhere in No 4 District-England					8		4		1	
Elsewhere in No 4 District-Wales			3		5		1		1	
Total born in No 4 District	11	67%	22	39%	30	36%	14	42%	6	35%
Born in No 3 District	2		10		17		3		1	
• Liverpool/Manchester			3		9		1		1	
Total Born in Western Command	**13**	**81%**	**35**	**61%**	**56**	**67%**	**18**	**55%**	**8**	**47%**
Northern Command			6		5		6			
Southern Command			4		7		1		2	
• Birmingham			1		1					
Eastern	2		4		6				1	
London District			1		3				1	
Scotland/Ireland					1				1	
Overseas					2		1			
Total Other Commands	**2**		**16**		**25**		**8**		**5**	
Location of Birth Unknown	1		6		3		7		4	
Total Deaths	**16**		**57**		**84**		**33**		**17**	

Table 22.6. Birth locations of soldiers of selected TF battalions who were killed/died between 1 July-30 November 1918.

Details of the birth locations are less conclusive, but the smaller numbers of deaths for 1/5th Cheshire, 1/4th RWF and 1/2nd Monmouthshire affect the percentages. The 1/6th Cheshire had also traditionally recruited just across the county border in Glossop and hence the men born in Northern Command. The figures for 1/4th KSLI also reflect the finding above that this was now a more mixed battalion than might have been expected given its late arrival on the Western Front. With the exception of 1/2nd Monmouthshire, over half of those who had died during this period in each period had been born within Western Command.

Conclusions

The members of the Army Council continued to blame the Government for the shortage of manpower, never fully accepting, even at this late stage of the war, the impact their continuing demands for men would have upon the nation's industries, including those heavily involved in the war effort. The Government's need was to balance the conflicting demands within the

12th Platoon, C Company, 1/4th RWF at Camblain-Châtelain in September 1918 (x is captioned on the back as Pte W. R. Hughes of Holyhead, aged 19) (RWF Archives)

prevailing political climate. There seems little or no evidence, however, that the Government had actively withheld men from the Army. It was more a case of delayed action, misleading statements and growing distrust on both sides.

The Cabinet had taken the decision to allow under 19-year olds to be sent to France during the immediate emergency earlier in the year. Many of those sent proved to be excellent material but although they had received longer initial training they lacked time to gain experience of the Western Front before being thrust into action. Nonetheless, many did extremely well and played their part in the successes of the 100 Days, although the perception that half the Infantry in the later months of the war was made up of 18 and 19-year olds is not supported by evidence from the units surveyed. There was a feeling of future capital being expended, however, together with an undoubted paternalism amongst senior officers at the sight of such youngsters in action. As a result, the tap was turned off at the end of August.

The BEF of the 100 Days is also often described as a conscript Army. That many of the men had been conscripted is undoubtedly true but the evidence gained from analysis of those killed in three battalions that took part in the Battle of the Selle in October shows that there were still

A Company 1/6th Cheshire at Wardrecques, near St Omer in late 1918 (Cheshire Regimental Archives)

many volunteers, some 40 percent, amongst their ranks. What is also apparent is that the TF continued to provide many of the replacements sent out in 1918, as it had done since late 1916.

It has long been thought that by 1918 battalions were made up of men drawn from all over the country. The evidence of the Marcher battalions surveyed does not support this, showing that well over two-thirds continued to have enlisted originally in Western Command. The surpluses obtained by the re-organization of divisions early in 1918 had been largely distributed to other battalions of the same Regiment whilst at home drafts for the BEF continued to be drawn as much as possible from the Reserve, TF and TR battalions of the parent Command. Although there were fewer men available for reinforcements in late 1918, those arriving in drafts would have found familiar accents and have talked about the same football teams as those of 1914, at least in the Marcher battalions.

Conclusions

It is difficult to obtain an accurate view of the size of the problem confronting the British Army's Manning authorities in the replacement of casualties during 1914-1918 since the statistics compiled after the war show figures reported up to March 1920. Furthermore, the figures for the wounded relate to the number of wounds and not the number of individuals wounded. Enough can be gleaned, however, to indicate the magnitude of the problem that had faced them in meeting the need for Infantry replacements for just one theatre of the war:[1]

Infantry Casualties on the Western Front				
	Killed	**Wounded**	**Missing**	**Total**
Regular Army	307,975	908,692	155,450	1,132,117
TF	91,558	287,649	46,968	426,175
Totals	399,533	1,196,341	202,418	**1,798,292**

Provision of Manpower

The fundamental requirement for the reinforcement process was obviously the availability of sufficient manpower. Initially the influx of volunteers provided ample resources but the recruiting downturn in late 1915 led to the introduction of a form of compulsion in 1916. The problem for the nation as a whole, however, was that the indiscriminate recruiting of earlier years had caused manpower shortages in various industrial sectors. It became necessary to regulate the occupations from which men were called up, but the mechanisms to do so were not in place. Furthermore, throughout 1917 the Government proved unable, rather than unwilling, to force the great Departments of State to release their manpower. The introduction of the concept of National Service early in that year proved ineffective, despite the creation of a Ministry of National Service and it would not be until later in the year that the appointment of a DGNS with Ministerial authority would enable any real co-ordination of the nation's manpower to become possible. By then, however, the situation had become critical.

1 War Office, *Statistics of the British Military Effort of the British Empire (SME)*, pp. 249, 240 fn 1.

The manpower crisis of early 1918 had thus been approaching since 1914 but the German Spring Offensive threw the shortages into stark relief. Since the end of Third Ypres the Army Council and GHQ had been demanding more men to replace the losses suffered during that offensive. The War Cabinet's problem was the distribution of manpower for the country as a whole; the large numbers demanded by the War Office ran the risk of destroying the nation's industries, including those required for the war effort, and plunging the country into an economic crisis. The Army Council appeared unable, or indeed unwilling, to recognise this, failing even to agree amongst its members:

> [A]ssuming a choice had to be made between a considerable reduction of men in the Army and a proportionate reduction in munitions and supplies, including those of our Allies, which would the War Office prefer? The Adjutant General of the day had always answered that they must have the men, whilst the Master General of Ordnance and the Quarter Master General had said that they must have the supplies.[2]

The Government and the Military hierarchy increasingly distrusted each other since neither accepted, nor even understood, the other's position.

Despite the views of the *Official History*, and Lloyd George's many comments on the subject, there is little evidence in Cabinet papers that the Government actively withheld men.[3] Other fronts had been opened up, all requiring manpower, and on the Government's insistence divisions had been sent to Italy in late 1917. The Government's real role was in the taking-up of men from civilian life. This had to be governed by the industrial requirements of the nation as a whole, and also by the increasingly difficult political climate of the time, with the growing Labour and Trades Union lobby. It was only the national emergency caused by the German Spring Offensives that enabled the two 1918 MSAs to be passed.

The calling up of men from civilian life was always a long-term measure. By the time notice had been given and men called up and trained, a minimum of four months would elapse before the earliest time at which they could be drafted. The men rushed to France to confront the German offensives were those already trained but who had been retained at home. The immediate decisions made at that time by the Cabinet related to the sending of under-age boys who had completed their training and the release of men from units earmarked for Home Defence, the latter bringing a complaint from Sir John French, the C-in-C Home Forces.[4] The rest of the manpower rushed to France came from men employed by different departments of the War Office. It emerged that some 1,400,000 men had in fact been retained on the Home strength of the Army whilst the Army Council had been pressing for the calling up of more men from civilian life.

2 TNA CAB 23/7: Minutes of War Cabinet Meeting 449 of 19 July 1918.

3 *BOH 1918 Vol.* 1, p. 52, fn. 1: 'It is obvious that the British Armies in France could have been brought up to full establishment before 21st March without unduly weakening the forces elsewhere had the Government so willed.'

4 TNA CAB 24/46: GT 4030 Troops Available for Home Defence dated 25 March 1918.

The Need for Greater Flexibility

There was early recognition of the need for greater flexibility in the use of manpower. One facet of this was the need to be able to transfer men to different units and arms within the Army, which required legislation to alter terms of service. This was passed for Regular soldiers in 1915 but the TF remained obdurate and consequently its usefulness both overseas and at home was curtailed. It would not be until the second MSA of 1916 that it would become possible to transfer TF soldiers without their consent not only between other TF units and corps but also into Regular units. The flexibility thus gained for the Army as a whole showed a willingness to make harsh decisions for the sake of expediency. The side-effect, however, was deep-seated resentment amongst the TF over the way in which their terms of service had been changed.

Apart from their normal and very valuable role in the treatment of casualties, the Medical Services also played a significant part in increasing both flexibility and the availability of manpower. Significant improvements were made in the rapid treatment of casualties, not only saving more lives but also enabling greater numbers of men to be returned to duty in theatre. The medical authorities subsequently calculated that some 64 percent of the wounded returned to duty in the front line and a further 18 percent returned to employment on LofC or garrison duties, or in sedentary occupations.[5]

The growing shortage of recruits also necessitated greater attention being paid to how and where men were employed. Medical classifications were reviewed several times in terms of the types of employment in which men of lesser fitness might be used, thus enabling the release of fitter men to fight. The monthly posting ACIs allocated men by fitness category and aptitude to appropriate parts of the Army. Men already serving and who were fit enough to fight were 'combed out' so that they could be sent to the front.

New Corps were also created, specifically to release fitter men to fight: the Labour Corps and the WAAC. Although fewer women joined up for service overseas than had been hoped for, those that did enabled thousands of men to be 'combed out' and sent to the front to fight. The women played a valuable part in the roles that they took over and their conduct during the March 1918 offensive won them recognition in the form of their name being changed to Queen Mary's Army Auxiliary Corps (QMAAC).

Reinforcement Process

The over-arching requirement was to provide sufficient reinforcements for units in the field as quickly as possible. Plans and procedures for this had been laid down pre-war, based on the requirements identified in previous conflicts but the demands of industrial warfare inevitably forced changes in the process. These might not have been as dramatic as developments in weaponry and tactics but nonetheless showed a steady evolution to meet changing demands.

At the start of the war a single Special Reserve unit serving the Line battalions of each Infantry Regiment (with occasionally an Extra Reserve unit for large regiments) prepared drafts when notified of requirements by the War Office. Once ready the draft would be despatched to the theatre concerned, to the Divisional IBD for the appropriate battalion. After several

5 *BOH 1918 Vol.* 5, p. 597.

days spent training at the Base the men would be sent forward to join their units, arriving in many cases almost a month, if not more, after they had been demanded. By the end of the war, the emphasis in the reinforcement system had changed from demand to supply. Regimental Reserve units, both Regular and TF, together with TR units affiliated to the Regiment's parent Home Command prepared drafts, informing the War Office as soon as they were ready. The Command concerned was then informed of their availability and called drafts forward as required. On arrival in theatre these drafts were moved rapidly forward to Divisional Reception Camps, close behind the fighting units, from where they could be fed into units as soon as they had time to absorb them. A speedier, more streamlined process had evolved.

Behind this evolution lay a willingness to change systems and organisations in the light of experience and in the interests of greater efficiency. Initial confusion arising out of the pre-war plans between the roles of the IGC and the DAG 3rd Echelon was resolved before Christmas 1914, with the latter assuming sole responsibility for the calling forward of drafts from home. The process of casualty reporting to GHQ and the 3rd Echelon was speeded up by late 1915 with the introduction of daily submission of estimated numbers. This remained unchanged for the rest of the war, with the sole refinement in early 1917 of the introduction, in the interests of accuracy and the avoidance of double counting, of running totals per unit for the phase of battle concerned. In France, the processing of drafts developed with the IBDs being re-organized twice to reflect changing circumstances. Firstly, in May/June 1916 it was decided in the interests of greater flexibility to reinforce by regiment rather than battalion. This necessitated the re-organization of Divisional IBDs into larger ones serving groups of Regiments from the same Military Districts. Subsequently, their size and role would be reduced in late 1917, effectively turning them into transit camps, simply receiving and posting men to units and then sending them rapidly forwards towards reinforcement units further towards the front. The cause of this later reorganization is said to have been the disturbance at Étaples in September 1917, but it also coincided with the move to situate reinforcements closer to corps and subsequently divisions. There is some evidence that the new IBDs were linked to the Home Commands.

Training

Adult recruits were posted on enlistment to draft-finding units for their training. New Reserve units had been created in 1915 to cater for New Army battalions and also for the TF but the anticipated increase in manpower with the introduction of conscription led to the creation of the TR. This did not replace the Regimental Reserve battalions but augmented them by taking surplus manpower within a Home Command after the former were filled. Despite perceptions in the Army at large, however, emphasis remained on preserving regimental affiliations. It still remained possible for a man to choose to serve in his local regiment and there continued to be acceptance of the value of *esprit de corps*.

Infantry training for the youngest recruits had evolved during 1917 with the introduction of new units. Later in the year these would become specifically YS battalions from which the youths would move to Graduated battalions, becoming part of the Home Army. Under normal circumstances, the youngsters would receive up to a year's training whilst adult Infantry recruits received a minimum of 14 weeks, long enough to train the man to at least the minimum standard required to take his place in a rifle section. What could not be imparted was the experience gained by being in action. Even in late 1914, the Army's perennial complaint had been heard that the new drafts were neither as good nor as well trained as those that had gone before. There seems little evidence that drafts later in the war were in fact any less well-prepared than before. What was lacking was time to acclimatize them to the front, and also the experienced officers and NCOs to lead them.

Composition of Armies during the 100 Days

It has frequently been assumed that the Cabinet's emergency decision of March 1918 enabling the drafting of 18½ year-olds to the BEF meant that half the men serving in Infantry units during the 100 Days were 'boys'. Analysis of the fatalities during that period has shown, however, that the average age of those who died was 24, and thus towards the middle of the optimum fighting ages of 21-28. This is not so very different from ages earlier in the war: rough analysis using CWGC data of the soldiers of 1st Cheshire who died between 8 August and 11 November 1914 provides 73 known ages, and an average age of 26-27.

It has also often been assumed that the army of 1918 was largely a conscript army. Again, analysis of those who died during the 100 Days indicates that some 40 percent had enlisted before the introduction of compulsion. Unfortunately, a lack of surviving Service Records prevents more detailed analysis of the Terms of Service of those who joined after that date. It may be accepted that the majority of those who took part in the 100 Days will have been conscripts but it is unsafe to call it a 'conscript army'.

Composition of Battalions

Before the war both the recruiting and the reinforcement organizations were based on territorial affiliations: Regimental recruiting areas, the Military Districts in which these were located and the parent Home Commands in which the Districts were located. It has long been assumed that by the end of the First World War these territorial affiliations had been seriously eroded and even that there had been a definite intention to 'destroy the Regiment … and nationalise the Army'.[6] Analysis of selected battalions of Regiments from the English/Welsh Marches for each year of the war, however, indicates that their composition remained largely the same as it always had been.

It is apparent that whenever possible efforts were made to send out drafts belonging to the same regiment or at least the same Military district or Home command. That is not to say that there were no instances of men being posted to cap badges other than their own because of course that did happen, particularly in times of great shortages such as during the Somme in 1916. Close analysis of these instances tends to indicate, however, that even then the traditional sources, namely the parent districts and commands, were being drawn upon as far as possible. The posting of Shropshire soldiers to the RWF, for example, was entirely within the existing procedures. What also becomes apparent from the analysis is that the earlier inability to transfer TF soldiers to other units and cap badges coupled with the existence of Home Service until after

6 Dunn, *The War the Infantry Knew*, pp. 245-6.

mid-1916 had the inadvertent but ultimately fortunate effect of effectively creating a huge pool of men that would be drawn upon, initially to replace the Somme casualties but also for the rest of the war, including during the 100 Days.

Overall, a soldier of 1914 would have found predominantly the same regional accents amongst those he served alongside in 1918, even though the individual battalions had been rebuilt several times.

Appendix I – Home Commands[1]

Commands	Districts	Counties
Scottish – • HQ Edinburgh	1 – HQ Perth	Aberdeenshire, Angus, Argyll, Banffshire, Bute, Caithness, Clackmannan, Dumbartonshire, Elgin, Fifeshire, Forfarshire, Invernesshire, Kincardine, Kinross, Morayshire, Nairn, Orkney, Perthshire, Renfrewshire Ross and Cromarty, Shetland, Stirlingshire, and Sutherland.
	2 – HQ Hamilton	Ayrshire, Berwickshire, Berwick-on-Tweed (Regulars and Special Reserve only), Dumfries, Edinburgh, Haddington, Kircudbright, Lanarkshire, Linlithgow, Midlothian, Peebles, Roxburgh, Selkirk and Wigtownshire.
Western – • HQ Chester	3 – HQ Preston	Cumberland, Isle of Man, Lancashire (except 40th Regimental District) and Westmorland.
	4 – HQ Chester	Cheshire, Herefordshire, Shropshire, that portion of Lancashire in the 40th Regimental District and Wales: Anglesey, Brecknockshire, Cardiganshire, Carmarthenshire, Carnarvonshire, Denbighshire, Flintshire, Glamorganshire, Merionethshire, Montgomeryshire, Monmouthshire, Pembrokeshire and Radnorshire.
Northern – • HQ York	5 – HQ York	Durham, Northumberland, Yorkshire, Berwick on Tweed, (except Regulars and Special Reserve)
	6 – HQ Lichfield	Derbyshire, Leicestershire, Lincolnshire, Nottinghamshire, Rutland and Staffordshire.

1 War Office, *Army List* (London: HMSO, August 1914).

Southern – • HQ: Salisbury	7 – HQ Warwick	Warwickshire, Gloucestershire, Worcestershire, Oxfordshire, Buckinghamshire, Berkshire (except Windsor for Regular troops and that portion of the County included in the Aldershot Command)
	8 – HQ Exeter	Devon, Somerset, Cornwall, Dorset, Wiltshire, Hampshire (except that portion included in the Aldershot Command)
Eastern – • HQ: Horseguards, London	9 – HQ Warley, Essex	Bedfordshire, Cambridgeshire, Essex, Hertfordshire, Huntingdonshire, Norfolk, Northamptonshire, Suffolk
	10 – HQ Hounslow	Kent, Middlesex, Sussex, Surrey (except portion included in Aldershot Command) and Woolwich (exclusive of Territorial Troops therein).
Ireland – • Dublin	11 – HQ Dublin	Londonderry, Antrim, Donegal, Tyrone, Down, Fermanagh, Armagh, Monaghan, Louth, Cavan, Dublin, Kildare, Wicklow and Carlow
	12 - HQ Cork	Sligo, Leitrim, Mayo, Roscommon, Longford, Meath, Westmeath, Galway, King's County, Queen's County, Clare, Tipperary, Kilkenny, Wexfored, Limerick, Waterford, Kerry and Cork.
Aldershot – • HQ: Aldershot		Parts of Berkshire, Surrey and Hampshire
London District – • HQ: Horseguards, London		The County of London, the Guards Depot at Caterham, Purfleet, Rainham Rifle Range, and (for Regular troops) Windsor.

Appendix II – Military Recruiting Areas for Western Command Infantry Regiments.[1]

Western Command

- Covered Cheshire, Lancashire, Shropshire, Herefordshire, Monmouthshire, Cumberland, Westmorland, the Isle of Man and the whole of Wales. Command HQ was in Watergate Street, Chester.
- Subdivided into two Military Districts, each containing Regimental Areas numbered according to the former Regimental Number:
  - **No 3 Military District** – covering Cumberland, Westmorland, Isle of Man and Lancashire (except 40th Regimental District). HQ in Preston.
  - **No 4 Military District** – covering counties of Cheshire, Flint, Denbigh, Anglesey, Carnarvon, Merioneth, Montgomery, Radnor, Cardigan, Brecknock, Monmouth, Pembroke, Carmarthen, Glamorgan, Hereford, Shropshire and that portion of Lancashire in the 40th Regimental District). HQ in Shrewsbury.

Infantry Regiments recruited in No 3 Military District:

- **The King's Own (Royal Lancaster Regt)**
  - Regimental Area No 4: Part of Lancashire (including Barrow in Furness, Lancaster, Morecambe and Ulverston)
- **The King's (Liverpool) Regiment**
  - Regimental Area No 8: Part of Lancashire (including Bootle, Liverpool and Southport) and IoM.
- **The Lancashire Fusiliers**
  - Regimental Area No 20: Part of Lancashire (including Bury, Middleton, Radcliffe, Rochdale and Salford).
- **The East Lancashire Regiment**
  - Regimental Area No 30: Part of Lancashire (including Accrington, Blackburn, Burnley, Clitheroe and Darwen)
- **The Border Regiment**
  - Regimental Area No 34: Cumberland and Westmorland
- **The Loyal North Lancashire Regiment**
  - Regimental Area No 47: Part of Lancashire (including Bolton, Chorley and Preston)
- **The Manchester Regiment**
  - Regimental Area No 63: Part of Lancashire (including Ashton-under-Lyne, Manchester and Oldham)

1 *Kelly's Directory of Cheshire 1914*, p 229; *Kelly's Directory of Shropshire 1913*, p 222; *Army List* - February 1915, *Army List* – January 1917.

- Infantry Regiments recruited in No 4 Military District: **The Cheshire Regt** Depot: Chester
  - Regimental Area No 22: covered County of Cheshire
- **The Royal Welsh Fusiliers (RWF)** Depot: Wrexham
  - Regimental Area No 23: covered Denbighshire, Flintshire, Carnarvonshire, Anglesey, Merioneth and Montgomeryshire ie North and Mid Wales
- **The South Wales Borderers** (SWB) Depot: Brecon
  - Regimental Area No 24: covered Brecknockshire, and Monmouthshire,
- **The South Lancashire Regiment** Depot: Warrington
  - Regimental Area No 40 – part of Lancashire including St Helens and Warrington

- **The Welsh Regiment** Depot: Cardiff
  - Regimental Area No 41: covered Cardiganshire, Carmarthenshire, Pembrokeshire, Glamorganshire ie South and West Wales.
- **The King's Shropshire Light Infantry (KSLI)** Depot: Shrewsbury
  - Regimental Area No 53: covered Counties of Shropshire, Herefordshire and Radnorshire (NB Herefordshire and Radnorshire came under Area 53 for Regular Recruiting but not for TF.

TF-only Regiments in No 4 Military District

- Herefordshire Regt
- Monmouthshire Regiment

Appendix III – Marcher Reserve Battalions (Regular Army)

Battalion	1915	1916	1917
3rd (SR) Cheshire	Birkenhead (Mersey Defences)	Birkenhead (Mersey Defences)	Birkenhead (Mersey Defences); December to Newcastle on Tyne
3rd (SR) RWF	Wrexham until May; then Liverpool	Litherland, Liverpool (Mersey Defences)	Litherland, Liverpool; November to Ireland
3rd (SR) SWB	Pembroke Dock; 4 coys in Edinburgh; June to Liverpool	Hightown, Liverpool (Mersey Defences)	Hightown, Liverpool
3rd (SR) KSLI	Edinburgh; March to Pembroke Dock	Pembroke Dock (Milford Haven Garrison)	Pembroke Dock December to Ireland
14th (Reserve) Cheshire	April: became a Second Reserve Bn in 11th Reserve Bde; Kinmel Park and then Prees Heath, Shropshire	September: became 59th TRB in 11th Reserve Bde at Prees Heath	May: became 225th (Grad) Bn in 203rd Bde, 68th Div at Halesworth, Suffolk; October: retitled 51st (Grad) Bn Manchester Regt at Yarmouth.
12th (Reserve) RWF	April: became a Second Reserve Bn in 14th Reserve Bde; Kinmel Park, N Wales	September: became 62nd TRB in 14th Reserve Bde at Kinmel Park	May: became 62nd (YS) Bn in 14th Reserve Bde; at Kinmel Park; October: retitled 53rd (YS) Bn Cheshire Regt
9th (Reserve) SWB	April: became a Second Reserve Bn in 13th Reserve Bde; at Kinmel Park	September: became 57th TRB in 13th Reserve Bde at Kinmel Park	May: became 282nd (Grad) Bn in 201st Bde, 67th Div at Canterbury October: retitled 52nd (Grad) Bn SWB
9th (Reserve) KSLI	April: became a Second Reserve Bn in 11th Reserve Bde; Kinmel Park and then Prees Heath, Shropshire	September: became 48th TRB in 11th Reserve Bde at Prees Heath, Shropshire	Remained 48th TRB in 11th Reserve Bde; at Prees Heath, Shropshire

Battalion	1915	1916	1917
17th (Reserve) Cheshire	August: formed as local reserve bn from Depot Coys of 15th (1st Birkenhead) & 16th (2nd Birkenhead) Cheshire in 17th Reserve Bde; at Prees Heath, Shropshire	September: became 74th TRB in 17th Reserve Bde; at Prees Heath, Shropshire	May: became 74th (YS) TRB in 17th Reserve Bde; at Prees Heath, Shropshire October: retitled 53rd (YS) Bn Manchester Regt; at Prees Heath but soon to 14th Reserve Bde at Kinmel Park
18th (Reserve) RWF (2nd London Welsh)	August: became local reserve bn in 14th Reserve Brigade; at Kinmel Park	September: combined with 20th (Reserve) bn to form 63rd TRB in 14th Reserve Bde at Kinmel Park	May: became 226th (Grad) Bn in 203rd Bde 68th Div at Halesworth, Suffolk October: retitled 51st (Grad) Bn Welsh Regt
20th, 21st & 22nd (Reserve) RWF	Formed in N Wales.	By April: in 14th Reserve Bde at Kinmel Park September: 21st & 22nd bns combined to form 64th TRB in 14th Reserve Bde at Kinmel Park	May: became 64th (YS) Bn in 14th Reserve Bde Oct: became 53rd (YS) Bn Welsh Regt
13th (Reserve) SWB	August: formed as local reserve bn from Depot Coys of 10th (1st Gwent) & 11th (2nd Gwent) SWB; at Kinmel Park	September: became 59th TRB in 13th Reserve Bde; at Kinmel Park	May: became 213th (Grad) Bn in 194th Bde 65th Div; at the Curragh, Ireland October: retitled 51st (Grad) Bn Cheshire Regt, remaining at the Curragh, Ireland
14th (Reserve) SWB	September: formed as local reserve bn from depot coy of 12th (3rd Gwent) SWB; at Conway	January: to 14 Reserve Bde at Kinmel Park September: became 65th TRB in 14th Reserve Bde; at Kinmel Park	Remained 65th TRB in 14th Reserve Bde; at Kinmel Park

Source: Brigadier E.A. James, *British Regiments 1914 – 18* (Uckfield: Naval & Military Press, 1998)

Appendix IV – Classification by Medical Categories.

Early 1916

In February 1916, it was announced that the medical fitness of men enlisting in the Regular Army for the duration of the war would be classified as follows[1]:

- i. Fit for General Service at home and abroad.
- ii. Fit for Field Service at home.
- iii. Fit for Garrison service.
  - a. Abroad.
  - b. At home.
- iv. Fit for:
  - a. Labour purposes (road-making, entrenching, Works Companies etc).
  - b. Sedentary work (clerks, storemen, batmen, cooks, orderlies, sanitary duty men).
- v. Unfit for any service.

May 1916

The categories were revised to give greater clarification of whether the man would be suitable for service overseas:[2]

A: General Service
B1: Abroad: Garrison service
B2: Abroad: Labour
B3: Abroad: Sedentary work
C1: At Home: Garrison service
C2 At Home: Labour
C3 At Home: Sedentary Work

June 1916

The categories were further revised with additional guidelines being added. This was intended to aid Medical Boards assessing the fitness of soldiers recovering from wounds[3]:

1 TNA: WO 293/4 ACI 290 of February 1916.
2 Ibid., ACI 1023 of May 1916.
3 Ibid., ACI 1241 of June 1916.

A: able to march, see to shoot, hear well and stand 'active service conditions'.
- A1: Men fit for overseas service in all respects: training, physically and mentally fit.
- A2: Recruits who will be fit for A1 as soon as trained.
- A3: Returned EF men who will be fit for A1 as soon as hardened.
- A4: Men under 19 years who should be A1 or A2 when 19.

B: free from serious organic diseases, able to stand service on the lines of communication in France or in Garrisons in the Tropics.
- B1: Abroad: Garrison service: able to march 5 miles, see to shoot with glasses and hear well.
- B2: Abroad: Labour: able to walk 5 miles to and from work, see and hear sufficiently for ordinary purposes.
- B3: Abroad: Sedentary work: only suitable for sedentary work.

C: free from serious organic disease, able to stand service conditions in garrisons at home.
- C1: At Home: Garrison service
- C2 At Home: Labour
- C3 At Home: Sedentary Work

D: Men unfit for service in A, B or C but likely to be fit in six months

E: Those not likely to be fit for service in A, B or C

April 1917

Category C was amended since it had been realized that there was very little difference between UK and North West Europe:

C: Fit for service at home or in North Western Europe, but not fit for General Service
- C1: In garrison or labour units.
- C2: In labour units or in Command, Garrison or regimental employments
- C3: Sedentary work: clerks, storemen, batmen, cooks, orderlies, sanitary duties etc. [4]

October 1917

All previous ACIs were cancelled and a new table of classifications published. The distinction between Categories B and C was also to be abolished with effect from 1 November 1917.[5]
- Category C soldiers would be placed in the corresponding sub-division of Category B.
- All soldiers serving at home (whether recruits, serving soldiers, or men who had been sent home sick or wounded from an Expeditionary Force or from a garrison abroad) were to be classified according to the categories shown in the table below.

4 TNA: WO 293/6 ACI 679 of April 1917.
5 TNA: WO 293/7 ACI 1606 of October 1917: Alteration of Classification of Men by Categories.

- In future, differentiation between those in categories lower than 'A' who were fit for service in North West Europe only and those fit to serve anywhere was to be made by special medical examination at the point at which they were actually required to proceed abroad.

Categories	**Standards**	**Guidance**
A Fit for general service.	(i) Men actually fit for general service in any theatre of war in all respects, both as regards training, physical and mental qualifications. (ii) Recruits who should be fit for A (i) as soon as trained. (iii) Men who have previously served with an Expeditionary Force, who should be fit for A (i) as soon as 'hardened'. (iv) Men under 19 years of age who should be fit for A(i) or A(ii) as soon as they are 19 years of age.	Able to march, see to shoot, hear well and stand active service conditions.
B Not fit for general service, but fit for service at home (and abroad in the case of men passed fit for service overseas)	(i) In field units (at home only) and in Garrison units, or on duties of an analogous nature. (ii) In Labour units, or on garrison or regimental outdoor employment (iii) On sedentary work as clerks, storemen, batmen, cooks, orderlies, on sanitary duties etc or, if skilled tradesmen, at their trades.	Free from serious organic disease; and in addition if classified under: - B(i) Able to *march* at least 5 miles, see to shoot with glasses and hear well. - B(ii) Able to *walk* to and from work a distance not exceeding 5 miles, see and hear sufficiently for ordinary purposes. - B(iii) Only suitable for sedentary work or such duties as storemen, batmen, cooks, orderlies, sanitary duties etc. Also, if a skilled tradesman, fit to work at their trades.

Categories	Standards	Guidance
D Temporarily unfit for service in categories A or B, but likely to become fit within six months, and meanwhile either:	(i) In Command Depots (ii) In Regimental Depots (iii) In any unit under or awaiting medical or dental treatment (who on completion of treatment will rejoin their own original category).	
E Unfit for service in categories A or B and unlikely to become fit within six months.	Awaiting discharge, re-classification or invaliding home from abroad.	

On the transfer of military recruiting to the MNS in November 1917, the responsibility for the training and posting of all recruits was retained by the Army. The MNS, however, found that it needed a simpler grading system to enable the men it obtained to be sent to the appropriate part of the Army's recruit training organization. The MNS system was introduced on 17 November 1917:[6]

Grade I Fit for General Service

Grade IILikely to improve with training

Grade III Only fit for labouring duties or sedentary work

Grade IV Permanently and totally unfit for any form of military service

NB This grading system did not replace the Army's own medical classifications. Once within the Army's recruit training organization, men would be classified according to the categories laid down in ACI 1606 of October 1917: Alteration of Classification of Men by Categories.

6 Ministry of National Service *Ministry of National Service Instructions Issued During November and December 1917, Nos 1–47 (inclusive) of 1917* (London: HMSO, 1919) – Instruction No 13.

Appendix V – Military Service Acts 1916 – 1918

Military Service Act, 1916[1]

An Act to make provision with respect to Military Service in connection with the present war:

- Conscripts all male British subjects, who had been resident in Great Britain and aged 18 – 40 on 15 August 1915 and who were unmarried or childless widowers on 2 November 1915.
- Provisions for certificates of exemption
- Schedule 1: Exceptions
- Schedule 2: Constitution of Tribunals

Passed: 27 January 1916
Appointed date: 2 March 1916

Military Service Act (No 2) 1916[2]

An Act to make further provision with respect to Military Service during the present War.

- Conscripts every male British subject who had been resident in Great Britain since 14 August 1915 and aged 18 – 40 from the 'appointed date'.
- Prolongs expiring terms of service for the duration of the war.
- Modifies exceptions given in the previous Act.
- Provisions relating to certificates of exemption
- Authorises transfers of officers and men of the TF without their consent to another Corps and/or their posting to regular units of their own or the Corps to which they are transferred.

Passed: 25 May 1916
Appointed date: 24 June 1916

Military Service (Review of Exceptions) Act, 1917[3]

An Act to enable the exception from Military Service of Men excepted on the ground of previous rejection, or the previous relinquishment of, or discharge from, Naval or Military Service, or unsuitability for Foreign Service, to be reviewed.

1 *Public General Acts, 5&6 Geo 5* (London: Eyre and Spottiswoode, 1916) Chapter 104.
2 *Public General Acts, 6&7 Geo 5* (London: Eyre and Spottiswoode, 1916) Chapter 15.
3 *Public General Acts, 7&8 Geo 5* (London: Eyre and Spottiswoode, 1918) Chapter 12.

- Enabled the call up for examination of certain categories of men who had been excepted under the 1916 MSAs: TF soldiers not suited for foreign service; men previously discharged from the Services on grounds of disablement or ill-health; men previously rejected on any grounds.
- Did not apply to agricultural workers employed on work certified to be of national importance or to men disabled as a result of wounds received during the present war.

Passed: 5 April 1917

Military Service (Conventions with Allied States) Act, 1917[4]

An Act to enable His Majesty in Council to carry into effect conventions which may be made with Allied and other States as to the mutual liability of His Majesty's subjects and subjects of the Allied and other States to military service.

- Allows for conscription of British subjects living abroad and of Allied citizens in Britain.
- Convention signed with Russia (July) and with France (October).

Passed: 10 July 1917
Effective date: 30 days after the Order in Council applying the Act

Military Service Act, 1918[5]

An Act to repeal subsection (3) of section three of the Military Service Act 1916 and to provide for the cancellation of certificates of exemption from military service granted on occupational grounds.

- On the expiration of certificates of exemption, only two weeks now allowed before the man is deemed to have been enlisted.
- Enables Director General of National Service to order the withdrawal of occupational certificates of exemption at any time. Applies to any certificates of exemption granted on occupational grounds by tribunals or Government Departments. Effective from fourteen days after the order, providing neither House of Parliament has objected within that period.

Passed: 6 February 1918
Effective date: 16 February 1918

Military Service (No 2) Act, 1918[6]

An Act to make further provision with respect to Military Service during the present war.

- Extension of conscription to men aged 41 to 50.
- Allows for extension of the age limit to 55 by future Order in Council.
- Allows for extension of conscription to Ireland by future Order in Council.
- Enables provisions as to applications for certificates of exemption and to calling up.

4 Ibid., Chapter 26.
5 Ibid., Chapter 66.
6 *Public General Acts, 8&9 Geo 5* (London, Eyre and Spottiswoode, 1918), Chapter 5.

- Power by proclamation to withdraw certificates of exemption in case of national emergency.
- Penalty introduced for avoidance, or assisting the avoidance of, service: up to six months imprisonment, with or without hard labour.

Passed: 18 April 1918
Effective date: Immediately.

Appendix VI – Infantry Recruiting, Training and Reinforcement Units at Home and in France

<table>
<tr><th>Home</th><th>France</th></tr>
<tr><td colspan="2">1914</td></tr>
<tr><td>Infantry Reserve Battalions<ul><li>Special Reserve battalions formed in 1908 from the old Militia units.</li><li>Usually designated 3rd (Reserve) battalions of regiments with two Line battalions eg 3rd (Reserve) Cheshire.</li><li>Or 5th & 6th (Reserve) battalions in regiments with four Line battalions eg Worcestershire.</li></ul></td><td></td></tr>
<tr><td>Infantry Extra Reserve Battalions
Some regiments had an Extra Reserve battalion: eg 4th (Extra Reserve) North Staffordshire.</td><td></td></tr>
<tr><td>TF Second Line Infantry Reserve Battalions
Second line TF battalions formed late 1914 as reserve for the First Line eg 2/4th Cheshire – Sep 14; 2/1st Herefordshire – Sep 14</td><td></td></tr>
<tr><td></td><td>Infantry Base Depots
Formed on arrival in France in 1914; one per division eg 5 IBD served Fifth Division.</td></tr>
<tr><td colspan="2">1915</td></tr>
<tr><td>Infantry 2nd Reserve Battalions<ul><li>April 1915 – the 75 battalions of Fourth New Army converted into 2nd Reserve Bns.</li><li>Role: to keep Service Bns supplied with men</li><li>14th Cheshire and 9th KSLI became 2nd Reserve Bns in 11th Reserve Brigade at Prees Heath.</li></ul></td><td></td></tr>
<tr><td>Infantry Local Reserve Battalions
Mid-1915 the Depot companies of Locally Raised New Army battalions expanded to form 68 Local Reserve Battalions.</td><td></td></tr>
<tr><td>Reserve Brigades
2nd Reserve and Local Reserve Battalions organised in 24 Reserve Brigades.</td><td></td></tr>
</table>

Home	France
TF Third Line Infantry Reserve Battalions • Third line TF battalions formed 1915 • 3/4th Cheshire – March 1915; 3/1st Herefordshire – February 1915 • Once recruited were to provide the TF Reserve; Second line TF battalions now became Home Service battalions with a Home Defence role.	
Infantry Provisional Battalions (TF) Formed summer 1915, from personnel of Second and Third Line TF Battalions not available for overseas service and soldiers of low medical categories.	**Entrenching Battalions** • Formed in France in July 1915 as holding units for drafts en route from base areas to units at Front. • Made available to RE as sources of labour, which also enabled familiarisation with conditions nearer the front.
Home Service Garrison Battalions Formed for garrison duties in Britain from those unfit for foreign service eg 3rd (Home Service) Garrison Battalion Cheshire was formed in November 1915. Served in UK until it became 11th Royal Defence Corps in August 1917. See Note 1.	
Convalescent Camps Insufficient hospital beds in UK so large Convalescent Camps established late 1915: Epsom, Blackpool, Dartford and Eastbourne. Very successful in preventing bed blocking.	
Command Depots Late 1915, Command Depots created to rehabilitate soldiers who were too fit for the Convalescent Camps but not yet fit enough to return to their units.	
1916	
	Labour Battalions Infantry labour battalions created, containing men of Reserve Infantry units who were not fit for service at Front and had no specialist trade or professional qualifications. By June 1916, 12 Infantry Labour battalions were in France. See Note 2.
Garrison Reserve Battalions Formed to train and supply men for Garrison and Home Service Garrison Battalions. The 3rd (Reserve) Garrison RWF was formed at Wrexham in February 1916.	

<table>
<tr><th>Home</th><th>France</th></tr>
<tr><td>1 September 1916</td><td rowspan="3"></td></tr>
<tr><td>Reserve, Extra Reserve and TF Reserve Bns
• Maintained their role as regimental reserves;
• To be kept at full strength, receiving recruits until full.
• Drafts required for battalions overseas to continue to be provided from regimental reserves. Only if insufficient trained men available, then taken from Training Reserve.</td></tr>
<tr><td>1 September 1916 – Training Reserve
• New organisation formed to receive and train recruits and send drafts abroad to battalions that could not be supplied from regimental reserves.
• Training Reserve Battalions (TRB) formed from 2nd Reserve and Local Reserve battalions. Affiliated to parent Home Commands and Districts.
• Filled with men surplus to requirements of Regimental reserves in parent Home Commands.
• Regimental designations discarded; TRBs became numbered battalions of the Training Reserve, from 1st to 112th.
• The 24 Reserve Bdes became Training Reserve Brigades.
• TF Reserve Battalions - Formed from 3rd-line TF bns in September 1916</td></tr>
<tr><td></td><td>Permanent Base Battalion
Permanent Base Battalion formed at Étaples in November 1916 to administer men found by Infantry Base Depots to be medically unfit (PB men).</td></tr>
<tr><td colspan="2">1917</td></tr>
<tr><td></td><td>Labour Companies
Formed early 1917 by 'combing out' men from TRBs. Immediately sent to France to work on road and railway maintenance, some also on unloading railway wagons.</td></tr>
</table>

Home	France
May 1917 Training Reserve re-reorganised and battalions became more specialized in their training role. **Young Soldiers Battalions** 14 formed in May 1917 to train soldiers aged 18yrs 1mth in Med Cats A4, B1 and C1. **Graduated Battalions** 28 formed in May 1917 to provide specialist training for those under age of 19 who had completed their Infantry recruit training. • Linked in pairs to each Young Soldier Battalion	**Creation of Young Soldiers unit** Under-age boys and 'immatures' removed from battalions and placed in new unit at Étaples for education and training. NB. Moved to No 5 Convalescent Camp at Cayeux in January 1918.
Summer 1917: Training Reserve again re-organized. **Senior Training Reserve Battalions** Became responsible for training med cat B and C recruits aged over 18years 8 months. **Junior Training Reserve Battalions** Formed summer 1917 to take in surplus 18 year olds from Young Soldiers Battalions, as well as those under 18yrs 8 mths who were of med cats B2, B3, C2 and C3. **Young Soldiers Battalions** A further 9 Young Soldiers Battalions formed (now 23). **Graduated Battalions** A further 18 Graduated Battalions formed (now 46) and numbered 201st onwards. To be used for Home Defence so posted to the eight Home Service divisions replacing 2nd Line and Home Service Territorial battalions.	**Permanent Base Battalion** In September 1917 became an Employment Base Depot.
October 1917: **Graduated and Young Soldier Battalions** All allotted to 23 Infantry Regiments: Graduated Battalions numbered 51st and 52nd; Young Soldier Battalions numbered 53rd.	

Home	France
November 1917: Transfer of Military recruiting to MNS. New recruits passed to military for disposal by: **Reception Battalions** • Infantry depots which received the new recruits and posted them to appropriate training units. **Recruit Distribution Battalions** • Formed to receive and post medical category B2 and B3 recruits.	**Entrenching Battalions** Entrenching Battalions had ceased to exist in France by end 1917 as result of need to 'comb out' all available men for the front line.
1918	
Early 1918 Home Service Divisions reduced to 4 and, except for one brigade, all their battalions were now Graduated Battalions.	**Entrenching Battalions** New Entrenching Battalions formed in February 1918 from surplus manpower thrown up by reduction of Brigades to 3 battalions. • All disbanded by end Apr 1918 because of need for reinforcements.
	Garrison Guard Battalions Formed 1918 from fitter Labour Corps men for line-holding duties.
	Young Soldiers Battalions Three separate Young Soldier battalions formed in France for young men with under-developed physiques.

Note 1. **Overseas Garrison Battalions.** Formed from Medical Category B men in the New Armies to relieve TF battalions on garrison duties overseas. The 1st (Garrison) RWF was formed at Wrexham in July 1915. It went to Gibraltar in September 1915 where it remained. The 2nd (Garrison) RWF was formed at Garswood Park, near Wigan in October 1915 and left for Egypt on March 1916.
Note 2. **Other Labour units.** By mid-1916 there would also be in France: 11 Labour battalions RE (elderly navvies and tradesmen employed on defence works, roads, water supply etc); 30 Labour companies ASC for the disembarkation of stores and the formation of depots); 3 RN Labour companies and 8 non-combatant labour companies.

Appendix VII – Infantry Base Depots (IBD) in France

On arrival in France in 1914, the BEF's IBDs were set up one per division in accordance with Field Service Regulations Part II. As successive divisions arrived their IBDs were set up in turn.

By May 1916 it had proved impossible to continue reinforcing by battalions and several New Army battalions had already had to be amalgamated due to lack of numbers. On 12 May the DAG 3rd Echelon was instructed that in future reinforcements were to be provided by regiment.[1] This would have been difficult to implement with the existing divisional IBDs so in mid-June the IGC, Lt Gen Frank Clayton, informed the War Office of GHQ's decision had to re-organise the Base Depots and enclosed a proposed scheme for amalgamating them by regiments and districts. Under the new organisation the IBDs would include reinforcements for both Regular and TF battalions. The proposed date of the change was to be 1 July 1916 and the War Office was requested to direct reinforcements sent out after that date to the new depots.[2]

The new system was implemented by 1 July, and a revised list of all Base Depots was sent to the War Office on 31 July 1916.[3] The new locations of all Depots and their responsibilities were as follows:

IBD	Location	Remarks
1	Le Havre	King's Royal Rifle Corps
2	Rouen	Devonshire, Regiment, Duke of Cornwall's LI, South African Regt
3	Rouen	Hampshire Regiment, Dorset Regiment, Wiltshire Regiment and Somerset LI
4	Rouen	Cheshire Regt, KSLI, Monmouth Regiment
5	Rouen	Royal Welsh Fusiliers, South Wales Borderers
6	Rouen	Welsh Regiment, South Lancashire Regiment
7	Le Havre	London Regiment
8	Le Havre	London Regiment
9	Étaples	Lincolnshire Regiment, South Staffordshire Regiment

1 TNA: WO 95/25 AG GHQ War Diary Entry for 12 May 1916.
2 TNA: WO 95/3969 IGC letter AD 2074 dated 13 June 1916.
3 TNA: WO 95/3970 Inspector General of Communications (IGC) letter to the War Office dated 31st July 1916. NB It is not clear why the IBD Numbers do not run in order but all Infantry Regiments in the BEF are covered.

12	Étaples	(Moved to Calais November 1916.) Leicestershire Regiment, North Staffordshire Regiments
14	Étaples	Nottinghamshire & Derby Regiment
15	Étaples	Suffolk Regiment, Essex Regiment, Cambridge Regiment.
16	Étaples	Irish Regiments.
17	Étaples	Norfolk, Bedfordshire, Northamptonshire, Hertfordshire Regiments
18	Étaples	Royal Highlanders, Gordon Highlanders, Seaforth Highlanders
19	Étaples	Argyll & Sutherland Highlanders, Cameron Highlanders
20	Étaples	Royal Scots, Scottish Rifles, Royal Scots Fusiliers
21	Étaples	King's Own Scottish Borderers, Highland Light Infantry
23	Étaples	Royal Lancaster Regiment, Lancashire Fusiliers
24	Étaples	Liverpool Regiment
25	Étaples	Border Regiment, Loyal North Lancashire Regiment
29	Rouen	Royal Warwickshire Regiment, Newfoundland Regiment, ? Coys N.C.C., Army Cyclist Corps
30	Étaples	East Lancashire Regiment, Manchester Regiment
31	Étaples	Northumberland Fusiliers
32	Étaples	Northumberland Fusiliers (cont), King's Own Yorkshire Light Infantry
33	Étaples	West Yorkshire Regiment
34	Étaples	West Riding Regiment, York and Lancaster Regiment
35	Étaples	Durham Light Infantry
36	Le Havre	Royal Irish Rifles, Royal Inniskilling Fusiliers, Royal Irish Fusiliers
37	Étaples	Yorkshire Regiment, East Yorkshire Regiment
38	Étaples	Royal West Surrey Regiment, East Surrey Regiment, East Kent Regiment
39	Étaples	Royal Fusiliers
40	Étaples	Royal Sussex Regiment, Royal West Kent Regiment
41	Étaples	Middlesex Regiment
45	Rouen	Worcestershire Regiment, Royal Berkshire Regiment
47	Le Havre	Rifle Brigade
48	Le Havre	General Base Depot for 47th and 56th Divisions (TF)
49	Le Havre	General Base Depot for 49th and 60th Divisions (TF)
51	Étaples	General Base Depot for 50th and 51st Divisions (TF)

55	Rouen	Gloucestershire Regiment, Oxford & Buckinghamshire LI, Bucks Bns [sic]
Guards	Le Have	Grenadier Guards, Coldstream Guards, Scots Guards, Irish Guards, Welsh Guards
MGC	Étaples	Machine Gun Corps
No 1 Territorial	Rouen	General Base Depot for 61st and 48th Divisions and Reinforcements for TF RAMC Units with Regular Divisions.
No 2 Territorial	Rouen	General Base Depot for 55th and 46th Divisions, and Reinforcements for TF RE Field Companies and TF Army Troops Companies.
Australian	Étaples	All Australians
New Zealand	Étaples	All New Zealand Personnel
Canadian	Le Havre	Canadian Base Depot
Royal Naval Division	Étaples	Royal Naval Division
Royal Marine Arty	Étaples	
RGA	Le Havre	RGA Base Depot
RHA&RFA	Le Have	RHA and RFA Base Depot
Horse Tpt	Le Havre	Regular and TF Horse Transport and Supply Personnel
RFC	St Omer	Royal Flying Corps
Signals	Abbeville	All Signal personnel
Mech Tpt	Rouen	Base Mechanical Transport Details
Pay	Rouen	Army Pay Corps
4 Gen BD	Rouen	No 4 General Base Depot for all Royal Engineers incl RE SR units
5 Gen BD	Rouen	No 5 General Base Depot for Cavalry, RAMC, Mounted and Foot Police, Yeomanry TF

In early 1918 the IBDs were re-organised again. They were reduced in number and lettered A to M. No trace has been found of which was which but there is some evidence indicating that they were linked to Commands: the Marcher battalion reinforcements of later in 1918 had generally passed through C IBD which could indicate a link to Western Command whilst D IBD sent forward drafts from Southern Command units. All Irish reinforcements passed through L BD whilst the Scots went through M BD, both of which were at Calais.

Appendix VIII – Changes to Military Recruiting under Ministry of National Service.

The new Recruiting organisation which came into being on 1 November 1917 was formalised by the following:

Instruction No 2 of 1917 dated 15 November 1917: *Constitution and Organisation of Regions, Regional Headquarters and Recruiting Areas, and Transfer of Recruiting to Civil Control under the Minister of National Service.*[1]

New Regional HQs were established to take over administration of respective regions wef 'midnight 31 October 1917'.

Organization of Regional HQs:

- Director of Recruiting: 'the principal representative of the Ministry of National Service in the Region so far as concerns all matters relating to the raising of men for the Armed Forces'.
- Deputy Director of Recruiting – assisted by Heads of Sections:
    - Official to deal with executive work of Recruiting machinery
    - Official to act as Legal Adviser
- Commissioner of Medical Services – assisted where necessary by Deputy Commissioner.
    - Deputy Controller of Registration – plus Assistant Controller where necessary.

New Regional HQs:[2]

Region	Location of Regional HQ
London	War Office (temp) then Newington Causeway
East Anglia	Paddington (82 Westbourne Terrace)
South Eastern	Paddington (84 Westbourne Terrace)
South Western	Bristol
Yorkshire & East Midlands	Nottingham
West Midlands	Queen's College, Birmingham
North Western	Liverpool University
Northern	Newcastle on Tyne
Scotland	Edinburgh
Wales	Cardiff

1 Ministry of National Service *Ministry of National Service Instructions Issued During November and December 1917, Nos 1-47 (inclusive) of 1917* (London: HMSO, 1919).

2 Ibid., Appendix 1 to Instruction No 2.

Overnight, the former Area Commanders of the Military Recruiting Areas became Assistant Directors of Recruiting, directly responsible to their regional Director of Recruiting for the efficient working and organisation of their Areas.

The new Regions covering Western Command Regiments were as follows:

Regimental Area	Recruiting Areas	Area HQ
North Western		
8th (Liverpool Regt.)	Liverpool	Seaforth
8th (Liverpool Regt.)	Isle of Man	Seaforth
22nd (Cheshire)	Cheshire	Chester
47th (Loyal North Lancashire Regt.)	N Lancashire (Preston)	Preston
47th (Loyal North Lancashire Regt)	Lancashire (Bolton)	Preston
20th (Lancashire Fusililiers)	Lancashire (Bury)	Bury
4th (Royal Lancashire Regt.)	Lancashire (Lancaster)	Lancaster
40th (South Lancashire Regt.)	South Lancashire (Warrington)	Warrington
30th (East Lancashire Regt.)	East Lancashire (Blackburn)	Preston
63rd (Manchester Regt.)	Lancashire (Ashton–u–Lyne)	Ashton-u-Lyne
West Midlands		
53rd (KSLI)	Shropshire	Shrewsbury
53rd (KSLI)	Herefordshire	Shrewsbury
Wales		
23rd (RWF)	Carnarvonshire	Wrexham
41st (Welsh Regt.)	Glamorganshire	Cardiff
41st (Welsh Regt.)	Carmarthenshire	Cardiff
24th (SWB)	Brecknockshire	Brecon
24th (SWB)	Monmouthshire	Brecon

The overall outcome was that No 4 District had been split three ways with the Cheshire and South Lancashire Regiments now coming under the North Western Region, the KSLI moving into West Midlands Region, and the Welsh regiments, almost certainly for political reasons, forming a region of their own.

Recruiting and Posting Arrangements – wef 1 November 1917.

- Men called up, and those enlisting voluntarily before being called up, continued to report to the local recruiting office for a primary Military Examination.

- Those not immediately rejected as unfit for any form of Military Service were attested and then sent to the National Service Area Headquarters for disposal according to the orders of the Assistant Director of Recruiting (the former Area Commander).
- Those found fit enough for General Service (MNS Grades I and II) would be sent to a 'Reception Depot'. This was a local Infantry Depot which took over recruits from the Area Headquarters and posted them to the appropriate training unit:
  - Regimental Infantry Reserves. (NB. These now included the Young Soldier and Graduated Battalions of the regiments.)
  - Training Reserve.
  - The Foot Guards, and arms other Infantry (eg RFA) entitled to receive them under the monthly posting ACI.
- Those placed in MNS Grade III (ie military categories B(ii) and B(iii)) would be sent to Recruit Distribution Battalions in the Training Reserve. There was one such battalion in each Command and their roles were to:
  - Post these men to appropriate units or employments (eg ASC).
  - Put through a course of physical training any who might be likely to attain B(i) classification within three months and then post them according to the result of the course.
- The War Office would continue to issue the monthly Posting ACIs which informed the Regions of the total numbers of men required each month, the number required to be provided by each Region and how they should be posted. For example, in January 1918, in addition to the Infantry, men were to be allocated as follows: 29,905 A(ii) and A(iv) men for other corps, including 15,615 for the RFA and RHA and 12,440 for the RGA; 3,600 B(i) men for the RFC; and 8840 B(ii), which included 6220 for the ASC.[3]

NB. It remained possible to volunteer. ACI 1731 of 28 November 1917 stated that: 'The term 'Voluntary Enlistment' applies to the enlistment of Group or Class men (whether they are or are not for the time being in possession of a valid form of exemption or protection) who present themselves for service before they are sent a calling up notice, or in the case of munition workers, before their names have been listed on MM82T'. In such cases, a note to the effect that the man was a volunteer was to be attached to his documents. 'Voluntary' and 'Direct' (men not liable under the MSAs) could be a) unconditional as regards posting or b) conditional on the man being posted to the corps of his choice. If he was not accepted for the corps of his choice and declined to serve in any other he would be allowed to return to civilian life.[4]

3 TNA: WO 293/7 ACI 1863 of 23 December 1917: Arrangements for posting to the Army men accepted for service during the month of January 1918.
4 Ibid., ACI 1731 of 28 November 1917: Arrangements for posting to the Army men accepted for service during the month of December 1917.

Appendix IX – Re-organizations/Movements and Arrivals of Marcher Battalions on the Western Front during 1918[1]

Regiment/ Battalions	1 January 1918 (Note 1)	Occurrences During 1918		11 November 1918
		February 1918	Rest of 1918	
Cheshire				
1st	Italy: 15th Bde in 5th Div	Italy: 15th Bde in 5th Div	April: returned to France	15th Bde in 5th Div; France
1/4th (TF)	Egypt:53rd Div	Egypt: 53rd Div	From Egypt: 1 July to 102nd Bde in 34th Div	102nd Bde in 34th Div; Belgium
1/5th (TF)	56th Div; Pioneer	56th Div; Pioneer	56th Div; Pioneer	56th Div; Belgium,
1/6th (TF)	118th Bde in 39th Div	6 Feb: absorbed 5 officers + 100 men from 16th Cheshire;	28 May to 75th Bde in 25th Div; 17 June absorbed 16 officers & 492 men from 11th Cheshire; 8 July to 21st Bde in 30th Div	21st Bde in 30th Div; Belgium
1/7th (TF)	Egypt:53rd Div	Egypt:53rd Div	From Egypt; 1 July to 102nd Bde in 34th Div	102nd Bde in 34th Div; Belgium
9th (Service)	58th Bde in 19th Div	Feb: moved to reconstituted 56th Bde	June absorbed personnel from 10th Cheshire	56th Bde in 19th Div; France

1 Brigadier E.A. James. *British Regiments 1914–18* (Uckfield: Naval & Military Press, 1998).

Regiment/ Battalions	1 January 1918 (Note 1)	Occurrences During 1918		11 November 1918
		February 1918	Rest of 1918	
10th (Service)	7th Bde in 25th Div	Feb: absorbed personnel from 13th Cheshire;	21 Jun reduced to cadre; spare personnel to 9th Cheshire. End June to England with 25th Div; July absorbed by 15th SWB.	
11th (Service)	7th Bde in 25th Div	Feb: absorbed personnel from 13th Cheshire;	17 Jun reduced to cadre; personnel to 1/6th Cheshire; 3 Aug **disbanded** in France	
13th (Service)	74th Bde in 25th Div	16 Feb: – **disbanded** in France; personnel to 10th & 11th Cheshire		
15th (Service)	105th Bde in 35th Div	6 Feb: absorbed 15 officers + 310 men of 16th Cheshire		105th Bde in 35th Div; Belgium
16th (Service)	105th Bde in 35th Div	6 Feb: **disbanded**; 5 officers + 100 men to 1/6th Cheshire; 15 officers + 310 men to 15th Cheshire; rest to II Corps Reinforcement Camp – later to 12th Entrenching Battalion		
23rd (TF)	At Home: in 224th Bde	At Home: in 224th Bde; > Garrison Guard Bn late Apr 18	May to France: 178th Bde/59th Div; June joined 121st Bde/40th Div	121st Bde in 40th Div; France

Regiment/ Battalions	1 January 1918 (Note 1)	Occurrences During 1918		11 November 1918
		February 1918	Rest of 1918	
RWF				
1st	Italy: 22nd Bde in 7th Div	Italy: 22nd Bde in 7th Div	Italy: 22nd Bde in 7th Div	22nd Bde in 7th Div; Italy
2nd	19th Bde in 33rd Div	6 Feb: to 115th Bde in 38th (Welsh) Div	115th Bde in 38th (Welsh) Div	115th Bde in 38th (Welsh) Div; France
1/4th (TF)	47th Div; Pioneer	47th Div; Pioneer	47th Div; Pioneer	47th Div; Pioneer; Belgium
9th (Service)	58th Bde in 19th Div	Feb: absorbed 5 officers + 147 men < 10th RWF	58th Bde in 19th Div	58th Bde in 19th Div; France
10th (Service)	76th Bde in 3rd Div	8 Feb: **disbanded**; 5 officers + 147 men to 9th RWF; others to 8th Entrenching Battalion		
13th (Service) (1st North Wales)	113th Bde in 38th (Welsh) Div	113th Bde in 38th (Welsh) Div	113th Bde in 38th (Welsh) Div	113th Bde in 38th (Welsh) Div; France
14th (Service)	113th Bde in 38th (Welsh) Div	113th Bde in 38th (Welsh) Div	113th Bde in 38th (Welsh) Div	113th Bde in 38th (Welsh) Div;
15th (Service) (1st London Welsh)	113th Bde in 38th (Welsh) Div	Feb: **disbanded**; men distributed among other battalions in 38th Division		
16th (Service)	113th Bde in 38th (Welsh) Div	113th Bde in 38th (Welsh) Div	113th Bde in 38th (Welsh) Div	113th Bde in 38th (Welsh) Div; France
17th (Service) (2nd North Wales)	115th Bde in 38th (Welsh) Div	115th Bde in 38th (Welsh) Div	115th Bde in 38th (Welsh) Div	115th Bde in 38th (Welsh) Div; France
19th (Service)	110th Bde in 40th Div	6 Feb: **disbanded**; men to 8th Entrenching Bn		

Regiment/ Battalions	1 January 1918 (Note 1)	Occurrences During 1918		11 November 1918
		February 1918	Rest of 1918	
24th (Denbighshire Yeomanry) (TF)	Egypt: 231st Bde in 74th Div	Egypt: 231st Bde in 74th Div	May: to France; 21 June joined 94th Bde in 31st Div	94th Bde in 31st Div; France
25th (Montgomery & Welsh Horse Yeomanry) (TF)	Egypt: 231st Bde in 74th Div	Egypt: 231st Bde in 74th Div	May: to France;	231st Bde in 74th Div; Belgium
26th (Service)	4th Garrison Guard Battalion	4th Garrison Guard Battalion	May: to 176th Bde in 59th Div; July became 26th RWF	176th Bde in 59th Div; Belgium
SWB				
1st	3rd Bde in 1st Div	Feb: 100 men from 12th SWB	3rd Bde in 1st Div	3rd Bde in 1st Div; France
2nd	87th Bde in 29th Div	Feb: 100 men from 12th SWB	87th Bde in 29th Div	87th Bde in 29th Div; Belgium
5th (Service)	19th Div; Pioneer	Feb: 50 men from 12th SWB	19th Div; Pioneer	19th Div; Pioneer; France
6th (Service)	25th Div; Pioneer	25th Div; Pioneer	2 July: to 30th Div as Pioneers	30th Div; Pioneer; Belgium
10th (Service) (1st Gwent)	115th Bde in 38th Div	115th Bde in 38th Div	115th Bde in 38th Div	115th Bde in 38th Div; France
11th (Service) (2nd Gwent)	115th Bde in 38th Div	Feb: **disbanded**; men reinforced battalions in 38th Div		
12th (Service) (3rd Gwent)	119th Bde in 40th Div	10 Feb: **disbanded**; 50 men to 5th SWB; 100 men each to 1st & 2nd SWB; rest to 9th Entrenching Bn		

Regiment/ Battalions	1 January 1918 (Note 1)	Occurrences During 1918		11 November 1918
		February 1918	Rest of 1918	
KSLI				
1st	16th Bde in 6th Div	Feb: received men from 5th KSLI	16th Bde in 6th Div	16th Bde in 6th Div; France
1/4th (TF)	190th Bde in 63rd Div	4 Feb: to 56th Bde in 19th Div; gained men from 5th KSLI	56th Bde in 19th Div	56th Bde in 19th Div; France
5th (Service)	42nd Bde in 14th Div	4 Feb: **disbanded**; personnel to 1st, 1/4th, 6th and 7th KSLI		
6th (Service)	60th Bde in 20th Div	Feb: received men from 5th KSLI	60th Bde in 20th Div	60th Bde in 20th Div; France
7th (Service)	8th Bde in 3rd Div	Feb: received men from 5th KSLI	8th Bde in 3rd Div	8th Bde in 3rd Div; France
10th (Shropshire & Cheshire Yeomanry)	Egypt: 231st Bde in 74th Div	Egypt: 231st Bde in 74th Div	May: to France;	231st Bde in 74th Div; Belgium
Monmouthshire				
1/1st (TF)	46th Div: Pioneer	46th Div: Pioneer	46th Div: Pioneer	46th Div: Pioneer; France
1/2nd (TF)	29th Div: Pioneer	29th Div: Pioneer	29th Div: Pioneer	29th Div: Pioneer; Belgium
Herefordshire				
1/1st (TF)	Egypt: 53rd Div	Egypt: 53rd Div	From Egypt; 30 June to 102nd Bde in 34th Div	102nd Bde in 34th Div; Belgium

Note 1. Battalions shown are in France and Flanders unless otherwise stated.

Bibliography

I UNPUBLISHED SOURCES

I.1 The National Archives of the United Kingdom: Public Record Office, Kew

Cabinet papers:

CAB 23: Minutes of War Cabinet
CAB 37: Copies of Cabinet papers
CAB 42: War Council and successors: copies of Minutes and Papers

War Office papers, including

WO 32: General
WO 33: War Office: Reports, Memoranda and Papers
WO 70/50: Summary of Principal Changes in Organisation and Administration of TF since Mobilization
WO 95: War Diaries
WO 106 DMO papers
WO 107 Minutes of meetings of QMG Department
WO 123 Army Circulars, Memoranda, Orders and Regulations
WO 158 War Office: Military Headquarters: Correspondence and Papers, First World War
WO 159 Material on Recruiting
WO 162 Commander-in-Chief and War Office: Adjutant General's Department papers
WO 163 Minutes of Meetings of Military Members of the Army Council
WO 293 War Office: Army Council Instructions

I.2 Imperial War Museum, London

General Sir Ivor Maxse Papers
Army Pay Souvenir

I.3 King's College London, Liddell Hart Collection

Field Marshal Sir William Robertson Papers

I.4 Cheshire Regimental Museum

Cheshire Regiment War Diaries
- 1st Cheshire
- 1/6th Cheshire
- 9th Cheshire

I.5 Joint Services Command & Staff College Library

Report of the Committee on the Lessons of the Great War (London: War Office, 1932)

I.6 Shropshire County Records and Archives

Minutes of Territorial and Auxiliary Forces Association of Shropshire (Ref. 1988/1-87)

II PUBLISHED SOURCES

II. 1 Official Publications

British Parliamentary Debates (Hansard)

Ministry of National Service, *Ministry of National Service Instructions Issued during November and December 1917, Nos 1-47 (inclusive) of 1917* (London: HMSO, 1919)

Public General Statutes 1914-16 (London: Eyre & Spottiswoode, 1916)
Public General Statutes 1916 (London: Eyre & Spottiswoode, 1916)
Public General Statutes 1917-18 (London: Eyre & Spottiswoode, 1918)
Public General Statutes 1918-19 (London: Eyre & Spottiswoode, 1919)

Soldiers Died in the Great War 1914-19 (London: War Office, 1921; N&MP CD Rom 2011)

War Office Training Publications:
- SS 109 Training of Divisions for Offensive Action (May 1916)
- SS 135 Instructions for the Training of Divisions for Offensive Action (December 1916. Reprinted with Amendments August 1917)
- SS 135 The Training and Employment of Divisions, 1918 (January 1918)
- SS 143 The Training and Employment of Platoons, 1918
- SS 158 Notes on Recent Operations on the Front of First, Third, Fourth and Fifth Armies (May 1917)

King's Regulations for the Army 1912 reprinted with Amendments 1914 (London: HMSO, 1914)

Manual of Military Law 1914

Regulations for Mobilization 1914 (London: HMSO, 1914)

Sequence of Musketry Training (London: General Staff, 1915 reprinted with amendments 1917; N&MP reprint)

Statistics of the Military Effort of the British Empire during the Great War 1914 – 1920 (London: The War Office, 1922; reprinted by The Naval & Military Press, 1999)

Welsh Army Corps 1914-1919: Report of the Executive Committee (Cardiff: Western Mail Ltd., 1921)

II. 2 Contemporary Newspaper, Journals etc

Chester Chronicle
Chester Courant
Chester Observer
Leominster News 1916
Macclesfield Courier and Herald
Shrewsbury Journal
Whitchurch Herald
Wellington News
Regimental Journals
The Oak Tree

II. 3 Diaries, Memoirs etc

Asquith, H. *Memories and Reflections Vol. 2* (Boston: Little, Brown, 1928)

Beauchamp, P. *Fanny Goes to War* (London, John Murray, 1919; reprinted by the Diggory Press, 2005)
Blake, R. (ed.) *The Private Papers of Douglas Haig, 1914 – 1919* (London: Eyre & Spottiswoode, 1952)
Blunden, E. *Undertones of War* (1928; London: Penguin Classics, 2000)
Bond, B. & Robbins, S. (eds.) *Staff Officer. The Diaries of Walter Guinness (First Lord Moyne) 1914-18* (London: Leo Cooper, 1987)
Bourne, J.M. & Bushaway, Bob (eds.) *Joffrey's War* (Nottingham: Salient Books, 2011)

Callwell, Major-General Sir C.E. *Field Marshal Sir Henry Wilson, His Life and Diaries* (London: Cassell, 1927)
Carrington, C. *Soldier From the Wars Returning* (Barnsley: Pen & Sword Military Classics reprint, 2006)
Charteris, J. *At GHQ* (London: Cassell, 1931)
Childs, Major-General Sir W. *Episodes and Reflections* (London: Cassell, 1930)

Coppard, G. *With a Machine Gun to Cambrai* (London: Cassell, 2003)
Cooksey, J. & Griffiths, D. (eds.) *Harry's War, The Great War Diaries of Harry Drinkwater* (London: Ebury Press, 2013)
Crozier, Brigadier-General F.P. *A Brass Hat in No Man's Land* (Oxford: Cape, 1930)

Dunn, Captain J. C. *The War the Infantry Knew, 1914-1919: A Chronicle of Service in France and Belgium* (London: King, 1938; Abacus reprint 1997)

Fay, Sir Sam *The War Office at War* (Wakefield: EP Publishing, 1973)
Feilding, R. *War Letters to a Wife* (London: Medici Society, 1929; Staplehurst: Spellmount, 2001)
Fussell, P. *The Ordeal of Alfred M Hale: The Memoirs of a Soldier Servant* (London: Leo Cooper, 1975)

Gordon, H. *The Unreturning Army* (London: Doubleday, 2013)
'G.S.O.' (Sir Frank Fox) *G.H.Q (Montreuil-Sur-Mer)* (London: Allan, 1920)
Gwynne-Vaughan, Dame H. *Service with the Army* (London: Hutchinson, 1942?)

Hankey, Lord *The Supreme Command 1914 – 1918* (London: Allen & Unwin, 1961)
Hanson, J.I. & Wakefield, A. *Plough and Scatter* (Yeovil: Haynes, 2009)
Hodges, F.J. *Men of 18 in 1918* (Ilfracombe: Stockwell Ltd, 1988)

Livermore, B. *Long 'Un – A Damn Bad Soldier* (Batley: Hayes, 1974)

Macready, General Sir Nevil *Annals of an Active Life, Vol. 1* (London: Hutchinson, n.d.)
Manning, F. *Her Privates We* (London: Serpent's Tail, 1999, re-issue of original unexpurgated version first published in 1930)
Maurice, N. (ed.) *The Maurice Case* (London: Leo Cooper, 1972)
Mellersh, H.E.L. *Schoolboy into War* (London: Kimber, 1978)

Nicholson, Col W. N. *Behind the Lines* (London: Jonathan Cape, 1939; reprinted Strong Oak Press)

Priddey, D. (ed.) *A Tommy at Ypres – Walter's War* (Stroud: Amberley, 2011)

Richards, F. *Old Soldiers Never Die* (1933; Dallington: Naval & Military Press, 2003)
Robertson, Sir W. *From Private to Field-Marshal* (Boston & New York: Houghton Mifflin Company, 1921)

St Clair, W. *The Road to St Julien* (Barnsley: Leo Cooper, 2004)
Sheffield, G. & Bourne, J. (eds.) *Douglas Haig, War Diaries and Letters 1914 – 1918* (London: Weidenfeld & Nicholson, 2005)

Taylor, F.A.J. *The Bottom of the Barrel* (London: Regency Press, 1978)

Terraine, J. *General Jack's Diary 1914 – 18, The Trench Diary of Brigadier-General J.L. Jack DSO* (London: Cassell, 1964; Re-issued 2000)

Voigt, F.A. *Combed Out* (London: Swarthmore Press, 1920)

II. 4 Official Histories

Becke, Major A.F. *History of the Great War: Order of Battle of Divisions Parts 1-4* (London: HMSO, 1935-45; N&MP reprint)

Edmonds, Sir J.E. (ed.) *Official History of the Great War: Military Operations France & Belgium* (London: Macmillan and HMSO, 14 vols. 1922-48)

Macpherson, Sir W.G. *Medical Services General History Vol. 3* (Uckfield: N&MP reprint, n.d.)

II. 5 Formation Histories

Hussey, A.H. & Inman, D.S. *The Fifth Division in the Great War* (London: Nisbet, 1921)

Kincaid-Smith, M. *The 25th Division in France and Flanders* (1918; Dallington: Naval & Military Press, 2001)

Munby, Lieutenant-Colonel J.E. *A History of the 38th (Welsh) Division* (London: Rees, 1920)

Ward, C.H. Dudley *History of the 53rd (Welsh) Division (TF) 1914 – 1918* (Cardiff: Western Mail Limited, 1927)

Whitton, Lt Col F.E. *History of the 40th Division* (Aldershot: Gale & Polden, 1926; Dallington: Naval & Military Press, 2004)

Wyrall, E. *The Nineteenth Division* (London: Arnold, 1932; Dallington: Naval & Military Press, 1999)

II. 6 Regimental Histories

Atkinson, C.T. *The History of the South Wales Borderers, 1914-1918* (London: Medici Society, 1931)

Crookenden, A. *The History of the Cheshire Regiment in the Great War* (Chester: Evans, n.d.)

Wood, Major W. de B. *The History of the King's Shropshire Light Infantry in the Great War 1914 – 1918* (London: The Medici Society, 1925; Dallington: Naval & Military Press, 2003)

Ward, C.H. Dudley *Regimental Records of the Royal Welch Fusiliers (23rd Regiment) (Vol. III) 1914-1918* (London: Forster Groom, 1921)

Wylly, Colonel H.C. *The Border Regiment in the Great War* (Aldershot, Gale & Polden, 1924)

I. 7 Unit Histories

Burgoyne A.J. *The 6th Battalion King's Shropshire Light Infantry 1914-19* (Ludlow, Burgoyne, 2000)

Burton, F. N. *The War Diary, 1914-1918, of the 10th Service Bn. Royal Welch Fusiliers* (Plymouth: Brendon, 1926)

Chalmers, T. *The History of the 16th Battalion The Highland Light Infantry (City of Glasgow Regiment* (Glasgow, McCallum, 1930; Dallington: Naval & Military Press, 2003)

Churton, Lt Col W.A.V. *The War Record of the 1/5th (Earl of Chester's) Battalion, The Cheshire Regiment, August 1914 - June 1919* (Chester: Phillipson & Golder, 1920)

Dixon, J. & Dixon, J. *With Rifle and Pick (1/3rd Battalion The Monmouthshire Regiment)* (Cardiff: Cwm Press, 1991)

Dixon, J. *Out Since '14. A History of the 1/2nd Battalion The Monmouthshire Regiment 1914-1919* (Abertillery: Old Bake House Press, 2000)

Langley, D. *Duty Done. 2nd Battalion Royal Welch Fusiliers in the Great War* (London: Chameleon Press, 2001)

Riddell, E. & Clayton, M.C. *The Cambridgeshires 1914-1919* (Cambridge: Bowes & Bowes, 1934; Dallington: Naval & Military Press, 2004)

Smith, C. *War History of the 6th Battalion, The Cheshire Regiment (TF)* (Chester: 6th Cheshire Old Comrades Association, 1932)

II. 8 Local Histories

Longbottom. F.W. *Chester in the Great War* (Chester: Phillipson & Golder, n.d.)

Sargeaunt, B.E. *The Isle of Man and the Great War* (Douglas: Brown & Sons Ltd, nd)

II. 9 General Works

Baker, C. *The Battle for Flanders* (Barnsley: Pen & Sword, 2011)

Beckett, I.F.W. & Gooch, J. (eds.) *Politicians and Defence, Studies in the Formulation of British Defence Policy* (Manchester: Manchester University Press, 1981)

Beckett, I.F.W. *The Amateur Military Tradition 1558 – 1945* (Manchester: Manchester University Press, 1991)

Beckett, I.F.W. *The Great War 1914 –18* (Harlow: Pearson, 2001)

Beckett, I.F.W. *The First World War, The Essential Guide to Sources in the UK National Archives* (Kew: Public Record Office, 2002)

Beckett I.F.W. & Simpson K. (eds.) *A Nation in Arms: a Social Study of the British Army in the First World War* (Manchester: Manchester University Press, 1985)

Bet-El, I.R. *Conscripts, Forgotten Men of the Great War* (Stroud: Sutton, 1999)

Bidwell, S. *The Women's Royal Army Corps* (Barnsley: Pen & Sword, 1977)
Boff, J. *Winning and Losing on the Western Front* (Cambridge: Cambridge University Press, 2014)
Bond, B. (ed.) *The First World War and British Military History* (Oxford: Clarendon Press, 1991)
Bond, B. (ed.) *Look To Your Front* (Staplehurst: Spellmount Ltd, 1999)
Bourne, J.M. *Britain and the Great War 1914 – 1918* (London: Arnold, 1989)
Bourne, J.M. *Who's Who in World War One,* (London: Routledge, 2001) (Taylor & Francis e-Library, 2002 – Kindle Edition)

Clayton, D *Decisive Victory, The Battle of the Sambre, 4 November 1918* (Warwick: Helion & Co Ltd, 2018)
Corrigan, G. *Mud, Blood and Poppycock* (London: Cassell, 2003)
Cowper, Colonel J.M. *A Short History of Queen Mary's Army Auxiliary Corps* (Guildford: WRAC Association, 1967)

Dallas, G. & Gill. D. *The Unknown Army: Mutinies in the British Army In World War 1* (London: Versoo, 1985)

Ekins, A. (ed.) *1918: Year of Victory* (Auckland: Exisle Publishing, 2010)

French, D. *Military Identities: The Regimental System, the British Army, and the British People, c 1870 – 2000* (Oxford: Oxford University Press, 2005)
French, D. & Holden Reid, B. (eds.) *The British General Staff* (London, Cass, 2002)

Gooch, J. *The Plans of War* (London, Routledge & Kegan Paul, 1974)
Gregory, A. *The Last Great War* (Cambridge: Cambridge University Press, 2008)
Grieves, K. *The Politics of Manpower, 1914-18* (Manchester: Manchester University Press, 1988)
Griffith, P. (ed.) *British Fighting Methods in the Great War* (London: Cass, 1996)
Griffith, P. (ed.) *Battle Tactics of the Western Front* (New Haven & London, Yale University Press, 1994)

Hart, P. *1918: A Very British Victory* (London: Weidenfeld & Nicholson, 2008)
Hawtin, W. Grist *The Law and Practice of Military Conscription under the Military Service Acts* (London: Harrison & Sons, 1917)
Hodgkinson, P. *The Battle of the Selle* (Solihull: Helion & Co Ltd, 2018)
Holmes, R. *Tommy* (London: Harper Collins, 2004)

James, E.A. *British Regiments 1914 – 1918* (5th edn. Dallington: Naval & Military Press, 1998)

King, A. *The Combat Soldier, Infantry Tactics and Cohesion in the Twentieth and Twenty-First Centuries* (Oxford: Oxford University Press, 2013)

Liddle, P. (ed.) *Passchendaele in Perspective* (Barnsley: Pen & Sword, 1997)
LoCicero, M *A Moonlight Massacre, The Night Operation on the Passchendaele Ridge, 2 December 1917* (Solihull: Helion & Co Ltd, 2014)

Lynch, T. *They Did Not Grow Old, Teenage Conscripts on the Western Front, 1918* (Stroud: Spellmount, 2013)

McCartney, H.B. *Citizen Soldiers* (Cambridge: Cambridge University Press, 2005)
McDermott, J. *British Military Service Tribunals 1916-1918* (Manchester: Manchester University Press, 2011)
Mansfield, N. *English Farmworkers and Local Patriotism 1900 – 1930* (Aldershot: Ashgate, 2001)
Mansfield, N. & Horner, C. *The Great War: Localities and Regional Identities* (Newcastle upon Tyne: Cambridge Scholars Publishing, 2014)
Messenger, C. *Call To Arms, The British Army 1914-18* (London: Cassell, Paperback Edition 2005)
Mitchinson, K.W. *Pioneer Battalions in the Great War* (London: Leo Cooper, 1997)
Mitchinson, K.W. *Defending Albion* (Basingstoke: Palgrave Macmillan, 2005)

Oram, G. *Death Sentences passed by military courts of the British Army 1914-1924)*, (London: Francis Boutle Publishers, revised 2005)

Philpott, W. *Bloody Victory: The Sacrifice on the Somme and the Making of the Twentieth Century* (London: Little, Brown, 2009)
Prior, R. & Wilson, T. *Command on the Western Front* (Barnsley: Pen & Sword reprint, 2004)
Prior, R. & Wilson, T. *The Somme* (New Haven & London: Yale University Press, 2005)
Prior, S. & Wilson, T. *Passchendaele, The Untold Story* (New Haven & London: Yale University Press, 2002)
Putkowski, J. *British Army Mutineers 1914 – 1922* (London: Boutle, 1998)

Robbins, S. *British Generalship on the Western Front 1914 – 18* (London: Frank Cass, 2005)

Sheffield, G. *Leadership in the Trenches. Officer-man Relations, Morale and Discipline in the Army in the Era of the First World War* (Basingstoke: MacMillan, 2000)
Sheffield, G. *Forgotten Victory* (London: Review, 2002)
Sheffield, G. & Todman, D. (eds.) *Command and Control on the Western Front* (Staplehurst: Spellmount, 2004)
Sheffield, G. *The Somme* (London: Cassell, 2003)
Simkins, P. *Kitchener's Army, The Raising of the New Armies, 1914 – 16* (Manchester: Manchester University Press, 1988)
Simkins, P. *From The Somme To Victory* (Barnsley: Praetorian Press, 2014)
Simpson, A. *Directing Operations: Corps Command on the Western Front 1914 – 18* (Stroud: Spellmount, 2006)
Spencer, W. *Army Service Records in the First World War* (Kew: Public Record Office, 2001)
Stevenson, D. *With our backs to the Wall* (Cambridge, Massachusetts: Harvard University Press: Paperback edition, 2013)
Strachan, H. *The Politics of the British Army* (Oxford: Oxford University Press, 1997)
Strachan, H. (ed.) *The British Army, Manpower and Society into the Twenty-First Century* (London: Cass, 2000)

Supple, B. *The History of the British Coal Industry Vol. 4: 1913-46 The Political Economy of Decline* (Oxford: Oxford University Press, 2004)

Turner, J. *British Politics and the Great War* (New Haven & London: Yale University press, 1992)
Todman, D. *The Great War, Myth and Memory* (London: Hambledon & London, 2005)

Weston, P. *Redan Ridge: The Last Stand* (Leominster: Orphans Press, 2005)
Westlake, R. *Kitchener's Army* (Staplehurst: Spellmount, 2003)
Whitehouse, C.J. & G.P. *A Town for Four Winters* (Brocton: Whitehouse, 1996)
Woodward, D.R. *Lloyd George and the Generals* (London: Associated University Presses Ltd, 1983)

II. 10 Biographies

Baynes, J. *Far From a Donkey: The Life of General Sir Ivor Maxse* (London: Brassey's, 1995)

Cassar, G. *Kitchener: Architect of Victory* (London: Kimber, 1977)

Sheffield, G. *The Chief, Douglas Haig and the British Army* (London: Aurum Press, 2011)
Spiers, E.M. *Haldane: an Army Reformer* (Edinburgh: Edinburgh University Press, 1980)

II. 11 Articles

Beckett, I.F.W. 'The Real Unknown Army: British Conscripts 1916 – 1919', *The Great War*, 2 (1) (November 1989)
Beckett, I.F.W. 'The British Army in the First World War: New Evaluations', *Commission Francaise d/Histoire Militaire Guerre et Societe en Europe Perspectives des Nouvelles Recherches* (Bucarest: Editions Europa Nova, 2004)

Cardinal-Harford, H. 'They Had Lied About Their Age', in Sir John Hammerton, ed., *I Was There Vol. 3* (London: The Amalgamated Press, 1939)
Cave, T. 'The Reserve and the Training Reserve', *Stand To!*, 70 (April 2004), pp.
Clare., R. J. 'Fit to Fight? How the Physical Condition of the Conscripts Contributed to the Manpower Crisis of 1917-18', *Journal of the Society for Army Historical Research,* 94 (379) Autumn 2016 pp. 225 – 244.

Dewey, P.E. 'Military Recruiting and the British Labour Force during the First World War', *Historical Journal*, 27 (1984), pp. 199-223
Douglas, R. 'Voluntary Enlistment in the First World War and the Work of the Parliamentary Recruiting Committee', *Journal of Modern History*. 42 (4) (December 1970), pp. 564-85

Fenwick, S. 'The Women's Auxiliary Army Corps (Postal) in BEF 1917-19', in *Forces Postal Historical Society Newsletter*, 247 (Spring 2001)

King, Lieutenant E. 'A Ripping Lot of Fellows – Letters from a Grenadier Battalion Officer', *Stand To!*, 70 (April 2004), p. 17

Lamm, D. 'Emily Goes to War: Explaining the Recruitment to the Women's Army Auxiliary Corps in World War I', in B. Melman, ed., *Borderlines. Genders and Identities in War and Peace 1870 – 1930* (New York & London: Routledge, 1998)

Millett, A.R., Murray, W. & 'The Effectiveness of Military Organizations', in Watman, K.H. *International Security*, 11 (1) (Summer 1986), pp. 37-71

Mitchinson, K.W. 'The "Transfer" Controversy', *Stand To!*, 36 (Winter 1992), pp.

Mitchinson, K.W. 'The Special Reserve', *Stand To!*, 70 (April 2004)

III INTERNET SOURCES

www.ancestry.com

http://www.awm.gov.au/histories/first_world_war Bean, C. E. W. *Official History of Australia in the War of 1914–1918 - Vol. 3 – The Australian Imperial Force in France, 1916* (12th edition, 1941)

www.cwgc.org

www.culpitt-war-diary.org.uk/index.htm Transcript made by his son of hand written book compiled by George John Culpitt from a number of entries in personal diaries kept whilst he was on active service during the First World War.

www.hansard.millbanksystems.com/sittings/C20

www.historicaldirectories.org/hd/

www.isle-of-man.com/manxnotebook/fulltext/gw1922/index.htm

www.nationalarchives.gov.uk

www.stockport1914-1918.co.uk/

Index

Formations/Units

Armies